W9-BIW-473

"A BOOK PACKED WITH INSIDER INFORMATION ABOUT THE POLITICAL PROCESS, a book that shows that politicians' feet are all too often made of clay." – *The Globe and Mail*

"If what Sawatsky ... reveal[s] about John Turner in this book is true, then the Liberals are in bigger trouble than most people think, and the rest of us better watch it ... RIVETING STUFF FOR POLITICAL JUNKIES." – *Montreal Gazette*

"**The Insiders** IS GOING TO BE ONE OF THE BIG POLITICAL BOOKS OF THE YEAR. If you're an insider, you'll hasten to the index. If you're on the outside maybe you owe it to yourself to find out who is doing what to whom in there, at what price and what cost." – *Toronto Star*

"PACKED WITH INTRIGUING VIGNETTES AND GOSSIPY INSIDE STORIES, the book exhaustively portrays a netherworld of Canadian political history and legend ... an entertaining choice." – *The Whig-Standard* (Kingston)

"A wealth of interesting biography in this EXCEPTIONALLY DE-TAILED survey." – *Report on Business*

"Sawatsky gives us a scenario of exits and entries AS ELABORATE AS A FRENCH BEDROOM FARCE ... The political bits in the book are already being talked about ... It's a situation comedy, made all the more vivid by being reported in such a matter-of-fact way." – *Vancouver Sun*

"A COMPELLING, WELL—CRAFTED account of a secretive little cottage industry of great importance." – *Regina Leader-Post*

"THE BEST CANADIAN POLITICAL BOOK so far published in the Mulroney era." *Halifax Mail Star*

"Sawatsky proves that THE REAL POWER IN OUR GOVERNMENT is not only in the hands of those seemingly in the driver's seat." – *Flare*

"Some books deliver less than their covers promise. This one delivers far more ... GRIPPING POLITICAL DRAMA." – *Windsor Star*

"If you've ever done business with government or wanted to do business with government, THIS SHOULD BE YOUR HANDBOOK." – *Saskatchewan Business Magazine*

Born in Manitoba and raised in Abbotsford, B.C., John Sawatsky went from Simon Fraser University to work for the Vancouver *Sun* in 1970. In 1975 he was sent to Ottawa, where he soon established a reputation as an investigative reporter, winning the Michener Award for public service journalism in 1976.

His first book, *Men in the Shadows*, came out in 1980, followed by *For Services Rendered*, which won the Periodical Distributors Award for Book of the Year in 1983. Since publishing *Gouzenko* in 1984, he has held the Max Bell chair of journalism at the University of Regina. Now resident in Ottawa, he teaches part time at Carleton University's School of Journalism. Since 1982, the man who got the Mounties to talk has turned his investigative talents loose on the shadowy Ottawa world of the lobbyists, on which he is now the acknowledged authority.

JOHN SAWATSKY

The Insiders

Power, Money, and Secrets in Ottawa

M&S

An M&S Paperback from
McClelland and Stewart
The Canadian Publishers

An M&S Paperback from McClelland and Stewart

First printing January 1989

Copyright © 1987 by John Sawatsky

Canadian Cataloguing in Publication Data

Sawatsky, John, 1948–
The insiders: power, money, and secrets in Ottawa

(M&S paperbacks)
Previous ed. published under title: The insiders:
government, business, and the lobbyists.
Includes index.
ISBN 0-7710-7948-6

1. Lee, Bill.   2. Neville, Bill.   3. Lobbyists –
Canada.   4. Lobbying – Canada.   5. Canada – Politics
and government – 1963–   .*   I. Title.
JL148.5.S29 1989   324′.4′0971   C88-094839-6

Cover design by Richard Miller, adapted by Kong Njo
Cover photo by Bill Brooks/Masterfile
Printed and bound in Canada by Webcom Limited
Hardcover edition published in 1988:

A Douglas Gibson Book
McClelland and Stewart
The Canadian Publishers
481 University Avenue
Toronto M5G 2E9

For
Marjorie Nichols
who introduced me to political reporting in Ottawa

With special thanks to

Professor Joe Scanlon
and the School of Journalism
Carleton University;

and the School of Journalism and Communications
University of Regina

Contents

Acknowledgements

This book is focused on one corner of lobbying in Ottawa – public-affairs consulting – and on the people who have played a major role in establishing the process and turning it into a lucrative profession.

During the time this book was being researched and written, many people made important contributions. None was greater than that of Professor Joe Scanlon, who invited me into his fourth-year journalism classroom at Carleton University and incorporated major portions of this research project as part of the students' work. As we taught together we made many discoveries in what was for both of us a dynamic process of analysing interview technique and incorporating it into practical journalism. It was a case where the professors learned as much as the students, hardworking and dedicated students. In the 1982-83 class I thank Jacquelynn Ellis, Paul Foy, Joyce Gaudet, Scott McClellan, Erin McKelvie, and Ruth McMahon; in the 1985-86 class Anita Boutzie, Harvey Cashore, Dan Conlin, Andrew Duffy, Sandra Berry Eagle, Mary Ann Horgan, Jennifer Kinnear, Tim May, Tim Moore, Shelley Page, Cathy Pruefer, Darlene Small, Jill Vardy, Laurie West, and Jonathan Whitten.

Outside the classroom, Suzanne Coté, Dan Conlin, and Luke Fisher helped me to gather material and did excellent jobs. Above all, Harvey Cashore did much of the research for Chapter One, and all the research for Chapter Twenty.

The School of Journalism at the University of Regina and the Max Bell Foundation appointed me Max Bell Professor of Journalism for 1984-85 and gave me a wonderful year and generous financial support which helped see this project through. I was proud to be part of the faculty.

The Library of Parliament again was an important source of material; Duncan Gray and Bob Blackburn especially went out of their way. Ralph Curtis again provided invaluable help with computers. I am also indebted to Ken Rockburn of CHEZ FM in Ottawa.

Special thanks are due to my publisher and editor, Doug Gibson, who, besides being cheerfully encouraging and always understanding, improved the manuscript immeasurably.

And finally, I wish to thank all the people who gave generously of their time in talking to me and my researchers and were amazingly open and helpful. These sessions often stretched on for hours and grew into multiple sittings. Truly, these are the people who made this book possible.

It is fitting that my first book on politics is dedicated to Marjorie Nichols, my Ottawa Bureau Chief at the Vancouver *Sun* when I arrived on Parliament Hill in 1975; she taught me how to cover politics in the capital.

John Sawatsky
Parliament Press Gallery
Ottawa
April 1987

ONE

THE SECRET RENDEZVOUS

"**W**here's Frank Moores?"

The question shattered the calm of the polite discussion in the dining room on the eighth floor of the Royal Bank Building overlooking the Prime Minister's Office. It was as if one of the lunchers beneath the chandelier had belched an obscenity. And in fact, to this assembled company of Ottawa lobbyists and consultants deftly picking their way through lunch, the name of Frank Moores was anathema. He was the one who had caused the trouble that had led to this top-secret meeting; at least that was how most of those at the table viewed it.

In the silence all eyes turned to the head of the rectangular table where Rob Parker sat. Parker was the Royal Bank's lobbyist in Ottawa, a former Tory MP from Toronto who had been an aide to John Crosbie, and a man whose owlish good looks and soothing deep voice had made him a successful television-commercial performer and public-affairs host. He had assembled this group and stressed and re-stressed the need for secrecy. Lobbyists, they all knew, had a bad image, and any government measure to regulate them would be applauded by the public as a healthy and welcome initiative. Parker did not want to be seen leading a group of lobbyists lobbying against lobby reform; hence the need for secrecy.

The stature of the people who had shown up in the Royal Bank's Room 800 that cold day in January 1986 pleased Parker and demonstrated how seriously the top practitioners viewed the possibility of public regulation of their profession.

The two most eminent lobbying consultants in Ottawa sat

on either side of him. Bill Lee, the dean of the group, perched somewhat impatiently on his right. Eighteen years ago Lee had helped Pierre Trudeau win the 1968 election. Only a year and a half earlier he had cleared John Turner's path to 24 Sussex Drive. In between those feats Lee had helped scores of private clients influence government. On Parker's left, sitting pokerfaced, was Bill Neville, whose backroom experience also spanned more than two decades. Neville had run Joe Clark's Prime Minister's Office and had come out of private industry for six weeks to ease Brian Mulroney's entry into office. Since then he had acted as part of the prime minister's unofficial brain trust, and collected big fees advising clients on how to deal with the Mulroney government.

The other members of the group were crowded around the rest of the table. There, sitting perfectly erect, was Susan Murray, the dynamic young lobbyist from Toronto with Big Blue Machine connections, who was expanding her operations to Ottawa. There was Jocelyne Coté-O'Hara who had left the Prime Minister's Office four months earlier to become B.C. Telephone's lobbyist. There were Barbara Smyth of the Canadian Bankers' Association, Bob Nuth of the Canadian Construction Association, and David Gibson of the Chamber of Commerce. Mike Gough, a lawyer with Osler Hoskin & Harcourt, sat sandwiched in the crowd. When the meeting's importance for the legal profession became apparent, Gough's senior partner, Ron Atkey, a cabinet minister under Joe Clark, joined the group.

And there was Pierre Fortier, the man who had asked the unwelcome question about Frank Moores. Fortier was the former national director of the Conservative Party, a lawyer who turned lobbyist when the Mulroney government took office, going into partnership with Paul Curley, another former national director, and quickly picking up a million dollars' worth of billings. Fortier was no shrinking violet and was not deterred by the silence that met his question. Before Parker or anybody else could reply, Fortier went on: "I think it is hypocrisy on our part to have these meetings and not invite GCI," Fortier said. "If you feel that GCI is the cause of all of this, they have the right to express their views if we're going to meet in concert."

The pause continued. Parker had deliberately excluded Moores and GCI from the guest list. Most of those around the table felt that inviting Moores would be like bringing an arsonist to a session on fire prevention.

CCI stood for Government Consultants International Inc., the lobbying company Frank Moores had established since Brian Mulroney became prime minister. Before September 1984 everybody knew Moores as the former premier of Newfoundland, a big, amiable, hard-drinking, hard-living man who was not overly busy. Since September 1984 he had become known more as a Mulroney crony, recently attending the christening of Mulroney's son Nicholas. Moores had worked diligently behind the scenes in the campaign to dump Joe Clark in 1983 and thus open the Conservative leadership for Mulroney, then had helped in the election campaign to make him prime minister. Between Mulroney's election victory on September 4 1984, and his swearing in on September 17, Moores moved his business address from Montreal to Ottawa; he soon acquired one of the highest profiles in town. He was one of the few men in Canada who could pick up the phone and call the prime minister.

Moores had been operating in Ottawa for about five months when a Canadian Press reporter named Bob Fife witnessed his effectiveness. In February 1985 Fife received a tip that an Israeli company had put in a bid to buy the ill-fated oil refinery at Come by Chance, Newfoundland. Moores had been premier when the New York industrialist John Shaheen built the mammoth Come by Chance refinery in his province. It never refined a single barrel of oil; it collapsed under the strain of escalating world oil prices, then was mothballed in 1976, and eventually wound up in the hands of the government oil company Petro-Canada. Now Fife called Moores and asked if he knew who was bidding.

"I'll get it for you," Moores promised.

Moores called back twenty minutes later with the names of the Israeli company and all the other bidders. Moores possessed the whole list. He seemed to have picked up the details of a secret tender.

Fife learned that Moores kept in close touch with Shaheen, who was competing against four other bidders to get his refinery back and who had once named one of his oil tankers the *Frank D. Moores*. Fife never discovered whether Shaheen was a Moores client – in fact he was not – but did find out that Shaheen seemed to know the details of the bids in advance. Shaheen showed so much confidence that he actually declared victory before Petro-Canada announced the result, but died before he could regain his cherished refinery; subsequently his heirs dropped the pursuit. It was impossible for Fife to believe that Moores didn't have his hand in there somewhere.

Moores's notoriety spread and started getting him newspaper ink, until for a while it seemed that he couldn't stay out of the headlines. The publicity started in June 1985 when Michael Harris of the *Globe and Mail* reported that Moores's firm had persuaded Fisheries Minister John Fraser to overturn his department's formal refusal to approve a fishing-licence transfer for a Nova Scotia fisherman named Ulf Snarby. The $3,000 fee GCI received for its services was so small as to be incidental to the growth and profitability of the firm – it had never lobbied such a small claim before – but the case was highly visible. The public saw Moores as the man who opened a minister's door for $3,000. Rightly or wrongly, the image stuck. Moores became the operator who fixed a commercial fishing licence for a fee.

In March 1985 the Mulroney government put Moores onto Air Canada's board of directors; in July Linda Diebel of the Montreal *Gazette* revealed that GCI acted as consultants for two competitors, Nordair Inc. and Wardair Ltd. It seemed unlikely that Moores could work for three competing airlines and do them all justice, especially in 1985 when the government was deregulating air travel and thinking of privatizing Air Canada. But Moores defended his ties to Nordair and Wardair and denied that they conflicted with his duties at Air Canada. His office issued a four-page statement saying that he saw nothing unusual or wrong as long as other people in his firm handled the Nordair and Wardair accounts. "I am confident that the firms of Bill Lee and David MacNaughton and others have a similar policy," his statement said. "All fair-minded people, including the media, will hopefully recognize and respect this." The explanation did not satisfy his critics. Two weeks later, when the chairman of Air Canada, Claude Taylor, advised him that there was indeed an appearance of conflict, Moores dropped his two private clients rather than give up his Air Canada directorship. He understood politics and realized that his cross-connection was giving Mulroney political trouble, but didn't see what the fuss was about.

A month after Moores resigned the Nordair and Wardair accounts Fife was told by a source that his connections with Messerschmitt-Bolkow-Blohm represented a potentially bigger conflict of interest than Nordair and Wardair. MBB, a Munich company, was a partner in a European consortium called Airbus Industrie, which wanted to sell wide-bodied A320 passenger planes to Air Canada as it replaced its fleet of Boeing 727s and DC-9s. When challenged, Moores said his firm represented only the helicopter division of MBB and had nothing to do with its other operations. But Fife learned that he had arranged a meeting with government officials on behalf of MBB in which the matters discussed included the sale of Airbus planes. If the story was accurate and if Airbus sold planes to Air Canada, whose interest was Moores serving: the buyer's or the seller's? Fife had started digging to confirm the tip when Moores learned that Canadian Press was checking into the story. He phoned Fife directly.

"Would you like a story?" he asked. "Come on down to my office."

Fife suspected that he wanted to trade stories and was wary when he entered his five-sided corner office on the thirteenth floor of the modern Metropolitan Centre, two blocks down the hill from the West Block.

"So you're onto Airbus," Moores greeted Fife. He tossed a statement across the desk. "Does it meet with your satisfaction?"

The statement announced his resignation from the Air Canada board. It claimed that the media were hounding him, and that he was not abusing the system but was being abused. "Unfortunately," it said, "certain forces seemed determined, by using innuendo, or slanting the facts, or both, to hurt Air Canada and/or the government and/or myself because of my Air Canada directorship." The statement also called for a "regulatory framework" for lobbyists, in other words for some sort of system for registering lobbyists.

"I just thought you'd want to read it because I'm not a very good writer," Moores said good-naturedly. "Well, I'm going to let you have it before anyone else. Just do me a favour, put it in the [press] gallery after you run your story."

"Thanks," Fife replied, "that's nice of you."

"Now," Moores smiled, "I suppose there's no need to mention Airbus, is there?"

That was the trade-off: the scoop on the Air Canada resignation in exchange for omitting the Airbus link. By wheeling-dealing standards it was a gentle offer, and made by an old pro. But Fife could not go along.

"I have to mention the Airbus," Fife insisted. "It's part of the story, part of the reasons why you're resigning. I'm going to have to mention it."

Fife stuck to his guns and they parted on friendly terms. Before Fife left his office Moores told him he hoped to get Nordair and Wardair back now that he had dropped Air Canada.

"If Prime Minister Mulroney is to retain any credibility as a foe of patronage sleaze, as he portrayed himself only a year ago in his first election debate, he will have to deal swiftly and convincingly with the matter of Frank Moores," the *Gazette* of Montreal wrote in an editorial on July 23 1985. "In all the years of Liberal patronage, it is hard to recall any appointment that raises quite the same smelly questions as those raised by Moores' membership on the board of directors of Air Canada."

The following month the fifteen ministers on the priorities and planning committee, effectively the inner cabinet, moved to the west coast and for three days holed up in the grand old Hotel Vancouver to prepare the fall legislative agenda. The government would soon meet parliament again and wanted to launch into its second year by proposing some impressive themes: social justice; economic renewal; reconciliation with the provinces; and trade. The committee approved one other theme: integrity of government. Controversial patronage handouts had blotted the Mulroney government's copybook. Only a year earlier, during the 1984 election, Mulroney had promised to depoliticize government largesse and to dispense patronage on the basis of merit and equity; in office he had been caught doing precisely the opposite. The law firms of the sons of Justice Minister John Crosbie received government legal work. Joe Clark's brother, Peter, was hired as lawyer for the 1988 Calgary Olympic Games committee, and the brother-in-law of Michael Wilson got a government advertising contract. These highly publicized incidents so early in the government's term gave the impression that the Conservative government was filling the pockets of relatives and friends. Then Frank Moores popped into the headlines as one of the prime minister's closest cronies. Mulroney had to deal with the Moores issue and the other ethical issues or see his image deteriorate further. On the issue of integrity, which he had used devastatingly against John Turner over patronage, he had to do something to regain the momentum. So out of Vancouver came proposed conflict-of-interest guidelines for executive staff and senior public servants as one measure. But Mulroney went a step further and advocated the registration of lobbyists.

Nearly a hundred reporters crowded into a press conference in the hotel's Vancouver Island Room where he announced this plan. He said: "I feel that it's important ... that you know who's sitting across the table from you and who he's representing, who's paying him and how much. If he is going to deal with the government of Canada – he or she – it seems to me fair that we know who he's speaking for, who he purports to represent and who he is representing. And the only way that you can do that, as I understand it, is to cause people to register pursuant to a statute which then, of course, would require a piece of legislation." By promising lobbying legislation, Mulroney had staged a great symbolic response and settled on a quick means for sanitizing his government's image.

Mulroney's announcement astonished and angered most lobbyists in Ottawa. Virtually all of them roundly opposed registration. They resented being listed in a central registry. They disliked even more having to reveal the identity of their clients, and absolutely bristled at the prospect of divulging their fees. Mulroney had included all three. Worse, he had not merely proposed a green paper to review options but was talking about legislation. When parliament resumed two and a half weeks later Mulroney stuck to his word and tabled an outline of seven reforms in public-sector ethics, including the registration of lobbyists.

"[It] is the undertaking of this government to introduce into the House of Commons, at an early date, legislation to monitor lobbying activity and to control the lobbying process by providing a reliable and accurate source of information on the activities of lobbyists," Mulroney told MPs and senators in an open letter on September 9. Mulroney said he had asked Consumer and Corporate Affairs Minister Michel Côté to prepare legislation "on an urgent basis." His letter included the line: "This government is simply saying that something so important should not be shrouded in mystery."

Having marched forward with guns blazing in September, the government retreated in December. Six days before Christmas, Côté issued not a bill but a sketchy "discussion paper". He announced that he had more questions than answers and wanted public input, and thus was referring the whole matter to a parliamentary committee for study. Evidently Mulroney had entertained second thoughts about the "urgent" need. This pleased the lobbyists, but they didn't care for the fact that a parliamentary committee was sticking its nose into the issue. They knew – it was their business to know – that parliamentary committees were uneven and unpredictable. MPs can get funny notions. Once the committee started public hearings there was no telling where it would go, which worried the lobbying profession, and led to the January meeting in the Royal Bank's executive dining room.

Fortier got little support when he advocated including Frank Moores. Most of the people around the table resented Moores's unabashed style. They felt that the image of lobbying had been rising steadily over the years until he came to town, and believed that his high-profile activities had tarnished everybody's reputation. His competitors felt that he had broken the unwritten rules to everybody's disadvantage and saddled them with a parliamentary inquiry. They believed that, by trading on his political connections, he was pulling them all inevitably towards a central registry that would require them to list their clients and perhaps even their fees. They abhorred the thought and called it the Frank Moores Bill.

After an awkward silence the subject was changed. The participants spoke up, and one by one they fell in behind Parker in his opposition to a public registry, which he called dumb. They saw its political appeal and understood why Mulroney supported it, but dismissed it as superficial and wrongheaded. Not surprisingly, a consensus emerged around the table that there was no substantial problem; if specific abuses existed they were caused not by misbehaviour on the part of lobbyists but by politicians and bureaucrats who gave improper access. They believed that Mulroney had reacted to an imaginary problem, not a real one. His registry was a response to an opinion of the media and the public but ignored the real problem, which was Moores and some other Tories. Bob Nuth, the grey-haired spokesman of the construction industry, said that Mulroney could solve the problem by passing the word around government to deny access to operators who sought to exploit personal or political connections. One simple decree would cut them off and shut them down. It seemed that Mulroney could not curb his friends, that he was being bombed by his own air force, and had rashly decided to move against everybody with a registry. They felt it was unfair to the majority of traditional operators that Mulroney was throwing all the apples into the same barrel. Some suspected he was covering up for Frank Moores.

An outsider in the room might have thought that many in the group had done rather well out of their own political connections. Back in 1968 Bill Lee had flaunted his connection with Pierre Trudeau and Paul Hellyer. Bill Neville had become hot when Mulroney became prime minister and, like Moores, had moved to Ottawa. Susan Murray had benefited from her Big Blue Machine connections, and Parker's ties throughout the Conservative Party didn't exactly reduce his clout as a lobbyist. They were not political virgins, and sensed that they should not protest too loudly. At the same time they felt that Moores had gone too far and overstepped the bounds of political propriety. They had used their reputations as "insiders" to get clients, not to exert influence, which they suspected Moores did. If Moores had done half the things ascribed to him he could justly be called the scourge of lobbying. The critics, however, though they had made plenty of allegations, had produced no evidence that he had opened any illicit doors.

At the next meeting, the following month, the group debated the significance of the fact that since the opening of Parliament in September Mulroney had kept remarkably quiet about his registry plan. Some maintained he was backing off. They advocated doing nothing while lobbying reform sank under its own weight. They said it might be different if the minister supported

Mulroney's registry, but everybody knew that Côté, a rookie MP with plenty of backroom experience, preferred to forget the whole thing. The issue was Mulroney-driven; once he retreated the plan would collapse.

Others were less hopeful. They agreed that Mulroney had lost his enthusiasm but maintained that he had committed himself in public and had to press forward whether he wanted to or not. They believed that Mulroney lacked the political courage to admit a mistake, particularly because of his reputation for breaking his promises; that while he could manage an about-face on some issues, the registry issue was too heavily intertwined with integrity to permit this. The very aspect of a registry that had appealed to Mulroney in the first place made it difficult to abandon.

The question was whether Mulroney had made a promise or not. If not, he might settle for industry self-regulation and the profession would be better off policing itself than letting government do it. It all hung on Mulroney's sense of commitment, and the group lacked sufficient knowledge for a sound judgement. It also needed a fix on the parliamentary committee and the public hearings that were soon to be held. Were the hearings serious, or a stall for time as Mulroney climbed off his own bandwagon?

The group decided to find out, and delegated Bill Neville and Jocelyne Coté-O'Hara to check with the Prime Minister's Office. They could hardly have picked two better-qualified emissaries. Neville was more than just a friend of Mulroney's, he was a political operator of the first order. From his experience as principal secretary to Prime Minister Joe Clark, Neville knew how a Prime Minister's Office operated. For her part Coté-O'Hara had only recently left the PMO. Together they would meet Bernard Roy who, as Mulroney's principal secretary and chief of staff, knew the prime minister's moods and attitudes better than anyone. Arranging such a meeting would not be hard. When Roy arrived in Ottawa sixteen months earlier he had been briefed on the pitfalls of his job by Neville, and Coté-O'Hara had worked as Roy's assistant. If Neville and Coté-O'Hara together couldn't discover Mulroney's thinking then nobody outside the PMO could.

Neville and Coté-O'Hara met Roy in the office that had once belonged to Neville. For half an hour they asked questions, raised problems, and described the issue – or, as they saw it, lack of issue. Neville complained that the mere fact that government was regulating lobbyists suggested that something was wrong, yet nobody had shown him there was a problem. He went on to suggest that a public registry would actually inhibit the government's freedom to make the right decisions, because everybody would keep scorecards and look for evidence of patronage. With lobbyists lining up in public, Neville reasoned, people would say: "Moores won last time and Lee the time before that. Now it's Curley's turn." For the sake of appearances the government would be tempted to overlook merit and would spread its decisions around in order to avoid charges of favouritism, introducing one more complication into an already tangled decision-making process. Neville also cautioned Roy that a wide net would catch lawyers and arouse the legal profession. That argument struck home because both Mulroney and Roy were lawyers.

Roy saw the problems and indicated that he understood what they were saying. But whatever sympathies he personally had with their views, the prime minister had made a promise. "When he makes a public commitment," Roy said, "our view is we've got to carry through." He added that they would rethink their position if the parliamentary committee rejected the registry but would not do so as a result of representations from the business community. For the moment the issue rested in the hands of the parliamentary committee.

Neville and Coté-O'Hara duly informed their colleagues that Mulroney felt obliged to follow through; the government would produce a lobbying bill of some sort. The news dashed the hopes of the Royal Bank group and undermined the reason for their meetings. Their third meeting was their last. The members agreed to deal with the parliamentary committee individually, and went their way. It was ironic that even the lobbyists could not kill the lobby bill.

TWO

THE BEST OF THE BACKROOM BOYS

"**T**he stupid bastards," snorted the minister of national defence, charging into his office. "They're going to do it."

At six feet four inches, Paul Hellyer was an imposing sight when he was angry, and he was angry now. He had hardly come through the doorway when he hurled his cabinet documents and briefing books across the room, where they hit the wall and dropped to the floor. His staff watched the normally sedate minister in open-mouthed astonishment. When he calmed down he told them that he was leaving the Pearson cabinet on the spot. He had just returned from a cabinet meeting where his colleagues had approved the Canada Pension Plan when they knew full well that the country lacked the wherewithal to pay for it. Hellyer supported the concept of a pension plan but had calculated the cost of this particular proposal and concluded that when all the factors were considered the country could not afford it quite yet. "And the people will fall for it," he huffed.

Bill Lee, Hellyer's right-hand man, moved quickly for an earnest tête-à-tête with his boss. As his executive assistant, Lee knew that Hellyer's objections were deeply felt and undoubtedly were fiscally correct; but Lee also knew that Hellyer's reasoning would not sell politically. If Hellyer had to make a stand on principle, Lee wanted him positioned on more politically attractive ground. He admired Hellyer as a public leader and valued him as a friend, but in these matters Lee weighed principally the politics of the matter. He laid out the hard political facts for Hellyer – that the public saw the Canada Pension Plan as a "free" pension and that his opposition, though reasonable, amounted to political suicide. History would vindicate Hellyer in a decade or two – as in fact happened – but that meant nothing in 1964. "You'll go back to the back benches," Lee warned him. "The name Hellyer will just disappear from people's minds. You'll be that crazy guy who resigned over a pension plan for all Canadians."

Paul Hellyer was one of the most decent and honourable people to enter Canadian politics. He tolerated none of the common political abuses associated with office, not even in the dispensing of patronage and advertising contracts. An idealist, he entered politics not to wield power but to better society with a series of tailored reforms. When idealism and politics collided – as they did with Hellyer – Lee jumped in, sometimes as a conciliator but more often as the spokesman for politics. He had talked Hellyer out of resigning before and would do so again. And he did it now by convincing Hellyer that he could not inaugurate his reforms from outside the cabinet room. The argument worked brilliantly. Hellyer, the visionary, had an agenda he longed to implement and the thought of having to abandon it cured his bouts of principle.

Lee looked like a whiz kid and performed like one. When he joined Hellyer in 1963 he was already almost 40 but his round, freshly scrubbed baby face, boyish grin, and thick mop of hair – fighting to annex the corners of his forehead – along with his energy, made him look twenty years younger. The same boyish style marked his office, which was cluttered with mechanical gadgets and forty-eight model aircraft; a dartboard hung on the door leading to Hellyer's office. He was flash with substance, a charmer with brains, someone always on the go and yet someone who always had time to talk. Lee would slap backs and trade quips with reporters, but he also gave them long serious briefings. He manipulated them, but usually in a way they wanted to be manipulated, by providing information rather than withholding it. He was the most open executive assistant on Parliament Hill and sometimes stunned reporters by producing Hellyer within minutes for an impromptu interview. When Hellyer couldn't make a speech, Lee stepped in and gave it for him right down to the post-speech television interviews. Lee promoted his man incessantly, keeping his name before the public, and perhaps pushed him further than he wanted to be pushed. The

Pearson years featured some outstanding executive assistants but everybody acknowledged Bill Lee as the king of the EAs or, as Judy LaMarsh later wrote, "the best of any of the backroom boys."

Lee's profile as a backroom boy rose with his minister's standing. Even though Hellyer was a strong minister and a star in the Pearson government, Lee eventually became a subject of public comment. "Has this been approved by Group Captain Lee?" John Diefenbaker sometimes heckled when Hellyer spoke in Parliament. Diefenbaker enjoyed using his position as leader of the opposition to denounce Lee's influence and to paint a picture of a mysterious group captain pulling the strings that controlled his puppet-like boss, "Corporal Hellyer". Lee belonged to the Royal Canadian Air Force and was on loan to Hellyer – that much the former prime minister knew. Lee thanked his lucky stars that Diefenbaker, who regularly cursed the traitors in the civil service who had betrayed his government and brought Lester Pearson and the Liberals to power, knew nothing more of his background. If Diefenbaker had been aware of Lee's air-force activities, his attacks would have taken on an entirely different character because a few years earlier, before he was officially in the political world, Lee had played a role in bringing down Diefenbaker's government.

As prime minister, Diefenbaker had shocked Canada's senior military officers in the latter years of his government with a flat order absolutely prohibiting nuclear weapons for the armed forces. The officers protested that Diefenbaker could not do that; only a few years earlier his own minister of defence had signed a NATO commitment accepting a nuclear inventory. Diefenbaker insisted there had been no commitment and left the generals sputtering with rage. They believed that the prime minister was misleading the public on a matter of grave national importance. They called in Bill Lee to dispense the truth.

Lee, at the time the RCAF's Head of Public Relations, mounted a campaign to win the support of the media. Dozens of journalists, including big names like Stanley Burke of the CBC and Blair Fraser of *Maclean's*, were flown to NORAD headquarters in Colorado on military aircraft for a tour and briefing on how Canada was shirking its legal obligation to NATO. The airlift even extended to prominent businessmen in the Conservative Party.

Lee's campaign produced spectacular results. Diefenbaker came under regular attack on the issue, and each time he repeated his claim it sounded less credible. Then came Lee's masterstroke.

Hardly anyone had noticed that General Lauris Norstad was due to visit Ottawa in January 1963. Norstad, a U.S. Air Force man, had recently retired as NATO's Supreme Allied Commander and planned to visit the capital for a few quiet goodbyes to old military colleagues. But Lee noticed. Realizing that Norstad was now free to talk, Lee saw his potential as a plain-spoken, respected military man, above politics, in a position to explode Diefenbaker's claim. He scheduled a press conference knowing exactly what questions reporters would ask, and how Norstad would feel obliged to respond. One reporter remembers the incident: "It was a beautiful set-up."

Norstad's flat statement that Canada was not fulfilling its commitment put Diefenbaker's minority government on the skids. The coup de grâce came four weeks later when a tough press release from the U.S. State Department – issued in Washington but circulated in the Press Gallery by Lee personally – virtually called Diefenbaker a liar. Defence Minister Douglas Harkness quit the cabinet and was soon followed by his successor, Acting Defence Minister Pierre Sévigny, and by George Hees. Diefenbaker's government fell, and in the ensuing election in April 1963 lost to Lester Pearson and the Liberals. Diefenbaker never regained office, and never lost his suspicion that the civil service had done him in.

Lee later claimed that he merely told the truth, that the campaign he ran was not politically motivated, and that he personally had no preference for the Liberals over the Conservatives. He had actually voted for Diefenbaker in 1958, and personally opposed nuclear weapons in Canada, but thought Diefenbaker should have renegotiated the commitment rather than deny the facts. But that would have required Diefenbaker to admit that his government had erred in accepting nuclear weapons in the first place, and Diefenbaker never admitted mistakes.

Lee was born to English parents who had immigrated to Canada as kids around the turn of the century. He grew up in a mixed neighbourhood of anglos and ethnics in Hamilton. His father, unilingual and lacking higher education, deliberately named his only son William Maurice Lee in recognition of the fact that his adopted country had two dominant languages. As he grew up Lee wanted to become a baseball player and idolized Bill Lee, pitcher of the Chicago Cubs, but Hamilton's Bill Lee showed more promise as a sprinter than as a ball player. He competed in inter-city meets and ran the 100-yard dash, the 220, the 440, and relays. He was in the Ontario track finals, and could have gone further had World War Two not intervened.

Lee graduated from high school in 1943 and promptly enlisted. His father's legs carried lifelong scars of trench warfare from World War One; the younger Lee did not relish similar exposure, so he volunteered for the air force instead of the army. Lee loved airplanes and, more than anything, wanted to be a navigator. He used to cut out airplane pictures, arrange them like a deck of cards, and have Chatty, his high-school sweetheart who later became his wife, flash them before his eyes. In a split second he could distinguish a Spitfire from a Hurricane, a Stuka from a Dornier, a Focke-Wulf 190 from a Messerschmitt 109; in fact, he could identify every plane in either the allied or the enemy fleets. In the air force Lee topped his class in everything, but especially amazed his superiors in the tests for aircraft recognition.

He flew as a navigator in the Ferry Command, visited exotic places like Casablanca and Beirut, and experienced a few near misses. But he also confronted the hard fact that he was mechanically inept – the tests revealed a strong creative bent – and knew he would never excel as a pilot. When he returned home, to his surprise, the air force offered him a peacetime position and stuck him behind an old wooden desk in Trenton as the "Public Relations Officer". Lee had never heard the term Public Relations Officer and didn't know what one did. Neither, it seemed, did the RCAF, but the staffing charts decreed there had to be one and Lee was it.

Public-relations theory did not exist in those days, but Lee's instinct told him to promote the RCAF rather than merely defend it, and that put him ahead of his time. A high-powered U.S. Forces public-relations course for senior officers really opened his eyes to the prospects, and to his abilities. At first the Americans tried to exclude him because he was only a flying officer and had no university degree, but Lee talked his way into staying. He topped the class, wowing everybody along the way. The Americans tried to keep him in the United States but the RCAF resolutely brought him back to Canada and promoted him to flight lieutenant after he came first across Canada in qualifying exams. After a stint in France, he returned to Canada to run RCAF Public Relations at headquarters in Ottawa.

Lee didn't just run public relations at the RCAF, he masterminded it. General Motors didn't promote the automobile as well as Lee promoted the RCAF. In the late 1950s and early 1960s, when big corporations such as Imperial Oil and Canadian Pacific employed maybe half a dozen public-relations officers, Lee created and ran an empire of 120 people with TV studios, radio studios, a weekly radio program, special displays and exhibitions, and the flash and drama of the RCAF Golden Hawks, an aerobatics team which he created as a promotional scheme. It all worked. Lee loved to brag that the RCAF hoodwinked the government out of more money than either the army or the navy, scooping up sixty per cent of the military budget while the other two services glumly divided up the remainder.

Whenever big international events came to Canada – a royal tour or President Kennedy's visit – Lee was borrowed from the RCAF to handle press arrangements. In 1963, when the NATO ministers met in Ottawa, accompanied by more than four hundred journalists, Lee gutted a group of offices in the West Block and assembled an awesome collection of electronic gadgetry, including a new gimmick called a closed-circuit television system, and an array of studios and direct radio and television links around the world. The elaborate arrangements drew whistles of amazement from everybody, including the new minister of defence, Paul Hellyer. A few weeks later Hellyer invited Lee to dinner and asked him to become his EA. Lee thought it over that night and the next day started to arrange a leave of absence from the air force.

Hellyer had been minister of defence hardly a year when he began to push for the amalgamation of the army, air force, and navy into one integrated force. The military opposed him bitterly, and some senior officers resigned in a blaze of publicity. But Hellyer pushed ahead, stared down opposition within his own department, and ultimately won. Hellyer was named Man of the Year both by *Time* [Canada] and *Maclean's*, but he knew that an entrenched bureaucracy could obstruct almost any changes that were big and significant and unpopular. Unification qualified on all three counts. "It was probably one of the most difficult things ever done in Canadian political life," Hellyer says today, "and it wouldn't have been possible without the support of someone like Bill Lee."

Lee had supported unification since he had witnessed the chronic waste brought on by duplication, and he knew all about the senseless tri-service competition for funds. From his earliest days in the service he had quietly despised those top officers who revelled in their chauffeurs and gardeners and other benefits. His military career had flourished; he was the youngest group captain in the air force and was certain to rise higher. But he worked loyally alongside Hellyer to impose unification, and his bureaucratic knowledge proved crucial to Hellyer's success. Now many in the military resented him. Some branded him an enemy. Returning to the military was out. So eighteen months after joining Hellyer he resigned his commission and entered the world of politics for good. Politics had opened new vistas for Lee. He liked rubbing shoulders with star cabinet ministers who were seen by his friends on television. But what really hooked him was the process – watching forces coalesce to create public policy; seeing which politicians had clout and which hadn't, and how that affected public policy. He enjoyed finding out which groups in society could make government sit up and pay attention, and why. And he loved the details of the wheeling and dealing needed to get a bill out of the bureaucracy, past the cabinet, into Parliament, and through committee for a final vote. Lee had found his true home in backroom politics.

The 1965 election tempted Lee to abandon the backroom for a spell in the spotlight. A group of businessmen, five of the biggest Liberals in Hamilton, offered to finance his campaign if he ran in Hamilton South, and Lee jumped at the opportunity. The time was right, and the prospect of becoming a cabinet minister was hard to resist. But then Lee checked with Hellyer, which stopped him in his tracks. Hellyer didn't like the idea and told the Hamilton businessmen he needed his executive assistant. Lee, ambitious but loyal, changed his mind about running. Always optimistic, he concluded that the only way he would get into the cabinet now was for Hellyer to become prime minister. He thought it would be fun to make Hellyer prime minister. First, however, he would have to convince him that being prime minister was a good idea.

"I didn't want this portfolio but I'm stuck with it," Hellyer grumbled when Pearson first appointed him minister of national defence in 1963. "There has never been a successful defence minister yet." The post Hellyer really wanted was Finance. He didn't just want Finance, he *craved* it; in Finance, he felt, he could introduce a new economic age and reduce both inflation and unemployment to zero. "I feel like the surgeon who has the answer to cancer and they won't let me in the hospital," he complained to Lee. "As minister of finance I could clear up these things. It's so obvious. We don't need unemployment. We don't need inflation. And we can have a hundred-cent dollar."

"Look," Lee replied, "I really don't understand your theories. Let's bite the bullet here. If you are ever going to get these strange theories in place you're going to have to be prime minister – because I can't see any prime minister allowing you to do this."

At first Hellyer pooh-poohed the idea. Being prime minister was not something he had seriously considered, but gradually the notion crept into his thinking. After the Liberals' disappointing minority victory in 1965 political insiders were quietly waiting for Mike Pearson to retire. A year later Hellyer set his sights above Finance and quietly gave Lee the go-ahead to start discreetly organizing his leadership campaign. Lee kept the title of executive assistant but delegated most of his functions so that he could concentrate solely on ensuring that Paul Theodore Hellyer would succeed Lester Pearson as leader of the Liberal Party and prime minister of Canada.

Lee recruited the best organizers in every province. Because Hellyer had started first, Lee got the best pick. The plan was to give Hellyer a running start that would put him out front the minute Pearson announced his retirement. Hellyer and Lee dared not campaign openly for fear of provoking charges of disloyalty. They could leave no footprints until the prime minister's job was officially declared open.

Hellyer worked hard and regularly stayed in his office until 11 o'clock, sometimes later, and worked every Saturday. "Thank goodness he's religious or he'd be there seven days a week," Lee's wife, Chatty, joked; but in fact, though Hellyer attended church on Sunday, he worked at home in the afternoon, often with Lee at his side. He saw issues looming on the horizon years ahead of time. In the days of cheap gasoline he wondered aloud about the wisdom of a single person's sitting in a car polluting the environment with potentially scarce resources; in those days neither pollution nor petroleum was an issue. And he had put his flair for prediction to good effect; as a University of Toronto student he had said: "The easy way to become a millionaire is to borrow money and accumulate a big tract of land, develop it, and sell it off for shopping centres and things like that." Which is exactly what he did. Being a millionaire by 25 allowed him the luxury of running for parliament in 1949 so that he could try to implement his agenda.

Hellyer also had huge drawbacks as a candidate. Nobody ever accused him of being a gladhanding politician who moved easily through a crowd shaking hands and winning votes. A big lumbering man, he looked stodgy and had the habit of throwing his head back, which made him seem to be looking down at the people he met. His oratory did not light up audiences. Lee knew that making him personally popular was going to require some packaging. Lee attended the Conservative leadership convention in September 1967 and received inspiration from the other side as he watched how Dalton Camp stage-managed the victory of the plodding Robert Stanfield over the attractive and articulate Duff Roblin. If Camp could sell Stanfield, Lee figured he could easily market Hellyer. Lee took copious notes at the convention and started keeping a diary. He made a deal with Longmans, the publishing company, to write a book called *The Making of a Prime Minister*, styled after the U.S. journalist Theodore White's book, *The Making of the President 1960*.

As Minister of Defence, Hellyer commanded a fleet of airplanes and could easily fly across the land and campaign discreetly for the party leadership. Lee did not think he could win the race from the defence portfolio, so Hellyer manoeuvred his way into Transport, which also had an airplane fleet, and gave him the chance to do politically popular things, like opening airports. At Transport Lee didn't even pretend to take possession of the EA's office. By this time the campaign had become more blatant than discreet and had already quietly recruited Robert Andras as the campaign chairman who, as soon as the official campaign got under way, would operate in the front room while Lee controlled events from behind the scenes. In the meantime Hellyer would fly into some region, do his ministerial business, and head over to meet future delegates at special Liberal meetings arranged by Lee. The people's names went onto file cards containing everything from the names of their children to descriptions of their political opinions. The overall plan was simple. Hellyer planned to meet, and impress, as many Liberals as possible before they became convention delegates when they would remember him as that nice guy with the ideas who also knew them and their constituency. It was a good foundation on which to build a campaign.

Hellyer's secret weapon was Arundel Lodge in the Muskoka Lakes in Ontario. Hellyer had honeymooned at Arundel back in 1945; he fell in love with the place and bought it. Now about half a dozen Liberals at a time flew in from all over the country for a free weekend at the rustic retreat and were treated to waterskiing and the sight of a senior cabinet minister flipping hamburgers. It was all going to help make Hellyer the next prime minister.

Lee expected tough competition from Hellyer's cabinet colleagues, especially Paul Martin. After losing to Pearson a decade earlier the perennial minister from Windsor had soldiered on loyally and effectively. Martin had longevity, political smarts, campaign skill, and fences that were always meticulously mended. Lee also expected a fight from Mitchell Sharp, who had business support, a strong Toronto base, a high profile, and in Michael McCabe an EA second only to Lee in effectiveness. When he looked at the race objectively, Lee placed Hellyer third. Hellyer had a good image as a strong, clean, and active minister, and his biggest advantage was his head start. But in Lee's mind – and the minds of the other pros – the two overriding question marks were Robert Winters, the tall, handsome businessman who looked like a prime minister, and Jean Marchand, the likable former labour leader who was the only credible Quebec candidate. Neither seemed interested in running but both had strong political bases from which they could vault ahead of Hellyer if they chose to run.

When Pearson's retirement seemed imminent in late 1967, Lee advised Hellyer to appoint a prominent francophone alongside Robert Andras as his official campaign co-chairman. Hellyer agreed and proposed Pierre Trudeau, an unknown from Montreal, who had been in the cabinet only six months.

"Come on, Paul, I'm talking about a big hitter," Lee argued. "Jean Lesage, Jean Marchand, Maurice Sauvé. Come on. Not that guy."

"You should see him in cabinet," Hellyer replied. "Boy, he is sharp."

"Okay, if you want him," Lee shrugged. "But he's not the calibre I had in mind."

Lee arranged a joint fishing trip at Arundel Lodge and Trudeau was all set to come, but urgent Transport business, now long forgotten, caused Hellyer to cancel. The fishing trip never did happen, and Trudeau never was approached. Later, when he was prime minister, Trudeau told Lee he would have co-chaired Hellyer's campaign if neither Marchand nor another Quebec candidate had entered the race. "I thought Hellyer was the best candidate of all of them," Trudeau said. A simple fishing trip might have changed Canadian history.

While he was awkward on the podium, Hellyer sparkled in little coffee klatsches, so as 1967 progressed and rumours of Pearson's retirement strengthened Lee kept him on the road, drinking endless cups of coffee as he met potential delegates. As Hellyer made his rounds Lee discovered that many of these likely delegates preferred Winters but switched to Hellyer because he had bothered to come. Lee knew that many would have committed themselves elsewhere had other candidates asked first, but Hellyer had put in an appearance. When Pearson announced his retirement in December 1967, with a leadership convention set for the following April, Hellyer started ahead of the rest. By this time Lee had compiled cards on eighty-five per cent of the party members who seemed likely to become convention delegates, and noticed a dramatic development: in the first-

and second-choice categories, Hellyer had risen from third to first. Hellyer had pulled in front. The organizing had paid off. The strategy had worked and the scenario was unfolding exactly as planned. It seemed that Lee was going to get his wish to make a Prime Minister.

Within a few weeks it seemed that half the ministers had announced their candidacies for the party leadership – Paul Martin, Mitchell Sharp, Allan MacEachen, John Turner, Joe Greene, and the former Quebec minister Eric Kierans. Jean Marchand backed out, and so did Robert Winters initially; when he changed his mind, much of his support had drifted elsewhere. Hellyer's prospects continued to look good. Then a new factor, which had completely eluded Lee's radar screen, swept onto the scene and upset Hellyer's carefully prepared scenario.

While declared candidates crisscrossed the country shaking hands and drinking coffee in search of delegates, Pierre Trudeau, the rookie MP who had become justice minister, sat at Pearson's elbow at the federal-provincial conference on the constitution in February 1968. Millions of Canadians watched on television as he locked horns with Quebec Premier Daniel Johnson. Trudeau handled himself with flair and gave an impressive performance. He had already leapt into the spotlight in December when he introduced amendments to the Criminal Code that legalized lotteries and therapeutic abortions and decriminalized homosexuality between consenting adults. "The state has no place in the bedrooms of the nation" became the phrase that symbolized Trudeau and the contemporary times.

The man in the Caesar haircut looked young, and was tough, intriguing, mysterious, bilingual, and obviously bright. Moreover, while Stanfield flirted with his two-nations theory, Trudeau, a French-Canadian Quebecker, unequivocally proclaimed himself in favour of Canada first. Above all he was fresh, new, and different. Trudeau popped up everywhere – on television, in newspapers, and, more importantly, on the tongues of most Canadians. When he declared his candidacy nine days after the federal-provincial conference, the race suddenly became exciting.

Youth was all the rage in 1968. The United States had the

Kennedy clan; Canada had a string of old prime ministers. The country wanted a young leader to match the spirit of the time, and Trudeau in sandals and open-necked shirts captured the mood. By comparison, Hellyer looked like a stodgy politician from the Saint-Laurent era. Lee, alarmed by this new kid on the block, visited the media guru Marshall McLuhan for insights into how Hellyer could stop Trudeau's momentum. McLuhan told him that Trudeau's mask-like face was perfect for television and predicted that he would win.

Lee tried a series of gimmicks. First he put Hellyer onto water-skis – Hellyer was a good water-skiier – in front of newspaper photographers to make him look young and athletic, like Trudeau. He had a group of Italian restaurateurs in Toronto piece together "the world's biggest pizza" with the pepperoni loudly spelling "44", Hellyer's age, compared to Trudeau's 46. (Trudeau was actually 48, but that detail was not exposed until after the convention.) Delegates didn't care who was born first; they thought of Hellyer as ten years older regardless of his birthdate. McLuhan was right. It didn't matter that Lee ran one of the most razzle-dazzle leadership campaigns in Liberal Party history. The country was being swept by a wave of Trudeaumania.

While Lee and the other campaign managers – Michael McCabe (Mitchell Sharp), Duncan Edmonds (Paul Martin), Tony Abbott (Robert Winters) and others – worked hard to get media interviews for their candidates, the Trudeau camp had Tim Porteous, whose job was to *turn down* media requests. Every time Trudeau opened his mouth another headline appeared.

Trudeaumania blossomed everywhere, but Trudeau had more going for him than popularity with the general public. He started with a big, solid block of delegates in Quebec. Marchand and Marc Lalonde told the Quebec caucus that Trudeau was Quebec's official candidate and that every Quebec MP would support him whether he wanted to or not. Quebec MPs who had already announced for Hellyer started coming to Lee and apologizing for reneging on their commitment. Hellyer lost more than twenty Quebec MPs when Trudeau declared. Only two defied the edict to "vote blood" on the first ballot, and both suffered the consequences. The rookie MP Jacques Tremblay was told to forget about running as a Liberal in the next election – not even to try for the nomination. Marcel Prud'homme, whose grip on his riding made him less vulnerable, never made the Trudeau cabinet in sixteen years.

In the weeks leading up to the convention, Lee kept hammering away at Trudeau's weakest point – that nobody really knew the man. Delegates were being alarmed by some of the vicious Trudeau rumours floating around, but Hellyer strictly forbade dirty tricks. Lee kept stressing that Hellyer was a good family man and people knew where he stood, and that the same could not be said for the swinging bachelor, Trudeau.

The Trudeau bandwagon shocked not only Lee but McCabe, Duncan Edmonds, and Tony Abbott, who started talking about forming a block-Trudeau alliance. They conceded that Trudeau would lead on the first ballot. The question was what to do after that. Whether Trudeau could be caught depended largely on the delineation of the later ballots. Whoever clearly occupied second place on the first ballot had the best chance to overtake Trudeau, but only if the other candidates dropped out. Otherwise Trudeau would ride to victory as the other candidates competed among themselves for the anti-Trudeau vote. Very informally, the EAs settled on the "discernible second" arrangement. They agreed to urge their respective bosses to drop out and, in the interests of blocking Trudeau, rally behind the candidate who was discernibly in second place.

When the convention opened in the Ottawa Civic Centre on April 4 1968, Lee expected Trudeau to capture 700-plus votes on the first ballot. (By this time Martin had slipped badly.) He expected Hellyer to be in the 450 range, enough for "discernible second", which made it likely that either Trudeau or Hellyer would win. Hellyer's second-ballot support would be strong – there had been enough trips to Arundel Lodge to ensure that – and would put him in a position to chase Trudeau once the other candidates started dropping off. Then, on the eve of the convention, the "discernible second" arrangement came partly undone. McCabe's man, Mitchell Sharp, withdrew and surprised everybody by announcing for Trudeau. His support gave Trudeau a big boost; but, on the other hand, it reduced the plausible alternatives to Trudeau to Hellyer or Winters. Everyone on all sides agreed that a lot rested on the candidates' speeches the day before the vote.

"What the fuck is he doing?" Bill Neville shouted. Quiet, almost shy, and always intense, the 32-year-old EA to Judy LaMarsh never shouted; but now, standing in front of a TV monitor in the Hellyer trailer outside the Civic Centre, he couldn't restrain himself. He was one of the best speechwriters in the business and figured he had drafted one of his better ones for Hellyer that day. But Neville could not believe his ears. Hellyer was not giving the speech. Instead he was laboriously plodding through some alien text that neither Neville nor the delegates could decipher. It was not a speech but a dry economic treatise. No punch, no laugh lines, nothing but dull economics.

A hundred yards away inside the arena, Lee reacted with equal horror. But unlike Neville he knew exactly what was happening. A few hours earlier he had dropped by on a good-luck visit to Hellyer's Ottawa home where the candidate was supposed to be resting for his speech. He found Hellyer in the living room with Bill Macdonald, a Toronto lawyer, and an aide, practising a speech written by the two visitors. Lee had already given Hellyer three speeches to choose from, including Neville's, and when he examined this latest speech he became apoplectic.

He had just left the hot and noisy Civic Centre and knew that the excited, clapping, chanting crowd was in no mood for an economics lecture. This new speech was so unusable, so wrong for the occasion, it couldn't even be fixed.

Lee motioned Hellyer into the kitchen where he told him the speech stank and ought to be scrapped. Hellyer disagreed, and nothing Lee said could sway him.

"Christ, we'll be murdered," Lee exclaimed in exasperation.

"Bill, I need this," Hellyer replied. "It's a crutch. I'm going to read this speech."

Hellyer returned to the living room. Lee, still in the kitchen, scribbled a note and taped it to the refrigerator: "Paul, if we've ever meant anything to each other, please don't read that speech. Please just go before the convention and say: 'I've been up and down this country in all the provinces and all the territories. You know what I stand for. I have been in this party, I have helped resurrect it since the St. Laurent defeat. Now if you think I'm the right leader, vote for me. And if you don't, I'll respect you and support your choice.' And sit down. They'll be so stunned I think you'll get one hell of a response for it. Bill."

Now, in agony, Lee and Neville listened to Hellyer tell delegates about the need to take into account the seasonal-average prices of fruits and vegetables instead of low-cost season-end prices when applying the anti-dumping laws. Hellyer later acknowledged that he could have won more votes by reciting "Mary Had a Little Lamb." After the convention he privately admitted his error, explaining to Lee that he never saw his note until the next morning, when it was too late.

That night – on the eve of the vote – Lee knew that the convention was lost and that he would not make Paul Hellyer prime minister. The field workers re-counted their delegates, while a second set of workers crosschecked their tallies independently. The results showed Hellyer barely staggering into second place. Hellyer was no longer clearly in second spot; that effectively killed the "discernible second" strategy, and with it any hope of catching Trudeau. The speech cost Hellyer 100 to 125 votes on the first ballot and drastically cut his second-ballot strength, thereby killing his prospects for growth. Lee knew that for almost twenty-four hours he would have to go through the motions while awaiting a verdict already decided.

Trudeau led on the first ballot with 752 votes, followed by Hellyer, 330; Winters, 293; Turner, 277; Martin, 277; Greene, 169; MacEachen, 165; Kierans, 103; and a nuisance candidate, Lloyd Henderson, 0. The vote shocked Hellyer, who was still hoping to top 500. Lee gamely approached the Winters camp: "Hey, guys, we're in second place, remember?"

"Discernible second?" was the sarcastic reply from Tony Abbott of the Winters campaign. "Come on, you're only 37 ahead of us." Lee didn't argue. There was no discernible second.

Lee looked for John Turner, who had left his box, and caught up with him near the washroom at the back. He tried to convince him that his future lay with Hellyer, but Turner would not deal.

"If Trudeau makes it," warned Lee, playing to Turner's ambition, "he's going to be in for a long time. Paul is going to be in for two terms – period."

"No," Turner replied, "[I'm] staying. Staying."

"If you do there'll be no way to stop Trudeau."

"So be it."

Lee moved over to Joe Greene, whose dynamic speech had

picked up many of the Hellyer votes, but he too hung tight. Paul Martin withdrew.

The second ballot was worse: Hellyer slipped to third, 8 votes behind Winters. Now the slide had started and the Hellyer box debated what to do next: stay for another ballot or withdraw and support Winters? Lee favoured neither.

"Quite frankly, Paul," he advised, "I don't think Winters can make it. I really don't. But the guy who can make it is Turner."

"He's just a kid," Hellyer responded, dismissing his 38-year-old cabinet colleague. Hellyer was toying with the idea of withdrawing but had not considered going to Turner.

As television cameras looked on, Hellyer huddled, football style, with Lee, Judy LaMarsh, and Léo Cadieux, the defence minister who had replaced Trudeau as Quebec co-chairman after the missed fishing trip. Hellyer's three top advisers unanimously agreed that the situation was hopeless and urged him to withdraw. Lee tried to block reporters' thrusting microphones with his hands and body but one managed to slip through and caught LaMarsh shouting the famous line: "Don't let that bastard [Trudeau] win it, Paul."

Hellyer conferred with his wife, Ellen, and a few loyal supporters who urged him to stay in the race. They stressed that only 8 votes separated him from Winters and that he could overtake him on the next ballot. But Lee knew it was hopeless. It didn't matter whether Hellyer trailed Winters by 8 or 800. Momentum is everything in political conventions, and Winters was rising while Hellyer was falling.

All eyes at the convention and the television cameras focused on Hellyer, awaiting his decision. He had remained cool and reserved throughout the second-ballot deliberations. Now he suddenly jumped to his feet, turned to his cheering section, flung both arms into the air, and with clenched fists pumping started chanting: "Fight, fight, fight." His supporters picked up the rallying cry.

The third ballot embarrassed Hellyer every bit as much as Lee feared. Hellyer dropped 244 votes behind Winters. Without hesitation or consultation, Hellyer stood up, walked over to Winters, and raised his arm. But it was too late to stop Trudeau, who won on the fourth ballot with 1,203 votes to 954 for Winters and 195 for Turner.

Lee and others still believe that Hellyer might have beaten Trudeau had he delivered a good speech. Despite Trudeaumania, which swept the public more than the political pros, Trudeau did not overwhelm the convention. He required four ballots and even then managed a majority of only 54 votes. His solid bloc of support was matched by an equally solid bloc of anti-Trudeau delegates who would vote for anybody but him. In between those blocs was another equally big bloc of neutrals who, as the choices narrowed, would eventually have to choose between Trudeau and the anti-Trudeau candidate. The neutrals held the balance and determined the outcome. As candidates dropped out one by one the anti-Trudeau delegates took too long to coalesce behind a single alternative. The fact that three of the four ballots were spent sorting out the discernible second gave Trudeau time to cut deeply into the neutrals and to pad his lead.

More crucial still, the discernible-second status ultimately went to Trudeau's weakest one-on-one opponent, the right-winger, Robert Winters. In the final ballot the choice for the remaining neutrals was clear: the left versus the hard right, at a time when the hard right was not where the country wanted to go. Significantly, seventy-five or so of Hellyer's supporters – led by Keith Davey – refused to follow him to Winters, and chose Trudeau instead. If Trudeau was beatable he was never beatable by Winters. Too many anti-Trudeau voters could not support an openly corporate candidate like Winters.

All this was cold comfort for Bill Lee, the failed kingmaker.

After the convention, Lee decided that he had been an EA too long. Most EAs lasted two years; he had been there five. The smart ones used the job as a stepping stone towards a greater career and not as a career in itself. But Lee had got locked first into the unification debate and then into Hellyer's leadership drive and before he knew it five years had gone. He had never earned much money. His air-force salary had reached about $13,500 a year (he had turned down two lucrative advertising jobs in New York for about double the money) and even his long hours as an EA fetched him a peak of about $15,000 a year. He was 44, had four kids nearing university, and felt the time had come to make some money. He informed Hellyer he was quitting to set up a consulting business.

Two weeks after winning the Liberal leadership in April 1968, Pierre Trudeau was sworn in as Canada's fifteenth prime minister and three days later he called a snap election to capitalize on his popularity. Lee planned to sit out the election and spend his time starting up his firm. He didn't care much for Trudeau and had reservations about his policies. His stop-Trudeau efforts during the leadership race had not gone unnoticed; Lee could still run in Hamilton, but he was sure that Trudeau would banish him so far into the back benches he would be touching the drapes at the back row. His standing was not helped when he briefly worked on the party's election platform and submitted what was basically Hellyer's old platform, only to have the whole thing scrapped for failing to reflect the new government's more interventionist plans. Lee had made an inauspicious start. His high-flying political days seemed to be over.

Meanwhile Trudeau's first week of campaigning left him steaming mad. He loathed campaigning at the best of times, and his first swing of the 1968 campaign started badly. The tour consistently ran late, denied him his precious breaks, pulled him out of bed too early in the morning, and got him back in bed too late at night. Trudeau grumpily let his handlers know he didn't care for being prime minister and had never wanted the job.

Lee was about to start cleaning out his desk in Hellyer's office when Marc Lalonde, his old sparring partner and Trudeau's new principal secretary, called.

"The boss is mad," Lalonde said, coming right to the point. "We know that you're a pretty good organizer. How would you like to become the campaign tour director and run the campaign tour?"

"The whole schmeer?" Lee asked.

"Yeah," Lalonde replied. "Just take over."

"Okay, but you're going to have to tell all the Trudeau people, Tim Porteous and Jim Davey and all that gang, that I'm in charge and what I say goes."

"Absolutely," Lalonde promised. "Just discussed it with him."

How political fortunes had changed. After spending months trying to thwart Trudeau "tooth, nail, and even knee," as one reporter put it, Lee now commanded the prime minister's campaign tour. He had leapfrogged over a coterie of loyal Trudeau aides who gasped at this dramatic turn of events and then swallowed their pride and returned to work to win the election. Lee became the czar on the plane, the fellow planning the tour and making it go. He controlled the prime minister's flow of information, in and out, on both party and government matters. For the next six weeks he was always at Trudeau's side and and became his most intimate adviser.

Lee and Trudeau had almost nothing in common. Lee spoke no French, operated pragmatically rather than intellectually, and generally was unversed in the subjects that interested Trudeau most, such as the constitution and French-Canadian literature. Yet he related well to Trudeau and, everybody agreed, handled him well and ran the entire operation with consummate skill. Election campaigns drain people's patience; everybody worked at the edge – Lee averaged three hours sleep a night – and the prospect of a flare-up always lay just beneath the surface. Trudeau was a prima donna, but Lee kept him in a good frame of mind, sometimes by stroking him and other times by challenging him. He read him expertly, simultaneously exerting authority and catering to his whims. "It was just the right approach," says one of the aides who had initially resented Lee. "... We couldn't have found a better person to do the job – and we had our choice."

At first Trudeau was a little distant, but as Lee briefed him in one hotel room after another, with the prime minister sometimes in nothing but undershorts, they developed a friendly, first-name relationship. Trudeau had his demands: no starts before 9 a.m., no finishes after 11, and a nap in the afternoon. Sometimes breakfast meetings were important and Lee would cut a deal: if Trudeau agreed to start at 8:30 Lee would have him to bed by 10:30. With his military background, Lee had no trouble keeping a rigid schedule. Once in Newfoundland he cut Trudeau's speech to one minute because Premier Joey Smallwood had made a long-winded introduction. Smallwood was furious, but Trudeau backed Lee.

Once Trudeau asked Lee something that clearly puzzled him. "Why would a guy as smart as you waste his time in the military?" asked Trudeau.

"There's a lot of pretty smart people in the military and they don't think it's a waste of time," replied Lee.

Trudeau had an aversion to the military, yet he liked military discipline and was impressed by Lee's clockwork efficiency and quick decisions. Sometimes the quick decisions were tough.

"Hi, Bill," said the voice on the telephone. "This is John Turner. I've got to speak to the prime minister right away."

"Well, John, he's having a nap. It's a hefty day."

"Bullshit," shot back Turner. "I'm solicitor general, God dammit, and I've got information to convey to him that is of vital importance. Wake him up. It's an order."

"No, John," replied Lee. "I'm not going to do that."

"You son of a bitch. Who the fuck do you think you are?" responded Turner, then and today a four-letter man. Later, he apologized.

Lee took care never to disturb Trudeau's rest periods. The only exception was when Bobby Kennedy was shot. On that occasion he woke Trudeau at 2 a.m.

For most of the campaign Trudeau rambled philosophically and promised little; the campaign was turning a little soft while Trudeau grew bored and tired. At that point, in Oakville, Lee ordered a size-34 men's bathing suit and talked Trudeau into taking a relaxing swim at the Holiday Inn pool. Meanwhile he secretly sent word for photographers to hide around the pool. When Trudeau stepped up to the water's edge in his lime-green trunks the photographers jumped out and started to snap pictures. "You son of a bitch," Trudeau muttered at Lee. Then he climbed onto the diving board and put on a show, starting with backflips and twists and finishing by spoofing the Stanfield bellyflop and the Douglas flip flop. Trudeau invited the lone sunbather, a blonde woman, to join him in the pool. The woman said she had no bathing suit. "Is that really essential?" asked Trudeau. More racy stuff. The next day Trudeau performed a somersault on the front page of virtually every newspaper in the country. *Time* magazine carried it, even the Washington *Post*. Image politics had arrived and Lee exploited it to the hilt.

When the press started grumbling about the lack of substance – Lee and the others were determined to keep substance out of the campaign – Lee orchestrated a similar stunt with Trudeau on a trampoline at a Vic Tanny's in Oshawa. Again Trudeau cursed Lee, and loved every minute of it as photographers captured him performing backflips and stunts that nobody could imagine his avuncular opponent, Bob Stanfield, ever doing.

Trudeau received help from an unexpected quarter when Quebec separatists rioted at the Saint Jean Baptiste Day parade in Montreal on election eve. Other dignitaries scattered before a hail of rocks and bottles as live television cameras watched. But Trudeau boldly held his position in the reviewing stand and impatiently warded off the Mounties' attempts to shield him, staring down the demonstrators and defying their attempts to intimidate him. Lee tossed him his rolled-up raincoat as padding in case the rocks came too close, but it was not needed. That single event probably turned a small Trudeau victory into a big one. Phone calls poured into Liberal Party headquarters from people who said they were switching their votes to Liberal. The next day Trudeau won an easy majority aided by a riot Lee had not staged.

The big victory celebration at the Château Laurier went on until the wee hours. At 2 a.m. Trudeau, with Lee at his side as usual, pushed his way behind the security guards out of the packed ballroom and into the waiting limousine. He slumped back in the seat and whacked Lee on the knee.

"We did it," he declared. "I'm going to run this country for a while. You are going to be in my office and will have a very key role."

"Pierre," Lee said quietly, "I'm not going to be in your office."

"What do you mean?"

"It really wouldn't work. You've got Marc [Lalonde] and you've got Michael [Pitfield], Tim [Porteous], Jim Davey, and all that group."

"I need somebody like you," said Trudeau. "I need a disciplinarian, somebody who can keep the thing moving."

"No, no," said Lee, shaking his head.

"Think about it for twenty-four hours," said Trudeau.

Lee knew he couldn't compete with the influence of Lalonde and Pitfield and was not interested in being number three. Moreover, he knew he couldn't work for Trudeau. The two got along well personally, but they were poles apart philosophically. Whereas bread-and-butter issues like unemployment and housing motivated Hellyer and Lee, Trudeau's raison d'être was the constitution. During the campaign Lee had noticed how patriation of the British North America Act had preoccupied Trudeau; Lee cared little whether the constitution lay in a dusty drawer in Westminster or in a dusty drawer in Ottawa. As for his own plans, Lee had passed up opportunities to earn big money and felt that now was the time to generate some private wealth.

Lee phoned Lalonde the next day with a message of "Thanks, but no thanks." What did he want, Lalonde wanted to know: director of communications? director of policy? Nothing, replied Lee. Just nothing.

"I would be fighting you and Michael all the time," Lee explained.

"The boss wants you in," Lalonde told him.

The next day Lee walked over to the East Block and across the prime minister's desk gave Trudeau his final no.

"What are you going to do?" Trudeau asked.

"Well," Lee replied, "I'm going to set up a business."

"A business?" Trudeau asked incredulously.

THREE

ESTABLISHING ECL

"Can you get me fifteen minutes with the minister for my client?"

"What do you want to talk to him about?" Lee asked. "Because he's very busy."

"Well, I don't know," came the response. "Just get him the fifteen minutes."

The agent was a professional door-opener who parlayed a personal acquaintance with Lee into a meeting between Hellyer and his client. The client, a businessman from Toronto, flew into Ottawa carrying a mammoth legal brief which neither Hellyer nor Lee had time to read. The client thought he was raising a crucial issue and believed that at the end of the meeting Hellyer would pick up the phone and fix the problem. In fact the problem was technical and so fraught with complications that Hellyer never did completely figure out what he was talking about. But Hellyer carried through with the charade, listening politely and promising to look into the matter. The businessman flew back home and boasted to his friends in Toronto that he had put his case directly to the minister of defence.

It happened in ministers' offices all over town.

"What was that all about?" Hellyer would ask once the businessman had left.

"I don't know," Lee would reply.

"Go straighten it out," Hellyer would say.

The businessman's brief, two inches thick, would go to the deputy minister, who bounced it down the line until it landed on the desk of a director or assistant deputy director who knew the issue intimately. The official would study the brief and transform the incomprehensible contents into a two-page précis, explaining how the problem fitted in with government policy – which usually meant that the bureaucrat, not Hellyer, determined the formal response that emerged from the system months later. Had the businessman gone to the bureaucrat in the first place the problem might have been resolved differently and more quickly. As it was, the bureaucrat would smile and put a mental black mark beside the businessman's name for going over his head. His two-page précis would be factually accurate but not very accommodating. Hellyer would eventually read it and instruct a staffer to draft a letter outlining department policy and recommending a meeting with the aggrieved bureaucrat. The businessman's task would now be tougher than when he started. The political fixer who had arranged the meeting with Hellyer had actually aggravated his client's predicament.

From a ringside seat in Ottawa, Lee watched the final disintegration of the once cosy relationship between government and business. During the Pearson years in the 1960s government grew more complex, more pervasive, and less intelligible to the great mass of businessmen, who yearned for the not-so-distant time when they could phone C. D. Howe and resolve their problems on the spot. In the old days of "élite accommodation" – as academics call it – businessmen and cabinet ministers lunched together. Élite accommodation broke down after the Saint-Laurent era, and business didn't fight the breakdown because it failed to realized that it had happened. Corporate executives still lunched with cabinet ministers, but somehow it no longer seemed to work. Government had grown and become a mass of policy-planning shops intertwined across departmental lines, so that even cabinet ministers didn't always know what was going on inside their departments. Outsiders had to study the new machine in order to learn how to prime it. Information became the vehicle of influence. Lee arrived in Hellyer's office just as the old order was going through its final collapse.

Before joining Hellyer, Lee had blindly accepted the prevailing notion that the captains of industry knew how to lobby and did it well. Five years as an executive assistant had opened his eyes and convinced him that business might have been good once, but had failed to adapt to the new reality. In fact Lee concluded that business was fundamentally incompetent in dealing with government, misinterpreted even its major intentions, and fared worse on the nuances. A lot of businessmen didn't even know which department to see. Lee concluded that business misunderstood Ottawa worse than Ottawa misunderstood business, and shook his head in dismay when businessmen constantly complained to him that government didn't listen.

Lee had a first-hand view of business's incompetence because anybody seeing the minister had to go through the EA first. From his vantage point he could see that business lacked not access but knowledge. Business lobbied incompetently because it didn't know government's agenda and was constantly caught by surprise over issues it should have foreseen and forestalled. Business too often set sail without first checking the political winds and blamed government when it got blown off course. Lee talked to public servants who had complaints of their own, especially that businessmen never talked to them until it was too late. Only after a law or regulation had become a fact did they show any interest, and then only to complain. The public servants confirmed that such lack of co-operation, such lack of advance warning about potential problems, seriously complicated their task.

Lee saw the problems from both ends and came to the conclusion that French and English were not the only two solitudes in Canada. Business and government needed each other and yet did not communicate.

He realized that he had stumbled into an opportunity. If two sides who needed each other could not get together on their own, somebody could earn a living doing it for them. Getting to know government took time, effort, planning, and, most of all, understanding. Since most businessmen lacked the time to understand government they needed an adviser to recommend what to do. He saw that with his background he could probably make a fortune by using his expert knowledge to provide industry with government intelligence and strategic advice. After a great deal of thought, Lee decided to establish a consulting company that would do two things: first, monitor government and alert his clients about impending problems, and second, coach his clients on how to deal with government – either in repairing immediate problems or in avoiding future ones.

Lee had faced big career decisions before. When he had quit the air force to join Hellyer he had walked away from the prospect of ending up as a general with a good pension. He had turned down Trudeau, and later a position with the new Department of Communications that probably would have made him a deputy minister. He had spurned generous offers in advertising and public relations. Now he decided to launch headlong into the area of business-government relations without knowing whether a market existed. He would have to convince the business community it needed him.

Lee had arrived at his decision four or five months before the Liberal leadership convention, and during the campaign he mulled over the names of potential partners. He seriously considered Dick O'Hagan, Pearson's highly regarded press secretary, and Mike McCabe, Mitchell Sharp's fast-track executive assistant, who had come out of Lever Brothers and knew marketing. Further down his list were Duncan Edmonds, EA to Paul Martin, and Ross Fitzpatrick with Citizenship Minister John Nicholson. Bill Neville, EA to Judy LaMarsh, was not on his list. Neville was known as a thoroughly competent aide and a brilliant speechwriter, but in terms of image had never graduated to the Super EA list. Neville, however, had written speeches and worked as a resource person in the Hellyer campaign and thus come to Lee's attention. Late one night, after a strategy meeting, he and Lee started comparing notes about life as an EA. Neville had lived through the same experience and come to the same conclusion about business and the new government environment, and how to correct the situation. They talked about the clutch of door-opening lawyers, senators, and old-style lobbyists they had met and how badly they served the business community, and about how things could be changed. They agreed on just about everything. Only one detail bothered Lee about Neville. He had been a first-rate journalist enjoying a flourishing career, and then had suddenly quit in mid-flight.

As the son of one of C. D. Howe's civil servants, William Henry Neville grew up in Ottawa. As a teenager he stood out among his peers because of an exceptional IQ, photographic memory, impressive vocabulary, and broad reading habits. In short, he was an egghead who wore thick glasses and, in school or out, always knew the answer. While fellow students traded meaningless banter Neville talked serious issues and chased after the logic of conversations to make sure it all fitted. During exams Neville would stare up at the ceiling and see the textbook page in his head. Nature had blessed him with an exceptional mind but had stinted a little on his body. He was skinny, physically frail, chronically shortsighted, and so highly strung that he sometimes shook with intensity for no apparent reason. He made the school basketball and football teams out of sheer determination; he seemed incapable of doing anything casually, even walking down a street.

He enrolled in journalism at Carleton University and promptly started pulling down As while a friend from a disadvantaged background was flunking out. Neville took his friend on as a special project and spent virtually every waking hour of the final two weeks tutoring him to a hard-won pass. Neville had taken journalism as a prelude to a law degree, but that all changed in 1956 when he got a summer job with the understaffed United Press International, then called British United Press, on Parliament Hill. Neville started out his student reporting career covering the infamous pipeline debate, the story of the decade. He had tripped into a wonderful opportunity and quickly made the most of it, becoming a first-rate reporter who enjoyed the excitement of breaking news and the reward of upstaging the better-staffed Canadian Press.

In his final year at Carleton Neville won the Kenneth Wilson Memorial Award for his thesis about the decline of the Conservative Party, in which he predicted that it would go nowhere. Neville argued that the party had failed to differentiate itself from the ruling Liberals, leaving the public to choose between the two parties on the basis of managerial competence, on which the Tories could not possibly win. Three months later John Diefenbaker destroyed the Louis Saint-Laurent government and led the Conservative Party to victory. It was not an auspicious beginning for a budding political analyst.

Neville stayed nearly a decade with UPI. He wrote so quickly and concisely that he spent only thirty or forty minutes a day behind his typewriter, banging out with flair in twenty words what other reporters sometimes needed fifty or a hundred words to say. He rose to be Ottawa bureau manager in 1960 and three years later, at 27, he moved to Montreal as news manager for Canada. UPI paid notoriously bad salaries, even by journalistic standards, and Neville by this time supported a wife and two children, but UPI's parsimony never seemed to bother him. What did bother him was bureaucratic nonsense like the day he fought New York's decision to send a reporter to Tallahassee, Florida, rather than put a photographer into Toronto. Neville quit after two years in Montreal and moved back to Ottawa. He worked temporarily at Canadian Press, but had already decided to quit journalism in favour of government.

Neville landed an interview with Paul Martin as a possible replacement for Duncan Edmonds, but Martin, the old constituency pro, turned him off by rambling on about Windsor. Neville then saw Judy LaMarsh, who swept in from a cabinet meeting and immediately started telling Neville in colourful detail what a bunch of nitwits her colleagues were. She hired Neville.

Neville had not been with LaMarsh a week when the Pearson government launched an investigation into the leak of a story in the Toronto *Telegram* about a $500-million health fund. The breach infuriated Pearson because he had been holding the announcement for the coming election campaign, when he planned to announce it with great fanfare. Neville sheepishly owned up to the act. The *Telegram*'s Fraser Kelly had asked him what the government planned to do, so naturally Neville told him. Neville realized that he was no longer a reporter and vowed there and then to stop acting like one.

Despite his shaky start, Neville quickly developed a rapport with LaMarsh that in some ways equalled the Hellyer-Lee match-up. LaMarsh was loud and fiery; Neville meek and almost shy. LaMarsh was famously partisan; Neville virtually non-partisan. Neville got to know LaMarsh's mood and could judge when to retreat and when to manipulate. He did everything he could for her, and above all remained patient and loyal even when LaMarsh became unreasonable. Even Neville's wife, Marilyn, became a devoted friend. Neville still calls LaMarsh one of the most significant politicians of modern Canada.

The devotion flowed both ways. LaMarsh thought of Neville as the quintessential EA and described him glowingly in her book: "He was a miracle, and from the time I hired Bill Neville practically all my staffing worries disappeared and many more besides.... His own judgment of issues was very often superior to mine, and I trusted him implicitly. He never tried to duck out of anything, never talked back when I blew up, talked me out of it when I was unfair to others, took my side and became my friend and closest adviser."

Neville came to work on the Hellyer leadership campaign more by accident than by plan, thanks to a fateful flare-up of LaMarsh's famous temper in February 1968. LaMarsh had decided to support Trudeau and was waiting for him to announce his candidacy when she and he tangled in cabinet over a judicial appointment. As justice minister, Trudeau had appointed a judge in her riding. LaMarsh opposed the appointment on the grounds that the person was a Tory and unqualified. When LaMarsh demanded that Trudeau rescind the appointment, he held his ground. LaMarsh, a hefty and imposing woman, was a bully in cabinet and literally terrorized her opponents – Paul Martin once became fearful for his physical safety. Now she turned up the volume and started shouting obscenities; Trudeau surprised her by shouting back. Their cabinet colleagues watched, white-faced. As LaMarsh got louder, so did Trudeau. In the end LaMarsh stormed out of the cabinet room and into her office, where she picked up the phone to tell Paul Hellyer she was backing him all the way.

Neville was already leaning to Hellyer but would not have been free to join his campaign as a volunteer had his boss been working for Trudeau. Now he was free and he happily joined Lee's team. Lee liked what he saw of Neville during the Hellyer campaign and found him a prodigious, reliable, and highly able worker. Neville's gift for writing enabled him to craft superb speeches, and his UPI speed meant that he could crank them out as fast as Hellyer could deliver them – or sometimes fail to deliver them. He was also highly articulate and a keen analyst of political developments. And he saw the commercial opportunities in Lee's proposed consulting firm, because independently he had been thinking exactly the same thing.

Lee's and Neville's mid-campaign chat was a meeting of minds. Before calling it a night the two had informally concluded a business partnership. Whether Hellyer won or lost, they agreed to start a company in which each owned fifty per cent of the shares; they would split salaries four to three in Lee's favour since his name would draw clients. The company's opening was delayed while Lee worked on the Trudeau election campaign, and delayed again after the election, as Lee helped Eric Kierans organize the new Department of Communications. In the interim Neville became executive assistant to Finance Minister Edgar Benson and then the $100-a-day secretary to Paul Hellyer's task force on housing.

Lee and Neville each went to the bank and secured a $10,000 personal line of credit. In September 1968 they hired a secretary-bookkeeper, bought a few desks, moved into a tiny fifth-floor office of the Burnside Building a few blocks below Parliament Hill, and opened for business under the name Lee-Neville Executive Consultants Ltd. The name was eventually shortened to Executive Consultants Ltd., or ECL. Like any new business, they faced the task of letting the world know they existed. Lee, who had not lost his gift for marketing, figured out a strategy. While still working on contract to the Department of Communications, he sent letters on Minister of Transport stationery to a series of prospective clients, shamelessly touting his connection with Hellyer and Trudeau, and Neville's connection with Edgar Benson. The letter ended:

"Before leaving government service, I wanted to thank you most sincerely for your courtesy and kindness to me. I very much appreciate our past relationship.

"As yet, we do not have a new business telephone but, if you should wish to contact me, I am sure the Prime Minister's switchboard (992-4211) or the Office of the Minister of Transport (992-9004), will relay any calls."

Lee had picked up some enemies in five years of hard-nosed political service; now he counted on them to react to this brazen letter. Sure enough, the *Globe and Mail* soon heard of it and ran a story about Lee's using his connection with the Prime Minister's Office to drum up business. The *Globe* reproduced the full letter, which had the effect of telling businessmen across Canada that Lee and Neville were two former EAs with good connections who were looking for clients. It was precisely the response Lee hoped to get. When the press demanded an explanation, that gave Lee and Neville a new round of publicity and another opportunity to explain what they were doing. The Toronto *Telegram* set up a "Lee Watch" to see how long the Prime Minister's Office would continue to relay telephone messages. Money could not have bought better advertising.

ECL paid its way from the day it opened. Lee's telephone-number caper stirred more interest than they could handle. Inquiries poured in. ECL's biggest problem was sorting out which clients to accept and which to turn down. Not surprisingly, people had the impression that ECL opened doors and did favours. Lee and Neville kept explaining that ECL didn't operate that way and that the client was further ahead doing his own lobbying on the basis of ECL's advice. No matter what Lee or Neville said, some clients failed to understand – or believe – the ECL concept. They wanted a government contract, a quick-fix solution, or a door opened. One businessman offered a $50,000 fee for a broadcasting licence. Several contractors, noting that the decision to build Mirabel Airport was made while Hellyer was Minister of Transport, wanted ECL to wave its magic wand in high places and produce construction contracts. Neville later joked to friends that they could have pulled down a fortune in the first year but then in the second would have had to flee to Mexico.

Some clients listened better than others, some worse. For instance, there was TRW, the giant Los Angeles aerospace company, which was keen to sell the Canadian government its civilian applications of NASA-related space technology. Lee and Neville met TRW's top executives in Los Angeles and advised them that they had to establish a bona fide Canadian presence and contribute to the country to win government sales. TRW's idea of a Canadian presence was an office in Toronto run by Americans. Lee and Neville warned TRW it would fall on its face trying to flog technology developed in Houston, and urged it to set up a Canadian plant and gradually introduce Canadian managers to run it. TRW paid the monthly $5,000 retainer but ignored ECL's advice and went on making requests for the very things Lee and Neville said they would never do.

Finally Lee and Neville concluded that they and their client held fundamentally different views on how to operate and flew to Los Angeles to confront the issue. "When we took this on you said you were going to follow our advice," Lee told TRW's two top officers. "That's what you hired us for. And all you've got is marketeers up there in Toronto. And you're getting nowhere. And you won't get anywhere. I don't care if your product is ten times as good as Bombardier's or somebody else's, you're not going to sell it in Canada. You're wasting your money, you're wasting our time. We're fed up with these marketing guys calling us and saying: 'Can't you do this, can't you do that?' You're doing nothing for Canada." The two sides agreed to terminate the contract. Lee and Neville downed a couple of stiff drinks and flew back to Canada. Aside from one contract with the province of Alberta, TRW never did get the government business it sought.

Lee and Neville drew up a set of rules when they agreed to form a partnership back during the Hellyer campaign days.

Rule number one: ECL would not lobby. Such a rule looked like heresy, in fact worse – suicide. After all, lobbyists were messengers to government – making representations was precisely what they did. It was like Bobby Hull vowing not to score goals. But Lee and Neville undertook not to be lobbyists and thereby set a new standard. ECL refused to do more than collect information and give advice. They gave clients a road map of government along with clear directions where to go, but they made them walk it themselves. Clients had to do their own lobbying.

Rule number two: ECL would never work for government. They refused to accept even those Crown corporations, such as Air Canada and Atomic Energy of Canada Ltd., which competed like private corporations. Some day they knew the Liberals would lose to the Conservatives and the Liberal image that helped so much at the beginning would return to haunt ECL. The company's ultimate success hinged on its ability to survive the comings and goings of governments. Lee and Neville wanted their company to last a long time, and that meant rising above the partisan wars.

Rule number three: ECL would charge hefty fees. No hourly charges, just one flat retainer of $1,500 to $4,000 or more a month plus expenses whether a client needed ECL that month or not. The fees were audacious – in 1968 the minimum $1,500 a month was equivalent to an executive salary, which meant that every new client added at least an extra executive-salary cost to the company's cash flow.

Rule number four: ECL would deal only with senior management, preferably the chief executive officer and definitely not the vice president of marketing. Lee and Neville felt their information was important and therefore should go to important people. That way ECL's advice would be treated with the respect it deserved.

ECL's rules could have scuttled the company – just as they ended the TRW relationship – but they did exactly the opposite. They separated ECL from the gaggle of lawyers and old-style door-openers, and underscored the genius of Bill Lee. Even Lee was amazed by the results. Lee and Neville held their breath when they quoted a fee for the first time and almost fell off their chairs when the client accepted without a blink. High fees enhanced their reputation. "If they're paying a lot of money they're going to pay attention," Lee was once advised. "If they've got you for peanuts, they'll think your advice is worth peanuts." Lee calculated that a company president would sooner pay ECL a sizable fee to keep a watching brief than open an Ottawa office to do the same thing. An Ottawa office even in those days cost more than $50,000, and many clients didn't want to know $50,000 worth. Lawyers on an hourly rate cost as much or more and didn't know as much. Associations were inexpensive but too broad to be effective. From a businessman's point of view ECL's hefty fees were not so outrageous.

Lee's and Neville's earnings surpassed their wildest expectations. ECL grossed $180,000 in its first year, and most of it flowed through to the bottom line. The company carried no inventory. Direct expenses were billed to the client and the indirect expenses consisted of rent at $2.50 a square foot and a secretary's four-figure salary. All ECL needed was a desk and telephone and invoice slip. Neither Lee nor Neville had earned more than $15,000 a year, and suddenly their incomes jumped four or five times. Their second-year incomes nudged close to $100,000, which was breathtaking in the late sixties. Suddenly they were among the highest-paid corporate executives in Canada and were talking to accountants about leasing cars and things like that. Neville would later joke that in the early days ECL consisted of him and Lee at one end of a phone with a government telephone directory and the client at the other end with a chequebook.

The decision to walk away from waiting government money enhanced ECL's image with the business community. The government offered Lee and Neville lucrative contracts to set up communications branches and mount public-awareness campaigns, but ECL could afford to turn down all propositions because it was doing so well. And it was doing well for its clients, too.

Xerox of Canada Ltd. each year sold the government from forty to fifty million dollars' worth of photocopying equipment and supplied the best product of its type, all manufactured in the United States. But as competitors moved into the photocopying field and began undercutting on price, Xerox started losing its share of government sales and the Department of Supply and Services started giving Xerox salesmen a cool reception. The company didn't understand what was happening. Eventually a friendly bureaucrat took one of the Xerox people aside and informally told him the company was doing things wrong and needed help from somebody who understood public policy. The bureaucrat suggested ECL.

ECL researched Xerox's problem and discovered why sales were dropping. Ottawa had adopted a new policy of using its purchasing muscle to boost Canadian manufacturing, and Xerox offered only imported equipment. ECL told Xerox that in order to continue selling the most expensive product of its type it needed more than just a sales office in Canada. It recommended three changes. First, establish a true Canadian manufacturing capability. Second, set up a research and development centre in Canada – initially run by Americans but always recruiting out of Canadian universities so that eventually Canadians would run it. Third, manufacture exclusively in Canada a particular Xerox product for the world in order to give the Canadian subsidiary an export market.

Xerox reacted dubiously at first and Lee visited the U.S. headquarters in Connecticut to make his pitch before the company agreed. When Xerox swung around, however, it did so with a vengeance: it built a plant, established an R&D Centre outside Toronto, hired a Canadian president, and set up a world product mandate for a document-handler which was incorporated into its worldwide product line and generated exports between $100-

and $200-million a year. The research and development centre got a world product mandate for paper, toners, and inks – and Xerox qualified as a Canadian supplier to the Department of Supply and Services. Without dropping its price, Xerox, the good corporate citizen, turned its government sales around. "That turned out to be a very successful story in responding to Canadian initiatives," says Xerox Vice President Peter Brophey. "They gave us good advice and helped us get a program up and running, and worked themselves out of a job while they did it."

ECL worked with NCR Canada Ltd. even before it got involved with Xerox. NCR did not want government sales as much as it wanted public financing. With ECL's help it got government grants to help establish a research, development, and production facility in Waterloo. In return NCR used the plant to produce decoding and encoding machinery for the high-speed processing of cheques, vouchers, and similar financial records. The Waterloo plant exported ninety-five per cent of its output and eventually captured three-quarters of the world market while creating seven hundred local jobs.

With the Xerox and NCR cases, ECL introduced the concept of moving into market dominance by shrewd use of public policy. The strategy was later picked up and perfected by companies such as Dome Petroleum, who first figured out what government policy was and then moved to get there ahead of the competition. ECL also advised clients to be open and truthful when dealing with the government and to act in the community interest; telling the truth was simpler than lying and did not require the company to remember what it had said in order to keep its story straight. For many businessmen it was a new way of operating.

By 1971 ECL was generating nearly half a million dollars in revenue a year, of which more than sixty per cent flowed through to the bottom line. The company now had about fifteen retainer clients and the load was beginning to strain the limit for a two-man operation. So Lee and Neville sold 20 per cent of the company – 10 per cent each – to Irv Keenleyside and took him in as a third partner. Keenleyside, who paid $130,000 for his 20 per cent, was nearing 60 and had long been a traditional lobbyist in Ottawa, representing mainly Acres, the dominant engineering company in Canada. Keenleyside carried no political affiliation and people joked that he wouldn't recognize the minister of finance if he fell over him. But everyone marvelled at his enormous network of bureaucratic contacts. Keenleyside, a slim, distinguished-looking man with grey hair and a small mustache, brought Acres with him as a client and for a brief time had trouble convincing Acres that with ECL he would no longer be lobbying.

In 1974 Lee and Neville wanted to put more money into the bank, and sold off additional shares. The company now had twenty-five to thirty clients and had become a valuable property, but each day the assets went up and down in the elevator. Lee or Neville could suffer a heart attack or be hit by a truck; or, as appeared likely, Robert Stanfield's Conservatives could win the next election. Despite ECL's policy of not employing political connections, it remained to be seen whether it could survive a change in government. ECL sold 10 per cent of the company to Tex Enemark and 10 per cent to Jack Struthers, each for $75,000, while 5 per cent went to Steve Markey, a researcher working his way up. Struthers had a public-relations background and brought two new clients: the Mining Association of Canada, which did not stay long, and Macdonald Tobacco. Enemark, a Vancouver lawyer who had been a special assistant to Ron Basford, brought no clients. Lee hesitated about bringing in partners without clients because it added another executive salary and limousine with no increase in revenue, but Enemark was bright and highly regarded and seemed to know about everything that moved in Ottawa.

Enemark soon proved his worth when he rescued Macdonald Tobacco from a sticky crisis over the launching of a new cigarette called More. Macdonald had poured millions into a razzledazzle ad campaign when a lawyer noticed at the last minute that More's fractionally increased length subjected the product to twice as much tax. The cigarette was correspondingly thinner, but the regulations taxed cigarettes not on volume but on length. The extra tax would destroy the product, and getting special relief would be difficult. It was not easy to get bureaucratic sympathy or to plead the public interest on something as unhealthy as smoking. There seemed to be no way out until Enemark took a copy of the regulations home for the weekend.

By Saturday night he had spotted a solution. The regulations defined a cigarette as a tube of tobacco and *mentioned nothing about filters*. The strategy became this: Macdonald Tobacco would claim that the regulations referred only to the tobacco portion of the More tube, which was short enough to fall within the regulations. In other words it was the filter and not the tobacco that violated the length! Any other interpretation, argued Enemark, warming to the work, would encourage cigarette manufacturers to reduce or eliminate filters and increase the risks of smoking *contrary to the public interest*. The bureaucrats accepted Macdonald Tobacco's argument, and the company launched More as scheduled. It was a classic case. The More cigarette lobby worked because it used one of the basic principles of successful lobbying: when pressing a case, always wrap it in the cloak of public interest. Successful lobbyists – like successful lawyers – do not necessarily advance the best case, but marshal the most effective arguments.

ECL developed a reputation for keeping its finger on the pulse of government. When the Trudeau government rattled the business community in 1971 with a sweeping new anti-combines bill, Lee, from his knowledge of the players, worked out half a dozen scenarios and concluded that the government lacked the will to push it through. The assessment seemed strange at the time but it proved to be dead on. The Japanese Embassy was a client whose main interest seemed to be the Foreign Investment Review Agency, on which ECL reported monthly. The Embassy pressed ECL for details of cabinet shuffles before they happened, so that Tokyo would know it kept on top of matters. Putting together hunch and guess, ECL forecast the six key shifts in the cabinet shuffle of August 1974 and was right on all but one. On August 29 1975, ECL surprised its clients with the news that Trudeau would soon introduce wage and price controls in violation of his election promise not to do so. Six weeks later Trudeau went on national television and did exactly what ECL had predicted.

ECL occasionally advised clients how to foil an unaccommodating politician. The Canadian National Millers Association returned to ECL's office to report that it had followed its advice and still failed to get Transport Minister Otto Lang to bend to a reasonable request. Lang was terminating a $20-million freight

subsidy on the export sale of flour, and the association merely
wanted some time to adjust. The executive of the association
tried to negotiate a five-year phase-out and then a three-year
phase-out with Lang, only to be spurned. Lang, a politician not
known for his flexibility, insisted on ending the subsidy in one
fell swoop. What was to be done? "Now we fuck up the system,"
ECL responded. Lang was a poor parliamentarian and ECL knew
that the bill ranked low on his priority list. Even more to the
point, it knew that the government House leader, Lang's colleague, would not invest much House time on a relatively small
piece of legislation. A few footdragging MPs determined to protest the unfairness of the measure could derail the whole thing.
After being briefed, a few regional MPs took up the cause and
passed the word that they would obstruct the bill. The government House leader dropped the legislation as not worth the
fight. Lang never knew what happened; he had been defeated by
ECL and his own intransigence.

What accounted for ECL's success?

The decision not to dirty its hands with lobbying made ECL
look virtuous, but the policy turned out to be as much pragmatic
as moral. If ECL had waded into the fight against Lang it would
have incurred the minister's longstanding enmity and harmed its
long-term effectiveness. Lee and Neville realized that ECL would
live longer and make more money in the long run by keeping its
hands clean. Lobbying required prepared briefs, endless meetings, and reporting back and forth, and those things consumed a
great deal of time. Giving advice used up only a fraction of that
time, which meant that ECL could sign up more clients and have
more retainers.

The no-lobby system not only made ECL more money but it
actually worked better all round. Properly briefed and advised, a
client could present a case more effectively than a hired gun
could. If Lee and Neville were to walk into a deputy minister's
office representing General Motors, they knew the deputy minister would wonder why General Motors itself had not come.
From their days as EAs they knew that Canadian decision-makers
wanted to deal with principals and would wheel and deal with
the president of a company much more freely than they would
with hired guns, who tended to get in the way. ECL's self-imposed

edict against lobbying turned out to be exactly what the system in Ottawa needed.

Lee and Neville, opposites that they were, made a perfect match. The qualities that made Lee a great salesman for Hellyer made him an excellent public-affairs consultant. He seemed to know everybody in government and spent his day on the telephone, exercising an uncanny ability to get people to tell him everything they knew. He knew the system, had a remarkable feel for events, was friendly and popular – but most of all he knew how to get clients. Neville, meanwhile, happily attacked the nuts and bolts of ECL's business and spent his time flying out to service clients or sitting behind his beaten-up manual typewriter and banging out briefs and memos with two fingers. Neville worked compulsively, going flat out until he crashed. Every six months or so his body buckled under the load and forced him onto sick leave. Then he would return and work away as intensively as ever.

Three times ECL branched off into sidelines and each time withdrew. First it saw a market opportunity in planning meetings and conventions for its clients and established Executive Convention Services. The venture made a modest profit but absorbed too much time and could not come close to matching ECL's profitability, so it was folded. Next ECL created a public-relations arm and then pulled back. It also seriously flirted with establishing a company called Asia Canada International to introduce Canadian companies to marketing opportunities in the Orient. Lee travelled throughout East Asia and had almost hired away a diplomat from External Affairs for the Hong Kong office before backing out entirely. These experiences, especially Executive Convention Services, convinced Lee not to stray from ECL's winning formula, although Neville was less convinced.

After ECL turned the corner into the 1970s, clients continued to come through the door, outnumbering those who dropped out, so that revenues continued to grow. Expenses rose, too, as ECL hired more research staff. Neither Lee nor Neville knew exactly where things were heading, but generally Neville wanted to expand the ECL concept whereas Lee preferred keeping things tight and running the profits out the other end. Neville never pressed the issue, but that divergence in philosophy remained one of the few differences in an otherwise remarkable chemistry.

FOUR

THE POLITICAL ITCH

On April 24 1969, well before ECL's first anniversary, Lee got a tearful phone call from Hellyer's personal secretary, Margaret Bulger, saying that Hellyer was drafting his letter of resignation from the cabinet. Lee dropped everything and raced over to Parliament Hill to talk to Hellyer before it was too late. As he hurried up O'Connor Street and onto the hill itself he reflected on the news and was not surprised. What had been a surprise was Hellyer's decision a year earlier to stay on with Trudeau and become his deputy prime minister.

On top of his cabinet duties Hellyer had formed his own seven-member task force on housing – a de facto royal commission – and had toured the country in search of solutions to Canada's housing problem. Lee and Neville had warned him not to run the task force because it would lead to an inevitable conflict of interest: when the task force reported to the government, which hat would he wear, the government's or the task force's? As deputy prime minister, which side would he ultimately support if cabinet rejected his task force? Hellyer didn't heed the warning, maintaining confidently that he had been given a mandate straight from Trudeau.

Trouble first loomed early in 1969 when the Prime Minister's Office tried to erase Hellyer's name from the report. Real trouble surfaced the day the report was published, when Trudeau's first words to Hellyer were: "Where would you rate this anyway in terms of our priorities? Twelfth? Fifteenth? Twentieth?" Hellyer turned white. Now, three months later, he was giving up on Trudeau. The housing issue symbolized two approaches to government: Trudeau viewed housing as a matter of provincial jurisdiction; Hellyer saw it as a pressing need requiring federal action. Exactly what Lee and Neville had warned Hellyer about had happened.

Lee arrived at the Centre Block and, without breaking stride, stomped through the reception area and straight into Hellyer's office.

"Don't do it, Paul," he warned. "Don't do it."

"You were right about Trudeau," Hellyer replied. "He doesn't care a fink about housing and he's not going to do any of the things that this task force has recommended."

"But I told you that," Lee said. "I told you not to head your own task force – if he doesn't do what the task force recommends you're dead. Even a man without principle would be dead."

"I just can't raise the hopes of people across the country," Hellyer said. "He's not going to do anything. He doesn't think it's relevant to the federal government."

Hellyer kept insisting he had no alternative and Lee could not persuade him otherwise. Hellyer was determined to quit, and wrote a searing letter of resignation. This intemperate letter received a stinging response from Trudeau. Realizing that Hellyer's future in the Liberal Party was finished the minute those letters were released, Lee met Marc Lalonde, Trudeau's principal secretary; like diplomats representing two hostile powers, they negotiated a compromise. Both sides agreed to withdraw their original letters. Hellyer would write a new letter of resignation, Trudeau issue a new response, and the two would be released as the exchange of record. The semi-truce ultimately made little difference. Hellyer eventually bolted the Liberal Party anyway. His political career would twist and turn in different directions, and would never again reach the old heights.

Having temporarily saved Hellyer's status in the Liberal Party, Lee began wondering about his own position. Despite advising Hellyer not to quit, Lee himself had serious reservations about Trudeau, and over the next few years they grew. Lee had always been on the right of the party. In fact he was never really a Liberal, becoming associated with the party only because Hellyer hired him. He agreed to be convention co-ordinator of the 1970 National Liberal Conference in Ottawa in order to move the party to the right where he thought it should be, but soon decided it was hopeless under Trudeau. His concerns continued to deepen. He believed that the 1971 Victoria Conference and the constitution so preoccupied Trudeau that for practical purposes he abdicated his role as prime minister and turned the country's affairs over to Marc Lalonde. Deep inside he felt that Trudeau could not be bothered with Canada's pressing economic problems. So when the Prime Minister's Office invited him to run Trudeau's campaign for re-election in 1972 he quickly begged off, saying that business commitments unfortunately prevented him from taking six weeks off to travel across the country.

Lee was relaxing in Nassau when Bob Andras, the new Liberal campaign co-chairman and a close friend, called with a long-distance proposal from Trudeau. Andras informed Lee that Trudeau appreciated his predicament and wondered if he could organize the tour from Ottawa while somebody else took his place on the plane and handled the daily details. The prime minister was asking, so Lee found it hard to say no. Once again he was manager of the prime minister's campaign.

Nobody expected Trudeau to repeat his sweep of four years earlier, but Lee figured a good campaign would secure a working minority of 125 to 128 seats. Reports from the plane streamed in daily, but Lee saw Trudeau only on weekends in Ottawa, which made it hard for them to duplicate the 1968 relationship. Trudeau was out of Lee's hands for the rest of the week when aides from the Prime Minister's Office had the minute-by-minute control of events. Lee saw the aides as Trudeau sycophants who ignored and mishandled Lee's strategies and, worse still, feared telling Trudeau anything bad. While they were busily assuring Trudeau how well his theme "The Land is Strong" was going over, sources from across the country were phoning to tell Lee that the campaign was bombing. With typical bluntness, he told Trudeau he was blowing the election. The prime minister retorted that Lee was sitting in a cocoon in Ottawa and missing the real thing, that his own reports showed precisely the opposite. Lee argued that the campaign was misfiring badly and started scaling down his predictions of 125-128 seats.

When Trudeau entered Liberal Party headquarters early on election night he walked straight over to Lee.

"Are you watching the results?" he asked, pointing to the early reports on the big board, which showed the Liberals gaining seats in Newfoundland and Prince Edward Island. "You and your doomsaying. You kept saying we were going to blow this election."

"We've still got the rest of Quebec, we've got Ontario and we've got the west to come, prime minister," Lee replied. "You sit and watch."

The early returns supported Trudeau. He quickly gained three seats in the Atlantic Provinces and held his own in Quebec but suddenly, when the Ontario results started streaming in, everything turned sour. Trudeau grew gloomier and gloomier as the returns moved west and the Conservatives picked up more and more Liberal seats. Trudeau dropped 28 seats in Ontario, 8 in the Prairie Provinces, and 12 in B.C. By B.C. Stanfield's Tories had caught up and the two parties briefly seesawed back and forth. Eventually the Liberals secured 109 seats to the Conservatives' 107 while the New Democratic Party, with 31, held the balance of power.

The next morning Andras invited Lee to breakfast at an East End shopping mall.

"What the hell do we do now?" Andras asked.

"Advise PET to do the right thing," Lee replied. "He caused this political crisis through his philosophical musings throughout the campaign, against our advice. Tell him to call a press conference, accept the responsibility, announce he is resigning and will ask the Governor General to call on John Turner to see if he can form a government that would gain support for a period in the Commons."

Above all, Lee wanted to avoid having the NDP dictate government policy; he figured that enough Tories would sooner support a Turner government than see the Liberals move left to make a deal with the NDP.

"Trudeau will throw me out the door of Sussex Drive if I tell him that," Andras responded.

"Tell him this is my advice," Lee said.

Andras thought Lee was crazy, but Lee insisted and Andras walked off, looking decidedly unhappy. At about 10:30 that morning Andras phoned and invited Lee to coffee at the Carleton Towers. Andras looked no happier now.

"Shit," he said, "it was awful."

"What did he say?"

"He said, 'Tell Lee to fuck himself.' "

According to Andras, Trudeau had decided that if the Liberals stayed ahead after the recounts he would have a couple of his left-leaning ministers strike a deal with the NDP; Lee said he was afraid of that.

Lee had burned his bridges with Trudeau. He was to stay out of Liberal Party affairs for more than a decade.

Like Lee, Neville also became disenchanted with Trudeau. Neville, a political centrist, was naturally more at home in the Liberal Party and yet he too became disillusioned. But his disillusionment sprang from different origins. While Lee, the rightwinger, was upset at Trudeau's neglect of the economy, Neville grew disturbed over Trudeau's combative style of leadership. He admired Trudeau and supported many of his ends, but disliked his methods of achieving them, particularly his predilection for finding villains to beat up on. Neville believed that Trudeau's approach was fundamentally divisive. Canada, he felt, was too easily divided as it was; political leaders should bridge divisions, not widen them. Neville, more a disciple of LaMarsh than a partisan Liberal, had no real ideological differences with either of the two major parties and believed that Canada should always be governed from the moderate centre. In his opinion Bob Stanfield, who appealed to Neville in the same way that Lester Pearson had, embodied exactly those prime-ministerial qualities Trudeau lacked. No single event pricked Neville's private questioning of Trudeau. It was just a feeling that kept growing. Neville let his feelings fester until Jim Gillies, a closet Liberal with his own doubts about Trudeau, defected and crossed over to the Conservatives.

Neville had first met Gillies when the York University business professor worked quietly – almost secretly – on the Hellyer leadership campaign in 1968. They became friends when Gillies sat as a member on the Hellyer task force on housing while Neville was secretary and report-writer. The two kept in touch. When Gillies ran for parliament as a Conservative in Toronto's Don Valley, Neville offered to help. This campaign became the vehicle that put Neville in touch with the Conservative Party.

Every weekend during the 1972 election Neville hopped down to Toronto to help Gillies's well-heeled campaign wrest a seat away from the Liberals. Ironically, while Lee managed Trudeau's campaign, his partner worked for the Conservatives although Neville's involvement was low-key and behind the scenes and limited to one riding. Few people paid attention or knew what Neville was doing, although some Tories wondered whether a spy had infiltrated the Gillies camp. On election night, while Lee argued with Trudeau, Neville celebrated Gillies's 6,000-vote victory over Robert Kaplan.

Gillies was one of the Tory stars of '72 and was destined for the cabinet whenever Stanfield won. Yet he lacked gut political instincts and could not deliver the one-line zingers in the House of Commons that focus an issue and grab the spotlight. His friend Neville worked to sharpen his performance, and many of Gillies's appearances in Hansard originated from Neville's typewriter. Clearly Neville possessed political instincts and skills that were superior to Gillies's, and at some point during the 1972-74 Trudeau minority government Neville started asking himself why he should not work toward becoming a cabinet minister. "Well, Jesus," Neville once told a friend, "if Gillies can do it, so can I." Neville had bolted from Trudeau on conviction; somewhere along the way he had acquired the political itch.

Lee saw what was happening to Neville and philosophically accepted the probability that his partner would run as a Tory in the next election. He assumed that Neville would select Ottawa West, a swing riding where he lived and stood a good chance of winning. So Lee was not surprised when Neville came into his office one fine spring day in 1974 and informed him of his decision to contest the next election. Lee was about to wish him well when Neville said something that almost left him choking. Neville told Lee he was running not in Ottawa West but in Ottawa Carleton. Lee was stunned. Running in Ottawa Carleton meant taking on John Turner, the minister of finance, who in 1972 had won by more than 8,000 votes when Liberals across the country were dropping like flies.

In his wildest imaginings Lee had never envisaged Neville

challenging Turner. It made no sense. For starters, the riding was unwinnable. The last Tory to represent Ottawa Carleton or the earlier riding, Russell, was elected in 1882 under Sir John A. Macdonald. The riding contained a strong francophone element. Turner spoke fluent French whereas Neville was unilingual. Second, Lee had become a fan of Turner. With Hellyer gone, Turner had taken over as Trudeau's heir apparent, and Lee had frequently said the only way he would get dragged back into Liberal politics was for Turner to run for the leadership. Now Neville was challenging Lee's Great White Hope. Third, it was clear that voters in Ottawa Carleton liked being represented by a cabinet minister and a possible future prime minister. Even among Conservatives there were many who hated Trudeau but liked Turner and wished he was a Conservative. Finally, Lee couldn't help wondering what Neville's attack on Turner would do to ECL. Alienating the minister of finance was, to understate the case, politically unwise. As things stood, Turner was an ECL friend who sometimes dropped by the office on Slater Street and occasionally phoned Lee for information and advice. That would change overnight if one of the founding partners tried to unseat him. The effects could be devastating.

"You don't have a hope in hell," Lee warned him.

"Oh yeah?" Neville replied, "We've done some quiet polling and he's an absentee MP as far as they're concerned. I've got a real shot at it."

"Bill, what if Stanfield doesn't win?" Lee asked.

"Come on, Trudeau is dead."

In 1974 Trudeau was hanging on with parliamentary support from the NDP. Stanfield had almost ousted him in 1972, and the polls now showed Stanfield winning a narrow victory.

Neville was self-confident, almost cocky. He had sought outside advice before breaking the news to Lee and was told by others that he was nuts, all to no avail.

Lee and Neville were more than business partners. They were friends, and the two seldom did anything so formal as exchanging memos. But on this occasion Lee wrote a note warning Neville he was forfeiting a six-figure income – in 1973 his income tax alone was $48,000 – to take a shot at something with the odds deeply stacked against him. Lee also asked what would happen to his family should the unthinkable – which, Lee argued, was the predictable – happen. The memo also mentioned that Irv Keenleyside had bought into the company a few years earlier and now was seeing half the team leave to skate off on thin ice. Lee had seen others get bitten by the political bug and go off and do irrational things, and he wanted to make sure that Neville understood the risks. Neville had lived a credit-card lifestyle, regularly flying off to New York with his wife on quick getaway weekends. Despite his high income he had not built a financial nest egg. Lee wanted Neville to be aware of the odds; having done so he accepted his action with good grace and when others asked about it he merely shook his head and muttered, "I love him but he's crazy."

The decision hit Keenleyside more heavily. He had borrowed to buy his shares and now, with money still owing, had reason to worry over the value of his investment. He consulted a lawyer to inquire whether Neville's withdrawal had altered the terms of his purchase. Realizing the problems he was creating, Neville put his shares into escrow under the control of Lee and Keenleyside, who reaped the dividends. Lee gave Keenleyside 60 per cent of Neville's profits and kept 40 per cent. The most shocked partner was Tex Enemark, who had just moved from Vancouver and taken out a loan to invest in ECL as well as buy a house. Enemark arrived for his first day at work to see a photographer taking campaign pictures of Neville. Only then did he learn, to his great dismay, that one of his partners had pulled out to run against Turner.

It was agreed that Neville could not go off and run against Turner and trot back to ECL after the election; he couldn't fight the Liberals one week and come back and deal with them the next. To protect itself the company had to divest itself of this instant political liability. He would have to leave. Neville concurred; as part of the formal departure he signed a no-compete agreement prohibiting him from competing with ECL for five years. Neville paid a stiff price for the dubious pleasure of challenging Turner: he surrendered his partnership in ECL, giving up the salary and dividends that went with it, and was barred from returning to his profession.

"Before you announce it," Lee asked him, "let me at least ring John up and tell him – to protect our company and my personal relationship with him."

Turner burst out laughing over the news.

"Neville?" he asked incredulously, almost sarcastically, when Lee broke the news. "If you were running against me I might be a little worried, but who the hell has ever heard of Neville?"

To Neville, Ottawa Carleton represented a natural choice. He had grown up there and still had many friends in the riding. Nobody expected him to win so he was a potential giant-killer. The riding had some solid Conservative support. The previous Tory candidate, Strome Galloway, was a retired colonel who advocated the return of the chastity belt to check the population explosion and still snared forty per cent of the vote. Neville knew that he could increase the forty per cent but could win only with the help of a national Tory trend. That suited him fine because he didn't want to be an opposition MP. Either way he felt he couldn't lose.

"You know," Neville told a colleague, "maybe it's just an ego trip." Then he added: "I think I might beat him."

Neville threw himself into the campaign with a vengeance, and Turner's cavalier attitude towards him soon changed. Neville took the offensive, hammering away at Turner's record as an absentee MP and never hesitating to point out that even during the campaign Turner was hardly in the riding. In the candidates' debates Neville overwhelmed Turner. He expressed his views more clearly and gave hard answers when Turner waffled. Old friends who remembered Neville as a slightly shy introvert were amazed at how outgoing and aggressive he had become and at how rapidly he had mastered campaign rhetoric. Neville brought Diefenbaker into the riding; he even had Judy LaMarsh, a Liberal, stumping for him against Turner. Through it all Neville created the impression that Turner was in trouble until even the CBC news program, The National, carried an item saying that Turner was in difficulties. In the final weeks Turner was forced to cancel his national campaigning to stay home and defend his turf in Ottawa Carleton. Turner even called Lee a few times to grumble about Neville's tactics. Lee was keeping strictly neutral throughout the campaign and didn't even post a campaign sign on his front lawn.

Stanfield started off the campaign a good bet to knock off Trudeau – until the Conservative party proposed wage and price controls as its major election plank. The Tories realized their blunder almost immediately, but the campaign was under way and there could be no retreat. As Tories contradicted each other from day to day trying to explain the policy, making their platform the issue rather than the record of the government, Trudeau took to the stump and ridiculed the proposal from coast to coast – "Zap, you're frozen!" – forcing the Conservatives onto the defensive. Trudeau swept in with a majority. Neville, whose only hope lay in a Stanfield sweep, lost by more than ten thousand votes.

Turner gloated about how he had whopped Neville better than he had the colonel, but in more serious moments accused Neville of running a dirty campaign. More dispassionate observers described the campaign as hard but not dirty. But that didn't matter as far as Turner was concerned. The campaign had given him a scare, had even embarrassed him, and had ever so slightly tarnished the glow of his golden-boy image.

ECL clients noticed that Neville was unemployed and quickly figured out he might be available to work for them. The Retail Council of Canada soon approached Neville about taking over as its president, since Tony Abbott, the old president, had just won election as a Liberal MP. Neville and the Retail Council knew each other well because the organization had been his client at ECL, and had been impressed by him. He was an ideal successor who could walk into the president's office and take control on the first day.

The Canadian Association of Broadcasters also moved to snap him up. The CAB needed an executive vice president and could not have designed a more qualified candidate. As LaMarsh's EA, Neville had practically written the Broadcasting Act, then had brought CAB into ECL as a client and proceeded to serve the organization for nearly six years. Neville's future seemed assured whichever job he took.

Then something happened. First the Retail Council opportunity evaporated without explanation, then the CAB prospect mysteriously disappeared. After some digging, Neville learned what had happened. Turner had gone out of his way to warn both organizations that hiring Neville would not be a good idea. As the lobbyist for all sorts of stores from Eaton's to little independent shops on the corner, the Retail Council had to get along with government, and simply could not risk alienating it. After thinking over Turner's warning, the Council concluded that it would be prudent to select another candidate. The CAB, meanwhile, as the voice of a regulated industry, lived under the government's shadow. In reference to Neville's appointment, Turner flatly told the broadcasters: "If I were a federally regulated organization that is the last thing I'd do." The CAB Board of Directors dearly wanted to hire Neville; but, like the Retail Council, it decided that it was more important to stay on good terms with the minister of finance.

Suddenly Neville had no job and no prospects. He could not return to ECL – that had already been determined – and his five-year no-compete agreement precluded him from starting his own consulting business. He could move out of town, or work for the Conservative Party. Neville took the summer off to think about it, and then joined Stanfield's office that fall as senior policy adviser.

Neville was long gone but there remained within ECL the question of what to do with his shares. They were in escrow and out of Neville's control, leaving him in a nowhere position, an absentee shareholder who neither participated in the company nor received dividends. Neville accepted the principle that non-participants should not own significant equity in the company, but at the same time nobody – not Lee or Keenleyside, and certainly not Enemark or Struthers, who could not finance it – wanted to buy him out. Relations were not helped by Neville's perception that Lee and Keenleyside had an incentive to let the problem linger because in the interim they were profiting from his dividends. Neville argued that he had to be either a shareholder or a seller, and that letting the state of affairs continue was unfair. It was an awkward period, and only several years later did Neville conclude a deal with Steve Markey, the most junior of the partners, who went heavily to the bank to buy his shares.

Lee and his partners sighed with relief to discover that Turner's vengeance was directed at Neville and not at ECL. Now they waited for the clients' reaction to Neville's departure. The clients seemed to think that Neville walked on water, so that his leaving represented a turning point. Would clients leave? ECL had to demonstrate that without Neville it was just as good as ever. Steve Markey moved up in the firm and took over part of Neville's load. Markey was bright, and good, but not ready to fill Neville's shoes alone. He simply looked too young. Besides, as ECL's first no-name consultant – lacking any experience outside ECL itself – Markey would not attract big fees. Enemark took over a big chunk of Neville's load and proved to be a gifted consultant but not a client-getter. Besides, he would soon become a deputy minister in the B.C. government. Struthers had a background in public relations rather than client servicing, and he would leave soon, too. The biggest single difference was that Lee worked a lot harder at client servicing.

ECL lost not a single client, and soon picked up a few more. Neville's departure had presented it with its first trial, and without doing anything dramatic the company had not only survived but actually boosted gross revenues. The experience indicated that it had transcended the era of Lee and Neville, "the plugged-in EAs", and had acquired a presence of its own. Whatever one thought of public-affairs consulting, the business was there to stay. Inevitably, this meant that others would copy the ECL formula and compete for business.

FIVE

STARTING PAI

Perhaps the most vivid image of the 1968 convention was not Pierre Trudeau with a rose in his mouth but the sorrowful sight of a group of elderly Liberals vainly struggling to hoist 64-year-old Paul Martin onto their shoulders like a victorious football coach after a Grey Cup victory. For what seemed like minutes, the minister of external affairs hung limply in midair while his supporters feebly fought to boost him the rest of the way up, and had to give up. It was unfair. Pierre Trudeau could not hope to match Martin's years of service to the party or his deep knowledge of politicking and government, and yet Trudeau had rewritten the book on political campaigning. Under the new rules Martin's decades of experience virtually eliminated him from the race, while Trudeau shone because he lacked experience. Delegates perceived Trudeau as a fresh hope and treated Martin as a caricature from the Thirties, the gladhanding master of circumlocution who, despite his record of achievement, had an image that was out of step with the times. Even Lee would have had trouble selling Martin to the Liberal convention in 1968; the task of finding a new bottle for this vintage wine belonged to Duncan Edmonds.

Edmonds, hunched over his perpetual pipe like a young North American Sherlock Holmes, had quit as Martin's EA three years earlier and was running a small consulting company in Winnipeg when Pearson resigned. Martin persuaded him to return to help him run for Liberal leader. Everybody expected Martin to lead the pack, or be close, but his campaign was a last-minute affair. Besides, time had passed him by. When he mus-ered only a fourth-place tie on the first ballot he promptly withdrew from the race.

As one of the Super EAs, Edmonds never enjoyed the relationship with Martin that Lee had with Hellyer or Michael McCabe had with Mitchell Sharp. Edmonds was articulate and quick, and familiar with the practice of planting stories with reporters, but he also had an intellectual side which made him less gung-ho. He never knew whether Martin would back him, yet he lagged only half a step behind Lee and McCabe as a mover and shaker on Parliament Hill. Edmonds knew how to wield power, but really preferred contemplating the implications of power. EAs like Lee, Neville, and McCabe came into politics from the business world; Edmonds arrived on Parliament Hill from the world of academe.

Edmonds grew up in Toronto and in high school at Etobicoke Collegiate earned first-class honours and became head prefect. As an undergraduate at the University of Toronto, he won the William Lyon Mackenzie King Travelling Scholarship and a raft of other awards in 1959 that permitted him to enrol at the London School of Economics where he went directly into a Ph.D. program. Edmonds chose the role of the leader of the opposition in Canada as his thesis topic, and in 1960 wrote to Lester Pearson – he already knew Jack Pickersgill – a long, pedantic letter inquiring about the operation of his office. Pearson returned a polite note saying he could get the answers to his questions by joining his staff as a research assistant for a year.

Edmonds accepted the offer, became a junior research assistant and speechwriter for $6,000 a year, and never returned to his thesis. When his year with Pearson ended he became an assistant professor of political science at Carleton University and kept his finger in politics by, among other things, writing speeches for Paul Martin. The day Martin was sworn in as minister of external affairs in 1963 Edmonds became his EA, an experience Edmonds subsequently found both rewarding and dreadful. Martin proved a difficult master and seemed on occasion to want a "gofer" more than anything else. He would commission six different people to write the same speech and then choose the one that suited his fancy. Edmonds didn't complain and never bad-mouthed Martin behind his back, the way some aides did their ministers. But by 1965 he had had enough and went off to organize the Canadian equivalent of the Peace Corps, the Company of Young Canadians. Later he did a variety of other things, and ran the Centennial International Development Program as executive director when it invented the Miles for Millions march in 1967.

Ambition drove Edmonds as much as any EA. He strove to get ahead and to exercise influence and accumulate wealth like the rest, but money and power never excited him as ends in themselves. He lived for ideas and was motivated by idealism. He was a small-l liberal who wanted government to serve all quarters of society sensibly and compassionately. He believed that reason and goodwill could solve most problems, allowing the human family to live happily on this planet. He admired Lester Pearson both for his international perspective and for his view that the political process ought to be a means for getting things done. The spirit and optimism of the 1960s and the Kennedy sense of purpose enthralled him and fed his interest in the Company of Young Canadians, Canadian University Service Overseas, and the United Nations. Edmonds had his detractors, but most people found him serious and sincere, and able to outline an issue brilliantly. Nobody questioned his idealism or his ability to conceptualize, but some wrote him off as a visionary and remained unconvinced of his ability to carry things through.

Edmonds returned to Winnipeg after Martin lost the leadership race. With Pearson retired and Trudeau the new prime minister his prospects in Ottawa had diminished. An incident during the campaign had ruined his relations with Trudeau. The Canadian Intelligence Service, a far-right fringe organization based in Flesherton, Ontario, had circulated hate literature portraying Trudeau as a Communist sympathizer. The Toronto *Telegram* columnist Ron Haggart successfully traced the distribution of the piece back to the Martin camp's mailing list. Edmonds at first denied the allegation in print. Later, when faced with the published evidence, he took the initiative to visit Trudeau at his suite in the Château Laurier. Edmonds was horrified and wanted to apologize; he sympathized with Trudeau because the same publication had once branded him a Communist for comments he had made after a trip to Rhodesia a few years earlier.

Edmonds told Trudeau that unauthorized people had evidently acquired a copy of the Martin mailing list. He assured him that the Martin camp had not participated in circulating the offending material, and that Martin personally deplored the incident. Instead of acting graciously, which as the frontrunner he could afford to do, Trudeau glared back and then picked up a copy of the article containing Edmonds's original denial. "Here's the article," Trudeau said. "You deny it." Trudeau refused to accept the apology and remained bellicose and hostile throughout the encounter.

Back in Winnipeg Edmonds took up management consulting with Peat Marwick, got elected to Tuxedo municipal council, and in 1969 ran for the leadership of the Liberal Party in Manitoba. He put on a creditable campaign and swept the youth and urban delegates, but lost among farmers and senior citizens and ultimately finished second. The loss disheartened him. He had offered himself for public service and had been rejected. His foray into provincial politics had blotted his copybook at Peat Marwick, which wanted to move him to Toronto. Edmonds quit instead, and after a brief fling at running his own consulting company in Winnipeg went off to Indonesia for a six-month stint with the United Nations.

He landed back in Ottawa in 1970 with his wife and two children but without money and with debts owing from the Manitoba leadership race. When Carleton University offered him a one-year contract to teach public administration he jumped at it. To augment his teaching income, Edmonds took his initials and incorporated a company called JDE Consulting Services Ltd., which he operated out of his house. He sought revenue wherever he could find it and promoted the company as "a consulting service to business and government".

Unlike Lee and Neville, Edmonds did not get his idea for a consulting practice from his experience on Parliament Hill. The notion of becoming a private consultant struck him only a few years later in Winnipeg during his time with Peat Marwick, which opened his eyes to the commercial value of consulting. He saw how traditional management-consulting firms billed clients and arranged their affairs; but most of all he came to realize that he could sell his services on the market, and command a good fee.

Edmonds was part of the Peat Marwick consulting team that conducted week-long seminars for federal civil servants on program planning, budgeting, and systems management. He immediately stole the show, effortlessly steering his audience through the issue under discussion, first building a framework, then evaluating individual components, their potentials and limitations, and finally reeling off conclusions as if accompanied by a drum roll. He melded together academic theory and political experience and wrapped them up in a dynamic delivery. He dazzled the civil servants. His seminar style impressed everybody, even, as he later discovered, hard-nosed corporate directors.

JDE Consulting started with a number of small clients such as Inspiration Drilling Ltd. of North Bay, Ontario, Durall Ltd. of Winnipeg, General Photogrammetric Services Ltd. of Ottawa, and half a dozen others. His biggest client at first was government: the federal, Manitoba and Saskatchewan governments, and the city of Winnipeg. But he did progressively less work for government and eventually gave it up entirely. His decision had nothing to do with philosophy. He disliked the fees, the restrictions, and the lack of results. He found he could do better in the private market, where he found no difficulty getting clients. The Canadian International Development Agency offered starter studies that paid travel expenses plus a small per-diem allowance for businessmen to explore business opportunities abroad. In helping clients pursue them, Edmonds travelled to Tunisia four times and to Indonesia twice, and also visited Nigeria, Brazil, Argentina, and Singapore.

His first big-retainer client was the TransCanada Telephone System, which wanted continuing advice on how to handle the new Department of Communications. Soon a TCTS member, Bell Canada, started contracting out spot jobs. Then he picked up his first major U.S. company, Boise Cascade of Boise, Idaho, which had two pulp mills in northern Ontario. The Canadian subsidiary of Boise Cascade not only became a client but put Edmonds on its board of directors. Next came Canada Safeway – another board appointment – and IBM, Monsanto, Shell, Amoco, and others. He charged what he thought were outrageous fees and quickly retired his campaign debts. By 1971 he had quit Carleton University – TCTS's $1,500-a-month retainer alone exceeded his university salary – and moved JDE Consulting out of his house and into a little office at 77 Metcalfe Street, up the street and around the corner from ECL on Slater Street.

JDE had taken off, and for good reason; the lecturing ability that had wowed his colleagues at Peat Marwick translated into boardroom qualities that impressed the hell out of businessmen. His performances soon brought opportunity to his door. He became the Canadian resource for the Public Affairs Council in Washington, a non-profit organization founded by Dwight Eisenhower as a bridge between business and government. Each fall he arranged a conference for thirty or forty Americans in Ottawa. The feedback from these sessions astonished him. The British parliamentary system puzzled American businessmen, who were accustomed to the open-door lobbying of Washington, and they relied on Edmonds for information and advice. He became an early board member of the Niagara Institute, a think-tank for Canadian business, and started giving seminars on its behalf. Sometimes he conducted sessions in Ottawa, arranging for presidents of major corporations to meet cabinet ministers and senior civil servants at formal gatherings during the day and in casual dinners during the evening. None of this did JDE Consulting any harm.

Soon industry associations, think-tanks, and corporations were inviting Edmonds as a speaker, and he became a hot number on the lecture circuit. The business community worried about the Trudeau government and wished to know what it was up to and what problem they could expect next. Edmonds spoke about "the business-government interface"; he started studying the issue as an academic discipline and was able to superimpose his analysis on the real-life problems he encountered through his consulting work.

Businessmen had specific objectives – to market a bar of soap or sell a bottle of beer – and they saw public policy as a narrow vista. Edmonds told them to broaden their perspective, instructing them that the first objective of any marketing campaign was to understand your client, and that the rule applied to their relationship with government too.

While Lee introduced the practice of public-affairs consulting, Edmonds introduced the theory. His lectures traced the historical development of the public-affairs function. Since World War Two, he told his listeners, the corporation faced several threats from its external environment, and in each case had responded with fresh management techniques: the personnel function in the 1940s introduced policies on recruiting, training, salary adjustment, promotion, and employee management because the labour force demanded them; the marketing function superseded the sales function in the 1950s because increasingly sophisticated consumers forced corporations to define markets and devise merchandising strategies; the systems function grew in the 1960s out of the flood of statistics accompanying the rise of industrial computers.

Edmonds warned that government encroachment on the corporation represented the external threat of the 1970s. Idealistic bureaucrats had moved into the civil service and were designing systems that increasingly held corporations to public account and did so with the support of the public, which no longer equated government planning with socialism. He told his audiences that the corporation would have to adapt to this latest factor, just as it had accommodated the previous three external threats. Corporations that did not take the public-affairs function seriously would suffer slow long-term reversals.

He cautioned his audiences not to react ideologically and not to make the mistake of substituting public relations for public affairs, because the two were different. Public relations sold the corporation to society, whereas public affairs educated the corporation about the outside world. Public affairs sensitized the corporation to what society wanted the corporation to do. Once the corporation had become sensitized – shaken off ideology, stupidity, and irrational behaviour and come to understand government's and industry's places in the larger society – it could design effective strategies to influence government; only then could it effectively protect its long-term interest.

Edmonds usually charged $1,000 for his speeches, but the fee was relatively unimportant. Each audience would include some company heads, and after the meeting one or two would usually come to the front and corner him about a specific company problem. They would chat briefly, exchange cards, and arrange appointments – and JDE would have a hot lead for another client. Edmonds never approached a prospective client cold. The client first had to be sold on the value of the service before Edmonds could begin to sell himself. The key was for the client to inquire first and, for Edmonds, his lecture opened the door.

By this time Edmonds had formed a loose consortium of single practitioners with Gorse Howarth, Lee Snelling, and Gordie Woods under the banner United Consultants International. Snelling and Woods saw the venture as an opportunity to cut costs by sharing office space and pooling secretaries, while Edmonds wanted to accumulate skills and build something resembling a partnership. The arrangement dissolved when Howarth left to join the Foreign Investment Review Agency. Edmonds continued to look for a full-time associate to help him build something bigger and better than a one-man bucket shop.

At this point Torrance Wylie, an insider with both Trudeau and the Liberal Party, happened to move into Edmonds's surplus space at 77 Metcalfe. Wylie, another former EA from the Pearson years, had hardly started in the consulting business but already had a few clients. Soon he proposed amalgamating their practices and working together as a full-scale partnership.

The two had first met when Edmonds had taught Wylie fourth-year political science at Carleton. Wylie learned a lot about political theory and analysis in Edmonds's class but that experience did not influence him as much as a book called *Why I Am a Separatist* by Marcel Chaput. The provocative arguments in that thin volume moved the 21-year-old Wylie and reminded him of Chute-à-Blondeau, a small francophone community at the eastern tip of Ontario where he grew up an anglophone across the river from Quebec. Wylie had trouble refuting Chaput's thesis and became convinced that separatism could be thwarted only if Canada introduced major changes to establish Quebec's rightful place in the country. Wylie knew that Prime Minister Diefenbaker, who believed he had answered Quebec's needs with simultaneous translation in the House of Commons, bilingual cheques, and the first francophone governor general, misunderstood Quebec's aspirations so fundamentally that he was incapable of addressing the issue even if Quebec was a priority for him, which it was not.

Something needed to be done. Wylie wrote to Lester Pearson

about the need to upgrade the status of French Canadians and the reasons why the Liberal Party must address the issue. Pearson wrote back inviting him to his Centre Block office, where he urged the fair-haired kid with the curls to get involved in the party if he felt that way. Pauline Jewett, then a Carleton professor and a Liberal, encouraged him to apply for a summer job with the party's national office. As a Liberal Party researcher, Wylie watched with satisfaction as the Diefenbaker government began to unravel. After the 1963 Liberal victory he became EA to the government leader in the Senate – first with Ross Macdonald, then with John Connolly – and after the 1965 election moved up to become Prime Minister Pearson's appointments secretary. He later quit and joined Molson Breweries in Montreal as assistant to the chairman. There he operated as the logistics person on the senior management committee and learned how a large corporation was run. Wylie loved the job and considered it a management-training course at the highest level, but didn't stay long. In 1969 Trudeau brought him back to Ottawa as national director of the Liberal Party.

Wylie ran the Liberal Party for three years and after the 1972 election chose to go into consulting. Experience in Ottawa had taught him that too many corporations failed to comprehend emerging developments in politics and society, and needed help in assessing what he called "the external environment". Corporations had internal departments to command capital, people, product design, and other things that they handled efficiently, but they lacked a public-affairs department for dealing with the external environment. He had watched the emergence of the public-affairs function in large American corporations and wondered why Canadian companies lagged behind in recognizing it as an important corporate function. It intrigued him enough to travel to the United States for a further look. Like Edmonds, Wylie believed that the failure of traditional management-consulting companies to pursue public affairs as a fully fledged service opened the way for new entrants like himself.

Wylie believed in descriptive corporate names; late in 1971, while still working for the Liberal Party, he registered Public Affairs International as the name of his company. The company itself was not incorporated until February 1 1973 and had hardly got started when Trudeau, as a consequence of the 1972 election débâcle, asked Wylie to postpone his business plans long enough to help out in the Prime Minister's Office. Trudeau knew that he needed to patch up his relationship with the Liberal Party if he was to enjoy political success, and picked Wylie as the man for the job. Wylie told him he would stay six months. He cancelled PAI's office lease, moved into Trudeau's office as his executive assistant, and hired his successor within a week. He stayed until the end of 1973, when he felt that he had met his obligations and was free to leave. One of his last acts was to convince Trudeau to bring back the banished Senator Keith Davey as the chairman of election campaigns in English Canada. Before Wylie got away Trudeau handed him a part-time assignment as chairman of the Federal Liberal Agency, to report expenditures and sources of revenue under the new revisions to the Canada Elections Act.

Wylie began as a single practitioner in a small office on Sparks Street a short block from the main gate to Parliament Hill. One of his first contracts was almost his last. Wylie was flying around the globe helping another consulting company, Public and Industrial Relations, of Montreal, investigate the image of the International Air Transport Association. He flew to the Ivory Coast in a last-minute switch in plans which left him no time for preventive treatment against malaria, and soon found himself in hospital with a nearly fatal bout of the disease. By the time his illness was properly diagnosed back in Ottawa it was too late for treatment. Wylie, a jogger with a wiry athletic build that carried no sign of fat, believed he pulled through at least partly because of his excellent physical condition.

A precise, organized man who held strong opinions, Wylie drafted a business plan with a specified objective: PAI, as Public Affairs International became known, would seek to attain intrinsic value as an institution, like a butcher shop or drugstore – something that could be bought and sold. Wylie did not see himself staying in the business forever, and wanted to make a capital gain when he sold out. That precluded him from building a practice based on selling personal contacts, because he needed to establish an enterprise that would survive his departure. Like ECL, the company would sell knowledge and advice about the government process and guide a client through the public-affairs environment. Unlike ECL, PAI would take government contracts. Wylie liked government business and, once PAI was up and running, usually had one or two government contracts on the go.

Wylie's entry into the public-affairs field didn't surprise Edmonds. He considered that Wylie's skills and experience made him a natural public-affairs consultant, and sized him up as analytical, articulate, and knowledgeable about the government process. Edmonds respected Wylie's range of contacts, which extended from Trudeau all the way to the common volunteers in the Liberal Party. When Wylie proposed a partnership, Edmonds said yes almost immediately.

Edmonds and Wylie took only three or four meetings to amalgamate their practices and were pleased to find that their clients could fit under the same roof without a single conflict of interest. They arranged a fifty-fifty partnership under the name Public Affairs International. For income-tax purposes each partner held back a major client in his personal holding company. Thus the revenue from Boise Cascade went directly to JDE Consulting, and the fees collected from the Canadian Tobacco Manufacturers Council, the tobacco lobby, went into Wylie's personal holding company, T.J. Wylie Ltd.

Like ECL, PAI sought retainers as its preferred source of income. It set retainer fees at about $2,500 a month – and never had difficulty negotiating a fee once a company decided to become a client. Private clients on retainer became PAI's backbone but not its only business, as Wylie kept some government contracts. Like ECL, PAI grew into a money machine which never needed to borrow money. The company moved to more upbeat offices and before long was able to hire consultants such as Sean Moore and Don Kelly, the former president of Quaker Oats.

Edmonds led PAI's marketing effort and could hardly have been a better ambassador for the firm. He devoted a third of his time to what he called "development work" – speaking at seminars and conferences – and displayed a natural gift for getting clients. PAI discovered what ECL already knew: that the stable of clients turned over continually, so that a perpetual influx of new clients was needed, some to replace old clients who dropped out and others to help PAI to grow. Edmonds sold a pricey and somewhat ethereal product and received many noes for every yes. Despite several trips to Chicago, he could not turn McDonald's Restaurants into a contract. Neither could he get Avon.

While Edmonds travelled the continent drumming up business, Wylie stayed in Ottawa and minded the store. Wylie didn't like being away from home. Edmonds preferred the boardroom level; Wylie showed no particular preference for any level. Wylie operated strategically and solved problems by being shrewd and tough. Edmonds freely mixed business and entertainment, whereas Wylie shunned social contact with clients and disliked working late. At the end of the day he wanted to to go home to his family.

Edmonds never sought to build a large consulting company, but PAI grew steadily nonetheless. He thought of it as a kind of way station, something to do because he enjoyed it, something that kept him busy speaking at conferences and solving problems and earning money. Despite his desire to accumulate skills, he had no grand design for PAI, no systematic business plan to develop the enterprise. His plan had always been to enter politics or join government at some point. Wylie, however, wanted to formalize the process and build a structure. He came up with the idea of producing a quarterly written report, a sort of newsletter. Edmonds and Wylie worked well together, their differences complementing the partnership rather than dividing it, and made up a formidable partnership that challenged ECL.

On one occasion Wylie neatly manoeuvred the Allstate Insurance Company through a crisis. Allstate came to PAI in 1976 complaining that the Quebec government was nationalizing its insurance business out from under it, and was driving it out of the province. The company had already suffered underwriting losses and now feared that it was going to lose the business itself. "We're going to be ruined," Allstate complained. "We might as well close the doors. We want you to stop that." Wylie said nothing. He knew it was almost impossible to stop a government from doing something it had decided to do. Wylie visited Quebec City and met the minister, the deputy minister, and the opposition critic and discovered virtually unanimous sentiment in favour of nationalization. It was an information-gathering trip, and from it Wylie learned all he needed to know. He realized that political reality required the Quebec government to undertake nationalization, and that it couldn't back down even if it wanted to. Fighting the government would be costly, harmful, and about as futile as resisting the setting of the evening sun. But he saw a silver lining: the province intended to nationalize only automobile insurance – the problem area where Allstate had in fact suffered losses – and to leave the money-making property insurance business to private insurers.

Wylie returned to Ottawa and advised Allstate that it would lose its auto-insurance business in about six months and had two options: it could either take a kick in the teeth or redesign its insurance policies for the new market. He counselled Allstate not to waste energy bemoaning the loss of auto insurance and to concentrate on the sixty per cent left on the table which, in any case, was easier to price and less vulnerable to underwriting losses. He told the company to act before its competitors woke up and did the same thing. The following year Allstate boosted its market share and earned a record profit.

Shortly after Quebec elected René Lévesque's separatist government in November 1976, with Quebec and the rest of Canada still reeling, Wylie phoned the premier's office and offered to do something good for his government. He proposed staging a two-day conference in Quebec City for the purpose of putting corporate executives in touch with the new government. It gave the Lévesque government a chance to calm corporate anxiety and to explain its agenda. The government quickly endorsed the offer and sent two cabinet ministers, Claude Morin and Bernard Landry, to the event as speakers. Claude Ryan, who would shortly become the Liberal leader, came as the luncheon speaker. Since Wylie invited both clients and prospective clients, the conference was good public affairs and great marketing for PAI, and was repeated annually for the next few years. Next to Edmonds's speaking schedule, conference-arranging became PAI's number one marketing technique. In 1978 PAI brought Finance Minister Jean Chrétien to the Pierre Hotel in New York for a session with American businessmen. The conferences made money but proved even more valuable to PAI as a way of attracting clients.

After one of Edmonds's talks to the Public Affairs Council, Cal Pond from Safeway's headquarters in Oakland, California, approached him about a troublesome problem the company had in Canada. Canada Safeway was facing criminal proceedings for monopolistic practices in Alberta. The company had already invested hundreds of thousands of dollars in lawyers and economists to fight the charge; now, with the case about to come to trial, Pond wondered whether Edmonds would look for another answer.

Edmonds scouted around in Ottawa, interviewed people in Calgary and Oakland, and advised the company to negotiate a settlement with the Crown in return for the dropping of the charges. The Safeway legal department in Oakland vetoed the suggestion. The Safeway lawyers, accustomed to the adversarial practices of the United States, refused to talk to Ottawa and at one point fired Edmonds on the spot for phoning the company from a government office. Edmonds was rehired two days later and eventually convinced Safeway that Canada operated differently. Finally, he got the two sides talking, although it was not always easy to keep them talking. Once, with negotiations bogged down, Edmonds, on an hour's notice, flew from Ottawa to Toronto, then to San Francisco before getting into Oakland at midnight for an 8 a.m. meeting with Safeway's lawyers. It took ten minutes to straighten out the three or four words that had snagged negotiations, and within an hour Edmonds was back at the airport for his return to Ottawa.

The two sides agreed to a settlement that set a legal precedent. The Crown dropped charges without Canada Safeway's admitting wrongdoing. In return Canada Safeway signed a prohibition order restricting its operations in Alberta for three years. Canada Safeway promised to tie its advertising budget to a formula, undertook not to open new stores in the province unless it closed one in Calgary or Edmonton, and gave an undertaking not to engage in discriminatory or predatory pricing. Edmonds joined Canada Safeway's board of directors, and the company became his longest-standing client.

Edmonds represented Canada Safeway before the Food Prices Review Board and later before the Anti-Inflation Board; he also walked many other clients through FIRA applications. Like ECL,

PAI protested, with hand on heart, that it didn't lobby, that it simply gave clients guidance, advice, and training, and told them how the system worked. That was the theory. In practice Edmonds often wandered knee-deep into active representation. If the corporation could not solve its problem alone, Edmonds, despite his virginal protests, would visit the government or do what was necessary to help the client. In such cases the client wanted a workable solution, not a lecture on the philosophy of government. Edmonds still saw himself not as a lobbyist, but more as a pragmatic social scientist who sometimes left the classroom. Others noted that he was a pragmatic social scientist with a big house in Rockcliffe Park and a condominium in Florida, and an expensive lifestyle to support.

PAI competed with ECL for prestige, but rarely if ever did the two go head to head in search of clients. Clients did not choose consultants the way they bought cars; they usually picked one or none at all. Both PAI and ECL engaged more in market development than in competition. Sometimes clients switched from one to another; Xerox, after its success with the world-product mandate, felt that it had picked ECL's corporate brain and swung to PAI to see what Edmonds and Wylie had to offer. But the competition was genteel. ECL and PAI referred to each other clients they could not accept for conflict-of-interest reasons. Edmonds and Wylie would bump into Bill Lee informally and they would swap information like old friends; once or twice they talked about amalgamating their companies, but the talks never got far.

Edmonds and Wylie worked well together, enjoyed a strong client base, and were starting to assemble a good and efficient staff. Politically they both belonged to the Liberal Party, but that particular kinship was deceptive, because they had different expectations of the party. Edmonds thought that bridging the gap between business and government was Canada's top priority, whereas Wylie still believed that reconciling the two major linguistic communities was of paramount importance. Edmonds and Wylie had talked often enough about Trudeau, but Wylie could never be persuaded that the prime minister was spending too much time on language policies at the expense of the economy. Never in a thousand years would anybody convince Wylie that too much had been poured into bilingualism. As far as Wylie was concerned Trudeau had spent the time needed to get a vital job done. Thus the very element that strengthened Wylie's loyalty to the party alienated Edmonds, who began distancing himself from the Liberal Party and especially from Trudeau. Wylie noticed that this was happening. Nevertheless he was taken aback when Edmonds announced in September 1977 that he wanted out of the firm. He had received an offer from the Conservatives to become senior policy adviser to Joe Clark, and had said yes.

SIX

THE NEED TO BE A PLAYER

Edmonds enjoyed nothing more than attending dinner parties with senior executives in the best clubs of Toronto, Washington, and New York and pushing back the chairs over brandy and cigars to talk current events. There, and in his other dealings as super consultant, he believed he was influencing industry's attitudes and changing its behaviour for the better. Rubbing shoulders with the corporate sector had moved him to the right, but in a typically thoughtful and purposeful way. The old CUSO director maintained his ideals, but now wondered about the capacity of government to deliver programs and contribute to the development of the economy. He had grown strongly pro-American, favouring multinational corporations as vehicles of the future; increasingly he entertained doubts about the growing role of government, believing that its scope should be reduced. He dismissed the government's talk of an industrial strategy as a socialist game, and advocated North American free trade long before it became acceptable.

Edmonds grew increasingly irritated with the Liberal government in Ottawa and especially with Pierre Trudeau. He believed that government and business were partners in society and that Trudeau had a duty to facilitate that partnership, instead of engaging in corporation-bashing, which he believed the prime minister was doing. Trudeau seemed to him to be narrow, disdainful, even arrogant, and he came to believe that the prime minister despised the business community. Edmonds voted Conservative both in 1972 and in 1974. John Turner had always been his idea of the ideal Liberal Party leader and by the time Turner walked out on Trudeau in September 1975, soon to leave Parlia-

ment for a life on Bay Street, Edmonds had become convinced
that Canada needed a better prime minister.

When Joe Clark succeeded Stanfield as leader of the Conservative Party in February 1976, he impressed Edmonds as fresh,
bright, and open to new ideas. Edmonds had met Clark through
his friend Walter McLean and later encountered him a few times
at conferences. Now that he occupied Stornoway, Clark lived a
few doors down the street, and often strolled past Edmonds's
front door. They had lunch a few times, and in late August 1977
Clark offered to make Edmonds his senior policy adviser. Clark
wanted him to assemble a blueprint of policies for the time he
became prime minister. Meanwhile he would act as Clark's liai-
son with the Policy Advisory Council and supervise the content
of Clark's speeches.

Edmonds took a few days to think it over but knew his
answer in advance. Clark's offer excited him. Edmonds knew that
he missed active involvement in the political process and
wanted back in. He had been looking for a bandwagon to climb
onto since his disaffection with Trudeau and now saw an opportunity to make a contribution to Canada. Clark had long political experience but, despite his favourable disposition towards
business, knew little about the business community and could
use his help. The following Labour Day weekend, with his wife
Nancy, Edmonds met Clark and Maureen in the backyard of
Stornoway to chat about the pros and cons of taking the job.
What about his background as a Liberal, Edmonds asked. Clark
didn't flinch. "If you can handle it, I can," he replied. With that
reply, Edmonds took the plunge.

Wylie disliked the thought of terminating such a successful
partnership, but knew that Edmonds was not the kind of person
who would stay in one place very long. Since his partner had
made up his mind, he never tried to talk him out of it. The two
remained amicable and handled the breakup in a businesslike
fashion. They had a buy-sell arrangement and instructed the
corporate lawyers and accountants to assess the value of the
company and arrange the sale of Edmonds's shares to Wylie. PAI
pulled down something under a million dollars' worth of revenue
and enjoyed a pre-tax net income of nearly half a million. But the

accountants' assessment downplayed its profitability and emphasized the lack of security, noting that PAI would become virtually worthless if clients suddenly failed to renew their contracts, as some did each year. So the accounting report assessed the company's worth very conservatively at three months of pre-tax earnings, which amounted to $120,000 for the entire company, $60,000 for Edmonds's 50-per-cent share. At around the same time a 10-per-cent share of ECL stock – which had survived a departing partner without missing a beat – sold for $75,000.

The PAI evaluation was absurd. The figure was so low that Wylie had been handed a bargain even if clients chose to quit. The $100,000-plus take-home annual income Edmonds was leaving behind could pay off his equity in six months, enabling Wylie to buy out Edmonds's share out of current revenues without borrowing. Wylie had to work harder and hire extra staff to cover Edmonds's workload. Nevertheless, his partner had left him well rewarded.

Edmonds left his lucrative practice with hardly a regret. He realized that he was leaving money on the table – about a quarter of a million dollars, as later events would show. He had lived on airplanes for five years helping develop PAI's profile to the point where new clients now walked through the door, and he knew that from a business point of view he was leaving at the wrong time. But money did not motivate him as much as public service or the need to be a player. Consulting had been good to him and he was prepared to make a financial sacrifice. Also he wanted to avoid heavy negotiations with Wylie because he saw the low purchase price as a quid pro quo for skipping out. Consulting companies are not worth a damn if people don't stay with them – and he was leaving. In short, Edmonds wanted as much money as he could get easily, and $60,000 happened to be the easy number. Yet the amount was important for Edmonds's finances. The Clark job paid about $40,000, while Edmonds still lived a six-figure lifestyle.

Naturally Clark had checked first with his chief of staff before offering Edmonds the post. The chief of staff knew Edmonds from years ago and realized that he had something to offer. What's more, he knew the kind of sacrifice Edmonds was making. In fact, the chief of staff was in a unique position to know the sacrifice involved, because three and a half years earlier he had done the same thing when he left ECL to run against John Turner. So Bill Neville agreed with Clark and supported the hiring of Edmonds.

After being effectively blackballed by John Turner's personal vendetta, Neville had taken the job Edmonds was assuming now, under the leader of the opposition, Robert Stanfield. Neville dearly wanted to be Stanfield's chief of staff, but his Liberal background meant that he had to settle for senior policy adviser instead. He soon moved on to become research director for the Conservative caucus, where he hired a bunch of whiz kids and co-ordinated the best and most aggressive research office the Tories had ever had. Every morning at 8:45 Neville helped devise the daily strategy for Question Period. His office assisted MPs in attacking government bills and also produced platform planks like the highly popular scheme for mortgage deductibility for homeowners. He introduced gumshoe tactics to the research office to help MPs like Elmer MacKay go on search-and-destroy missions against the government. Scandals like the Sky Shops affair gave him the most fun, and caused the Liberal government the greatest embarrassment. Neville's performance attracted attention, and one of the people who noticed was a relatively junior MP named Joe Clark.

In the final days of the 1976 Conservative leadership campaign, when he felt that he was picking up momentum, Joe Clark sent feelers to Bill Neville inquiring whether he might be interested in joining Clark's staff if he won. He made no mention of what job he had in mind, and it was only the morning after Clark's victory that Neville learned that Clark wanted him as chief of staff. In some ways the appointment was as surprising as Clark's come-from-behind victory the day before. Clark had risen through the Young Conservatives from his university days, knew everyone in the party, and could have selected any number of old soldiers from earlier wars. Instead he opted for someone he knew only casually who had been a public Tory less than two years. But Clark had seen Neville operate as research director and liked what he saw.

Neville never believed that Claude Wagner or Brian Mulroney, the two favourites, could win, and predicted that both would start fast and then sputter for lack of wide support. So confident was Neville that he laid down a few hundred dollars in bets that either Flora MacDonald (his choice on the first ballot) or the unlikely Clark would win, depending on which placed ahead of the other on the first ballot. On February 22 1976, events unfolded exactly as Neville predicted. Clark placed third on the first ballot, behind Wagner and Mulroney but well ahead of MacDonald, and on successive ballots overtook first Mulroney and then Wagner. Somewhat richer after the convention, Neville accepted Clark's offer immediately. He was a political junkie addicted to the public-policy process.

Clark needed somebody like Neville. He had moved from being an obscure backbencher from Alberta to national leader in one big jump. Suddenly he was expected to give instant but flawless answers on every conceivable issue, to negotiate disputes in a traditionally fractious caucus, and to produce a strategy for victory in the next election. American presidential candidates assemble teams of advisers long before they step into the spotlight. Clark had no team worth mentioning. In Ottawa he was an outsider once he left Parliament Hill; the big bureaucrats were only names to him. Neville, by contrast, knew most of the key players personally, had one of the best political minds in Ottawa, and could help the new 36-year-old leader of the opposition become prime minister.

As Clark's top man, Neville ran an office of forty to fifty people and acted as Clark's administrator and key strategist on everything. Clark would not take a single line of attack in the Commons without first consulting him. Every speech had Neville's hand in it somewhere, and he played a major role in managing the Conservative Party bureaucracy. The job was most demanding and, typically, he threw himself into it. Typically too, like Judy LaMarsh a decade earlier, Clark was soon not only his boss but a close friend.

Neville stimulated Clark intellectually and became his idea man. Neville's mind worked both conceptually and tactically; he started each issue from a broad theoretical base and broke it down into components, moving inexorably from the theoretical stuff to the strategic heart of the matter, until, by the end, he was a pure tactician, overlaying each choice on top of the political colouration of Canada's different regions. Meanwhile Clark tossed in ideas and together they kicked them back and forth. Above almost everything else, Clark was a good listener, and he revelled in their sessions, admiring Neville's ability to combine ethical theory with hard-nosed politics. What particularly endeared Neville to Clark was his ability to take an idea and fashion a workable strategy out of it. Clark found the sessions not only rewarding but enjoyable, and in some ways savoured them as the essence of politics. For his part Neville loved nothing more than policy-making, which made him an oddity as a chief of staff. Most backroom operators concentrated on day-to-day politics and left the framework questions to somebody else. Neville did not, which made Edmonds's arrival especially interesting, because Edmonds too liked to cut a broad policy swath.

The nature of the Clark-Neville relationship suggested that Edmonds faced a tough challenge in becoming senior policy adviser in more than name as he moved into Room 416 of the Centre Block. It was exactly the same office he had shared with a co-worker seventeen years earlier as junior assistant to Pearson. Now Edmonds had the office to himself. His appointment had caused a brief stir in the press, which seized upon the fact that a Grit had defected to the Tories, but the story blew over quickly. Some partisan Tory diehards were shocked, and others remained suspicious; Edmonds took solace in the fact that Conservatives were suspicious by nature.

Once he had settled in, Edmonds, as his first priority, picked up a pet theme he had been developing in his business seminars – free trade. Only now he took it a giant step further by advocating a far-reaching compact with the United States. He drafted a long memorandum proposing a Treaty of North America which would establish a supranational parliament called the Council of North America, comprising Canadians and Americans and, eventually, Mexicans. The Council would oversee a Permanent Joint Board of Defence to supervise greater military integration, a Joint Economic Council to co-ordinate a common industrial strategy, and a series of other joint councils. Edmonds maintained that Canada needed more than free trade, it needed a framework treaty to rationalize its entire relationship with the United States. The Treaty of North America was courageous and exciting to proponents – and politically dumb and outright scary to opponents. Whatever their conclusion, everyone agreed that the idea was big and bold.

Edmonds expected that his proposal would encounter short-term resistance, but that didn't worry him. He believed in getting the policy framework correct first and worrying about the political marketability later: if the concept was sound, eventually it would sell. But first he had to sell it to Clark. He hoped Clark would pick up his theme as a basic analysis for Canada's future and use his status as leader of the opposition to develop it.

Clark's response disappointed Edmonds deeply. Clark didn't develop the theme. He didn't advocate it. He didn't even express sympathy for it. In fact, he never discussed it with Edmonds, not even to acknowledge its existence or merely to say he had received it. Clark said nothing and Edmonds wondered whether he had even bothered to read it. Edmonds's only ally was Jim Gillies, who was chairman of the Conservative caucus policy committee, and he enthusiastically endorsed it. Others wrote it off as intellectual, idealistic, and politically foolish. If neglect meant anything, Clark seemed to agree.

Strangely, Edmonds never pushed his beloved proposal or even jogged Clark's memory about it, but simply let it slide in the face of Clark's polite rebuff. The memorandum in a sense was peripheral because both Clark and Edmonds soon realized that the relationship was not working anyway. Edmonds tried to arouse Clark to attack the size of the then $10-billion deficit and got only a limp reply. Edmonds travelled to the Middle East with Doug Roche, MP, in the summer of 1978 and returned urging Clark not to advocate recognition of Jerusalem as capital of Israel, but would eventually lose on that one, too.

During those years in opposition, Clark's office felt like a bunker in the middle of a war zone. Clark fought to overcome the "Joe Who?" image but went from one setback in the press to another. Working in Clark's office was painful for everyone, even Neville, who found the most frustrating part of his job was trying to undo the image the media had affixed to Clark, and give the electorate the chance to look beyond it.

Edmonds's efforts to overcome Clark's poor image with chief executive officers involved him in arranging the sort of formal dinner parties that he himself enjoyed so much. The endeavour never worked. Clark was obviously out of place at these sessions. He listened politely to all views rather than plunging into the give and take of discussion. On one occasion in Toronto the after-dinner cigar smoke drove Clark out of the room and made him throw up. The unfortunate incident symbolized their different styles.

Clark felt that Edmonds was not particularly useful, and Edmonds felt unneeded. There was no personality conflict or ill will on either side and there were certainly no blow-ups. Perhaps the relationship lacked the dynamism for a blow-up. In the end, after a year, Edmonds left Clark quietly and amiably in the fall of 1978 with a warm exchange of private letters but with no public statement and without the press's knowing about it. Edmonds slipped away so unobtrusively that other office workers hardly noticed.

Edmonds could have hung on for the impending election and would probably have received a plum appointment, but that did not particularly motivate him. He didn't believe Clark would make a great prime minister and had no desire to be part of his government. He reactivated JDE Consulting and returned to his old profession, where he enjoyed the the freedom of life as a consultant. He kept up a positive face, but occasionally sank into a low mood and grumbled to friends that Clark had not used him properly. Clark, he complained, had no interest in policy; leaving PAI to work for Clark was the biggest mistake of his life. At other, happier times he described Clark as intelligent and decent and possessing elements of greatness. His greatest regret, he said, was not that he had left PAI but that he had failed to be helpful to Clark.

Edmonds was happy when Clark was sworn in as Canada's sixteenth prime minister on June 4 1979; he started sending him memos on a variety of subjects and keeping in touch as an informal adviser.

After Edmonds left to join Clark, PAI continued to perform well. Wylie was relieved to find that clients did not react to Edmonds's departure in a way that affected the company; they commented on it, but none of them walked out. The short term was secure. The long term was another matter. Wylie realized that, given the client turnover, PAI would either grow or shrink, but was not likely to stay static.

Wylie himself had crossed a personal Rubicon with respect to PAI. He found that the increasing administration of an expanding company like PAI bored and even irritated him. Business-government affairs interested him but managing people did not. At the same time his three consultants – Sean Moore, Don Kelly, and Carl Baltare – were pushing for stock in the company. Wylie increasingly resented the business invasion of his private life because it robbed him of family time. He didn't like to lunch with clients, and certainly didn't want to have dinner with them. Wylie decided that he wanted to sell. Building a capital gain had always been one of his objectives, and not long after Edmonds's departure he figured he was in a position to achieve it.

SEVEN

ENTER MACNAUGHTON

At the same time as Duncan Edmonds left PAI to work for Joe Clark, David MacNaughton left his job as EA to External Affairs Minister Don Jamieson to try public-affairs consulting. MacNaughton had already met his friend Steve Markey for lunch at the Four Seasons to sniff out his prospects at ECL. MacNaughton liked how Bill Lee and the others at ECL were educating business and was interested in joining the company. But Markey, who had emerged as a highly regarded consultant, was not encouraging, and MacNaughton concluded that ECL was too profitable and too established to open a senior position to him. So he decided to set up his own company and launch out on his own. ECL would regret the loss. If Bill Lee was the father of public-affairs consulting and Duncan Edmonds the great marketer, before long Mac-Naughton would become the great innovator and the greatest driving force of all. He would take Lee's innovations, build upon them, and market the concept with Edmonds's aggressiveness.

MacNaughton dressed neatly and looked somewhat like a prim schoolboy. Nothing about his looks or personality suggested any hint of adventure or risk-taking. A stranger meeting him for the first time would describe him as a pleasant person who would fit comfortably into the head office of an insurance corporation. He was polite and agreeable, maybe a little bland, and people who dealt with him regarded him as decent, thoughtful, and fair. He lacked the larger-than-life character flaws that bedevil high achievers. The superficial signs all pointed towards ordinariness.

Looks were deceiving. MacNaughton was anything but ordinary. His sedate exterior hid a reservoir of ambition which he combined with shrewd aggressiveness in the business world. He was the sort of entrepreneurial gambler who would wager his entire fortune on a business deal so that he could reap a bigger one. His energy was controlled and spurted out in rational flows rather than ups and downs. Decisions came easily. He was not only bright and articulate but also possessed the knack of making highly strategic moves without appearing cold or calculating.

As a fresh high-school graduate out of hometown Hamilton, MacNaughton spent much of 1967 and 1968 teaching junior high school in the south of France. Living abroad during Canada's Centennial touched him patriotically, enough to write a letter to Prime Minister Pearson declaring how proud he was to be a Canadian. Unlike Edmonds and Wylie, MacNaughton did not receive a job offer but did get a nice reply which thrilled him. He returned to Canada in May 1968, just after Trudeau had become Prime Minister and while he was campaigning for election. MacNaughton had never heard of Trudeau before but he liked what he saw; quickly catching the spirit, he walked into the campaign office of Colin Gibson, a Liberal candidate in Hamilton, and volunteered his services. In no time MacNaughton became Gibson's youth organizer and chief door-knocker, and loved it.

The University of Western Ontario had accepted his application for that fall but MacNaughton felt too close to home there and could tell from the size of the Mustangs' linemen that he would never make the football team, so he promptly enrolled in commerce at the tiny University of New Brunswick. As a UNB Liberal Club delegate he attended the Atlantic Provinces Student Liberal Convention in his second year, and on the eve of the vote for president realized that the race was wide open. Quickly filing his papers, he pulled together an instant campaign team and the next day won his first official position in politics.

That weekend influenced his life in another way; back in Hamilton his father, vice president of sales at Stelco, suffered a stroke. After three decades with the company, he went onto a fixed disability income. MacNaughton had resented how his father had sacrificed family time for Stelco and now that he was disabled the company swept on without him, impervious and unnoticing. His father had little equity in the company. Mac-

Naughton decided that he wanted to be an owner instead of an employee.

The next spring Colin Gibson, the MP he had helped to elect, arranged two summer-job interviews in Ottawa with cabinet ministers. The prospect with Hamilton's John Munro evaporated when Munro failed to show for the interview, but MacNaughton saw Don Jamieson's executive assistant and landed a job as special assistant.

MacNaughton started at the bottom. His first assignment was to pick up some fresh salmon Jamieson had brought back from Newfoundland and distribute it among various people. MacNaughton showed up at the Ottawa airport with green garbage bags, stowed the salmon into the back of the car, and successfully apportioned the supply. Mission accomplished. He soon showed the kind of daring that suggested he was cut out for more than delivery work when he talked Jamieson into holding a young people's Think-Tank in his southeast Newfoundland riding. One thing led to another and before long MacNaughton had snared Trudeau himself as a participant. MacNaughton pulled off the Think-Tank magnificently, and at the end of the summer Jamieson offered him a full-time job when he graduated from UNB next spring. MacNaughton started in the spring of 1971 at $8,000 a year.

Jamieson soon singled out MacNaughton for a special job, one that crucially affected Jamieson's political future. The minister needed a rescue job in his Newfoundland riding. The constituency polls showed Jamieson either tied or slightly behind the Tories – with no Tory candidate. An election was expected in the following year and something had to be done to turn matters around. MacNaughton had to look after the riding and help Jamieson mend his fences before the election.

MacNaughton moved to Newfoundland and rented an apartment in St. John's. From there he drove countless miles across the Burin Peninsula and along the south coast. Jamieson had about a hundred communities in his riding and MacNaughton visited each one, camping in local bed-and-breakfasts and building a list of contacts. Newfoundland politics are unique, and the fact that Jamieson's emissary was a kid, a political greenhorn, and from Ontario was extraordinary. But it proved to be an astute move. As an outsider MacNaughton in some ways saw more clearly

how the forces were changing in Newfoundland and realized that
Jamieson could no longer get by with a visit to the parish priest
and the local merchant before jetting back to Ottawa. He broadened Jamieson's normal contacts to include people like
teachers and union representatives. On election night in 1972,
while Liberal candidates across the country went down to defeat
or clung to precarious leads, Jamieson nearly tripled his 1968
margin and won by more than nine thousand votes. A few weeks
later he appointed MacNaughton his executive assistant.

As the 51-year-old Jamieson and the 23-year-old Mac-
Naughton travelled together for two months during the campaign Jamieson had come to trust and rely on him implicitly,
and that reliance continued and strengthened in Ottawa. Mac-
Naughton was not only Jamieson's executive assistant but a
close friend and adviser. He sat in on any meeting he wanted,
travelled with the minister everywhere, and more often than not
joined the Jamieson family for weekends at home in Swift Current, Newfoundland. During 1975 MacNaughton spent all but
half a dozen of fifty-two weekends with Jamieson. Both worked
hard, played hard, and above all consumed politics.

As an EA MacNaughton was to the seventies what Bill Lee
had been to the sixties. The up-front wheeler-dealer EAs from the
Pearson years had given way to Trudeau-era EAs who were less
visible but could be equally important and powerful. Few people
played the system as well as MacNaughton. On one occasion a
wharf in Jamieson's district needed fixing but went unrepaired
for lack of funds. The repairs budget had run out of money.
MacNaughton instructed a coastal-boat captain to take a run at
the wharf to damage it further – enough to qualify the damage as
new construction, because the construction budget still had
money.

As people figured out that MacNaughton made things
happen, the stack of phone messages on his desk seemed to grow
with his reputation. Jamieson wanted MacNaughton at his side
most of the time, so that he was rarely around to take or return
telephone calls. A new stack of phone slips awaited him each
time he returned to his office. His failure to call back grew
legendary, and when he finally left Jamieson the invitation to his
farewell party was inscribed on an oversized government-issue
yellow telephone slip.

Like other EAs, MacNaughton treated his position not as a career but as a stopping-off place on the way to something else. He had planned on staying two years but remained longer when Jamieson moved to Industry, Trade and Commerce because that portfolio excited him more than any other. He had stayed through four portfolios in all and concluded he had done as much as he would ever do. In his fifth year, in 1977, he told himself to grow up and find a real job, that what he was doing could not last and was not conducive to a long-term marriage. He had married the year before and with the birth of his first daughter had decided that the time had come to get out, since he could not simultaneously work for Jamieson and raise a family. By this time Jamieson had moved to External Affairs, which didn't excite MacNaughton. He got to visit the capitals of the world in first-class style and to meet the likes of Ferdinand Marcos, but he found his scope as EA restricted. He viewed External Affairs as spectators watching spectators watching a game; he wanted to be a player rather than a watcher.

MacNaughton cast about for something to do. He had opportunities in the public service, but could not picture himself as a career civil servant. He tried to parlay a connection with the chairman of the Toronto Dominion Bank into a high-level job but lost interest when the bank wanted to start him as a management trainee. Then his lunch with Steve Markey dashed his hopes for a senior post with ECL. MacNaughton suffered a common problem for executive assistants. After handling the biggest problems at the highest levels, how do you find satisfaction in the humdrum world of middle management? As his options dwindled, MacNaughton started thinking for the first time about launching his own public-affairs company.

MacNaughton grew up hearing his father talk about business as virtually the sole productive element in society. He could not count the number of times "government creates nothing" had been drummed into his mind, and it had stayed with him until life as an EA in Ottawa changed his thinking. Despite the foibles of government bureaucracy he became impressed at how intelligent, hardworking, and supportive of business many public servants were. At the same time he was surprised, even amazed, at how stupidly most businessmen represented themselves to government. Businessmen might be experts at financing, manufacturing, and marketing, but nobody could convince MacNaughton they knew much about government relations.

MacNaughton remembered how Dave Mundy of the Air Industries Association of Canada had made himself persona non grata in Jamieson's office until Jamieson refused to meet him, even though the government would soon spend more than a billion dollars for a fleet of Long Range Patrol Aircraft. Mac-Naughton finally convinced Jamieson that he had to see Mundy, if only for the sake of appearances, because the Air Industries Association had a vital stake in the decision. "All right," Jamieson conceded. "Schedule him for twenty minutes but make sure that he doesn't babble on for the whole time – or else." Mac-Naughton huddled with Mundy before the meeting and advised him to put away his flip charts and to keep his presentation simple and down to ten minutes, and then invite questions. He explained that Jamieson didn't like flip charts and didn't need them because he knew the basic facts. Mundy seemed to agree. But he had hardly entered Jamieson's office before he was hauling out his flip charts, flicking the pages, and talking incessantly. Jamieson stood up after twenty minutes and walked out of the room saying other business demanded his attention. Mac-Naughton could almost see smoke coming out of his ears.

With notable exceptions, business executives still used the sledgehammer approach to government relations, alienating even pro-free-enterprise ministers like Jamieson who were their natural allies. MacNaughton sat through meetings thinking how easily most businessmen could accommodate Jamieson, while yielding almost nothing, and wondered why the executives didn't approach him with the same attitude with which they approached their customers. He concluded that there existed a market opportunity for him to pursue. The complexity of government had created the environment for ECL in the 1960s; government had grown even more tangled since. With his inside view of the departments of Transport, Industry, and Regional Economic Expansion, MacNaughton could see the opportunity for a consulting firm to try to find simple solutions out of complicated circumstances.

MacNaughton was arranging the details of a Liberal fundraising dinner in Newfoundland when he happened to ask Rod Bryden what kind of problems he could expect setting up a consulting company. Bryden, a former ministerial aide, knew what consulting companies were all about and how to set one up. He himself had established an economic-consulting practice and then expanded into other fields, and when MacNaughton asked for advice was in the process of becoming one of the most sophisticated financiers in the country. Bryden was always on the lookout for business opportunities and like MacNaughton saw a vacuum in how business handled its relations with government.

"Are you thinking really seriously about it?" Bryden asked.

MacNaughton said yes but admitted that he had no experience getting corporate loans and doing the various things needed to start off a business.

"Why don't we see whether we can strike some sort of a deal?" Bryden replied.

Bryden taught law at the University of Saskatchewan until his dean, Otto Lang, joined the Trudeau cabinet and brought him to Ottawa as his special assistant. Bryden's raw intelligence and capacity for seemingly effortless work earned him the role of a firefighter whom the Trudeau government parachuted in to stamp out political brushfires. First he tackled a grain crisis in the west, then confronted unemployment in Quebec and elsewhere (establishing the imaginative Local Initiatives Program) and finally was assigned to clean up Canada's wasteful regional economic incentive grants. He quit the government in 1973 and moved into a tiny office on Laurier Street with only him and a secretary; a decade and a half later he presides over eleven companies, seven thousand employees, and a billion dollars in sales.

The high-powered Bryden saw several opportunities in MacNaughton. He saw first a potentially profitable investment, since MacNaughton seemed to possess the right ingredients to run a successful public-affairs company, and, second, an invaluable source of strategic planning that he, as a venture capitalist, could use for business purposes. He also saw a tax write-off. Bryden was winding down a failed Montreal public-relations company called LaPierre, Thomas & Associates Ltd. fronted by the broadcaster Laurier LaPierre when MacNaughton chanced on him. LaPierre, Thomas had produced nothing but red ink, and Bryden figured he could recoup a tax loss by changing the company's name and fitting MacNaughton into the corporate shell under the name KinMac Consultants. KinMac brought together MacNaughton and Kinburn Capital, Bryden's company.

As in almost everything else he did, Bryden financed KinMac creatively. Bryden started as the sole owner and put Mac-Naughton on salary at $5,500 less than his EA salary. Bryden would pay MacNaughton $2,000 a month and supply an office and modest secretarial help. If after six months KinMac failed to stand on its feet MacNaughton would return half his accumulated salary – $6,000 – to Bryden. Thus each principal stood to lose an equal amount of hard cash. If KinMac was paying its way after six months MacNaughton instantly acquired 25 per cent of the stock and moved up in salary to the $70,000 Deputy Minister 1 level. Bryden would act as silent partner; he became very much involved in the executive affairs of the company but few would know he was the majority owner.

MacNaughton moved into a cubbyhole down the hall from Bryden Ltd. at 161 Laurier and borrowed Bryden's secretary for spot duty. It was August 1977 and he had no clients; he quickly learned that he had to go out and find some because nobody came to him. After being deluged with phone calls for five years he finally experienced the phenomenon of a silent phone. Mac-Naughton sent letters to the people he had met as an EA and followed up each letter with a hard approach. His status as a former EA gave him enough standing to get appointments but not clients. Businessmen who once flattered him and invited him to see them when he left Jamieson had changed their mind. Clients were tough to get.

MacNaughton was not deterred; he planned to build the largest firm in Ottawa and would overcome the obstacles. He and Bryden talked about building a unique consulting company, one based not on personalities but on corporate appeal, that would be the definitive government-relations company in Canada. Like ECL and PAI, it would look at the total environmental influences on government, but it would offer something they did not – specialist advice from a battery of public-affairs issues experts. KinMac would set up regional offices keeping in touch with provincial governments across the country. With luck the company would get into public-opinion analysis to further define the influences on government. But all these goals needed staff, which he could not afford to hire. For the moment KinMac was a one-man bucket-shop operation competing against ECL and PAI, who had big clients and solid reputations.

KinMac aimed for retainers of $2,000 to $3,000 a month. Retainers would allow MacNaughton some breathing space to plan his empire, and would act as a safety net for the day he would have payrolls to meet and no projects on the go. Much as he wanted retainers, MacNaughton did mostly project work at the beginning. He needed cash flow and could not afford to wait for a retainer clientele to build up. But handling projects kept him constantly off balance. He could not keep an eye on government while completing the projects in progress and simultaneously beating the bushes for new clients; there were not enough hours in the day for him to promote KinMac and service the contracts he already had. KinMac had to grow and reach a "critical mass" where everything could be pursued concurrently. For instance, if KinMac had two or three oil companies on retainers it could hire an energy specialist, which would attract still more oil companies. One energy specialist cost the same whether he serviced one oil company or a dozen. MacNaughton would lose money hiring an energy specialist for only one client, but would reap a windfall with a string of clients. The theory was fine, but KinMac lacked the base to invest in an energy specialist, so MacNaughton ran around covering the bases the best he could.

It took MacNaughton little more than six months to hire his first two employees, a researcher and a secretary. By this time KinMac, along with Bryden, had moved to a plush suite of offices in the Metropolitan Life Building on Bank Street which gave the company an upscale image. But the nice new offices didn't seem to help him recruit partners. He originally offered a partnership to Jim McDonald, another high-powered EA, but McDonald figured that somebody who never returned phone calls would not succeed in business. MacNaughton tried to entice a number of other EAs to join KinMac, but there was too big a gap between his rosy projections and the existing balance sheet. After more than a year of coaxing, MacNaughton persuaded Michael Robinson, Judd Buchanan's EA, to take a $5,000 salary cut and borrow $15,000 for a slice of KinMac. MacNaughton sold Robinson his vision of the future despite the tenuous nature of KinMac's early balance sheets.

Robinson, short and slightly pudgy, looked like a cherub and was universally well liked. His constant smile and friendly manner sometimes masked his abilities. Some regarded him as the best manager on Parliament Hill, and he had excelled in keeping the wheels of Buchanan's office turning and the employees happy. As an EA Robinson had choked a few times as he listened to businessmen complaining to Buchanan for twenty minutes about too much government interference in the economy – and then heard them ask for a handout. He had seen a multinational consortium invest $150-million in an application to build a natural-gas pipeline along the Mackenzie Valley and lose out to a hastily conceived, ill-prepared, and underfinanced rival through bad lobbying. The Arctic Gas consortium was confrontational and talked about rates of production and netbacks while its successful competitor stressed social and environmental matters, and commitment to the government's public-policy agenda. So he felt confident that KinMac had a useful and profitable role to play.

The energetic Robinson kept on top of the Ottawa political world, but KinMac's biggest asset was MacNaughton's salesmanship. Because he believed that the most alienated and out-of-touch businessmen lived in western Canada, MacNaughton wore out a few pairs of shoes selling KinMac to companies in Alberta and British Columbia. He learned through Bryden that the British Columbia Development Corporation, a Crown corporation set up a few years earlier by NDP Premier Dave Barrett, had no friends in Ottawa and could not get enough federal assistance for its huge northeast coal development. BCDC turned to MacNaughton, who signed up the company as KinMac's first retainer. Next were Burrard Drydock of Vancouver, Progas Ltd. of Calgary, a consortium of natural-gas producers seeking an export licence, and the Canadian Motion Picture Distributors Association.

MacNaughton bumped into a representative of the Canadian Motion Picture Distributors Association on an airplane and learned that the organization was worried about the coming of Pay-TV. He quickly arranged an appointment in Toronto, knowing absolutely nothing about the film or television business. He later flew to the appointment from Vancouver on the midnight flight, planning to catch some sleep on the plane and arrive in Toronto at 7 a.m. in time for his morning presentation, but ran into a friend on the plane, talked all night, and arrived in Toronto in terrible shape. He checked into a hotel for a fast shower, went into his meeting, and signed up the association as a retainer client.

By early 1979 KinMac had collected a handful of retainer clients and had generated $190,000 in billings in its first full year, which produced a profit of about $60,000. MacNaughton never exercised his option for a deputy minister's salary. He could not afford to pay himself $70,000 and hire the employees he needed to expand KinMac. Instead he awarded himself about $45,000, while the extra money was set aside for hiring the next employee. Dividends were out of the picture, and were not even discussed. KinMac operated on such a tenuous cash flow that the company missed payrolls when clients' cheques arrived late. There was a period when strategic planning meant issuing cheques that didn't bounce. But KinMac grew steadily and had good prospects of one day reaching the status of ECL and PAI, a remarkable achievement – but not remarkable enough for Mac-Naughton, who was in a hurry. He felt KinMac could grow more quickly and, given a chance, he wanted to speed up the growth by acquiring another company. He had not figured out how, because neither ECL nor PAI was for sale – at least so he thought, until a phone call from Jamie Deacey changed his mind.

In January 1979 Torrance Wylie had finished lunch with Jamie Deacey of the Canadian Petroleum Association and was walking with him back towards the office when he casually dropped a little bombshell. Wylie said he wanted to do something different and was thinking of getting out of PAI. Deacey was so surprised that his first reaction was to ask Wylie if he was serious. Wylie assured him he was. Deacey, a former EA and now a well-connected lobbyist for the big oil companies, asked if he could pass on the word. He was eager to tell MacNaughton, because he knew about his ambitions and could visualize his reaction.

MacNaughton reacted quickly and dramatically. Back on the

the eleventh floor of 99 Bank Street, he couldn't wait to call Bryden and Robinson together and discuss strategy in meeting Wylie. Until now, MacNaughton had never set his sights on PAI. ECL had interested him a lot more, and he was biding his time waiting for the right moment: KinMac needed a better base, and MacNaughton needed some sign that ECL was available. The KinMac trio met Wylie several times over the next few weeks and they started to talk terms. Wylie wanted a good price and as they discussed details shrewdly let it out that others were interested in buying PAI, namely his own employees as well as one of his clients, Public and Industrial Relations Ltd., of Montreal, a public-relations firm wanting to expand into public affairs. Others were interested, but Wylie had no real offers.

Wylie proposed a price: $350,000 – almost three times the value on which he had based his payments to Edmonds a year and a half earlier. The figure would net Wylie a healthy windfall, but represented a good deal for KinMac. PAI turned in excellent profits and Wylie's price more than met the rule of thumb for evaluating the worth of a personal-services company: between 0.8 and 1.2 annual sales – depending on the stability of the client base – if the company generates pre-tax profits of 20 per cent on annual billings, more if the company's earning potential is particularly good. By these standards, Wylie's price looked like a bargain. As far as MacNaughton and Bryden were concerned, $350,000 was good value providing the clients were happy and likely to stay.

The purchase was hardly risk-free. A personal-services business is hard to evaluate at the best of times. Its fortunes hinge on client relationships, and these can change for a variety of reasons, especially after a shift in ownership. The PAI client base looked stable, but there were no guarantees that some clients would not leave a month after the takeover. Wylie allowed Robinson to sound out a few PAI clients about their reactions to new ownership, but was understandably touchy about KinMac's probing too far, for fear that they would disturb his clients and then back out. Robinson duly reported that the two clients he saw were solid. MacNaughton already knew that one other client, Hudson's Bay Oil and Gas, was happy; not long before he had tried to entice the company over to KinMac and had failed.

Thus reassured, MacNaughton and Bryden made little effort to bargain down Wylie's price. The negotiations soon narrowed down to how much down, how much in payments, and over what period. The two sides started talking in February and the deal was wrapped up in April.

Bryden devised a financing package that met the terms but ensured that the cash that went into Wylie's pocket wouldn't come out of his. He leveraged the debt so that payments came out of earnings and would be paid out inside three years. The debt was financed by the bank and guaranteed by the four new shareholders, who were now Bryden (through Kinburn Capital) 51 per cent; MacNaughton, 24 per cent; Robinson, 15 per cent, and Don Kelly, a PAI consultant who plunked down $25,000 for 10 per cent. All four shareholders guaranteed the loan on the basis of their shareholding, but the key was Bryden. No bank would have touched the deal without his guarantees.

PAI moved lock, stock, and barrel into the KinMac office at 99 Bank Street, and settled in across the hall from Bryden's coffee room. PAI was legally absorbed into KinMac, which changed its name to Public Affairs International. KinMac had a total office staff of four, where PAI had a dozen. A small fish had swallowed a big fish and could expect indigestion. MacNaughton became president of the new PAI and ran the company, while Wylie stayed on as the figurehead chairman.

As chairman, Wylie dispatched a "good news" note to all clients proclaiming that PAI had merged with one of the fastest-growing firms in Ottawa in order to serve clients better. The announcement portrayed events as a merger rather than as the outright purchase that it was. PAI's clients would figure out the truth soon enough, but MacNaughton hoped that by that time the new company would have captured their loyalty. He planned to service the clients up and down, backwards and forwards for the first six months while the relationships jelled. Meanwhile KinMac didn't hesitate to trumpet the real story to its old clients, boasting how it had taken over PAI. "The news was managed a little," one insider acknowledged. "It depended on who the audience was."

MacNaughton held his breath and waited for clients to react. He knew that the key would be Wylie himself, so during the negotiations he had extracted a commitment from him to stay on at least part time. Wylie had some longstanding, almost personal clients who paid retainers mostly for the right to phone him at will for his insights into public policy. MacNaughton planned to steer PAI away from this kind of relationship where the attraction was an individual. In contrast to ECL and the old PAI, MacNaughton wanted clients to be lured by the company and its vast resources and specialized expertise, rather than by one individual in the company. MacNaughton guessed that approach would cost PAI some clients in the short run, but would ultimately attract more clients and give PAI a competitive advantage over ECL. In the meantime he had to keep as many clients as possible or risk finding that he had bought the PAI name and not the business. So Wylie had to stay aboard and remain prominently identified with PAI to get it through the transition stage.

The PAI takeover quadrupled the size of MacNaughton's operation overnight, and gave him the resources to expand the way he wanted. He acquired a healthy cash flow and a roster of clients who paid their bills every month, which meant that "critical mass" was in sight. He had also bought credibility and a profile, which in some ways were the most important acquisitions of all. Whereas KinMac had been one of a dozen two-man shops in town, PAI had the kind of reputation where new clients walked in off the street.

In a year and a half MacNaughton had propelled himself into the number two position in public-affairs consulting in Ottawa. As far as he was concerned he had only started; PAI was not a destination but a springboard to bigger things. He was in a hurry to become number one because other dreams waited beyond that. Overtaking Bill Lee was merely a short-term aspiration. His long-term plans went far beyond.

After taking over PAI, MacNaughton drafted a five-year business plan. By 1985 PAI was to have fifty clients, $2-million in billings, and a ratio of retainers to project billings of 70-30. To some those figures seemed unrealistic, but MacNaughton believed they were conservative if anything, and that the market still held plenty of potential. He wanted to hire experts in energy, transportation, communication, and international trade. He also wanted to buy a few more rivals and take a run at buying ECL. He planned on making a major push into the provinces, the goal being to open offices coast to coast and build the first "national" public-affairs consulting firm. According to the plan, PAI would open at least one branch office each year and would seek the capacity to deal with every provincial government by the beginning of 1981-82. After that it would expand internationally.

EIGHT

THE PUNK POLLSTER

Mike Robinson was living in Edmonton and working on the 1972 Liberal election campaign in Alberta when his roommate introduced him to a long-haired 20-year-old University of Alberta student named Allan Gregg. Gregg was not in politics – he was working as a summer playground supervisor for the city of Edmonton – but he struck Robinson as profane, outrageous, intriguing, and fun. Even in the accommodating culture of the early seventies, Gregg looked like a misfit, from his earring to his scuffed shoes, but Robinson sized him up as capable and uncommonly bright and somebody who was clearly going places.

Two and a half years later Gregg dropped by to see Robinson in Ottawa, where Robinson by then had become EA to Judd Buchanan, the minister of Indian affairs and northern development. Gregg said he had moved into town to start on a Ph.D. in political science at Carleton University and needed some work; he wondered if Robinson could find him something. Although Gregg had married and become a father, otherwise he was the same brilliant oddball Robinson had known in Edmonton. Robinson made a few phone calls and found nothing. He sent Gregg to Blair Williams, the national director of the Liberal Party, but openings there too were scarce, since graduate students looking for part-time work sprouted like summer weeds. The Liberal Party turned away many students every year, but would later regret saying no to this one.

Gregg next tried Richard Clippingdale, a Carleton history professor who was impressed by his superior abilities and his spirited if somewhat irreverent performance in seminars. Clippingdale was giving Gregg a crash minor in Canadian history and enjoyed watching his mind work. He was struck by Gregg's exceptional insights and noticed a sense of adventure, which few graduate students shared. He also could see that Gregg possessed an uncanny knack for selling himself that effectively erased his outlandishness; besides, he liked him.

Clippingdale, an active Conservative, made a single phone call. Reaching Robert Stanfield's office, he told his friend Bill Neville that an exceptionally bright student needed work and could help the Tory party. Neville was soon to take over as the Conservative caucus director of research and happened to be looking for a social-policy researcher, somebody who could cover housing, income security, immigration, and related issues, so he arranged a meeting with Gregg in the cafeteria of the Confederation Building. If the locale was unusual for a job interview, so was the candidate. Gregg arrived without a tie, because he didn't own one, and his hair reached halfway down his back. He never apologized for his appearance. Indeed, he revelled in it and used it to grab attention. Being out of fashion was his cachet and reflected his personal culture; more than almost anything else in life, Allan Gregg really wanted to lead a rock band.

Neville asked the standard questions about why he wanted to work for the opposition research office, and Gregg mustered an academic reply: Parliament was important and misunderstood; a pluralist society needed a healthy and viable opposition. The answer didn't excite Neville because he didn't plan on staying in opposition long. For Gregg's part, "the notion of helping those fuckers move from opposition to the government was a long way from my mind," as he later told Robert Fulford in *Saturday Night*. Neville hired him anyway. Only after Gregg started the job did Neville realize what a catch he had made; soon Neville was telling his wife that the world would hear from Gregg some day.

The Conservatives gave him a desk in the Confederation Building and an $11,000-a-year researcher's job for the summer of 1975 which was continued for two days a week after he returned to Carleton in the fall. Gregg attacked his work with a dedication and enthusiasm that left him no time to sit around the office. The job introduced him to caucus, took him around Parliament Hill, and kept him on top of events in the Commons. Whenever the Liberal government introduced a bill with health, welfare, or social-income issues Gregg quickly dug into the issues and wrote a research critique to help Tory MPs launch their attack in the Commons.

Gregg arrived at the research office shortly after the Tories had become disenchanted with the polling of Bob Teeter. The high-flying Teeter was probably the top pollster in the United States; from his Detroit base he had polled for Richard Nixon and Gerald Ford. But the feeling in the Conservative Party was that he tended to rerun his last U.S. Republican presidential campaign in Canada, oblivious to differences in the political culture, and some Tories suspected that he looked at the Canadian data only after he stepped on the plane to Toronto. It offended Neville and others that one of Canada's national political parties relied on an American to tell it what Canadians were thinking. Besides, Teeter didn't come cheaply; after Stanfield's shattering loss in 1974 the Conservative Party faced an austerity period, and it was decided to save money on polling. The party set up a makeshift in-house polling program to replace Teeter, which was run out of the office of Michael Meighen, the party president. It was strictly amateurish. Ian Green, Meighen's EA, rounded up volunteers and started calling people randomly on the free long-distance telephone lines belonging to the House of Commons.

Green's polling activity piqued Gregg's interest. Polling had fascinated him ever since, at 18, he had worked on the 1970 mayoralty campaign in Edmonton. He had dabbled in polling and studied behaviouralism under Professor Thelma Oliver in his undergraduate days at the University of Alberta. Survey research and quantitative methods had always given him his best marks in university.

Gregg introduced himself to Green and offered to help. Green asked whether he could run data on a computer. "Sure," Gregg replied, "no problem at all." Soon he was drawing samples and helping design questionnaires. The polling program grew and became almost formal. Gregg and Stephen Probyn, Green's original helper, printed up covers and promoted the results as hot merchandise. Professionals could have quibbled, but the product was fundamentally sound and proved good value for the money; for $40,000 the party got survey data that would have cost six figures under Teeter.

In 1976, after Joe Clark won the party leadership and

appointed Neville his chief of staff, Green joined Neville's staff as Clark's executive assistant and Gregg moved up to be Meighen's EA. Meighen took Gregg around, introduced him to the party, and installed him as a legitimate and key person. Gregg had by now acquired two ties but couldn't actually tie them. His father tied them once and Gregg kept them knotted, slipping them over his head when the occasion required. By this time Gregg's polling had become organized, regular, and statistically fairly rigorous. Parts of the job were being farmed out to private companies.

After slumping badly and falling behind Clark, Trudeau jumped ahead in the polls after the November 1976 victory in Quebec of the separatist Parti Québécois. Expecting Trudeau to exploit his government's sudden popularity with a snap election in 1977, Clark picked Lowell Murray, the baby-faced former Stanfield aide who looked more like a hesitating assistant than a chief, as director of campaign planning to pull together a campaign that could roll into action the minute Trudeau struck. Murray had not even thought about a national campaign secretary until he noticed this long-haired character playing with statistics like a mad scientist. Gregg's wizardry so impressed Murray that he snapped him up as the first member of his campaign team when Meighen stepped down as party president, and let him write his own job description. By this time Gregg had found that real-life political science on Parliament Hill stimulated him a lot more than the textbook variety; he abandoned his Ph.D. program and moved into the office next to Murray at Conservative headquarters.

Trudeau toyed with the idea of calling an election in 1977, but put it off; he hated campaigning and didn't want to be seen as taking advantage of events in Quebec. He considered an election again in the spring of 1978 but by then the polls were swinging back to the Tories, so Trudeau and Jim Coutts and his other advisers concluded that he couldn't win. Both parties were now following public opinion closely as a critical element in their electoral strategy, the Liberals relying primarily on a private pollster, Martin Goldfarb, and the Tories on Allan Gregg.

Gregg's new job put him in direct touch with Clark, who soon fell under his spell; in time Clark would call him the best analyst of public opinion in Canada. Clark's most important campaign planners were Murray, Neville, Nancy Jamieson, and Gregg – and Murray asked Gregg's advice whenever he faced a tough decision. In two years Gregg had jumped from part-time researcher to high party mandarin and key strategist at party headquarters. He had joined the Tories as a job only after trying for work with the Liberals. But he made friendships and built alliances with like-minded people in the party and became a loyal follower of Joe Clark.

Gregg had not wowed Neville, Murray, and Clark through happenstance. He profoundly impressed people wherever he went. Party workers whispered about how terrifyingly bright he was and wondered how somebody so smart could still be affable and approachable and interested in what they had to say. Colleagues stopped noticing his appearance after a while and began realizing that his cloak of eccentricity concealed a cache of diplomatic skills. Gregg pricked balloons but rarely alienated people. He gleamed with self-confidence and said outrageous things, but almost never provoked antagonism or resentment. Quite the reverse. People liked him and trusted him with their secrets. He wielded the English language with an ease and precision most politicians would kill for, using even four-letter words precisely and mixing them naturally into a polysyllabic vocabulary. His sentences came out in edited form with no useless words filling the air. Gregg made every syllable count.

As Murray assembled his campaign team Gregg became the indispensable "systems man". He demonstrated a knack for putting systems into place that matched the strengths of the people they were designed to fit, and showed a sensitive touch for handling people. Gregg later confided to a colleague that he always took on the character of his boss so that it became ingrained. He did it with Neville and Meighen and did it with Lowell Murray more than anybody else.

Of all Gregg's skills, none impressed his colleagues more than his talent for interpreting polling data. Gregg awed everybody by the way he moved blocks of data around, interchanging one set of numbers for another to capture insights into voters' intentions. Gregg believed that most polls measured the wrong things, that they counted noses and tallied up the result without looking at people's attitudinal antecedents. For Gregg, attitudes were the key, and he tried to find out all he could about them.

Knowing that the Conservative Party had 35 per cent of the vote was only the beginning of the story. Knowing how much of the 35 per cent support was soft, and what the party had to do to hold it, told a lot more, as did knowing why 15 per cent remained undecided and how it could be enticed to support the party. Knowing these things allowed the Conservatives to design a campaign with maximum appeal.

Gregg went further. He believed that a key to successful polling – and to electoral positioning – was not only understanding *what* people felt but *why* they felt it. Society had become fickle and always seemed to be changing its mind; the Conservative Party might take a popular position on an issue and a month later watch the public reverse itself. Gregg wanted to know not only how public opinion was changing but why it was changing. He believed the "why" related to people's values, which varied surprisingly little. The party that best understood public values stayed closest to the mood of society. Shrewd polling to discover the "why" would allow the party to build a strategy that remained consistent while constantly adapting to changing public preferences.

In the summer of 1978 Neville nominated Gregg for an exchange program sponsored by the U.S. State Department for a ten-day consulting tour of the United States. Gregg submitted an application proposing a tour of visits with leading American pollsters and political consultants. The State Department liked the idea and arranged interviews with the top practitioners in the country. Gregg spent five days in Washington, two in Texas, and the rest of the time in California seeing people like Peter Hart, Pat Caddell, Lance Torrence, Matt Reese, Stu Spencer, and Richard Wirthlin. "What's new in American politics?" Gregg would ask. "Tell me the most exciting thing you know that's happening." His American hosts poured out their knowledge and Gregg felt he was living a dream. The pollsters he visited all operated highly successful businesses in public-opinion research; they were modern gurus in hot demand who indulged their creative passions, influenced public policy, and made big money. The work and the lifestyle appealed to Gregg. A light bulb lit up in his mind after he returned to Canada amazed and excited and ready to put his new knowledge to use – and was unable to find a Canadian company to handle the polling requirements of the Conservative Party. It struck him that other Canadian users of data must be in the same position. "Maybe there's a real market niche out there," he told himself. At that moment Gregg decided to go into the polling business after the election.

What impressed Gregg most was how much the American pollsters relied on "tracking" as an indispensable part of public-opinion analysis. Tracking meant that they surveyed continually during elections, turning around data overnight and rolling totals into cumulative trends that allowed them to follow public-opinion trends with stunning precision. Gregg's ten-day trip seriously influenced him and convinced him that the Conservative Party had to start tracking the minute the next election was announced.

Gregg started twisting the arms of Neville and Murray. "Look," he told Murray, "we can't run this in-house polling program any more. It's crazy." He was right. As things stood, Gregg wrote the questionnaire, printed up copies at party headquarters, and submitted the forms along with a sample design to a company called Canadian Facts, which did the telephone interviewing. Gregg then had party volunteers code the results, tucked the coding sheets under his arm and delivered them to Ottawa Keypunch for processing into computer cards and, finally, carrying boxes full of cards, stood in line for the computer at Carleton University. The Progressive Conservative Party of Canada, which hoped to form the next national government, ran its political data off Gregg's graduate-student account at Carleton. Gregg protested that the Clark team was trying to run the Conservative Party like the YMCA – on the basis of volunteerism and Christian zeal. "This just isn't going to work," he complained.

Gregg was convinced that tracking represented the biggest breakthrough in election campaigning since television. It could virtually dictate the details of an election campaign, by uncovering moods and divulging trends. When public opinion shifted during the campaign the party could reposition itself to meet the change. A party could emphasize some issues and drop others with pinpoint effect as the campaign developed. By looking at numbers on a sheet of paper, politicians could watch one

region firm up while another turned soft and change the campaign itinerary accordingly. Used correctly, tracking could be an
astonishingly potent weapon. But it required next-day capability
and Gregg's in-house polling program took nearly a month to
produce data.

Murray agreed and told Gregg to hire a professional polling
company. Gregg interviewed virtually every reputable polling
company in Canada except Goldfarb Associates, the Liberal
firm. He returned discouraged. None of them could do the job to
his standards. He gave them good marks for counting heads,
conducting taste tests for things like Jello, and determining
advertising recall. But he flunked them for their lack of understanding of issue-based polling, since they had so far failed to
grasp public-affairs research and how attitudes determined people's decisions. Gregg also challenged their methodology and
concluded that they couldn't tell a regression analysis from the
man in the moon. He dismissed them as marketers who equated
the choice of the country's fiscal policy with selecting a brand of
dog food, noting that their sample frames coincided with postal
codes and census areas instead of political boundaries. Gregg
reported back to Murray that the Canadian companies were "no
god-damn good" as far as the Conservative Party was concerned.
The Americans were light years ahead. Murray told him to try
the United States.

The Conservative Party returned to the United States somewhat sheepishly, since it was admitting that it couldn't go it
alone and that perhaps it had acted precipitately in dropping
Teeter. The most sheepish part was yet to come. With an election staring the party in the face, it had little time to form new
links. So Neville, Gregg, and Murray agonized for a while, swallowed hard, and hired Teeter again.

Teeter's people conducted their interviews from a phone
bank in Toronto off a questionnaire drafted by Gregg, and then
fed the responses into a computer at Wayne State University
outside Detroit. The data rolled off a terminal in Gregg's office
in Ottawa where he interpreted the results. While Teeter
gathered the data and tabulated them, Gregg manipulated the
figures and worked out what they all meant.

From the start the data revealed that Canadians generally felt
worse off than before, and pinned the blame at least partly on the

country's political leadership. Gregg, Murray, and Neville used the findings to mould a campaign strategy. They would seek, as Jeffrey Simpson wrote in *Discipline of Power*, to plant the "right" question into voters' minds when they entered the polling booth on election day.

It took some doing. Choosing between Clark and Trudeau, the voter would choose Trudeau, because the data revealed that Trudeau scored higher than Clark as a leader. Choosing on the basis of the local candidate, the voter would select Liberals more often than Conservatives because the Liberals, as the government party and with a majority of MPs, enjoyed higher visibility. Choosing between the Liberal and Conservative parties, the voter opted for the Liberals because more Canadians instinctively identified with that party.

The Conservative campaign had to avoid these comparisons and had to focus instead on getting the voters to ask themselves the "right" question: "Do you really want four more years like the last eleven under Trudeau?" The Tories would win the election if voters entered the polling booth thinking of that question; the Conservative campaign needed to keep linking Trudeau to the problems of the country.

When Trudeau called an election for May 22 1979 the Conservative Party needed only to turn the key to start the election machine and shift into gear the polling apparatus that went with it. Clark took to the hustings and Neville travelled at his side, while Murray ran the campaign from Ottawa with Gregg as his right-hand man. At headquarters, Murray made the decisions and Gregg was often tagged to carry them out, throwing in ideas along the way. Meanwhile the Liberal strategy revealed that the Liberal tacticians had reached the same conclusions as Gregg and his colleagues had. Trudeau downplayed his record and emphasized Clark. "Don't compare me with the Almighty," Trudeau warned voters. "Compare me with the alternative."

After their federal counterparts dropped him in 1974, the provincial Conservatives in Toronto had continued to stick with Teeter. Premier Bill Davis nearly lost the election the following year and in February 1976 Teeter told a small circle of local Tories that Davis "will never be an asset to a political party again".

Teeter's sweeping assessment instantly raised the hackles of Davis's supporters. One of them was Tom Scott, of Sherwood Communications, who believed that Davis was anything but politically dead. He suspected that Teeter had dashed through the polling numbers on the plane to Toronto and wouldn't have the foggiest idea what he was talking about if the flight from Detroit had been any shorter. Scott, a short, balding, bearded advertising man with a reputation as a whiz-bang, concluded that Ontario Conservatives needed a different pollster instead of a new leader, one based in Canada and with a sense of the country.

When Scott quietly looked for somebody to replace Teeter, he discovered what Gregg learned a year or so later, that a capable Canadian polling company didn't seem to exist. He decided that if he could not find one he would start a new one that would operate in the private marketplace and be on call to the Conservatives – and would be at least as sophisticated as what the Liberal Party had in Goldfarb Associates. Through Rich Willis, a Tory friend, Scott stumbled across a pollster in Santa Ana, California, named Richard Wirthlin who measured public opinion for Ronald Reagan and other Republicans. Wirthlin impressed Scott instantly. As an advertising executive Scott had been around survey research for years and had been a big buyer of polls, but after talking with Wirthlin he realized how badly Canadians had been served. Wirthlin excited Scott and within thirty minutes the two agreed in principle to set up a 50-50 joint venture in Canada. Sherwood Communications would supply start-up money and Wirthlin's company, Decision Making Information, would contribute the technology and run the new Canadian company, Decima Research Ltd.

Meanwhile Scott had come to know Gregg well enough to see that he would give Decima a competitive advantage and decided he wanted to launch the new company with Gregg as a partner. Slouched in Scott's living room in Oakville, with their feet up, Scott and Gregg talked far into the night. Like everybody else, Scott was impressed by Gregg and never doubted his ability to fit into a corporate mould. He pictured Gregg creating a market for Decima faster than anyone else could. His dress, long hair, and four-letter words would attract instant attention; Scott figured the market was ready for a punk pollster.

Scott announced to Wirthlin that Gregg had to be cut into the company. Wirthlin had met Gregg during his 1978 trip and liked him, but he disliked the idea of surrendering equity. What did he offer that they didn't have or couldn't purchase? Scott replied that Gregg offered freedom from competition, warning him that Gregg would make an unbeatable rival, so much so that without him he would reconsider investing in Decima. The choice was to accept Gregg as a partner or face him as a competitor, and he wanted Gregg on the same side. Given Scott's feelings, Wirthlin agreed to cut in Gregg to a one-fifth share, leaving Decima with a 40-40-20 ownership split.

Scott's instinct proved deadly accurate and not a bit premature; when he relayed Decima's offer to Gregg about two weeks before voting day during the 1979 election campaign, Gregg was weighing an offer from PAI.

MacNaughton, whose business it was to know these things, had learned soon enough about the splash Gregg had made inside the Conservative Party. He quickly realized Gregg's potential in the market, so quickly that he had been pursuing Gregg since the KinMac days of 1978. Now, as the election campaign rolled along, he and Mike Robinson outlined PAI's ambitions for the future to Gregg and invited him to establish a polling division within it. When Scott learned of MacNaughton's overture he assured Gregg he would match PAI's salary and they could discuss details after the election. For the first time in his life Gregg had people chasing him with job offers.

Even before Decima and PAI started competing for his services, Gregg had informed Murray that, win, lose, or draw on May 22, he was leaving the Tories after the election. On election day, with everything finished except the counting, Gregg plunked his resignation on Lowell Murray's desk. Thanks to the "right" question, Joe Clark won a minority victory, and Gregg decided to join Decima. Exactly two weeks after Clark was sworn into office, Gregg moved to Toronto to begin his new career.

Decima Research opened its doors in Toronto in July 1979 and to no one's surprise became the official pollster for the Conservative Party. Nobody had given him any guarantees, but

Gregg never doubted he would land the party account. Who else would the party hire? He knew that the rehiring of Teeter had irritated and embarrassed both Neville and Murray, who felt it a national disgrace for the party to rely on an American firm for polling. Neville and Murray also valued Gregg's abilities and wished him well; his business success would be helpful to the Conservative Party's political success and provide them with a prosperous and friendly pollster. They had encouraged him to go into business. So nobody blinked when Decima was chosen to conduct the post-election study of why people had voted the way they did. One of Decima's first contracts was to advise Prime Minister Joe Clark about the meaning of the 1979 election results.

NINE

THE STUMBLE FROM POWER

On June 4 1979, when Joe Clark was sworn in as Canada's sixteenth prime minister, Bill Neville moved to the Langevin Block and took over Jim Coutts's old office, overlooking Parliament Hill and about eight doors down the hall from Clark. Neville's office budget doubled to $2-million, while his staff grew to nearly a hundred. Neville still met Clark and a few senior aides every morning at 8:45 to oversee the critical operations, but now that he ran the country Clark leaned on Neville more than ever, rarely moving without checking with him first. Neville remained Clark's unquestioned number one political adviser. Below him the pecking order grew less clear; either Jim Gillies, Neville's old friend and Clark's policy adviser, or Lowell Murray, his political strategist, followed next as number two.

Working long hours under pressure was not new to Neville, but the demands and pressures of the Prime Minister's Office burdened him as never before. Besides grappling with the structure of government and the operations of cabinet, he had to deal with the five or six major decisions that faced Clark's inner cabinet each week. Neville was not only the ideas man who thought out the government's approaches but also the co-ordinator who chaired the meetings that brought the processes together. And while he had a large staff of speechwriters and other aides, Neville could not stop himself from writing many of Clark's speeches. "He did everything in Clark's office except run the photocopier," Jeffrey Simpson wrote.

Neville arrived in the office each morning around 8:15 and worked through to about 7 p.m. when he scooped up a pile of documents for what amounted to a second day of work at home.

Other chiefs of staff dodged, delegated, or diverted the paperload. Neville confronted it. Each evening he diligently waded through a pile of reports, underlining the salient points as his mechanism for committing to memory what he read. Around 11:30 p.m. he took the documents to bed and even there he continued to pore over them. His wife joked that she once slipped a note into his pile of paper saying "Let's make love" – and he underlined and filed it.

Neville's underlings swore by him. He allowed them major roles and didn't look over their shoulders or start second-guessing. Even better, he listened to their advice, made quick decisions, and, unlike others who have occupied the chief-of-staff position, never hoarded his access to the prime minister. He worked hard, took his laughs when he could get them and backed up his staff. He could be abrupt and was naturally tense, but never raised his voice or cracked under pressure, and generally set a quiet style in the hottest office in the country.

After sixteen years of opposition the Tories suddenly found themselves in government without knowing how to govern. Since Clark had chosen to ignore the old Diefenbaker veterans, virtually the entire cabinet needed crash training on how to run a department, and none knew how to run the country. Clark himself lacked government experience and of his twenty-nine-member cabinet only Finance Minister John Crosbie and Solicitor General Allan Lawrence had even been provincial ministers before. Health and Welfare Minister David Crombie had been a mayor. That left Neville, the ex-Liberal, as the only team member with federal-government experience. It made his role especially important.

People expected Clark to stumble occasionally but nobody, least of all Neville, expected him to trip up within twenty-four hours of taking office. At his first press conference as prime minister, Clark announced that Canada was moving its embassy in Israel from Tel Aviv to Jerusalem. Clark told reporters he would instruct the Department of External Affairs to proceed forthwith and would discuss only logistics and not its "appropriateness". Flora MacDonald, the new minister of external affairs, learned about Clark's statement at a reception and was simply aghast, knowing that it would enrage the entire Arab world.

Neville was equally aghast. He had carefully briefed Clark

beforehand on what issues to hit, but somewhere between the briefing and the start of the press conference Clark decided to demonstrate that the public service – in this case, External Affairs – was not pushing him around and picked Jerusalem as his "tough guy" issue. Ironically, it was Neville who, during the campaign, had sold Clark on the Jerusalem policy without fully appreciating the international political repercussions. Neville in turn had been persuaded by Ron Atkey, the Tory candidate in the Toronto riding of St. Paul's, and to a lesser extent by Rob Parker, the candidate in neighbouring Eglinton-Lawrence. Both candidates were running neck and neck with tough Liberal opponents in ridings with big blocs of Jewish votes and they persuaded Neville that the Jerusalem policy would sweep both ridings. Polls showed Clark teetering on the brink of a majority, and Neville believed these two ridings might boost him over. So in mid-campaign Clark announced that his government would do what few other countries did: move the embassy in Israel to the disputed capital of Jerusalem.

The Jerusalem policy plagued Clark from the start. It didn't give him his majority. It didn't even sweep the two target seats; Atkey won and Parker lost. And the policy proved to be so controversial across the country that it may have hurt the Tory campaign. The international consequences of actively planning the move were not debatable. Only a dozen or so junior countries kept embassies in Jerusalem. Even the pro-Israeli American government refused to do it. It was clearly bad policy.

The Jerusalem issue died down after the election, giving Neville time to look for a political solution. He saw Jerusalem as a low-priority item in the first term of the Clark government. Delay was good because the passage of time defused the issue; the government would talk about the goal and await a quiet settlement. The Department of External Affairs, however, exercised no such patience and was urging Clark to reconsider the policy even before he was sworn into office. The intervention angered Clark, who decided to show External Affairs that the cabinet – not the bureaucracy – determined foreign policy. So he announced the policy at his opening press conference and in doing so rekindled the debate.

A variety of groups rose up to confront Clark over Jerusalem.

Canada's NATO allies opposed him, while Arab countries threatened to cancel the contracts of Canadian corporations in the Middle East, which in turn stirred up Canadian business. Even some Jews, who saw the debate turning anti-Semitic, quietly advised the government to bail out. But bailing out was not easy. The way that Clark had announced the policy caused as much difficulty as what he had announced; since he had presented the issue in terms of who was running the government – the politicians or the bureaucrats – it was now hard to retreat without losing face. Before long Clark dug up Robert Stanfield as special envoy to examine the issue, for the purpose of allowing the government to retreat.

Clark stepped onto another land mine at the same press conference when he announced that he planned to appoint trustees to evaluate the worth of Petro-Canada. Once again he reopened an old wound. If Jerusalem had failed to deliver Clark a majority, his stand on Petro-Canada had probably denied it to him in the first place. If Clark had backed Petro-Canada, or even remained relatively neutral, there might not have been a need to chase those seats with the Jerusalem policy. The public supported Petro-Canada in 1979 as the only honest broker in the oil patch, but Clark spent the entire election campaign ridiculing it and challenging its right to exist. Clark held progressive views on most things, but not on Petro-Canada. On this issue he resembled the typical Alberta MP and defiantly remained among the most conservative members in the Tory caucus. He flatly opposed public ownership in the oil industry.

Neville didn't even try to change Clark's position, although he spent months, including the entire 1979 election campaign, trying to get him to moderate his language on Petro-Canada, to no effect. Clark became even more bellicose as he continued to assault Petro-Canada with every verb and adjective in the financial dictionary. Neville had learned many years ago that any political position based on ideology spelled trouble, no matter what the position or the ideology. Nor could Allan Gregg stifle Clark with a memo saying the Conservatives were being perceived as obstacles to an energy solution. Gregg warned that changes to Petro-Canada must be presented as something more than a knee-jerk commitment to free enterprise. The public resented Clark's manifest ill will to the Crown oil company, and wondered whether Tory ideology would overcome practical decision-making.

But now, in his first press conference, Clark announced the imminent dismemberment of Petro-Canada, and did so without cabinet support. His new cabinet split several ways over what to do. Some ministers, like Clark, wanted to sell it outright, while others wanted to offer shares to the public, and still others wanted to leave it alone. Compromise appeared out of easy reach, so the cabinet did nothing. Yet Clark's statement created expectation and caused various lobbies to rally to Petro-Canada's defence and in the process paint the government as autocratic and right wing. Petro-Canada hung on like a bad cold and dogged Clark throughout the life of his government. Clark finally retreated a little and proposed offering Petro-Canada stock to the public, a measure which had some popular appeal. But months of fruitless struggle made the government look paradoxically stubborn and weak, and ultimately wrong.

Before the election, the public wondered about Clark's competence, and that nagging doubt more than anything denied him a majority. Clark's physical awkwardness, lack of personal grace, weak chin, pretentious vocabulary, and overblown sentence structure – "What is the totality of your land?" he asked a farmer in India – created an unreassuring image, and now that he was prime minister the public waited for more substantial evidence. Clark's inability to handle Jerusalem and Petro-Canada confirmed the image. Twice Clark had fought for impractical measures and been forced to back down. The public saw his handling of the issues as incompetent and concluded it had erred in electing him.

At the same time Clark delayed recalling Parliament, where he could introduce bold new initiatives and appear daily in the role of national leader. Neville and others wanted cabinet ministers to learn their departments and devise a solid legislative plan before facing Parliament, which meant that in the interim the government was seen as limping along for nearly five months without a comprehensive agenda. It made it appear weak before it ever did anything.

Jerusalem and Petro-Canada denied Clark his honeymoon and robbed him of the so-called "halo effect" that traditionally blesses new prime ministers. As if he didn't lack criticism already, he also lost popularity in squabbling with the provinces over oil prices. Clark held a First Ministers' meeting on energy in mid-November, knowing that his Tory cousins in Ontario would devastate the federal position on oil pricing. "We let Bill Davis beat the shit out of us believing their election [Ontario's] would come before ours," a Clark insider explained. That, plus the fact that energy negotiations with Premier Peter Lougheed of Alberta went badly, added to the impression that Clark was not running things smoothly or well.

Clark also alienated some support within his party because of his snail-like pace in handing out patronage. The prime minister's office was compiling a centralized list of order-in-council appointments along with a computerized list of potential recipients. The latter undertaking proved to be immense and got so bogged down in administration that very few appointments were being made.

Before Clark stumbled over Jerusalem and Petro-Canada, Neville had already concluded that he faced an uphill fight for re-election unless there was a major shift in voting patterns. The Tory problem, as he saw it, was simple; the Liberals fundamentally enjoyed broader support than the Conservatives and at any given time, all things being equal, would beat the Tories at the polls. Over the years the polls showed that there was a gap of about eight percentage points between the two parties. The voters in that eight per cent margin did not blindly follow the Liberals. They moved around, and when they did the gap widened or narrowed depending on the current mood. But when nothing bothered them, they "parked" their support with the Liberal Party. Neville knew that Canada had what some people called "a one-and-a-half party system". This fact of political life kept the Tories out of federal office – unless the Liberals did something to alienate their natural supporters, as Louis Saint-Laurent did in 1957 and as Pierre Trudeau had just done.

Neville never kidded himself about the meaning of the Conservative victory. He knew that Joe Clark hadn't won, Pierre Trudeau had lost. Now that the Liberals no longer controlled the levers of power they were bound to stop alienating their political supporters, who, having vented their frustration, would automatically return to their old political nesting place. In effect, even while Clark was being sworn in as prime minister, the Conservative Party was returning to its traditional minority status. To win re-election Clark had to broaden Tory support, and the fastest way to do that was by demonstrating managerial superiority over the Liberals.

The official post-election analysis from Decima Research supported Neville's assessment. Allan Gregg's first report as Tory pollster informed Clark that the Conservatives had not established an image that would enable the party to break out of its minority ghetto. The statistics showed that the electorate had not voted for real change, and instead had merely vented its spleen. The public supported most of Trudeau's policies, but felt he lacked competence and, worse, didn't care.

"The research showed again and again that the reasons for voting PC were negative six to one over positive," Gregg wrote. "Equally, our core support – that is, 1979 voters who identify with the PC Party and claimed that they always voted PC – comprised a mere 18% of the electorate, or about one-half of our May 22nd support. There was nothing in the data to suggest that our forming the Government would do anything to change this, which would lead me to the conclusion, based on two years of research, that the PC electoral position was weaker on May 23rd as a consequence of forming the Government than it was on May 22nd as a consequence of being in Opposition."

Neville wrote a long memo outlining a survival plan in which he mapped out a strategy to shore up Clark's shaky mandate and ultimately keep him in office. It was not so much a memo as a flow chart of actions to raise the government's standing by spring 1980. Assuming that Trudeau would soon resign, the government would get the unpopular things that needed to be done out of the way early while the Liberal Party was preoccupied with looking for a new leader. Then the government would switch gears around mid-January 1980 with a series of popular measures designed to win public confidence. Parliament would see one "goody" after another through the winter and into the spring, leading into the Liberal leadership convention. Each new measure would boost the popularity of the government and portray Clark as an attuned and popular prime minister. By the time the Liberals had a new leader and were ready to bring down the government, the Clark team would have overcome its initial difficulties and be ready for an election.

Neville's survival plan hung on one crucial assumption; he took it for granted that the government was safe from parliamentary defeat while the Liberals looked for a leader to replace Trudeau. He could not imagine the Liberals jumping into an election campaign without somebody to lead them. It would be suicide. The party would have to recall Trudeau and face annihilation with a leader the country had just finished repudiating. But, more than that, Neville believed that a large enough group of Liberal MPs so disliked the prospect of running under Trudeau and regarded him as such a liability to the party and themselves that they would not force an election, and would be conveniently out of town for critical votes. So he concluded that Clark had a de facto majority until the Liberal leadership convention in March 1980. It was this reason that led Clark to make his proclamation that he planned to govern as if he had a majority.

The Clark team felt so confident that it actually turned down an opportunity to build a slim working majority. The Conservatives had 136 seats, the Liberals 114, and the NDP 26. The 5 Social Credit MPs held a razor-thin balance of power. In the fall of 1979 they offered an informal alliance to backstop the government in Parliament. (They were already sitting on the government side of the House, as the opposition side was overcrowded.) Social Credit support would give the government 141 votes, whereas the Liberals and NDP could combine for only 139 (not counting the Speaker, a Liberal, who voted only in the event of a tie). Two seats hardly constituted a comfortable margin but it would allow the government to squeeze through, at least temporarily. The Social Credit offer, however, came with a price, which varied from day to day; sometimes they wanted a cabinet seat, at other times special concessions for Quebec.

Had they been in government, the Liberals would have jumped at the opportunity, as they did from 1972 to 1974 with the New Democratic Party, in the alliance that had so disgusted Bill Lee. But now the Tories, by contrast, rebuffed Social Credit. They had little time for this ragtag collection of rustic MPs who were living on borrowed time, and they dismissed their support as too expensive at any price. Neville and others in Clark's office felt that the Conservatives had a chance to grow in Quebec and were being blocked by Social Credit, which siphoned off the Quebec votes the Tories would otherwise get. Social Credit faced extinction in one more election, which would be good news for the Tories in the long run, and an alliance now would only prop it up. Neville mistakenly believed it had collapsed even as a parliamentary unit to the point where its support was unreliable. In the end Clark concluded that he could not negotiate a reasonable deal with Social Credit and dismissed the option entirely.

The Conservatives didn't merely ignore the Social Credit MPs. They ostracized them. They could have courted them but sought to crush them instead. The government denied them recognition in Parliament as a party, thus refusing them funding for research staff and barring them from meetings of House Leaders. Despite this, Parliament had been sitting only a month when David Kilgour, the freshman MP for Edmonton-Strathcona, reported an unexpected break; Social Credit had agreed to backstop the government in the Commons for eighteen months *without conditions*. Besides being parliamentary secretary to House Leader Walter Baker, the bilingual Kilgour was seatmate to a Social Credit MP, Armand Caouette, and worked as an informal link with the five Quebec MPs. While Clark's office was crushing them, Kilgour and Baker gently courted them. The new offer astounded Kilgour; the government had made life miserable for Social Credit MPs and they reciprocated with the offer of a blank cheque. The government had nothing to lose, and now merely had to consummate the deal with a meeting between Clark and the Social Credit leader, Fabien Roy.

The Social Credit olive branch did not impress Clark, Neville, or Murray – and the two party leaders never met. The arrangements that could have secured the government bogged down on details of who was phoning whom and where to meet. After a few false starts Roy realized that Clark had no real interest in his support and broke off communications in irritation.

The decision to act like a majority government proved the Tories' biggest political faux pas since they endorsed wage and price controls in 1974. It exposed the government's most vulnerable flank, its precarious status in the House of Commons, and made it an easy target when John Crosbie tabled his first budget on December 11. Crosbie had earlier unveiled a program of tax credits for the mortgage interest and property taxes paid by homeowners. On budget night he revealed an array of incentives for different groups. That was the popular part. He also raised taxes $3.7 billion in an attempt to cut the federal deficit in half within four years. Most notably he introduced an eighteen-cent-a-gallon jump in the excise tax on gasoline, which won him no accolades.

Opposition MPs called it a hard-times budget. Consumers recoiled at paying eighteen cents more for gasoline, which was the news that grabbed the headlines. The fact that the government was striving for energy self-sufficiency by 1990 didn't matter. Neither did the fact that Crosbie was returning at least part of the eighteen cents to lower-income families in the form of an energy tax credit. No offsets made the eighteen cents palatable. Allan Gregg's Decima Research had recently done a poll for the Department of Energy, Mines and Resources which revealed that short of gasoline rationing the government could do nothing more unpopular than hike gasoline taxes significantly. The mortgage tax-credit program earned some applause but did not erase the hostility to the gasoline-tax jump. After Crosbie introduced his budget the opposition introduced a non-confidence motion and Liberal MPs talked bravely about bringing down the government. Neville dismissed it as bluster and refused to believe that the Liberals were nuts enough to mean it.

Meanwhile Jim Coutts, Neville's opposite number with Trudeau, worked actively for the government's defeat. The prospect of being caught leaderless in an election campaign didn't worry Coutts. On the contrary, he saw this as an opportunity to keep Trudeau as leader. He had never accepted Trudeau's wish to retire, had tried to talk him out of it, and had refused to give up even after Trudeau formally announced his retirement on November 21, and even after the Liberal National Executive set March 28-30 1980 as the date of the leadership convention. Coutts, a management consultant in Toronto before Trudeau made him his top political aide in 1975, operated from the back room with as much craft as Bill Lee had in the previous decade. He saw everything in partisan terms and immediately seized on the Crosbie budget as a device to destroy Clark and restore Trudeau.

The weekly meeting of the Liberal caucus happened to fall on the morning after the Crosbie budget, and the members debated how far to push the government. The non-confidence motion was due for a vote the evening of the next day, and the caucus had to determine whether to go all out or merely go through the motions. Trudeau didn't help when he said that the government should be defeated, but that he would not lead the Liberal Party into the election if it was. Having said that, Trudeau left the meeting.

As a backroom boy Coutts didn't attend caucus, but he showed up in spirit. Led by the wily Allan MacEachen, Liberal MPs one after another stood up to support a full-scale assault, until the caucus had worked itself into an oratorical passion, and decided to go all out to bring down the government, calling in every vote and accepting no pairing with Tory MPs. Coutts and MacEachen had done a marvellous job, telling Liberal MPs the stories they wanted to hear, even if the story for one MP failed to match the story for another. Pro-Trudeau MPs believed Trudeau was staying. The ones who wanted him out expected a leadership convention right after the government's defeat. That night, in the ballroom of the West Block, inebriated MPs at the packed and noisy Liberal Christmas party boasted to anybody who would listen – and journalists were listening – how they planned to stick it to the government the next evening.

While the Liberals were partying, Neville was perusing his nightly pile of documents, oblivious to the gathering storm. He first learned of the Liberal plan on Thursday morning – the day of the vote – at an early-morning breakfast meeting with staff. Nancy Jamieson had heard the talk, checked it out, and concluded that the government faced trouble. Neville dismissed it as posturing and did not raise it later at his regular 8:45 a.m. meeting in Clark's office where the following week's First Ministers' Conference on the Economy devoured most of the agenda. Near the end, after routine business, Clark asked for items around the table. The meeting had nearly ended and people were gathering their papers together when he came to Jamieson at the far end of the table.

"Sir, the government is going to be defeated tonight," Jamieson blurted out.

"Why?" Clark asked.

"Because we don't have the numbers," Jamieson responded.

"What do you mean?"

Jamieson explained that both the Liberals and the NDP planned to support the non-confidence motion, and between them could muster enough votes to win regardless of what Social Credit did. Six Conservative MPs were absent, and that made the difference. Clark turned to Neville, who stuck to his theory that the government was safe until the Liberal leadership convention in March. Neville predicted that some Liberals would fail to show up, and Lowell Murray backed him up, though with less confidence. Clark concurred. The entire exchange lasted only a few minutes and unfolded like an afterthought. The meeting had dragged on too long and thrown Clark behind schedule for a flight to Burlington where he was delivering a lunch-hour speech. Given the implications of Jamieson's news, the meeting broke up with what in retrospect seems amazing tranquillity. The delay in Clark's departure for Burlington seemed more urgent and important than facing the gang-up in the Commons.

The government had the option of putting off the vote until after Christmas. Delay would give it time to round up all its MPs and, if it wanted, to strike a quick deal with Social Credit. After Christmas, the Liberals would be one month closer to their leadership convention, making it practically impossible for them to pursue their non-confidence motion seriously. But this option was not discussed in the morning meeting, and came up only fleetingly later in the day, when it was promptly dropped. Postponement would save the government, but Clark equated postponement to chickening out and did not want to be seen vacillating. A few weeks' delay would derail the popular mortgage-interest tax credit for 1979 because forms had to be printed for the 1979 income-tax returns. A few weeks' delay would mean a full year as far as the program was concerned, and the government was counting on the mortgage tax-credit program to bolster its public standing. So Clark, with only a moment's thought, resolutely said no to a postponement and gave orders for the vote to proceed that night.

The Social Credit members were the only opposition MPs with anything good to say about the budget. Like everyone else, they opposed the eighteen-cent excise tax but praised the mortgage tax credits. Reporters spotlighted the Social Credit MPs and pressed them for answers on how they planned to vote. At first they hedged, waiting for the government to give them a face-saving excuse to support the budget, but the Tories gave no response, no signs of encouragement. The Social Credit MPs finally announced that they would abstain; with that the government's only hope of survival evaporated.

That night, before the vote, Clark, Neville, and Murray dined in the Parliamentary Restaurant and for the first time they seriously pondered the prospect of defeat. Clark said he wanted to call the election in the minimum time. They discussed ways of getting the campaign off to a fast start. There was no sense of doom or panic. They looked at various scenarios, but none of them examined the ultimate question: whether the government could win an election.

By 10 p.m. the public galleries of the House of Commons were jammed with spectators, and the corridors outside the chamber were lined with television crews as everyone awaited the fate of the 31st Parliament. Just as Neville believed the Liberals would fold, many of the observers expected the government to pull a last-minute trick out of its sleeve. They refused to believe that it would surrender its mandate so casually. Doubts about the determination of the Liberal caucus disappeared when Claude Lajoie shuffled painfully into the chamber. The 51-year-old Liberal MP for Trois-Rivières had undergone a double-hernia operation a week earlier and the desks on either side of the aisle became his crutches as he worked his way to his seat. Another Liberal, Maurice Dionne, had to sign himself out of hospital before hobbling into the chamber, while Pauline Jewett of the NDP dragged herself out of her sickbed. Only one opposition MP failed to show.

The Conservative whip had rounded up everybody he could and had whittled the six missing Tory MPs down to three. Alvin Hamilton lay plugged into a kidney-dialysis machine in an Ottawa hospital and could not be moved. Lloyd Crouse was in

Australia and out of touch, while External Affairs Minister Flora MacDonald was stranded at an airport in Paris. She had been attending a NATO meeting in Brussels and earlier had been told not to bother returning. By the time her instructions were changed it was too late; the last transatlantic flight had left. These absences meant that Social Credit no longer held the balance of power, and could not save the government even if it wanted.

Minutes later the Members of Parliament stood up to vote on the motion of non-confidence as Bev Koester, the Clerk of the House of Commons, called out their names. Liberal MPs let out a thunderous cheer when Trudeau got to his feet, but instead of acknowledging it he covered his face with his hands and quietly sat down. At 10:21 p.m. the clerk announced the results: Yeas, 139; Nays, 133. The hypercharged chamber was frozen silent for a split second and then exploded into cheers and flying paper. Clark stared stiffly down at the top of his desk. Across the aisle, directly opposite, Trudeau pensively leaned forward with both elbows on his desk and his chin resting on his cupped hands. MPs on both sides looked genuinely surprised. The country had stumbled into an election that nobody wanted. All four parties had reasons for avoiding a campaign, and everyone in the House dreaded going onto the hustings in the dead of winter.

"Mr. Speaker," Clark stood up to announce, "I rise on a point of order. The government has lost a vote on a matter which we have no alternative but to regard as a question of confidence. I simply want to advise the House that I will be seeing His Excellency the Governor General tomorrow morning."

Clark sat down and the Commons erupted into more cheers and catcalls, as both sides taunted each other for having blundered. Clark retreated through the curtain behind him and stepped into the MPs' lobby. He took off his jacket and stepped onto a couch to give the gathered Tory MPs a fighting speech. "We presented a responsible budget and we showed we were a responsible government," he declared. "We're going to show 'em. We're going to show 'em."

Bill Neville told the CBC that the Liberal Party had made the biggest mistake in its history in thinking it could win with a recycled leader rejected by the people seven months earlier. It was fine blustering bravado for the Tory troops. But Neville also believed it. Clark, Neville, and the inner cabinet gathered in the boardroom of Clark's Centre Block office amid excited partisan prophecies of how they would stick it to the Liberals in the coming election campaign. Trudeau, they crowed, was a lame duck and the Liberal Party was finished.

The next morning, Friday, Clark visited the governor general and announced an election for February 18 1980. He launched his campaign on Monday. He started in Montreal, with a week-long swing through Kitchener, Yellowhead (his home riding in the Rocky Mountains), Vancouver, and finally Winnipeg. On the return flight to Ottawa his staff decked the plane with Christmas decorations, passed around gifts, and uncorked some champagne. "This is my tenth election and I've never been so up," Neville told journalists in the back of the plane. "I really want to kill them this time."

While the Tory campaign got off to a flying start, the Liberals wallowed in a leadership crisis. The battle had begun, and the party didn't know who would lead them into combat. The Liberal caucus huddled the day after the Commons vote. After eleven hours of soul-searching and arm-twisting the caucus "unanimously" asked Trudeau to continue as party leader. The following day the Liberal National Executive, furious at the caucus for forcing an unwanted election for which the party was clearly unprepared – some Executive members demanded the dismissal of Coutts – fell into line and also urged Trudeau to continue. Trudeau took the weekend to think about it and prudently checked with the latest Goldfarb poll. "It is my duty to accept the draft of the party," he finally announced. The poll showed the Liberals far out in front.

While Clark stumped the country, Allan Gregg, who had not polled for the federal Tories since August, scrambled to check the public mood. Ten days before the government's fall a Gallup poll had revealed that in November the Tories had dropped from 36 per cent to 28, and trailed the Liberals by no fewer than 19 points. Clark, Neville, and Murray had seen the poll and dismissed it as a blip or, at worst, as a measurement of how people felt, and not how they intended to vote when choosing between Clark and Trudeau. During the Christmas break, at the end of

Clark's first full week of campaigning, Gregg joined Clark, Neville, Murray, and Paul Curley, the party's national director, in the living room at 24 Sussex Drive.

Gregg confirmed the validity of Gallup's 19-point Liberal lead. In fact, he reported, the government had grown *more* unpopular, not less, since the November poll. His data put the Conservatives a full 21 points behind the Liberals and showed them trailing everywhere except Alberta. More ominously, he saw no prospect for a turnaround in two months. The overwhelming issue in people's minds, he reported, was not Trudeau, not fair play, but competence, namely Clark's competence, and the outlook was hopeless. Gregg was the doctor who told the patient he had terminal cancer. The campaign had hardly started and he had already pronounced defeat. For the first time Clark and Neville realized that the parliamentary game of chicken had been a huge mistake.

How Joe Clark, Bill Neville, and Lowell Murray had convinced themselves a government so unpopular would be re-elected remains a mystery. All three were astute observers and lifelong political junkies who should have known better. They expected the public to exercise fair play and even adopted the campaign slogan "Real Change Deserves a Fair Chance." Everybody had assumed – including Allan Gregg – that the country still hated Trudeau and could not countenance bringing him back. Now Gregg was telling them that they had all been wrong.

Clark accepted the news calmly. Even the angel Gabriel couldn't overturn such a lead so quickly, but that merely seemed to stimulate Clark's determination to fight. Neville travelled at Clark's side with a sinking feeling in his gut as he watched him bravely remind voters not to forget the man they threw out of office eight months earlier. Clark campaigned superbly, even flawlessly, demonstrating his tremendous personal growth since he became prime minister. Had he campaigned in 1979 as he did in 1980 he might have amassed a majority that would have prevented this election.

Clark's combination of savvy and epic composure started paying off late in the campaign. The media, which had unfairly eviscerated him over the last several years, grudgingly admired his performance. They began to sympathize with him and to redirect their fire towards Trudeau's peek-a-boo campaign where, two or three times a day, he popped into public view long enough for the television cameras to get their required footage, and then, just as quickly, disappeared without answering questions. With the campaign heading into the home stretch Gregg uncovered a ray of hope. His polls detected unrest among Liberal voters and a swing of sorts to the Conservatives. Trudeau's 21-point lead had shrunk to 11. Clark still trailed but seemed to be moving up. Gregg dispatched a memo outlining the "best", "worst" and "most likely" scenarios. The "most likely" scenario was that Trudeau would win despite the late trend for Clark. The "best" had Clark closing the gap and winning.

The news injected much-needed late momentum into the Clark campaign. Neville pictured the trend growing and Clark possibly squeaking out a minority victory. On the next flight Neville "worked" the reporters at the back of the plane, telling them that a substantial shift in public mood had pulled Clark within striking range. At first the reporters dismissed his claim. They were starting to come around when news reached the plane that a new Gallup poll showed Clark stuck 20 points behind and clearly going nowhere. Gallup detected no upward shift, not even a trace, and that devastated Neville's account. It also threatened to kill the morale of party volunteers who, on the basis of Gregg's findings, were being urged to redouble their efforts as they closed the gap.

Neville had never much respected the Gallup poll and now he respected it even less. He called it one of the great Canadian myths and put this one down as another bad Gallup poll that ought to be debunked. Normally, political parties jealously guard the secrecy of their private polls, but this time Neville decided to challenge Gallup in public. Four days before the election he asked Gregg to meet reporters and unveil *his* findings.

Gregg faced the television lights and for the next half hour the fate of the Conservative campaign rested on his shoulders. The right words could breathe life into the Conservative corpse, while the wrong ones could nail the coffin shut. Gregg faced a dilemma and a professional conflict of interest. What should he do: lay out the cold numbers, or advance the Conservative Party? As a key Conservative strategist he could not fail the party in the face of an election. As a professional pollster he could not compromise the figures. "I refused to lie," Gregg later explained to Robert Fulford of *Saturday Night*. "But I fudged and back-pedalled." It was the first time anybody had seen Gregg pushed into a corner.

The media refused to believe Gregg. But four days later the election results proved him correct and Gallup wrong. Clark lost by Gregg's 10 points rather than by Gallup's 20. The Liberals swept into power with 147 seats for a majority government; the Conservatives won 103 seats and the NDP 32, while Social Credit was shut out. Neville found little consolation in the fact that Clark had cut a 21-point lead to 10 and had outperformed Trudeau on the campaign trail. Eleven points represented an incredible swing during an election period. But the result that counted was that Clark and Neville moved out of the Langevin Block and Trudeau and Coutts moved back in.

Fighting an uphill election for two months had been difficult, but Neville found the period after the election worse. The Monday-morning quarterbacks started second-guessing the bad decisions and missed opportunities. The party had chased power for sixteen years and Clark and Neville had blown it in eight months. Four more years would pass before the party got another crack. Party members everywhere pointed fingers and demanded an accounting. The disappointment, the frustration, the anguish, and the bitterness caused the Tory caucus to look for a target.

At first they hesitated to challenge Clark directly and targeted the people around him, especially Neville. The party wanted him sacked. Neville had stayed away from Parliament and sometimes ignored the caucus rank and file, who mistook shyness for aloofness and depicted him as a snob on the throne. MPs resented Neville's non-elected influence and sought revenge for the times he had said no. Neville sometimes lapsed into momentary gruffness when irritated and became abrupt. Some MPs disliked his red-Tory tinge. Moreover, the caucus wanted to know why Neville had not foreseen events, why the government had not bought off Social Credit, why it had not delayed the vote and – dammit – why it had doled out so few patronage appointments while it was in power. Party members called Clark the worst-advised prime minister in the history of Canada and charged that Neville had not given Clark one piece of good advice in eight months.

Neville was an easy target. As a servant of the party he couldn't fight back, although Clark loyally defended him and rejected demands for his dismissal. Neville shrugged off the criticism as part of the furniture that came with the office and allowed himself to be a whipping boy. In fact he offered himself up in that role. Much as he disliked it, he saw himself as a lightning rod who would deflect criticism from Clark. The hardest part of the post-defeat trauma unfolded in spring 1980 during the regional party meetings, which Clark used to flush the frustration out of the party's system. Before every meeting Neville steeled himself for the tirade he would be facing from just about any party member with a complaint.

The criticism was often abusive and usually unfair, but the critics made some telling points. Only on the Petro-Canada issue was Neville blameless. That particular mess originated entirely with Clark. But Neville had contributed to the other fiascos, particularly the Jerusalem embassy débâcle and the government's failure to meet Parliament for the first four months of its term. Neville had urged Clark to take his time learning government during the summer of 1979 and not to meet Parliament until the fall. Given the government's lack of experience, the advice made sense, but it hurt Clark politically. The decision – along with Jerusalem and Petro-Canada – made his government appear to be avoiding the scrutiny of elected representatives, and contributed to its image problems. Neville deserved a measure of blame for two out of the three identifiable issues that damaged the government's credibility.

The *big* mistake, however, was letting Parliament bring down the government when defeat could have been avoided. Clearly, Neville had not kept his finger on the pulse of Parliament. The government House leader and other MPs should have rung the alarm bells, but it was Neville's survival plan that dictated Clark's strategy to govern as if he had a majority. Clark had been given a minority Parliament to work with and he chose to ignore that fundamental reality. He even spurned a stopgap arrangement with Social Credit. And when the strategy seemed to be heading for disaster Neville misread the mood on Parliament Hill, failed to postpone the vote, and let the government slide into an election as a 20-point underdog.

How much blame belonged to Neville became a point of debate. Clark was the leader and made the decisions. Some thought Neville was made the scapegoat; others argued that he was the architect. Neville had sold himself on the paralysis of the leaderless Liberal Party and nothing budged him. Even in retrospect, after replaying the parliamentary events of December 1979 in his head, Neville did not retract his strategy.

Except for the one big mistake, Neville might have become a great principal secretary. The job made impossible demands, left no margin for error, and inflicted enormous consequences upon failure. Nobody could learn it in eight months, and Neville didn't have the luxury of a honeymoon or a majority government as his predecessors had most of the time under Trudeau. He was saddled with a minority government, inexperienced colleagues, a fractious party that devoured its young, and a boss who was surprised at being prime minister. It remained an open question whether Neville possessed the Right Stuff to excel in the biggest back room in the country.

A month before the Conservative Party's Annual General Meeting in Ottawa in March 1981, when Joe Clark's leadership was to be endorsed or rejected for the first time, Neville contracted an illness which he initially dismissed as a stomach virus. The affliction hung on and eluded diagnosis. He kept getting cramps and diarrhea, began losing weight, and generally felt awful. His nerves were shot but he kept going because Clark's leadership was up for review. As chief of staff, Neville presided over the campaign to bolster Clark's support at the convention but found himself rushing to the washroom every half hour. Clark fared worse. He limped through the weekend with a questionable 66.1 per cent endorsement, and would be facing another review vote at Winnipeg in two years. Meanwhile, his grip on the party remained unsteady.

Neville flew to Bermuda after the convention but soon fell gravely ill and became convinced his time would soon be up. He hurried back to Ottawa where tests finally diagnosed Crohn's disease, a genetic weakness that caused the lining of the small bowel to ulcerate. He had come down with an incurable illness that would come and go and could flare up any time, but would always live with him.

His bout with Crohn's disease convinced him that he needed a change in lifestyle. His body could no longer match the strain of the job with Clark. He was 45 and a heavy smoker, and he needed, as he told friends, a long lunch hour. He had been thinking of quitting, but this setback clinched it for him. He notified Clark of his plans and was gone before the end of spring. He did nothing for most of the summer of 1981 and that fall picked up odd bits of consulting work. Premier Bill Davis of Ontario offered him a job, but Neville wanted to return to private business. David MacNaughton tried to coax him into joining PAI, but Neville's non-competition agreement with his former colleagues at ECL had not expired.

Brian Mulroney, who was a director of the Canadian Imperial Bank of Commerce, introduced Neville to Russ Harrison, the bank's chairman. Harrison, a right-winger and a dictator at the Commerce, thought all politicians were idiots and immediately chewed out Neville for Clark's tardiness in replying to an invitation he had once sent him. Nevertheless, Harrison was quickly impressed by Neville and hired him as vice president and his assistant on public affairs and strategic planning. Neville moved to Toronto and worked in the Commerce Tower in the heart of Bay Street. He loved his new job and later became senior vice president of marketing, where, among other things, he ended Anne Murray's contract as the advertising voice of the Commerce. Neville enjoyed Toronto, but his backroom days in Ottawa were not over. In a few years both David MacNaughton and Brian Mulroney would call on him again.*

---

*For some details this chapter has relied on Jeffrey Simpson's excellent account of the short-lived Clark government, *Discipline of Power: The Conservative Interlude and the Liberal Restoration*, the winner of the 1981 Governor General's Award for non-fiction. Readers wanting a more detailed account of the Clark interregnum will wish to read this book.

TEN

A MATTER OF ENERGY

David MacNaughton ate, breathed, and slept politics, and in 1979 he knew that a federal election lurked around the corner and would probably defeat Trudeau. Yet, in his haste to buy PAI, he had never stopped to consider the political consequences of a change in government. The ink on the purchase agreement with Torrance Wylie had hardly dried when Trudeau dissolved Parliament in March 1979 and called a general election.

Clark's victory over Trudeau in May 1979 frightened MacNaughton, and he didn't frighten easily. He had invested everything in PAI and suddenly the political landscape he had always known as Liberal had become Tory, and PAI had a decidedly Liberal look. MacNaughton, the president, Mike Robinson, his right-hand man, and Torrance Wylie, the figurehead chairman, had all risen out of the Liberal labyrinth, and remained active in party affairs. PAI's only Conservative was a former Ontario cabinet minister, Sid Handleman, who kept an eye on the Tory government in Toronto.

MacNaughton and Robinson visited all their clients to reassure them that they could serve them as well under the Tories as they had under the Liberals. Clients took a wait-and-see attitude, sticking with PAI for the moment but making no promises about the future. MacNaughton and Robinson resolved to service their clients as never before, particularly clients whose contracts were soon up for renewal. They soon learned that they had cause to worry, after hearing from Taft Broadcasting, an American company that was planning to build Canada's Wonderland north of Toronto and needed corporate sponsors as well as permits and approvals from Ottawa. Taft had agreed to become a retainer client and was about to sign a one-year contract with PAI when Trudeau lost to Clark. Believing that PAI was too close to the Liberals, Taft gave notice that it had changed its mind about signing the contract. It intended to look for a Tory firm.

MacNaughton had no friends in the Clark cabinet and needed a minister to champion the building of a floating dry-dock in Vancouver on behalf of Burrard Drydock. MacNaughton had helped the company apply for federal money for the project, and the application had seemed to be working its way through the federal bureaucracy when the Tories took power. Now it faced a rough ride in cabinet without the active support of a minister. It was time to pull strings. A friend of MacNaughton's who knew John Fraser phoned the Vancouver minister at his Ottawa home, and Fraser invited both of them to dinner that evening. At around 11 p.m., with the meal long over and the three relaxing over cognac in Fraser's living room, MacNaughton briefed Fraser on the drydock issue. "If those are the facts," Fraser responded, "why don't you see if you can get them on the phone?" MacNaughton called the head of Burrard Drydock from Fraser's living room and on the spot put Fraser directly in touch with the company's chief executive officer. Fraser became a champion of the project and stickhandled it through cabinet, securing final approval a few days before the Clark government fell.

The Burrard Drydock case convinced MacNaughton that PAI could indeed work under a Conservative government. But that political fact mattered nothing if clients didn't believe it, and most companies clung to the view that you needed special connections to wield clout. The day-to-day reality mattered less than the marketplace opinion. A firm that was conspicuously Liberal could expect few new clients in a Conservative period.

Other than Taft Broadcasting, PAI escaped the Clark period without a single client loss. But it had been lucky; the Clark interlude lasted for only a few months, whereas clients planned in years. The Clark government was open and easy to deal with, and had no craving to overturn the bureaucracy and the system. Things might have gone differently if Bill Neville had not been there to set a friendly tone, and PAI could not count on such breaks in future. Trudeau had returned with a majority government, which made MacNaughton safe for at least four years, but that didn't matter, because sooner or later the Tories would return. "Okay," he asked, "how do we get a Tory in here?" He made it his top priority to hire some established Conservatives.

About a month after Trudeau was sworn in again as Canada's refurbished prime minister in March 1980, MacNaughton hired his first Tory. He was Harry Near, freshly out of work as EA to Ray Hnatyshyn, the energy minister in Clark's government. Near looked to the world like PAI's token Conservative, but that impression faded as MacNaughton and Robinson added more Tories. Soon half a dozen Conservatives adorned PAI's staff, until people speculated whether MacNaughton was de-Liberalizing or semi-Toryizing.

Harry Near became PAI's first energy consultant and was deliberately recruited first, because MacNaughton believed that energy was destined to become Ottawa's next big-ticket item and would require a full-time specialist. Immediately after Clark's defeat MacNaughton and Robinson flew to the West Coast to advise Hudson's Bay Oil and Gas on its five-year corporate plan. Around a Vancouver boardroom table piled high with elaborate documents projecting financial growth, MacNaughton and Robinson warned HBOG that the new Trudeau government would probably intervene dramatically in the energy field, throwing the company's forecasts out of whack. They reported that the Liberals had set two targets for the petroleum industry: increased Canadianization, and a higher federal cut of the revenue flow.

The news should have scared the daylights out of the HBOG executives because their company was foreign-owned and planning to expand, and since both these factors clashed directly with the government's objectives they seemed destined to give the company trouble down the line. HBOG instead dismissed the warning and challenged its authenticity. What did a pair of 32-year-old Grits know anyway? HBOG stuck to its five-year plan and MacNaughton and Robinson returned to Ottawa, telling colleagues they had been virtually run out of town. HBOG was to regret its decision before the year ran out. The resurrected Liberals were indeed about to start drafting the National Energy Program which would radically affect the future of the company.

PAI's decision to hire Near raised some eyebrows. As a partisan Tory he had no connections with the government or with Energy Minister Marc Lalonde. Quite the reverse. But Near proved to be an inspired appointment. He was intelligent, personable, and ambitious, and also a good salesman. Before his spell with Hnatyshyn, he had worked for Imperial Oil and had acquired a strong technical background which he combined with policy insight and a sense of political reality. Like Mac-Naughton and Robinson the month before, Near foresaw the coming of the National Energy Program and realized its potential effect on the petroleum industry. Relying on much the same sources as MacNaughton and Robinson had used, namely Trudeau's statements during the 1980 election campaign and, subsequently, the words of senior bureaucrats, Near learned that the program would feature a mammoth Canadianization program involving grants based on the nationality of ownership. He warned oil and gas companies that the government would do something soon and do it big, but nobody believed his message of doom. Most of the companies were too busy making money to pay attention. They suspected his motives, figuring it was a ploy to get their business. But they failed to realize how jealous Ottawa had become for a share of the revenue.

When Marc Lalonde introduced the National Energy Program on October 28 1980, he sent the industry into panic. Even PAI underestimated the impact. Nobody, including Near, had predicted that federal grants would reach 80 per cent or that holdings would be subject to a retroactive 25-per-cent back-in, which gave the Crown the right to buy a quarter of any petroleum discovery, even those found before the NEP. Trudeau and Lalonde had never disguised their intentions, and Trudeau had broadly spelled it out during the election campaign. Yet when the program was announced, petroleum executives couldn't believe their ears. Despite warnings from PAI, Trudeau, Lalonde, and the bureaucrats, the NEP caught the industry completely off guard.

HBOG had been one of the strongest and best-managed companies in the industry but was marching out of step with government. Now its fortunes collapsed overnight. One stroke of the public pen cancelled months of corporate planning and reams of financial projections. The new rules turned foreign-owned oil companies into takeover targets. Had HBOG taken measures to boost its Canadian ownership above fifty per cent it would have prospered. Instead it was devoured six months later by Dome Petroleum with the active encouragement of the government.

MacNaughton, as was his wont from time to time, dropped his adviser's role and jumped in to lobby directly to save HBOG. He tried to convince old friends in government, but Ottawa unwaveringly backed the Dome purchase. Dome had received so much federal aid in taking over HBOG that it bit off more than it could chew and eventually choked to death. But HBOG went down first, a victim of the NEP – but ultimately of its own shortsightedness on public policy.

The HBOG lesson demonstrated the folly of disregarding the impact of government. Government policy could kill a company. Bill Lee and his colleagues at ECL had predicted the coming of the NEP as early as the mid-70s but, like PAI, had encountered skepticism in the oil patch. Petroleum executives didn't like being told that Ottawa hated their guts. The only ECL client to heed the warning was Atlantic Richfield, which sold its Canadian assets to Petro-Canada. Atlantic Richfield was no more perceptive, however, than its competitors; it sold out because its American head office needed cash and wanted to withdraw from Canada anyway.

Once it had wakened up, the oil industry reacted with fury. Calgary wanted to know what had happened, which politicians and bureaucrats were the culprits, and how to defeat them. The industry started throwing money at the problem and hiring anybody – even competing firms – who could help it. The activity generated a mini-boom for consultants of all varieties, and PAI got the biggest slice.

MacNaughton had hired Near expressly to exploit the coming boom but had never imagined how lucrative it would become. Suncor signed on as a client, then Norcen Energy Resources, Dome Petroleum, the Independent Petroleum Association of Canada, and so on. Before long PAI had accumulated a dozen energy companies, plus a handful of companies with strong energy interests. Soon oil executives in the dining room of the Petroleum Club in Calgary were quoting the PAI line on the latest Ottawa developments. The fact that the NEP exceeded PAI's warnings strengthened its credibility. Oil's bad fortune became PAI's good fortune and its engine of growth. The NEP boosted PAI's revenue as nothing had before, until it overtook ECL as the biggest public-affairs consulting firm in town. In two years MacNaughton had catapulted PAI into first place.

For a while PAI had so many energy clients that Near could not service them all. When energy billings had reached almost half a million dollars, PAI hired Marjory Loveys away from Marc Lalonde's office to help service the client list. Loveys, with prematurely grey hair in startling contrast to a youthful face, was one of the few women in Canada to wear an engineer's ring. As a Liberal working alongside Near, she gave PAI political balance in energy, so that her appointment seemed normal. In fact it was hardly normal. If the hiring of a Tory like Near seemed unconventional, in 1980 the employment of a Liberal like Loveys raised just as much curiosity. Loveys suddenly had to work with the industry that loathed and despised her former boss, Marc Lalonde, for introducing the hated NEP. To make matters worse, she didn't back off from her support of the NEP and was not shy about defending the program. Her plight was not helped by the fact that she once had been a Pollution Probe worker and was also an advocate of women's rights, in the face of possibly the most male-chauvinist business community in Canada. For the first year and a half Loveys didn't set foot in Calgary without Near at her side. The industry treated her appointment coldly at first, but came to accept her.

PAI advised clients to avoid rhetorical combat because an outright war with Ottawa was something they could only lose, while they could win small battles with the use of strategy. It meant holding their fire on the NEP's two basic principles: Canadianization, and a bigger revenue share for Ottawa. Everything else was negotiable. PAI counselled its clients to say in effect: "We support Canadianization; however, you'll achieve the same objectives and hurt us less if you do it this way."

The Independent Petroleum Association of Canada rejected the advice. IPAC, which spoke for Canadian oil companies, wanted to fight on ideological grounds even though it was the chosen vehicle of the NEP and, in relative terms, had the most to gain from the program. PAI tried cajoling IPAC, saying it had special clout with government, which wanted to develop Canadian ownership in the industry. Instead IPAC harangued the government and even resorted to a full-page newspaper ad portraying Marc Lalonde as a liar and a thief. It was not a smart move. IPAC effectively ostracized itself from government circles, and Lalonde warmed up to the multinational-dominated Canadian

A MATTER OF ENERGY **143**

Petroleum Association, the NEP's original target. CPA, the 1970s bad boy, had upgraded its act and now held more influence than the association the government originally favoured. PAI and IPAC soon parted company.

PAI soon achieved MacNaughton's coveted "critical mass" in energy, but when energy grew to account for twenty-five per cent of billings he and Robinson became concerned that it could become too successful, making them too dependent on one sector, as they had been on the Liberal Party. PAI would never turn down energy clients, but MacNaughton used the revenue from the energy windfall to build up critical mass in other sectors. Having successfully specialized in energy, PAI moved into other fields of specialized knowledge about particular sectors of government.

Everybody at PAI became a specialist, even old hands like Carl Baltare, who dated back five years to the Wylie-Edmonds era and had always been a generalist. Now Baltare started specializing in consumer policy and health protection. Sean Moore took over the social-policy envelope, which included pension reform and employment equity. Rising ministerial aides were brought into PAI for their specialized knowledge. Pat Ross came from the Department of Transport to become PAI's transport specialist. Joe Thornley left Communications Minister Francis Fox's office to handle communications and Alf Chaiton, who had been with Industry, Trade and Commerce Minister Herb Gray, looked after industrial development. Brian Mersereau quit the Department of Supply and Services to advise PAI clients on how to bid on government contracts, and Tom Burns, a public servant in foreign trade for thirty-two years, left the Canadian Export Association to counsel companies about selling abroad. An outsider could not help but think that the locksmiths who had designed the locks were being hired for their ability to pick them.

The specialists were told to concentrate on developments in their fields, acting as a distant early warning system, and not to worry about government's overall agenda. The senior officers would track the overview. The Chairman (Wylie), the President (MacNaughton) and the vice presidents (Robinson and Don

Kelly and later Harry Near) would brief clients every two or three months about where government was headed.

MacNaughton argued that specialization gave clients faster service and better information. If specialization was good for clients, it was great for PAI. The firm left day-to-day servicing to specialists at smaller salaries and thus lowered its cost per dollar of revenue. Lower overhead meant higher earnings. Meanwhile executives concentrated on marketing and administration. The company could grow without overburdening its senior partners, the traditional problem for most personal-service firms like law offices and accounting firms and, most notably, ECL. With three partners, ECL couldn't handle PAI's client load because Bill Lee, Steve Markey, and Irv Keenleyside could spread themselves among only so many clients.

Specialization helped PAI in another way, too. It kept clients longer, and that boosted revenue. Both PAI and ECL often worked themselves out of a job; once they had finished tutoring clients on how government operated, the clients often failed to renew their contracts on the assumption that they no longer needed advice – at least not $60,000 a year's worth. PAI could brief a client only so many times about the next cabinet shuffle or the upcoming budget. Now it sought to keep clients longer by digging more deeply into each client's specific concern.

PAI never declared a dividend. Whenever the company reached a positive cash flow, MacNaughton hired another consultant on the assumption that the added expense would translate into four more clients down the road. The policy usually paid off. Word spread that PAI was the firm to see, and eighty per cent of its new clients arrived unsolicited. MacNaughton didn't know how they had learned about PAI, he only knew that nobody had walked through the door when he was a one-man shop at KinMac. Now everything was rolling his way.

On September 1 1982 Torrance Wylie, who had helped smooth the ownership transition three years earlier, stepped down as chairman. He remained a director and kept an office at PAI but spent most of his time consulting for his own small company. He had been easing out of PAI to return to the kind of consulting he enjoyed, which featured a strong personal relationship with a few clients who sought his counsel. MacNaughton replaced Wylie as chairman and Robinson moved up to be president. Harry Near joined Don Kelly as vice president. The well-liked Robinson got on well with both clients and colleagues, and MacNaughton relied on him to run the operations while he himself increasingly looked at outside opportunities. Robinson fixed problems, soothed bruised egos, and kept clients happy while MacNaughton undertook strategic planning.

When the 1981 recession struck and the economy slumped, PAI held a gloomy management meeting where they froze salaries, talked about staff layoffs, and even drew up a contingency plan for the loss of clients. Six months later they unfroze salaries, hired new people, and finished the year with more clients than ever. Most companies suffered but PAI, seemingly immune from the vicissitudes of a bad economy, experienced thirty-percent growth.

How long could PAI continue to grow? The management committee asked itself that question every summer at its annual business-planning session. Billings had been growing twenty-five to thirty-five per cent a year, and each summer somebody on the committee predicted that this would be the year it would end, that the saturation point had finally been reached, that this was the year to budget for less growth. Business prudence suggested good reasons why the historical growth pattern could not persist: conflicts of interest, increased competition, the threat of economic recessions, the growth of public-affairs groups inside companies. Sooner or later the market would run out of corporations willing to pay substantial fees to firms like PAI. It made sense, but it never happened. Every year PAI grew another thirty per cent, as the PAI officers debated what constituted optimum size.

When would PAI stop reinvesting its earnings into future growth and start milking the cow? MacNaughton always opted for more growth. He had not finished yet.

ELEVEN

THE DECIMA POINT

After Decima Research opened its doors in 1979 and started looking for clients, Allan Gregg might have been expected to soften his personal style. In fact the business world didn't tame him one bit. His profile grew more brassy, not less. He got into leathers and a semi-punk hairdo, and complemented his wardrobe with burgundy shoes or whatever happened to be unfashionable. People never knew what to expect. Sometimes he walked into a boardroom with a leather jacket and half-bare chest and the next time arrived in three-piece pinstripes. Plain black T-shirt or regular suit, his outfit for the day depended not so much on his audience as on his mood, and he enjoyed the ripples he caused.

Gregg, the nonconformist with chutzpah, could not have invented a partner whose personal style contrasted more with his than Richard Wirthlin, the shrewd California pollster. Gregg screamed defiance; Wirthlin oozed compliance. Wirthlin wore conservative suits and couldn't be loud even if he worked at it. A Mormon, he never uttered a bad word and was the essence of restrained social behaviour. Some described him as vanilla ice cream. By comparison Gregg stuck out as a wild combination of raspberry and double chocolate. Yet the two clicked when it came to the business of polling.

Although he had originally opposed Gregg's partnership, Wirthlin came to realize that the firm could succeed only with a Canadian front man, to avoid the Bob Teeter syndrome – an American telling Canadians what they thought. Wirthlin quickly recognized Gregg's usefulness as quasi-figurehead, but as he got to know him, he came to value his intelligence and abilities and desire, and particularly his salesmanship. He also liked him, and the prospect of his exploding onto the scene excited him. Wirthlin became the teacher and Gregg the ideal student. "Allan," he said, "we're going to make you the number-one pollster in this country. You watch."

Wirthlin envisaged Gregg as the pollster and his own company, Decision Making Information, as the operator of Decima, while Tom Scott through Sherwood Communications bankrolled it from the background. Wirthlin moved his vice president of administration from California to Toronto and sent a technical wizard to get the computer and its unique software up and operating. But soon after Decima started to operate, Wirthlin realized that his people were not running the company. Gregg was. From day one he took over as top salesman, administrator, schemer, and organizer, and through sheer force of presence emerged as the boss. He strutted around as if Decima were his personal company, which in some ways it had become.

Decima opened what amounted to a polling factory at Summerhill and Yonge in uptown Toronto. The day it opened Gregg could rightly boast that they had the best polling apparatus in Canada. Wirthlin's state-of-the-art technology gave Decima better computer systems, better software, and more sophisticated methodology than anyone else. Seed capital from Sherwood Communications underwrote the up-front costs of physical plant: a big phone bank, office space that soon expanded to nine thousand square feet, and Wirthlin's computer plant, not to mention an army of casual labourers and the astounding long-distance phone bill their surveying incurred. A lot of money went out the door before the first dollar came in, and the whole extravaganza was being directed by Gregg, who hardly had a personal credit rating with which to get a Visa card.

Bob Teeter, the Detroit-based pollster who had been used by the Conservative Party, had sniffed out the prospects for setting up a branch in Canada. Teeter concluded that a political polling company was doomed to failure north of the border because the Canadian market lacked sufficient volume, even with the Conservative Party as a client. Canada had only eleven governments compared to fifty-one in the United States, which meant fewer elections and less revenue. Americans spent a whole lot more on polling than did Canadians, so Teeter stayed out.

His decision was good news for Decima, but Gregg never disputed his business assessment. He agreed that political polling in Canada was fundamentally uneconomic and that big bucks from the Conservative Party could not by themselves keep Decima afloat. One could even argue that the Conservative Party account hindered, rather than helped, its economic base. During an election the party suddenly needed about fifty telephone lines to track public opinion because the data had to be turned around in one night. The day after the election the party needed zero telephone lines. Federal elections provided quick windfalls, but did not sustain the expensive infrastructure they created.

Gregg faced that very problem a few months after Decima opened for business in the wake of Joe Clark's victory. When Clark quickly fell into another election, Decima was forced to build plant faster and larger than it could afford, and just as quickly the Conservative government – having given Decima only two contracts, as well as two from the party – lost the election and was driven from power. Suddenly, the Tories had no money for polls, and no election to contest. Decima would wait more than four years for the next federal election. The feast-or-famine syndrome was no way to build a business.

If the Conservative Party account brought problems it also bestowed great benefits. The fact that Gregg was the party pollster gave him a profile in the private sector that delivered polling contracts in the corporate market. The Conservatives governed most provinces and Gregg's federal connections helped him get all that business – except, ironically, in his native province of Alberta, which stuck to an American firm. The provincial Conservative parties evened out the ups and downs of federal elections and helped offset the cost of some of those telephone lines.

Decima needed private clients if it was to survive. Gregg must either hustle up some private contracts or see it fold. In his search for clients, he followed the well-worn trail taken by Bill Lee and Duncan Edmonds a decade or so earlier. He spoke to seminars, think-tanks, any group that would listen, especially organizations with a heavy business membership like the Niagara Institute. He spoke about the need for business to use public-opinion research, but otherwise delivered essentially the same message that Lee and Edmonds had given: business must understand the external environment to thrive in modern society.

Gregg decided early on never to release anything that didn't meet his finicky standards of perfection. He figured that Decima could do a hundred things right and still get killed doing number 101 badly. So when Decima landed a contract to test Stouffer's TV Dinner, he refused to use the traditional "mall intercept" technique of stopping passers-by on a street corner. This method, he maintained, lacked sufficient methodological rigour and introduced biases of shopping patterns and locations. Instead he bought the Dun & Bradstreet lists of all retail establishments selling food, for a random probability selection. Random probability turned up butcher shops that never carried frozen dinners and overlooked stores where they sold caseloads. A surveyor in Manitoba phoned Toronto complaining of standing in the cold for three days without finding a single purchaser of Stouffer's TV Dinner. It turned out that Stouffer's didn't distribute in Manitoba. Gregg concluded that Decima's standards were not conducive to market polling and quit that kind of work, but not before Decima spent $60,000 finishing the $16,000 Stouffer's job to his satisfaction.

He then vowed to stick exclusively to his expertise – attitudinal surveying. He would refuse Labatt's if the company wanted him to compare its beer with Molson's, but would accept if Labatt's wanted to learn what the public thought about beer and why it was losing market share to other alcoholic beverages.

In the late summer of 1980 Jamie Deacey, the Ottawa lobbyist of the Canadian Petroleum Association, gave him a lucrative one-time contract to survey the public's attitude towards the oil industry. Gregg reported disturbing results. The numbers revealed that Canadians saw oil companies as rich, money-grubbing, overbearing, and untrustworthy. They thought of them as foreign tax-dodgers who could not be counted on to supply Canada's energy needs. The news shocked some of the executives in Calgary boardrooms but didn't surprise Deacey, who had no illusions about the level of public disdain for the industry.

Deacey was fascinated by watching Gregg sift through the numbers to interpret how the public arrived at its opinions. "It's always magical to watch Allan do that part of the business," Deacey says, "and you can't help but learn something about how he views the world when he takes a set of numbers and really plays four-dimensional chess with them, moving them around and discovering the opinion blocs and where they are coming from. . . . He looks at the world in a totally different way."

Gregg continually amazed people with his interpretative skills and instinct. Polling was one part art and one part science. Almost anyone with a few university statistics courses and some computer know-how could draw a valid sample – the science part. Asking the right questions was more challenging, but it was in interpreting the data – the art side – that Gregg particularly distinguished himself. What did the numbers mean? How should the data be used? The numbers themselves sometimes revealed little. But Gregg could take them, lay them on top of each other, and craft a strategy for his client, whether he was advising the Canadian Imperial Bank of Commerce on the introduction of automatic-teller machines, or fashioning an election strategy for the Conservative Party. Gregg could pull together a bunch of variables and tell his client, "The real message is here."

On the basis of Gregg's findings, the Canadian Petroleum Association launched a national advertising program fronted, in the early years, by a former CBC television newsman, Ken Colby. As Decima continued to poll for shifts in public attitude, the CPA tailored its advertising both in newspapers and on television to target the latest weak points. The oil industry's "honest" rating rose from 32 to 54 per cent in three years; the proportion who thought it was run by Canadians jumped from 27 to 53 per cent. The one-time CPA poll grew into a continuing program, providing a cash flow for Decima of about $350,000 a year.

It soon became clear, however, that Gregg's genius didn't carry over from deciphering trends into administration. Decima had developed the knack of making sales and rolling up impressive revenue figures, but didn't turn a profit. Its budgeting and management were haphazard. It expanded sales continuously but accumulated additional debt faster than it picked up new revenue. Consequently, the more Gregg sold the deeper Decima fell into debt. The situation could not continue, yet none of the financial reversals deterred Gregg for one minute, or diminished his vision of the future. His partners wondered where it would lead. Meanwhile Gregg watched David MacNaughton's innovations at PAI with an admiring eye, and kept in touch with Mike Robinson, his old friend from Alberta.

Decima had hardly started when Gregg hit upon an idea he thought would be good for Decima, and for PAI, and would earn a lot of money. He planned to poll 1,500 Canadians 18 years and older randomly every March, June, September, and December for a continuing picture of the mood of the country, and publish the results in a subscription series called *The Decima Quarterly Report*. It meant probing more deeply into society's thinking, going beyond the "what" and exploring the "why" – much as he did for clients in custom polls, only the *Quarterly* would be ongoing and would cover many issues instead of one. The *Quarterly* would not ask people who they were voting for, but would probe the insecurities that led them to their choices. The questions would relate mostly to values, systems, beliefs, and attitudes and would cover issues from Acid Rain to Work-Sharing.

The *Quarterly* could revolutionize public-affairs consulting. Used perceptively, it could give subscribers an inside peek into government thinking, since Ottawa spent big money measuring public opinion and studied the secret results carefully. The data – if published – would reveal the forces and restraints facing the bureaucracy on every major issue and allow lobbyists to figure out government's agenda, removing much of the hunch, guess, and gossip from government relations. The *Quarterly* would be the next best thing to reading government's own confidential polls. For the first time the client could see the total environment the government saw.

Gregg had no idea how many subscribers the venture would attract, and somewhat arbitrarily set the subscription price at $20,000 a year. The field work cost $60,000 each quarter, which meant that he needed twelve subscribers to cover the fixed costs. Each new subscriber above twelve would represent almost pure profit, giving the *Quarterly* almost unlimited earning potential.

One major impediment blocked it – seed money. Start-up costs would be high and in the early years subscribers might be few. By its nature the *Quarterly* could not start with small polls and expand as the number of subscribers grew. It was an all-or-nothing enterprise. It cost as much to provide the subscription service for one user as it did for a hundred, which meant that for the first few surveys $60,000 would be going out the door with little coming back. Succeeding surveys would lose progressively less money as subscribers joined, until the *Quarterly* crossed the break-even point on its inexorable path towards profit. But the shakedown period promised to chew up chunks of cash when Decima was already losing money on custom polling. Economics and prudence suggested that Decima delay the *Quarterly* until the company turned profitable, but Gregg expected it to sell like hot cakes and decided to proceed immediately.

He went to MacNaughton and Robinson at PAI, and over drinks proposed that they launch the *Quarterly* as a 50-50 joint Decima-PAI venture. "I'll do all the research," Gregg offered, "you do all the marketing and all the client servicing." MacNaughton jumped at the idea. The two companies represented a good fit: PAI had the client base and marketing ability, and Decima had the research capability; Decima would monitor public opinion and PAI would monitor government. MacNaughton saw the *Quarterly* as another device to differentiate PAI from its competition. He also saw it as a revenue-generator and as a means to sell existing clients more things. The client-getting prospects had not passed him by, either. PAI and Decima could use each other as marketing tools to get each other's clients, and together they could get new clients neither would get alone.

The *Quarterly* took to the field with its first survey in March 1980. At the same time Gregg launched a subscription drive with great fanfare, pushing the *Quarterly* in a major speech in Ottawa and putting on a slide demonstration at the Harbour Castle Hotel in Toronto. Nothing happened. Buyers of all sorts sat on their hands. Evidently business didn't place the same value on this exclusive product that Gregg did, and balked at shelling out $20,000 a year for something without a track record. Gregg claimed that the *Quarterly* was building up a historical data base whose value would grow with time. In that case, prospective buyers replied, come back in five years when you have something to show. Only Allstate and Labatt's signed up, plus three government departments that took up Gregg's half-price offer to government departments on the theory that the federal government was really one client.

The *Quarterly* finished its first year with three and a half

clients for revenue of $70,000 and entered the second year
$170,000 in the hole. Nobody could see anything but further
losses. The *Quarterly* was draining both Decima and PAI, and
grew into the number-one crisis on Gregg's turbulent calendar.
Even MacNaughton started to worry. "It will work," Gregg
insisted. "Hang in. Hang in."

The *Quarterly* was heading straight for collapse when a few
changes pulled it back from the brink. PAI brought in Rick Anderson, a young whiz kid and former aide to Judd Buchanan, on a
two-month contract in a belated effort to make the venture
work. Anderson duly reported that PAI and Decima should
decide to underwrite another eighteen months of losses – or
scrap the whole project immediately. Anderson advocated sticking it out. He believed that the concept was fundamentally
sound but needed more time, patience, and money. Mac-
Naughton and Gregg agreed, put Anderson onto the *Quarterly*'s
payroll, and told him to find subscribers.

Sales picked up, but one of the most effective sales strategies
was discovered by accident. Oddly, the thought of the federal
government as a major source of revenue had not crossed Gregg's
mind, and it occurred to him only as an afterthought, even
though government far outstripped everybody else in the country as a buyer of polling data. The *Quarterly* had always been
aimed at corporations but now it needed every subscriber it
could get. Gregg and Anderson discovered that bureaucrats were
easier to sell than businessmen, partly because of the half-rate
discount, but mostly because government officials quickly saw
the value of the *Quarterly*. Soon half a dozen government departments subscribed (as well as some provincial governments),
which bolstered the *Quarterly*'s subscription revenue a little.

But that was nothing compared to what else it did. The government gave the *Quarterly* something nobody – not Gregg,
Anderson, MacNaughton, or Robinson – had expected. It gave it
clout in the private sector. When the corporate world realized,
somewhat belatedly, that government read the *Quarterly* for
public-affairs trends it got curious, too. If the *Quarterly* contained data that influenced the bureaucracy, businessmen
started to think that they ought to take another look. It seemed
that influence with government yielded influence with business. Gregg had conceived the *Quarterly* as a window into gov-

ernment, but had never thought it would require government subscriptions for business to sit up and take notice.

Everybody who saw the *Quarterly* agreed that it made absorbing reading. The forty-page Executive Summary was designed so that businessmen could read it on the plane from Toronto to Ottawa, and bore no resemblance to a bunch of dull statistics. In fact one PAI executive complained that some businessmen read it for the wrong reason, that they were more interested in men's-club chatter than in information on which to base business plans. The Executive Summary paraded splashy charts, graphs, and illustrations. Each issue featured regular departments like "The Mood of the Country", "Assessments of Government", "Confidence in Institutions", "Specific Issues", plus a feature in-depth study of a different issue in each publication.

Before long the *Quarterly Report* had accumulated an invaluable data base which Gregg used in speeches and seminars. On twenty minutes' notice he could talk authoritatively on any issue because he had the data, whether it related to public attitudes towards the union movement, women, or almost any other topic.

One other thing helped sell the *Quarterly*. Every subscriber got a two- or three-hour free briefing from Gregg and Anderson, whether its office happened to be down the street or across the country. The free briefings added to the start-up cost, but over the long run enhanced the *Quarterly*'s value and enticed subscribers because they advertised the *Quarterly*'s strongest asset – Allan Gregg. A Gregg performance was something to behold. He walked into a room and within minutes turned skeptics into believers. He was entertaining, thoughtful, and eloquent, and he manipulated numbers the way a veteran bridge player shuffles a deck of cards, breathing life into statistics. He spoke colourfully, forcefully, and always for a purpose. If he had one weakness it was racing ahead of his audience, and even that enhanced his image for brilliance as his listeners scrambled to catch up. Gregg's mind ran so fast he sometimes forgot that not everybody operated at his speed.

Anderson played a role too. Gregg reported the latest public attitude towards foreign investment, Anderson chimed in with hot news about upcoming changes to FIRA. Gregg examined how public attitudes had caused the changes and Anderson gave details of the impact on industry. Sometimes Anderson reported an upcoming change that had yet to be announced and Gregg pulled data from the *Quarterly* to predict its fate. Sometimes he said public opinion supported the measure. Other times he said it didn't. And sometimes he said that the government had gone too far and might have to back down. Clients saw the link between public opinion and politics. Nobody else could produce such juicy intelligence about Ottawa.

Sometimes the intelligence proved to be uniquely prescient. As early as June 1982 Gregg was confidently advising clients to stop worrying about the Parti Québécois because the government was dead; despite its recent re-election it had no hope of victory. "The next time, they're gone," he said. "Count on it." Gregg's polling during the recession detected what he called the "post survivors' mentality". Concluding that the old rules no longer worked, people had turned dramatically against government intervention and had begun relying more on the private sector, including voluntary associations. The status quo, and any politician defending it, were judged non-viable and in trouble. The "post survivors' mentality", Gregg said, had caused Quebeckers to rethink their values, and abandon protectionism and parochialism in favour of expansion. Separatism had lost its clout because it no longer made sense. Quebeckers had stopped seeing the PQ as a protest movement and started to regard it as a vested government that taxed excessively, created undue conflict, and failed to govern well. On the basis of these new attitudes Gregg proclaimed that the PQ was dead no matter how it handled the remaining three or four years of its term. Time would prove him right.

Gregg grew into a guru of sorts and developed a loyal following among Canada's most prestigious business élite. For the $24,000 price of a subscription – it had been raised – bank chairmen, oil company executives, and the like got access to the oracle. His persona enhanced the value of his advice. Some businessmen got a kick out of watching this odd but brilliant character, some wanted to show open-mindedness, and others simply desired to be in the forefront of public analysis.

Despite his radical image, Gregg was not radical, merely unconventional. Beneath the hair and the clothes was a conservative person with traditional values not unlike his research profiles of a typical Canadian. Gregg's dress was his way of showing that he could play on the establishment's turf and embrace its values without sacrificing his individuality; it was his personal statement that he could not be bought. He could comfortably discuss business trends with any client and talked rates of return and margins as if he belonged to the corporate world, which he did. He still used obscenities, but even they had moderated and were tailored for the occasion. Even his gold earring stopped surprising new clients. Once Gregg developed a reputation everybody – whether he had met them before or not – expected the earring, and felt disappointed if he forgot it, so that his colleagues had to reassure their clients that he really did wear one. His conduct and dress never cost him business; businessmen concluded he must be outstanding if he became successful looking like that, and paid him more attention in jeans and a T-shirt than if he had been wearing horn-rimmed glasses and a Brooks Brothers suit.

Gregg exploited his eccentricity to good effect but never faked it. He displayed a cavalier attitude towards many things in life, as if they didn't matter, but rock music was different. Even as he grew older, rock music continued to consume him and was the thing that most noticeably aroused his passion, so that his personality changed when he listened. He showed the same intensity for it as do teenagers, and thereby hung a tale. Gregg abhorred the prospect of growing old and tried to hold onto the trappings of youth. He couldn't halt the aging process but could stop the processes accompanying it. He refused to divulge his age. "I'm not growing old gracefully," he told Robert Fulford. "I don't even have birthday parties. I just don't like getting as old as I'm getting." Gregg kept close to rock bands, financially supporting one in Vancouver, and owned part of the rock magazine *Music Express*.

In the *Quarterly*'s second year Anderson sold ten subscriptions, which finally pushed the publication into the black. The subscription list grew to twenty the following year and by that point it made money, even after Gregg internally expensed his briefings at $1,000 a day. The *Quarterly* mushroomed to more than forty-five subscribers, including a dozen federal-government departments and half a dozen provincial governments, and revenue reached a million dollars a year. Just as Gregg had predicted, the *Quarterly* turned lucrative, and became the single most successful subscription research product in the world. The United States had the Roper and the Cambridge reports, but nothing that could match the profitability of the *Quarterly*.

Lucrative as the *Quarterly* was, custom polling remained Decima's top revenue-producer, with five dollars in project work coming in for every dollar received from the *Quarterly*. The economic fate of Decima was yet to be determined, and custom polling would make or break it. Decima earned $800,000 in revenue in the first year, $1.8-million in the second and $2.4-million in the third – and yet showed red ink on its financial statements. Its losses grew as impressively as its sales revenue.

Decima's fortunes hit bottom in the the winter of 1980-81. The Tories were long out of power, Clark had come under internal attack as Conservative leader, and Gregg was juggling two money-losing operations: the *Quarterly* and Decima's custom polling division. Interest rates topped twenty per cent, driving up the cost of the money that Sherwood Communications advanced as shareholders' loans. Every year the company sank deeper into debt. Tom Scott at Sherwood Communications suffered most of all because he shouldered the investment burden but had no operational control. Gregg wondered how much longer Sherwood Communications would tolerate the losses.

That winter Ronald Reagan moved into the White House, and that affected Decima's fortunes. Suddenly Richard Wirthlin, hitherto an unsung California pollster, was the pollster to the president of the United States. *People* magazine featured the quiet Mormon as a centrefold. Gerald Ford asked him to meet the presidents of General Motors, Ford, and Chrysler to develop a strategy for saving the North American automobile industry. Wirthlin became hot property overnight and could spare little time for helping Gregg project Canadian riding results from a national sample. Had Wirthlin known in 1977 that Reagan would run for president in 1980 he would not have committed himself to Decima in the first place. Wirthlin's regret over Decima coincided with Sherwood Communications' growing unease that Decima had become a bottomless money pit.

Gregg was not happy either. He had singlemindedly thrown

his energies into Decima and built up big revenues, and still had nothing but a pile of debt to show for it. He bemoaned his fate one night in 1981 while visiting David MacNaughton at his home in Almonte outside Ottawa. MacNaughton's wife, Sheila, was out for the evening and MacNaughton threw some steaks onto the barbecue. Over cognac Gregg talked about the paradox of Decima: the company attracted plenty of business, generated good revenue, and seemed on the verge of turning the corner, yet constantly floundered in the red. There seemed to be no end in sight. Meanwhile Wirthlin had no time, and Sherwood Communications was losing its enthusiasm. Gregg lamented that he would be lucky to see a dividend before his first Canada Pension cheque.

"I bet you I can get Bryden to buy all the other guys out," MacNaughton said.

"Why would Bryden want to do that?" Gregg asked.

"Look at the fabulous synergies we've developed off the *Quarterly Report*," MacNaughton replied. "We can do it in everything."

"Holy Jesus," said Gregg, "that might be everyone's answer."

Bryden had been MacNaughton's silent partner when he first started out in KinMac and had financed the takeover of PAI in 1979. Bryden had taught MacNaughton the ins and outs of the business world and had always shown great confidence in him. But he didn't share MacNaughton's enthusiasm over Decima and thought that this time his reach had exceeded his grasp. He believed buying Decima was silly. Although both Sherwood Communications and Wirthlin were willing to bail out with only their skins intact, Bryden considered even such a fire-sale price too high. He balked at Decima's debt load, and even the tax loss didn't tempt him. MacNaughton assured him that stronger internal management and the passage of time would solve Decima's problems and make it profitable. Bryden remained unconvinced. But in the end he agreed to indulge MacNaughton's wish the way a father surrenders to a pestering son, although he warned him that he had better be right.

PAI had earlier allowed Bryden's company, Kinburn Capital, to gobble it up too. In 1980, PAI had become a box in the Kinburn organization chart alongside some unusual other boxes, most notably SHL Systemhouse Inc., a booming high-tech firm, and

Paperboard Industries Corporation. Kinburn had grown so fast that Bryden had offered a private share issue of Kinburn stock at an attractive price, and the lure of windfall gains enticed Mac-Naughton and his PAI partners to convert their PAI shares into Kinburn stock, so that now MacNaughton and Robinson owned stock in Kinburn, which in turn owned PAI. Systemhouse stock shot up like a rocket and generated a tidy capital gain for Kinburn stockholders. PAI's owners – MacNaughton, Robinson, and Don Kelly – had seemingly pulled off a coup in attaching their company to Bryden's rising star.

Decima ceased to exist as a corporation in 1981. It continued operating as before, but legally became a division of PAI, which by now was a wholly owned subsidiary of Kinburn Capital, which purchased Decima's outstanding debts at face value and converted it into one of Bryden's tax losses while PAI bought the company for a dollar. Gregg received an option to buy Kinburn stock at $10 a share and join in the Systemhouse spoils.

Rumours of the Decima takeover raced through the informed echelons of the Conservative Party. People mused about it in tones of amazement and even crisis: the Liberal Party had bought the Conservative Party's polling company. Bryden, Mac-Naughton, and Robinson belonged to the Liberal Party and now they controlled the fate of Decima and had access to Tory polling data. So the talk went. It was Bryden, more than Mac-Naughton or Robinson, who worried the Tories. He raised funds for the Liberal Party and made corporate donations to it through Kinburn. Now he and Gregg were business partners. The Conservative right wing went into a fury, treating Gregg like a spy who had crossed the Berlin Wall with party secrets.

Gregg's response only intensified the outcry. Officially he ignored the furore; unofficially he said his detractors could go to hell. He reasoned that if people couldn't understand what had happened they were dumb and that was too bad for them. Had he tried, he might have isolated the grumbling to the hard-core right wing. Instead he permitted it to fester and spread into the middle reaches of the party where there was quiet concern that Gregg had walked into an intolerable conflict of interest. Even Clark worried about the question of cross-ownership and briefly kicked around the idea of having the PC Canada Fund buy fifty-one per cent of Decima, or, if that was not possible, commissioning the Fund itself as party pollster. Gregg, meanwhile, calculated that the controversy would blow over and disappear. It did not.

The matter moved to the executive committee of the National Executive where a motion was made calling on the Conservative Party to cease and desist from all relations with Decima Research. The party's supreme body leaned toward sacking Decima as official pollster, but before the committee could vote someone pointed out that at least it should hear Gregg's side before firing him. The executive committee referred the matter to the treasury committee for investigation.

Gregg had never fitted the party mould, and this made some members uneasy. They didn't like his manner or his attitude, but this investigation involved more than met the eye; the fact that the executive committee handed the matter to the treasury committee said a great deal about the nature of the inquiry. The treasury committee was controlled by the party's Dump-Clark conspirators as a vehicle to harass Clark and undermine his authority. It had the authority to investigate any expenditure of money, and that allowed it to probe virtually anything it wanted. It used that power to isolate and weaken Clark by taking out the loyalists around him, and Gregg and Lowell Murray topped the hit list. Clark's leadership would come up for review in Winnipeg, and the pro-review people were determined to deny him the advantage of his pollster. Like a grand inquisition, the treasury committee – comprising the caucus chairman, Ron Huntington, the party treasurer, Peter Vuicic, and the national vice president for Ontario, Dr. John Balkwill – hauled in Gregg and demanded an explanation of what happened to the party's polling data.

When Gregg arrived at party headquarters on Laurier Street and sat down before the three-member board he was in an ugly mood. The mere fact that the committee dared question his integrity enraged him. Gregg defended himself defiantly and conceded nothing. He outlined the security and access procedures to Decima's computer and told his inquisitors that only he and the man who ran his computer division could obtain access. Specifically, he added, neither MacNaughton nor Bryden nor anybody else connected with the Liberal Party could gain entry.

Vuicic, a former Dump-Clark advocate who had switched sides, appeared satisfied. But Huntington and Balkwill wanted to know what "guarantees" the party had. Balkwill said party officials had penetrated his computer by telephone link during the 1980 election when they needed data in a hurry. If the party could do it over the phone nothing could stop insiders like Bryden or MacNaughton. Gregg shot back that it was a matter of "common fucking sense" and exploded into a fit of rage. "You people", he lashed out, "are either very stupid or very malicious – one of the two. Because you think that either I or David MacNaughton would sacrifice our entire fucking business when our business is based on reputation, a major part of which is confidentiality, in exchange for a glimpse at an open kimono."

Huntington and Balkwill stood their ground, protesting that the issue was not personal conduct but ownership and conflict of interest and that if Gregg could not recognize the problem there was no point in continuing the meeting. The encounter broke up with Gregg yelling at Huntington and Balkwill and them yelling back.

The committee leaned towards bringing in another pollster to share Gregg's duties and act as a check on his figures, but submitted a short list of recommendations ranging from doing nothing to firing Gregg outright. Gregg dashed off a furious letter to Clark telling him it was not a question of whether the Conservative Party fired him, but whether he resigned the account. He informed Clark that he would not have his reputation sullied any longer, and demanded a vote of confidence; otherwise he was gone. Clark tried to stay out of the issue but, faced with this ultimatum, entered the fray to keep Gregg. Clark went to the executive committee and politely told them that the pollster reported to the leader and he was the leader and that was the end of it. Gregg's funding came out of Clark's budget, which lay beyond the control of the executive committee, and that put Gregg out of reach.

MacNaughton faced trouble of his own over the PAI-Decima alliance. Some Trudeau aides already resented MacNaughton's sometimes disloyal advice to his business clients with respect to the government. Now they wanted to know what he was doing pulling Gregg out of financial trouble, so that the Tory's biggest asset could knock them silly at election time. MacNaughton did not face the inquisition Gregg encountered and emerged mostly unscathed. But he didn't care, in any event, if he had fallen out of favour with the Trudeau Liberals; by this time he had become disillusioned with them.

MacNaughton's disenchantment had started during his final EA years when Trudeau introduced wage and price controls. His alarm grew as Trudeau and the core people around him centralized power increasingly in the Privy Council Office and picked fights with the country's regions. MacNaughton gave an impassioned speech advocating party renewal at the 1979 Liberal reform conference in Winnipeg after the party's defeat by Joe Clark. PAI became identified with the anti-Trudeau wing of the Liberal Party, and when Trudeau withdrew his resignation in December 1979 to stay on as party leader, MacNaughton essentially dropped out of active party involvement.

The handling of the Foreign Investment Review Agency and the National Energy Program particularly irked MacNaughton. He supported the objects of both FIRA and the NEP – and defended the principles of each of them to hostile clients. But he thought that in pursuing them Trudeau had abandoned the Liberal Party's traditional moderate pragmatism in favour of ideological objectives. Philosophically MacNaughton was a social liberal and an economic conservative, who could not see how owning a string of gasoline stations helped the state provide services for people in need.

He flirted with the idea of switching to the Tories and joining some of his best friends, people like Allan Gregg, Bill Neville, Nancy Jamieson, and others, but could not get himself to make the switch. Switching was hard. Party affiliation involved personal relationships and he was not sure the Conservative Party had enough room for him to play the active role he craved. Besides, the Tories were going through the process of shooting their leader. So MacNaughton stayed.

Gregg, by contrast, who looked like a candidate for disenchantment with the Conservatives, never experienced similar alienation because he was not a Tory and never had been. His party roots were tied to loyalties and friendships, to people like Lowell Murray and Joe Clark.

By merging their stock with Kinburn, MacNaughton and Gregg figured they had been the smartest guys in the world and had pulled off a real deal. The transaction had made MacNaughton a millionaire several times over, thanks largely to the value of Systemhouse shares, and Gregg planned to become one shortly. Their euphoria didn't last long. Within weeks the price of Systemhouse stock plummeted from $14 to under a dollar, and the company teetered on the edge of bankruptcy. As in a chain reaction, Systemhouse's troubles crippled Kinburn, and that in turn afflicted PAI and Decima.

Suddenly the fates of both PAI and Decima rested on a company that at any minute might see the bailiff at the door. MacNaughton had surrendered his interest in PAI and Gregg had relinquished his part of Decima for stock which had proved almost worthless. MacNaughton tried to dump some Kinburn stock for $2 but found no takers. Gregg had no stock; he had traded his Decima stock for an option to buy Kinburn shares at $10, which had sounded good when they traded at $14, but became meaningless at 87 cents. Aside from personal avarice, MacNaughton and Gregg had joined Kinburn for its pool of capital, which was supposed to finance their growth. The pool had vanished and, if anything, PAI and Decima would have to bail out Kinburn as everyone sank together.

Gregg lost his assets but at least owed nothing. MacNaughton, on the other hand, faced personal bankruptcy. He had gone nearly a million dollars into personal debt the previous year, borrowing over a quarter of a million dollars to buy Kinburn and Systemhouse stock, and using the paper strength of Kinburn's capital gain to borrow another $600,000 to build a mansion outside Ottawa. The house had just been completed when the Kinburn stock collapsed, leaving MacNaughton strapped. It was serious. MacNaughton's wife had gone shopping and filled her basket with groceries when the store bounced her cheque and told her to put the items back.

Ironically, Kinburn fell just as PAI and Decima were performing better than ever. PAI had always made money and now Decima had finally edged into the black. The new corporate structure brought Decima new management and accounting techniques and a belt-tightening the company sorely needed. Decima saved $100,000 a year by purchasing the computer it had previously rented. A few staff members were fired, and a new system of financial controls enabled Decima to gauge its costs more accurately, and to improve its abysmal collection record. Gregg had not bothered with these business details; now Decima turned the profit corner while hardly adding a nickel to sales. But this impressive turnabout would go for naught if Kinburn didn't survive.

"We've got to do something," Gregg implored MacNaughton. "This is crazy."

The former PAI-Decima owners – MacNaughton, Gregg, Robinson, and Don Kelly – met Bryden and politely told him that they wanted out. Led by MacNaughton, they said they could not remain part of Kinburn any more, and asked him if they could buy their companies back. Bryden promised not to stand in their way, and offered to sell PAI and Decima for $1.5-million. By any standard, $1.5-million was a bargain. Both companies were profitable and still growing, and together generated more than $4-million in revenue. An arm's-length negotiation would have fetched Bryden twice the figure or more, but he wanted to preserve a good relationship.

The price may have been a steal, but bargains are no bargains to those who cannot afford to buy. MacNaughton and his group didn't have $1.5-million and couldn't raise it. MacNaughton figured that together they could swing half that amount through personal loans, and could raise another $500,000 internally – but couldn't scrape together the final $250,000. The deal was consummated when Bryden agreed to waive the $250,000 unless real growth in Canada's Gross National Product exceeded 3 per cent. The price effectively dropped to $1.25 million if the economy fell flat.

MacNaughton borrowed $450,000 for 60 per cent of common shares while Gregg and Robinson each borrowed $150,000 for 20 per cent of the shares. PAI and Decima employees kicked in $350,000 for non-voting preferred shares paying an automatic 10 per cent dividend. The final $150,000 was raised through company debt. If MacNaughton had not imprudently overindebted himself buying Kinburn stock he and his partners would not have raised the $750,000 down payment. Like Brazil or Poland – or, later, Dome Petroleum – MacNaughton wallowed so deeply in debt that the bank had to prop him up to protect its earlier loans.

MacNaughton, Gregg, and Robinson formed a holding company called Public Affairs Resources Group – PARG – and made PAI and Decima Research its two subsidiaries. PARG started business in the fall of 1983 with its three partners each so deeply in debt that they were paying more interest than they collected in salaries.

Unlike PAI, which MacNaughton institutionalized without making his personality part of it, Decima remained the embodiment of Gregg, even when it became the General Motors of public-affairs polling in Canada. Clients demanded Gregg personally, and some refused to hire Decima without him. Ian McKinnon, Gregg's right hand and alter ego, had certain methodological skills that outstripped Gregg, yet it was Allan Gregg who reigned as the analyst, the salesman, and the driving force behind Decima. A million-dollar insurance policy protected Decima in the event that death or incapacitation deprived the company of Gregg. One could tell his holiday scheduling by looking at a graph of Decima's cash flow. The revenues dropped two months after Gregg took time off; if he took December off, Decima scrambled to catch up in February.

Only once did Gregg's personality cost Decima business. In the summer of 1983, after the Conservative Party leadership convention, Brian Mulroney, the new leader, decided that he did not want somebody as outspoken as Gregg in his circle.

TWELVE

THE MULRONEY FACTOR

The political fortunes of Pierre Trudeau after his electoral triumph over Joe Clark in 1980 showed how fickle political popularity had become in modern society and how quickly winners became losers, and vice versa. Trudeau's winning 44 per cent on voting day in February 1980 climbed to 47 the following month and a heady 49 the month after that, then dipped briefly before peaking at 50 per cent in September 1980. At that point he started a long and uneven slide that brought him down to a virtual dead heat with Clark by September 1981. Clark jumped ahead with an 11-point lead in the spring of 1982, and at one time that summer he led by as much as 19 points. The poll positions of Trudeau and Clark had flip-flopped in less than two years.

The numbers flashing up on Allan Gregg's computer screen more or less confirmed Gallup's findings and by the summer of 1982 Gregg decided that Pierre Trudeau would lose the next election no matter what he did. Gregg found that public disenchantment now extended beyond Trudeau and carried into the Liberal Party as an institution. He concluded that the Liberals were finished and that virtually nothing could resurrect them in the short term. Although Joe Clark still suffered severe image problems, the public was willing to overlook them for the moment. Gregg joked that even somebody like himself could lead the Conservative Party to victory in the next election.

But while Clark was sweeping the polls, the Conservative Party could not overlook the image of its leader so easily, and refused to forget or forgive the 1980 defeat. No matter how high he soared in the Gallup poll, the 1980 albatross hung around his neck. The fiasco had badly shaken the party's confidence and had made Tories secretly wonder whether they really could run the country better than the Liberals. Clark's continuing presence symbolized these internal doubts, and many Tories actively undermined his leadership in an effort to topple him from power.

Gregg had personally felt the wrath of the Dump-Clark Movement following Decima's merger with PAI. Now the conspirators were working harder than ever in anticipation of their big opportunity at the Conservative Party's January 1983 General Meeting in Winnipeg when Clark's leadership would come up for another automatic review. The most active dump-Clark faction sprang out of Brian Mulroney's entourage, and it had been quietly working for months. Mulroney himself carefully avoided overt links to the endeavour, but at the same time made it clear he was interested in seeking the leadership should Clark tumble. He undertook a national speaking tour in the fall of 1982 and dropped in on Conservative riding associations across the country in an apparent effort to bolster his standing as an alternative to Clark.

Then, in early December 1982, Mulroney discreetly informed Finlay MacDonald, a personal friend who happened to be Clark's policy adviser, that he would back Clark for the upcoming Winnipeg meeting. All Clark had to do was come to Montreal and receive the endorsement. On December 6 1982 reporters flocked to the Ritz Carlton in Montreal to watch Brian Mulroney declare his support for Joe Clark. Mulroney's endorsement pleased some party members and bewildered others. Some saw it as a positive step to unify and strengthen the party. More skeptical observers saw Mulroney distancing himself from the behind-the-scenes plotting to bring Clark down.

The dump-Clark leaders did not expect to get a majority at the review vote in Winnipeg, but hoped to garner enough strength to pressure him into calling a leadership convention which, they believed, would throw him out. Most of Clark's own caucus supported the drive to unseat him. Clark well understood what to expect in Winnipeg and arrived for battle with a sophisticated high-tech audio-visual presentation on 40-foot screens and a 120-foot stage. The Clark forces were determined to pull out all the stops in order to impress delegates and seduce them into voting "No" to a leadership convention.

Clark had to score measurably better than the 66.1 per cent he had received two years earlier in Ottawa for him to maintain his grip on the party. Like almost everybody else attached to the leader, Gregg expected him to beat off his detractors with a 75 to 77 per cent vote. Such an endorsement would stop the dissidents, dispel the doubts, and preserve Clark's tenure through the next election. Gregg had done no polling – with only 2,406 delegates, the size of the universe was too small – and was relying on the results from Clark's sophisticated system for tracking delegates.

Most delegates arrived on Wednesday, January 26, for the five-day conference; some arrived as early as Tuesday. Everybody waited for the big vote on Friday night. Clark's speech early that evening went well and the mood of the convention seemed to suggest that he would breeze through the vote. As delegates on the floor – and a national television audience – waited for the results of the vote, news spread across the hall that a CTV exit poll gave Clark 76 per cent. Flora MacDonald, a Clark supporter, led a dance as the band played "I'se the B'y That Builds the Boat". Anti-Clark workers started to concede defeat and shook hands with Clark organizers and hoped there would be "no hard feelings".

Meanwhile Clark was waiting in the manager's office of the Winnipeg Convention Centre. The room contained Senator Lowell Murray; Finlay MacDonald, the "silver fox" from Nova Scotia; Terry Yates, Clark's chief fundraiser, and his wife Brenda; Erik Nielsen, the hard-liner from the Yukon; Tony Saunders, Clark's British Columbia campaign chairman, and his wife Valerie; Manitoba's Jake Epp and his wife Lydia; Peter Harder, who had succeeded Neville as Clark's chief of staff; and David MacDonald, the red Tory from Prince Edward Island. Marcel Danis, in charge of votes from Quebec delegates, joined the group last. "You've won Quebec, sir," he announced as he sat down. Everyone felt confident but during the long wait Maureen McTeer, Clark's wife, mentioned that she was wearing her wedding dress for good luck, whereupon Clark pulled a red rabbit's foot out of his pocket as his good-luck charm.

Finally, an official from the accounting firm Touche Ross & Company entered the room and formally handed Clark the results. He stared at the paper and his hand started shaking uncontrollably. Everybody knew what it meant. When he blurted out "66.9," the already hushed room turned stony silent. One participant said he had never been in such a silent room all his life. Then Terry Yates uttered "Jesus Christ" and McTeer broke into tears. "I guess it's not so lucky after all," Clark said as he put his rabbit's foot back into his pocket.

At that moment the Gallup poll was finishing a survey that would put Clark 18 points ahead of Trudeau. According to the bizarre consensus that had seemed to emerge, more than 67 spelled victory for Clark and less than 66 per cent amounted to defeat (to the disgust of Dalton Camp, who proclaimed that victory should require "50 per cent plus one"). With typical Tory bad luck, the vote fell into that narrow and uncertain no-man's-land, leaving everybody perplexed. As delegates waited for the announcement, Clark and his group pondered the meaning of 66.9, knowing that he had an important decision to make, and little time in which to make it. He would soon have to mount the platform and face the convention and announce his response. So he had to decide quickly whether or not to try to reinforce his base with a leadership convention. Since the last convention's 66.1 per cent, he had struggled to maintain his grip on the party, and had spent the last two years fending off attacks; he could expect worse in the next two years. The core of the anti-Clark resistance lived inside his parliamentary caucus, and possessed the strength to immobilize him. Clark asked for opinions around the room. One by one, most of his advisers sadly recommended that he call a leadership convention.

While Clark deliberated, Bill Neville sat in the CTV television booth doing analysis of the convention with Lloyd Robertson and Bruce Phillips. Neville, who had always admired Clark's deeply rooted beliefs, figured that the two-thirds vote would allow him to hang in long enough to win the next election. He vehemently opposed a leadership convention and, fearing that Clark at that moment would be receiving contrary advice, he desperately wanted to warn him not to succumb. But Neville was stuck in front of the CTV camera and could not rush off to Clark's hideaway to present his argument. Meanwhile Gregg was tied up with Barbara Frum in front of the cameras at the CBC booth; he also opposed a leadership convention but, like Neville, could not advise Clark at this crucial moment.

Neville and Gregg watched from their respective television booths as Clark walked onto the podium. With rising hope they heard him tell the convention he had received a clear majority of the vote. It looked as if he would stick it out. Then he dramatically announced that his majority was not enough. "It [the majority] is not clear enough to enforce the kind of discipline and to achieve the kind of unity that this party requires," he said amid a cacophony of cheers and hollers. "My friends, we know that the greatest enemy this party faces is uncertainty about our unity." As a consequence, he declared, he was recommending a leadership convention – and he would be a candidate.

"Well," Gregg said, reflecting on his own fate as much as on Clark's, "we're into the glue now."

In this case, television influenced the outcome of events in a way that eluded the medium's critics. Clark's decision could well have been different if television had not taken such influential advisers as Neville and Gregg out of the back room and into the studio when he needed their advice.

Neville visited Clark's hotel suite that night and saw him convince himself that he relished a knockdown fight with his detractors. He had faced repeated adversity and had always survived. But Neville knew that Clark was finished. A leader could not quit and expect the party to re-elect him. The system didn't work that way. Later, Clark confessed to friends that he woke in the middle of the night saying, "My God, what have I done?"

In the campaign that followed, eight Tories ran for the leadership of the party. Only three held realistic hopes of winning: Joe Clark, Brian Mulroney, and John Crosbie, the droll orator from Newfoundland. The polling data showed that on most factors the delegates preferred Crosbie and regarded him as the candidate with the most to offer. He was best liked, best respected, and judged the smartest. Despite a bad flub in which he equated fluency in French to fluency in Chinese, he also ran the best campaign. The data put him on top in most categories. Trailing badly in almost every category was Mulroney, whom delegates judged poor in trustworthiness, image, policy, and much else, while Clark fell in between those two on most issues. Crosbie should have swept the convention, but delegates were not looking for a perfect leader. They wanted a winner, and in the "winnability" column Mulroney topped everyone. Delegates distrusted and even disliked Mulroney but they saw him as the party's ticket to power. Conservatives had been losers so long that on June 11 1983 the delegates in the Ottawa Civic Centre swallowed their misgivings and on the fourth ballot elected Brian Mulroney the leader of the Progressive Conservative Party by a vote of 1,584 to 1,325 over Joe Clark.

Gregg wore a Clark button and voted for Clark on all four ballots. He never disguised or downplayed his loyalty to Clark and never hid the fact that he liked him both personally and politically. If anything he flaunted his support, not deliberately, though Gregg's personality made everything he did seem deliberate. He couldn't burp without attracting attention, and that fact helped convey the impression at both the Winnipeg and the Ottawa convention that he had bolstered Clark more than he actually did.

Decima itself did no work for Clark once he resigned to run as a candidate in January. A decision was taken to keep Decima clean for post-convention work. The Conservative Party had no leader during the interim stage and when Clark ceased to be the leader Decima ceased to have him as a client. After Mulroney's victory Gregg resigned his position on the party's policy committee, as was the proper thing to do. A new leader could not be blamed for wanting to fill party positions with his own people. Gregg received a one-line reply thanking him for rendering useful service to the party.

Decima had no ongoing contract with the Conservative Party. When the party wanted a poll it signed a contract and plunked down 50 per cent of the purchase price. Decima produced the results and collected the remaining 50 per cent. The formal relationship ended when the project ended, which meant that Decima's status as the Conservative Party's pollster depended on the whims of the party leader. With Mulroney as leader the party stopped offering Decima contracts. Months slipped by after Mulroney's victory, and Gregg heard nothing officially from party headquarters. Unofficially he learned that he had been frozen out by the new régime and could expect to stay in the cold as long as Mulroney was leader.

The Mulroney camp thought Gregg had supported Clark too

openly and too enthusiastically, in fact the new incumbents saw him as foe. Gregg was undeniably a red Tory, dressed oddly, and was tarred by the Clark brush, and all three facts worked against him. Mulroney had won by putting together a coalition of "outs" and the attitude around the Mulroney camp was that any confidant of Clark deserved permanent exile. It had never occurred to Gregg that Mulroney saw political activity in such "them and us" terms. As far as Gregg was concerned he supported Clark personally, but in his professional capacity as a pollster he worked not for Clark but for the party leader. It never dawned on Gregg that Mulroney viewed him as an enemy, as someone out to undermine him. Gregg's supporters and admirers in the party, alarmed at the loss of a talent like Gregg and that the tracking of public opinion had stopped, tried to change Mulroney's mind and warned him he was mistaken about Gregg. "That son of a bitch," Mulroney railed, showing his vindictive side, "he sat on television cutting me up. Now you want me to hire him?"

After Mulroney's victory Gregg hurt his cause further with his own lack of discretion. Gregg said in public what he believed, and never shied away from venturing an opinion about Mulroney's strengths and weaknesses, expressing himself emphatically and clearly. It made wonderful copy. And each time it alienated Mulroney a little more.

The two had hardly met and had never really had a substantial conversation. Gregg, along with hundreds of others, had shaken Mulroney's hand at the 1976 leadership convention when Gregg was a nobody. He had since phoned Mulroney twice as president of the Iron Ore Company of Canada to flog a subscription to the *Decima Quarterly* and both times had struck out. Those three encounters made up their total contact.

Gregg telephoned Mulroney's office and left a message, hoping to arrange a meeting. Mulroney ignored the message. Gregg then called Charley McMillan, Mulroney's top policy adviser, whom he had known through Michael Meighen, and invited him to the Decima office for a look at the data. Gregg told McMillan he had possession of several years' worth of good statistics belonging to the party and needed the leader's instructions on what to do with it. McMillan said he would ask Mulroney and get back to him, but never called. Mulroney made it clear he could do without Gregg and Decima. McMillan ran some survey questions through the Gallup organization and dabbled a little with polling, but otherwise Mulroney let the subject of polling slide.

That fall *Contenders: The Tory Quest for Power* appeared on the bookstands and climbed aboard the bestseller list. *Contenders* covered the recent Tory leadership convention in detail, and pulled no punches, taking the reader behind the scenes of the major leadership campaigns and exposing the foibles and heavy-handedness that inevitably beset such campaigns. Clark and Crosbie were criticized for various misdeeds, but the toughest comment was directed at Mulroney. The book left the impression that a bunch of sleazy characters who operated without finesse surrounded Mulroney throughout the campaign. It also exposed the Mulroney camp's participation in the Dump Clark Movement, and how some of Mulroney's aides continued to agitate against Clark despite Mulroney's public endorsement of his leader. As a media junky, Mulroney read everything written about him, and he read *Contenders* with mounting fury. After telling an interviewer that he had not read the book, a few questions later he went on to complain that he had not realized he had won by the time he finished it. Three people had a hand in writing the offending book: Patrick Martin, an award-winning journalist with the *Globe and Mail*, who was the lead writer, George Perlin, a professor of political science at Queen's University, and Allan Gregg.

"It's just me," Gregg said later when asked for an explanation, arguing that the book gave an accurate rendering of events. It happened to be true, but to Mulroney and his enraged advisers that was not the issue.

Contenders moved Gregg to the top of Mulroney's hit list. Anything Gregg had done before, real or imagined, paled in comparison. As far as Mulroney was concerned the book confirmed every suspicion he had ever held of Gregg, and he proclaimed that he was finished. He vowed that as long as he was party leader Gregg and Decima would not get another federal Tory contract. In fact, he declared, the most important qualification the next Conservative pollster needed was *not* to be Allan Gregg. Even Gregg, who operated with an amazing naiveté, acknowledged that his prospects looked grim.

Despite their preoccupation with loyalty, and their suspicion of supporters of the other candidates, the Mulroney people had a point; it seemed inappropriate for the party pollster to dig out and analyse in public the entrails of the Conservative Party. Gregg, for his part, explained his reasons simply: he had a responsibility to help advance the collective knowledge of society about the most important system in the country. Canada, he said, suffered from a dearth of authoritative and interesting books on domestic politics. None of his friends doubted Gregg's social conscience, and most believed that idealism motivated much of what he did. But some felt that something else also drove him to such an unusual act. Gregg liked publicity and could not resist an opportunity to see his name in print. They felt that he needed a media fix every so often.

The turning point in Gregg's political fortunes came when Mulroney appointed Norm Atkins as his campaign chairman for the coming election that would most likely be held in 1984. Atkins, an avuncular figure, came from Ontario's famous Big Blue Machine and regularly used Decima for provincial polling with great success, and he was convinced it could be just as successful for Mulroney. Atkins told Mulroney that Gregg belonged to his team, that nobody else would do and that it would be crazy to use another pollster. Mulroney refused to budge. Atkins argued that the Conservative Party had made an investment in Gregg, who now possessed knowledge and background the party needed and could not get elsewhere. Besides, he added, Gregg was the best in the business. Mulroney said no. Atkins told Mulroney he didn't have to like Gregg, only to recognize that nobody could help him more. Mulroney still said no.

Gregg had his detractors within the party, but his friends outnumbered his enemies. As the polling debate widened, Tories across the country, including the party establishment, intervened with Mulroney on Gregg's behalf. At least three provincial premiers – all Decima clients – counselled Mulroney to use him. Bill Neville spoke up for him, and so did Lowell Murray and Pat Kinsella. They all said he was the industry standard, and the Conservative party should not settle for less. Mulroney replied that he was a jerk. His defenders said it didn't matter whether he was a jerk or not if he could help them knock off the Liberals in the next election. Mulroney told people to stop bugging him.

Things might have gone better had Gregg extended an olive

branch, but the operation on his behalf received little help from him. He talked to friends who tried to act as conciliators, but refused to call Mulroney or do anything to ingratiate himself with the Tory leader. He told anybody who would listen that the Conservative Party accounted for only 15 per cent of Decima's business and couldn't expect to claim 100 per cent of his profile. Instead he turned his attention to commercial sales, which were booming, with Decima growing 50 per cent that year. Gregg might have been on the outs politically, but Decima's balance sheet had never been better.

Mulroney, who often promised revenge with the phrase "His time will come," could afford to be intransigent. The Gallup poll showed him leading Trudeau by a country mile; while the Tory leader registered in the mid-50s sometimes, Trudeau hobbled along in the mid-to-upper 20s. Mulroney did not need the kind of detailed breakdown and analysis that Decima offered, or the expertise of an Allan Gregg, when he led his chief rival two to one. Nothing reduces the influence of a pollster as much as an intoxicating lead.

But Gregg had time as an ally. As the clock ticked and an election drew nearer, Mulroney's resolve showed signs of cracking. Sooner or later he would need a pollster, and the longer he waited the tougher it would be for Gregg's successor to get up and running in time for the campaign. February 29 1984 proved to be a watershed, because on that day Trudeau announced his retirement. Mulroney realized that, suddenly, all bets were off. He could only guess how this gigantic event would affect his fortunes and had no idea how his existing lead would fare against a new prime minister. He had no detailed polling breakdown of the individual weaknesses of the major Liberal candidates nor a strategy for exploiting them. Mulroney did know one thing for sure – that the coming Liberal leadership convention would give his opposition an awful lot of free publicity, boost Liberal popularity, and cut his lead. Mulroney needed a comprehensive poll to tell him where he stood and how to react.

In a few days Atkins sensed a change in Mulroney's attitude; the leader was ready to admit that he didn't really know Gregg. He still balked at employing a pollster who was likely to say things that could damage his prospects, but Atkins said he could fix that. Mulroney finally succumbed, giving Atkins the go-ahead to commission a single poll from Decima if he could promise to gag Gregg. Gagging Gregg was more easily said than done. Atkins sat down with him and told him he had to promise to button his lip and make no press statements on the political fortunes of Mulroney and the party through the next election. Gregg said he would remain silent, but only with regard to the federal Tories and only until the polls closed in the next election. It was his sole concession during the nine-month standoff. Gregg could live with that. So could Mulroney.

Atkins commissioned Decima to undertake a major baseline nationwide poll that examined the image of the Tory party and its leader as well as probing into a range of issues. Atkins knew that one poll would dispel Mulroney's doubts and convince him he needed Decima; Gregg would sell Mulroney the way he did everybody else. Atkins was right. When Gregg and Mulroney met in Mulroney's Centre Block office to analyse the results, Gregg poured out a series of numbers and proceeded to craft a political strategy that would take the Conservative leader into and through the next election campaign. Mulroney was amazed and impressed. Decima had returned as the Tory pollster.

THIRTEEN

BATTLE FOR SUPREMACY

David MacNaughton did not wait long to make his move for control of ECL. In 1980 he had been running PAI for only a year when he sent out feelers via ECL's Steve Markey that he was interested in making a deal. Both he and PAI were deeply in debt, but that did not stop him from making a lunge for control of ECL, at the time the biggest public-affairs consulting firm in Ottawa. He counted on continuing market growth and the financial backstopping of Rod Bryden's deep pockets to make the deal work.

The two sides met in the cocktail lounge of the Four Seasons. Bryden and MacNaughton represented PAI and Bill Lee and Steve Markey appeared for ECL. Bryden, the whiz-bang financier, drew organizational charts on a piece of paper and when the page ran out continued drawing boxes on a paper napkin as he tried to illustrate the intricate financial setup of Kinburn Capital. PAI entered the picture in the third tier of boxes. Lee and Markey never really understood where the different shareholders stood and why.

Bryden did most of the talking. He proposed buying ECL for a combination of cash and Kinburn stock. Lee would become PAI chairman, MacNaughton the president, and the four vice presidents would be Mike Robinson and Don Kelly of PAI and Steve Markey and Irv Keenleyside of ECL. The new firm would become probably the biggest public-affairs firm in North America, possibly in the world. Lee said he wanted a salary twenty per cent higher than MacNaughton's, which was okay with Mac-Naughton as long as he got to be chief executive officer and ran the combined operation; he cared less about whether Lee got more money and a better title than about control. He insisted that the name of the new firm would be PAI and not ECL. He was prepared to give Lee big money for an interest in his company but would not bend over the corporate name.

In 1980 ECL had grossed a million dollars a year and because of lean management amassed more than half of that as profit. In 1980 PAI had hardly started to grow, had yet to hit the million-dollar mark, and already seemed burdened by high overhead. It still accepted a few government contracts – a policy Mac-Naughton and Robinson would change over the next year or two – whereas ECL righteously and unwaveringly shunned all forms of government business. ECL was not only bigger but felt morally superior, which did not augur well for the take-over.

The two sides met again, this time in the more formal surroundings of a dinner hosted by ECL in the restaurant in the Inn of the Provinces. By this time they had reviewed each other's books and client lists, checked each other's earnings, and examined the potential for conflicts of interest that would come from mixing clients. Some conflicts were head-on, and would require the dropping of a few clients. Others were manageable. But Markey worried over trading control of a proven moneymaker for a small slice of a conglomerate like Kinburn. In effect he was moving his equity out of the consulting business, which he knew well, and into software and paper enterprises in the Kinburn corporate complex, about which he knew little. The ECL partners felt uncomfortable with the offer, believing that Bryden and MacNaughton operated too aggressively. In the end Lee and Markey consulted financial advisers, talked it over, and decided no. They sent word back to PAI that the deal was off.

The failed negotiations revealed a fundamental difference in philosophy. Lee instinctively went for profit; MacNaughton for control. The individual preferences accounted for the corporate difference in the companies they ran. ECL sought first to make money, stuck to the traditional formula that had served it so well in the sixties and early seventies, and dismissed PAI's new range of services as inconsequential. Meanwhile PAI strove to grow big. It was building for the future, sacrificing immediate profit in order to build capacity, and in the process had assembled specialists for energy, trade, communications, government procurement, transportation, and social policy.

While PAI became a firm of specialists, ECL remained a company of generalists and continued to reap lucrative profits – which had increased every year since the firm started in 1968. ECL kept operations small. Its full-time personnel consisted of a few senior partners – Lee, Steve Markey, and the aging Irv Keenleyside, until he retired in 1981 and sold his shares to Rick Bertrand, a former vice president of Ottawa Cablevision – and a handful of support staff. ECL did make some informal concessions to specialization. Lee looked after National Defence, Transport, and some Finance; Markey kept an eye on the House of Commons, CIDA, Northern Affairs, and some Transport; Bertrand looked after Communications, FIRA, Consumer Affairs, and broad economic policy; and Keenleyside, until he left, handled Supply and Services. But they were not specialists. They were partners who serviced all clients on all subjects. Who did what often depended on which partner happened to be in the office when a client called. Lee filled ECL's labour needs with retired part-timers such as Harry Boyle, the former chairman of the CRTC; Bob Stead, a former member of the National Energy Board; Jack Rutledge, a former assistant deputy minister of industry, trade and commerce; and Don McDougall, a former executive assistant to various deputy ministers of transport. They came in several days a week and were solid personnel, but all of them were veterans who had retired from the bureaucracy, while Mac-Naughton, for the most part, audaciously hired young, energetic aides with political backgrounds. ECL made a lame attempt at stringing together a network of part-timers in some provincial capitals, but soon abandoned it when the expense proved unrecoverable.

ECL missed out on the energy-client boom that PAI exploited so brilliantly when the government introduced the National Energy Program in 1980. By all rights ECL and not PAI should have bagged the majority of clients, since ECL had been the first to warn about the coming of the NEP. But PAI was aggressive while ECL remained complacent. It had no Harry Near or Marjory Loveys to exploit the moment and by default allowed PAI to market itself as *the* energy consultant.

Soon ECL's reign as the king of the consultants came to an end. PAI surpassed it in billings shortly after the failed merger talks. Nobody knew exactly when. Some said as early as 1981, others pegged it in 1983, while most put it into 1982. The spurt in energy consulting propelled PAI past ECL and the acquisition of Allan Gregg's Decima secured its lead. Of all PAI's innovations, the marrying of public-opinion intelligence with public-affairs intelligence did the most to separate it from the competition. ECL could claim nothing equivalent, could not offer clients insights into public attitudes as PAI could through the Decima *Quarterly*. PAI hung out a very flashy shingle and that, plus the aggressiveness of the principals, appealed to clients. But it was the acquisition of Decima that raised it above ECL in stature. PAI boasted the most comprehensive service in town and became the public-affairs model that ECL once was.

One of ECL's biggest shortcomings was, simply, that Lee scrimped on operations. He hired people only reluctantly and worked so hard at cutting costs that at times he seemed more preoccupied with squeezing existing revenue than in looking for more. ECL still operated out of the Burnside Building where Lee and Neville had begun as a two-man bucket shop in 1968. The premises were far from lavish but the rent was only six dollars a square foot, so ECL stayed and acquired more space as it was needed.

Lee's parsimony dated back many years. He had tasted the Great Depression and had never forgotten the experience. His father had a white-collar job with International Harvester as an office supervisor; one day he returned home with red hands and a blue collar. The company had laid off most of its executives and had put him to work in the twine mill. The Lee family started to eat a lot of bread fried in bacon drippings, and later his father had to tell Lee that he could not send him to university. MacNaughton, by comparison, although also from Hamilton, grew up during the booming fifties and sixties in an upper-middle-dle-class family and after high school took a year off to live in France before enrolling in university. Lee and MacNaughton were products of different generations – and so were ECL and PAI.

Critics alleged that Lee worked so hard keeping ECL lean that he had forgotten to keep an eye on the market, which had turned a corner while ECL kept going straight. By the 1980s, they claimed, many of the companies that were big enough to pay the kind of fees ECL charged had grown sophisticated enough to handle most government problems on their own, and demanded more than general advice and the latest poop on which cabinet ministers were up and down. While PAI cultivated the market, ECL tended to slide along on its charm.

Others said that Bill Lee was too quick and astute to miss a turn in the market; if ECL had fallen into second place it must be because of a deliberate decision by Lee about how he wanted to work. He still dealt with the petty details that MacNaughton had long shrugged off, giving instructions to secretaries and doing things himself. Growing bigger would mean offloading responsibilities on new staff, and would also mean less control, possibly new partners, higher overhead, and interrupted profits, since growth required investment. Lee had been in mid-career when he started ECL, had become a millionaire, and now, nearing 60, had reached the age where he wanted to maximize his take and minimize his risk. The fire in his belly for risk-taking had vanished. Consulting had already been his third career and he had always planned to start a fourth one rather than stick around and innovate. He had never planned to stay as long as he did at ECL and therefore, unlike MacNaughton, had never bothered mapping out a long-term plan. Consequently, ECL, which had the right product in the late sixties and early seventies, grew sleepy regarding innovation just as PAI burst forth with lots of razzle-dazzle.

ECL had one exclusive service that PAI could only dream about. It administered an informal association of associations that operated in secret and was arguably the greatest source of public-policy intelligence in Ottawa. PAI had lost its opportunity to land it before MacNaughton's time, and he rued the day, because PAI had nothing comparable.

In the mid-1970s, the national trade associations woke up to the fact that they all spent a lot of money gathering information on government, but never systematically exchanged it among themselves. The bankers' lobbyist would spend time and money hunting down a piece of intelligence only to go for a drink and discover that his friend, the manufacturers' lobbyist, had had the intelligence in his filing cabinet all along, having gone through the same chase the previous month. Bruce Macdonald of the

Canadian Chemical Producers' Association concluded that associations like his own were spending vast sums in duplicating the intelligence-gathering activities of others, and started pushing for an informal national intelligence pool. Macdonald invited the heads of half a dozen industry associations into the Gold Room of the Rideau Club for sessions to swap notes on the latest developments. It turned out that Macdonald knew what was happening in Energy, Mines and Resources; Andrew Kniewasser of the Investment Dealers Association of Canada was aware of events in the Department of Finance; Ernie Steele of the Canadian Association of Broadcasters had in-depth knowledge of Communications and Secretary of State; and Sam Hughes of the Chamber of Commerce was up to date on several departments. Assembled under one roof and supplemented by a few others with specialized access, they could unearth more secrets than the KGB.

After meeting informally a few times the group invited Lee, of ECL, and Duncan Edmonds, then of PAI, into a Gold Room session and asked each of them to submit proposals for a more formal mechanism. Lee sketched a three-part format and suggested the name "Business Association Interchange". The group liked Lee's plan and appointed ECL as its secretariat. BAI, as it came to be called, grew to comprise twenty-five members and developed into one of the most exclusive clubs in the city, keeping such a low profile as to be almost invisible. The *Financial Post* once mentioned its name in a short item, but otherwise it remained free from journalistic exposure. It took no positions on anything and never lobbied. It merely provided a forum to exchange information so that individual members could lobby more effectively on behalf of their associations.

Each month, except in summer, BAI members assembled in the evening in a private room in the Château Laurier. (In 1986 the venue switched to the newer, more lavish Westin Hotel.) The members swapped their latest findings on government and exchanged views in a free-wheeling round-table discussion. At 7:45 the next morning the group reassembled for an off-the-record breakfast with a guest, usually a senior civil servant or politician. The guest sat at the table with the group, without a podium or a microphone, and was free to say whatever he

Even in the 1960s Bill Lee was a familiar figure on Parliament Hill, a man who knew his way around the corridors of power. (*Photo by Ted Grant*)

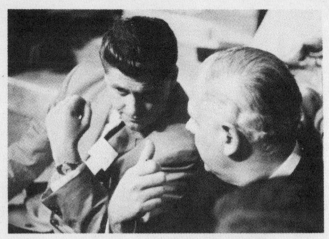

As Paul Hellyer's campaign manager, Lee (*left*) was constantly at Hellyer's side during the Liberal convention in 1968. But for a missed fishing trip Pierre Trudeau might have been in the Hellyer camp, and Canadian history very different.
(*Photo courtesy of Bill Lee*)

Even Judy LaMarsh (seen here with Lee) was unable to persuade Hellyer to combine forces to stop "that bastard" Trudeau. (*Photo courtesy of Bill Lee*)

Lee was promptly hired to run Trudeau's 1968 campaign tour, and was the man behind the stunts that kept Trudeaumania rolling. (*Photo by Inn Studios Ltd.*)

By 1972, although he ran his campaign tour, Lee had become disillusioned with Trudeau, who was less receptive to Lee's advice and to his news that the campaign was not going well. (*Photo by Duncan Cameron*)

As an idealistic young man Duncan Edmonds (*left*) was a moving force in the creation of the Company of Young Canadians. He is shown here in 1965, with (*centre*) Dr. Francis J. Leddy, the chairman of the organizing committee of the CYC, and Prime Minister Lester B. Pearson. (*Photo courtesy of Duncan Edmonds*)

By 1972 Edmonds had become a public affairs consultant and a lecturer who impressed business audiences across the country with his skill in explaining the Ottawa scene. (*Photo courtesy of Duncan Edmonds*)

As Executive Assistant to Don Jamieson, young David MacNaughton gained wide experience. Here he appears (*second from right*) with Jamieson and CN workers at Port aux Basques, Newfoundland. (*Photo courtesy of David MacNaughton*)

MacNaughton (*left*) even accompanied Jamieson to Moscow in 1975, in the course of the Minister's time at External Affairs. All of this was useful background for MacNaughton, now the head of PAI, with ambitions to make it the largest public affairs company in the world. (*Photo courtesy of David MacNaughton*)

After Joe Clark became leader of the Opposition in 1976, he turned to Bill Neville – with Lee, the original Ottawa insider – to run his office, and help him become Prime Minister. The inscription reads: "To Bill – With thanks for your friendship and help. Joe Clark." (*Photo courtesy of Bill Neville*)

To Bill – Just keep 'em laughing. Joe

At Prime Minister Clark's 40th birthday party in June 1979, as his chief of staff Bill Neville (*left*) was one of the main celebrants, along with Maureen McTeer and Catherine. Within six months Clark's government would fall. The inscription reads: "To Bill – Just keep 'em laughing. Joe" (*Photo courtesy of Bill Neville*)

Future lobbyist Paul Curley (*right*) in his role as PC national director looks on while Marcel Masse (*left*) and Don Mazankowski discuss the 1981 party convention in Ottawa. (*Canapress Photo Service*)

ABOVE, LEFT Two of the major Tory backroom figures were Lowell Murray (*left*) now elevated to the Senate, and Allan Gregg, the pollster turned down by the Liberals who became the Tories' secret weapon. (*Photo courtesy of Allan Gregg*)

ABOVE, RIGHT Former Newfoundland Premier Frank Moores, one of Brian Mulroney's closest friends, helped dump Joe Clark and make Mulroney the Tory leader. Later he would become the most free-wheeling Ottawa lobbyist of them all. (*Canapress Photo Service*)

Campaign Director Bill Lee (*left*) had just taken John Turner to victory at the Liberal leadership convention in June 1984 when this triumphant photograph was taken. Within two months he and the new Prime Minister had abruptly parted company in the course of the disastrous election campaign. (*Canapress Photo Service*)

After Brian Mulroney's sweeping victory in 1984, Bill Neville, a keen supporter of the St. Louis Cardinals, received this signed photograph from the new Conservative Prime Minister. The inscription reads: "Bill – Baie Comeau is not St. Louis but the Cards never won this big! With gratitude Brian and Mila"
(*Photo courtesy of Bill Neville*)

wanted, but could not give a speech or read from a prepared text.
BAI kept the atmosphere informal and encouraged the guest to be
candid, promising absolute anonymity for anything said, since
the mere fact that he appeared was classified as a secret. The
guest usually – but not always – spoke briefly and then threw
the session open to questions. The secrecy and informality
encouraged openness and worked amazingly well. Ministers
described fights in cabinet and revealed hidden agendas that
they would deny in public. The anonymity rule was never violated and BAI never lacked for guests, sometimes entertaining
two guests and occasionally three. Politicians and mandarins did
not need to be persuaded to come. They often asked to appear.
The president of the post office, for example, outlined plans for
cutting costs and dealing with unions. When Trudeau returned
to power in 1980, Michael Pitfield, the clerk of the privy council,
gave details of the government's priorities and sketched its
agenda. There was hardly a minister or deputy minister who did
not appear at least once before BAI, and most showed up several
times.

After the guests withdrew, BAI moved into routine business
and around 10:30 a.m. ECL swung into action with its Ottawa
Overview. For an hour and a half Lee, Markey, Bertrand, and later
Sandra Severn used slides and an overhead projector to run
through the government's legislative schedule and relate how
different bills were faring in the Commons pipeline. The Ottawa
Overview served up a potpourri of news on what was happening
on the political agenda and on which ministers or bureaucrats
were rising and falling in the game of political snakes and
ladders. It covered everything from the Prime Minister's Office
to the Department of Veterans' Affairs.

In terms of revenue, ECL earned the equivalent of about one
good client – about $70,000 in 1986 – from BAI members, but
money was almost a peripheral benefit. BAI helped generate new
clients for ECL, which was far more valuable than a single fee,
giving Lee's company access to a broad range of association managers who recommended ECL when their member companies
were looking for strategic advice on government. BAI also netted
ECL free intelligence. As the secretariat, ECL sat in on the round-
table and picked up some information that had escaped its net.

To some extent BAI provided ECL with in-house specialists because the members themselves were specialists in the major sectors of government.

No other firms in Ottawa could really compare themselves to PAI and ECL. Corporation House Ltd., founded in 1945 and led by Eric Hehner for much of its history, grossed more than $500,000 in 1980 and represented a range of big corporations, but concentrated on the public service and stayed out of the political field. Specializing mainly in technical matters, such as tax and tariff items, it acted primarily as an advocate, often appearing before official boards and tribunals on its clients' behalf. ECL sometimes referred clients to Corporation House and occasionally worked on joint cases, but did not compete with it. They both helped clients who had problems with government, but otherwise were in different businesses.

Most public-affairs firms operated as one- or two-person shops, and tended to specialize. Many came and went; others did exceedingly well, such as Marshall Crowe, the former chairman of the National Energy Board, now an energy lobbyist who kept a low profile and had clients like Dome Petroleum and Mobil Oil in New York. Most of the competition in Ottawa came from lawyers who lobbied under the guise of practising law.

Reisman and Grandy Ltd. showed initial signs of emerging into a major force. The company started with flair in 1975 when Simon Reisman, a loud, arrogant, and obnoxious, but effective, deputy minister of finance, quit the public service and formed a partnership with Jim Grandy, an equally effective but quiet deputy minister. Together they took on big clients. Reisman and Grandy were opposite personality types who clicked as a team, but in one important area they did not differ; at the time both were mid-fiftyish former civil servants more interested in earning big fees than in pushing the frontiers of innovation. Consequently Reisman and Grandy Ltd., with clients like Lockheed and Weston, became an economic success – and a public-affairs also-ran.

At the same time Tom d'Aquino launched himself as a force in public-affairs consulting. D'Aquino, a prematurely balding, fashionably dressed whirlwind of energy and ambition, came to

Ottawa in 1968 as EA to Minister without Portfolio Jim Richardson, and a year later joined Trudeau's office as a special assistant until 1972 when he went to Europe as a lawyer-consultant. He returned to Ottawa in 1975 and set up Intercounsel Ltd., an élite public-affairs consulting company that dealt only with chief executive officers. The hyper-active d'Aquino picked up blue-chip clients like the Royal Bank and Gulf Canada and such foreign-based giants as Mars, Time Inc., and Unilever. He also acquired a string of U.S. border broadcasters unhappy with Canadian restrictions on advertising. On behalf of another client, the Business Council on National Issues, he did a study on parliamentary government which later became a model for a Commons committee studying parliamentary reform. Intercounsel grew to eleven people, including support staff, and had started challenging ECL and PAI when d'Aquino's client, BCNI, hired him as its full-time president in 1981, thus making him the highly visible spokesman for 150 or so of Canada's top chief executive officers. D'Aquino pared down Intercounsel into a small and discreet sideline, until five years later he disbanded it entirely. With the withdrawal of Intercounsel, PAI and ECL had the market sewn up between them. They were the only two firms of significant size, and competitors could do little more than nibble for crumbs around the edges. In the eighties, however, a pocket of competition started growing out of Toronto, most notably from a new entrant named Susan Murray.

Like Lee and MacNaughton, Susan Murray came from Hamilton, but there the similarity ended. She graduated from the University of Western Ontario in 1976 in honours political science with an interest in public housing as an issue, and leaning towards a career as a civil servant. She landed a job as researcher for the Conservative caucus at Queen's Park in Toronto, and that job introduced her to the pillars in Ontario's Big Blue Machine. The following year she ran the Tory youth campaign in the 1977 Ontario election and then moved up to become a vice president of the Conservative Party in Ontario. Her stint at Queen's Park convinced her that business carried such ill-conceived notions of government and came so poorly prepared that it usually lost out to smart, well-prepared public-interest groups like Pollution Probe.

The lack of understanding between business and government

bothered her. She couldn't understand how corporations operating in a country like Canada, with such a strong history of government intervention, could lag behind virtually every other country in awareness of public policy. So she decided to become a broker between the two camps, and in 1980 joined with the veteran consultant Jon Kieran to form Kieran and Murray Inc. Murray handled the marketing, which seemed a little odd because she barely looked her 27 years, was thin on experience, and possessed no hot leads in the search for clients. She happened to be a blonde bombshell who at first blush seemed better suited for a beauty contest than a boardroom; her petite size, soft voice, and shy manner seemed unlikely to persuade a hardheaded chief executive officer that he needed her expensive advice.

Murray read the newspaper and assembled a list of prospective clients by working out which companies, in her opinion, needed a government-affairs strategy, and then started making cold calls. She got a lot of rejections. But then she happened to phone Victor Rice, the chairman of Massey-Ferguson Ltd., just as the banks were threatening to foreclose on his company. Rice needed $200-million to stave off bankruptcy, had exhausted all the private options, and now concluded that his only hope lay in government assistance. Massey-Ferguson had no director of government relations and lacked even a strategy for approaching government. Murray met Rice for lunch the next day and within twenty-four hours signed up her first client. She started her lobbying career working on what was until then the largest corporate refinancing in Canadian history, and in doing so showed that she was determined, shrewd, and brimming with down-to-earth common sense.

Both Ottawa and Ontario flatly rejected Massey-Ferguson's appeal for funds. Chrysler, Dome Petroleum, and a couple of western banks had yet to tumble, so Massey-Ferguson's demand for government backstopping attracted controversy and created outraged headlines. Murray and Kieran first assembled a strategy to contain the political shellshock for government, and then, after long sessions with Rice and his management team, developed the case that, with seven thousand jobs at stake, the economic and social cost of bankruptcy outweighed the cost of a bailout. The strategy also consisted of asking not for a loan guarantee but for an equity guarantee, whereby government would buy Massey-Ferguson stock as the banks called in their loans.

The negotiations dragged on for months. They involved two hundred banks around the world, as well as the U.K. government, because of Massey-Ferguson's big interests in Britain. Murray became emotionally involved in the rescue effort and jumped in to lobby; she personally petitioned every federal cabinet minister in Ottawa, and every provincial minister in Toronto, so that when the deal ultimately reached their respective cabinet tables, she could count on more yesses than noes. The federal government, however, kept changing its position, and seemed to be foot-dragging. About 48 hours before the Ontario Tories called a provincial election in late winter 1981, Murray called her old friend and adviser Tom Scott, and asked if the collapse of Massey-Ferguson in the middle of an election campaign would hurt the government. Scott said it would indeed. Murray then asked if somebody from Ontario could exert pressure on Ottawa. This was done. At times only twenty-four hours separated the company from bankruptcy, and on one occasion Premier Bill Davis had to intercede directly with Trudeau to keep the talks from foundering. At one point Murray spent four days in a hotel room, locked in almost constant negotiations. Ultimately Ottawa acceded, but not before extracting a series of concessions, including the requirement that Massey-Ferguson should move all U.S. plants and jobs to Canada. But Susan Murray had pulled off the impossible.

The two-year contract with Massey-Ferguson was about to expire when Murray largely did herself out of a job by recommending that the company hire a director of government relations. After Massey-Ferguson, nothing intimidated Murray; she wanted to expand, while her partner Kieran wanted to keep things small, so in August 1982 she struck out on her own as S. A. Murray Consulting Inc. and opened a small office on Front Street in Toronto with herself and a secretary.

There she spent her first three months without a client. For eighteen months she had done almost nothing except Massey-Ferguson, and now she had no cushion to fall back on.

As a volunteer project on behalf of the Ontario Conservative party, she happened to be organizing a seminar on government relations for senior executives with Premier Bill Davis, Larry Grossman, and Allan Gregg among the speakers. More than a hundred corporations signed up, including Carling O'Keefe, the brewing company which wanted to introduce long-necked beer bottles to help stave off competition from white wine and other beverages, but was being stymied by an unwilling Ontario government. Carling O'Keefe retained Murray, who put together a lobbying package that portrayed the beer industry as a declining area which might have to lay off workers within eighteen months. First she got the bureaucracy on side and then won over the minister, and within six months got the regulations loosened so that brewers could abandon the stubbies. Carling O'Keefe launched Miller Beer in 1983 and captured ten per cent of the market within three months, which made it the most successful launch ever. Long-necked bottles boosted sales for all companies.

Carling O'Keefe remained her only retainer client for almost a year, but soon word spread that she had saved Massey-Ferguson and shored up the brewing industry, and thereafter her volume doubled each year. Murray acquired clients like the Royal Bank, Eli Lilly, Duracell, CARA, and the Insurance Bureau of Canada. Tom Scott joined as a silent partner in much the way he invested in Decima Research at the beginning, and in November 1983 S.A. Murray Consulting Inc. hired its first consultant, the former journalist Diana Crosbie, and moved to better quarters. Murray would soon hire more consultants and in a couple of years would staff an Ottawa office and begin to compete directly with PAI and ECL.

ECL might have slipped, but Lee still had the personal touch that had made the company successful in the first place. A colleague complained admiringly that he once thought up a brilliant idea which he honed and fine tuned and then unveiled at an ECL management meeting. Lee played with it for a second, adding one or two deft twists that reshaped it ever so slightly into something absolutely perfect. The originator pounded himself on the forehead and asked: "Why didn't I think of that?" Lee had the magic touch, but he also reeked common sense and understood what drove a client, and clients still asked for him. Sometimes clients came in to transact business with Markey or Bertrand, but they liked to know that Lee was around, just in case. Some clients waited for Lee to return from Florida before asking ECL for strategic advice.

While PAI chose to become bipartisan – with MacNaughton and Mike Robinson tied to the Liberals, while Allan Gregg and Harry Near moved with the Tories, ECL deliberately moved toward neutrality and withdrew from the political wars. In the 1980s Bill Lee no longer cut the broad swathe he had in the 1960s. Since his split with Trudeau after the 1972 election he had distanced himself from the Liberal Party and was politically inactive in the 1974, 1979, and 1980 election campaigns. He still kept in touch with his network of contacts, of course, and knew more about what happened inside government than many plugged-in Liberals, but he also spent increasing time with conservative (and Conservative) business colleagues. Political neutrality was safe, but it was dull and didn't do much to capture clients. A neutral firm could dig up information and offer advice as well as any other, but could not market itself as easily, since clients still believed that firms with the right political connections offered an inside track.

ECL's image as a political neutral would soon change dramatically. Bill Lee was about to come roaring out of political retirement and return to the centre of power in a way that would upstage PAI and his other rivals.

FOURTEEN

TURNER FOR LEADER

Shortly after John Turner quit the Trudeau cabinet in 1975 to practise law in Toronto he phoned his friend and close adviser, John deB. Payne. Two of his clients, Bechtel Canada Ltd., the Canadian subsidiary of the multinational engineering-construction giant, and Racetracks of Canada Inc., needed public-affairs counsel. He wanted to know whom to choose: Bill Lee at ECL or Torrance Wylie at PAI. Payne recommended ECL because he believed it provided better all-round service. By taking that piece of advice, Turner started a long-term business connection with Lee, which led to other fields and other clients.

Turner was now a lawyer and operated out of a law firm, but he didn't practice conventional law. He acted more as a super-salesman, slapping backs around boardroom tables, and as a consultant marshalling together groups of lawyers on big items. He often needed Lee's advice on public affairs. Lee worked with Turner and his partner, Bill Macdonald, on strategy for the Independent Petroleum Association of Canada (after IPAC left PAI) in its attempts to overturn the hated National Energy Program. Lee grew to know Turner better as a lawyer in Toronto than he had as a cabinet minister in Ottawa. Turner, meanwhile, used Lee to keep himself abreast of political developments in Ottawa, and introduced him to Toronto business circles.

Many observers regarded Turner's return to Ottawa as inevitable and wondered when, not if, he would come back to claim the throne from Prime Minister Trudeau. Turner wondered, too. In 1983, with Quebec secure, and the constitution home in Ottawa, Trudeau had completed the tasks that had most compelled him. The press began openly speculating about his retirement and started guessing the date.

"Look," Turner told Lee over the telephone late in the summer of that year, "there are rumours around that the old bastard is finally going to retire."

Turner was uncommonly polite that day. He usually called Pierre Trudeau worse than "the old bastard"; four-letter words rolled off Turner's lips the way hamburgers streamed off McDonald's grill, especially when the subject was his old rival Trudeau.

"I'll believe it when I see it," Lee replied.

"I'm putting together a small group of trusted people to meet with me in Toronto every three weeks or a month," Turner explained. "No agenda. Just to help me make up my mind what I should do if the old bastard does retire."

Turner's invitation meant a return to active politics, and Lee had little desire for another term on the political battlefield. He was nearing 60, was wealthy, and had started spending time at his condominium in Florida. Taking political sides again after twelve years of partisan celibacy made no corporate sense. Lee now had almost as many connections among senior Tories as among Liberals, and at this stage of its development ECL's best interest lay in staying clear of the political roller coaster. Lee had every reason to say no, but said yes.

Something still tugged the old political warhorse towards one more joust. He had once signed an undertaking to write a book called *The Making of a Prime Minister* on how he had triumphantly propelled Paul Hellyer into 24 Sussex Drive. Circumstances – the sudden rise of Pierre Trudeau, coupled with Hellyer's last-minute flub – had spoiled the plan and killed the book, but the wish to make somebody a prime minister still lived. He had nearly pulled it off in 1968 with an ungainly candidate. Now he wondered what he could do with the Hollywood looks, blue eyes, winning smiles, and personal magnetism of John Turner. Turner, the Rhodes Scholar who had danced with Princess Margaret, looked irresistible. He carried an aura of glamour, and combined freshness with years of experience. Turner had so much going for him that he was not so much a candidate as a weapon.

Another reason compelled Lee to say yes. He genuinely believed that Canada needed John Turner as prime minister and that nobody else could match his unique qualifications for the job. Lee mourned September 10 1975 as a black day – the day Turner, at the peak of his power, had quit the cabinet and walked out on Pierre Trudeau. On that day, Lee felt, Canada had lost the last major voice of moderation inside the Trudeau cabinet. From then on he saw the government shifting irretrievably away from creating wealth to distributing it. The unexpected return of the Trudeau government in 1980 ushered in what Lee described as a horrible period where the cabinet capitulated completely to economic nationalism and interventionism. Only Turner possessed the stature and the will to move the government back and set things right. What better way to culminate a career than make a prime minister out of a philosophical soulmate, and replace Pierre Trudeau at the same time?

As a cabinet minister Turner had occupied the conservative side of the pragmatic centre, but eight years in Toronto had moved him so far right that he was now the darling of the corporate world. Turner's close friend, Bill Macdonald, the man behind Paul Hellyer's infamous speech, recruited him into McMillan Binch and opened the door to a string of board memberships. He also helped Turner write some ill-advised newsletters that got him into trouble with Jean Chrétien, the Trudeau government, and a good portion of the Liberal Party. A man who leaned so far right that people constantly wondered at what he was doing in the Liberal Party, Macdonald influenced Turner politically too. Turner entered McMillan Binch as a middle-of-the-roader and during his time there grew into a true-blue spokesman for the corporate community.

Lee wasted no time getting to work. He took soundings in the Liberal caucus and asked party members across the country who they would support if Trudeau stepped down. Some MPs resented Turner for those dumb newsletters but also calculated that only he could beat Mulroney. Trudeau's fall in the Gallup poll made Turner's leadership much more palatable for many Liberal MPs. The public favoured the Mulroney-led Conservatives by margins reaching thirty points. Turner, the only credible candidate not tied to Trudeau, held the best chance of turning the polls around and keeping the party in power. The same MPs who had once resented Turner for walking out on them now saw things differently. Turner's biggest liability had become his greatest strength, a turnaround that convinced Lee that Turner could win the party leadership.

Beginning in September 1983, Turner periodically rode the elevator down from the thirty-eighth floor in the Royal Bank Building and walked through the busy underground tunnel that led directly into the Royal York Hotel. There, on the mezzanine floor, he secretly met Lee and five other confidants in the old-fashioned spendour of the hotel's Newfoundland Room. He kept the meetings secret from his law partners and, more particularly, from his wife Geills. "For God's sake," Turner cautioned his advisers at the outset, "let's not let this out of this room. Geills doesn't know I'm even thinking about this yet."

Besides Turner and Lee, the room included Payne, Turner's alter ego, who had been advising him since he first ran for Parliament from Montreal in 1962; John Swift, a Vancouver lawyer and his former EA; Rick Alway, the warden of Hart House at the University of Toronto; Irene Robinson, a longtime Toronto Liberal pro; and, surprisingly, Bob Foulkes, the former EA to Judd Buchanan who a decade earlier had brought PAI's Mike Robinson to Ottawa. Foulkes worked in Calgary as an executive for Petro-Canada, the company that Turner vehemently opposed.

The meeting studied the results of a custom survey by Peter Hart, the U.S. pollster who worked for the Democratic presidential candidate Walter Mondale. Hart found good name recognition in Turner, but without much content. The recognition hinged largely on an old memory people had of Turner as the best minister in Trudeau's government. He registered solidly as a man of integrity and substance, which was impressive for somebody out of the news for most of a decade – but not too much could be read into that, because Trudeau also showed up well on those counts. Turner came on most strongly with older male Liberals but faded noticeably with women. He fared unsatisfactorily among young Canadians who, as a group, hardly remembered him; they had heard about this legendary prince in exile, but generally associated him with board memberships and the Toronto business establishment.

The Hart figures did not conflict with Gallup's findings showing the Liberals lagging far behind the Conservatives; in fact Gallup had done the poll on Hart's behalf. But Hart went one step further than Gallup and, after asking people how they planned to vote, asked which party they preferred. Here the numbers broke out differently. The Liberals scored a stunning 52 per cent as Canada's party of preference. Voters preferred the Liberals as the governing party even when they voted against it. The results confirmed the Liberal-majority phenomenon that had dogged Joe Clark four years earlier, and supported Lee's long-held opinion that Turner had to distance himself from the current government to win. Turner had to avoid links with Trudeau and appear to be substantially different from him, which for Turner was as easy as spitting out another four-letter word.

Lee reported to the group that Trudeau was leaning toward retirement but was being pressured to stay on by senior advisers such as Senator Keith Davey and Tom Axworthy. He also reported that Jean Chrétien had quietly begun his campaign and was actively rounding up MPs, that Don Johnston was setting up an organization, and that even Gerry Regan, the former premier of Nova Scotia, was sniffing around. Others around the table followed with their reports. Turner asked questions and traded quips but kept his intentions to himself, forbidding everyone to do anything to tip his hand. He wanted no footprints, even if it meant entering the campaign from a standing start. Turner repeated that Geills knew nothing and made it plain that he wanted it to stay that way.

Turner could feel his options dwindling. The allure of being prime minister enticed him, but he wanted no risks. He had much to lose and wanted to be assured of winning before plunging into the race. He would be trading a huge salary, ten corporate directorships, and a good social scene for life in a fishbowl and a 20- or 30-point deficit in the Gallup poll. Yet he had promised his mother he would be prime minister someday, and that covenant compelled him towards tackling the challenge. The obligation burdened him even more after Alzheimer's disease disabled his mother, as if it was one thing he could do to lessen her plight.

On the other hand Turner lacked the fire in his belly, the compelling ambition a politician almost inevitably needed to force his way into the highest post in the land. Opportunity had knocked in 1979 when Trudeau resigned – temporarily as it turned out – but hours of soul-searching could not convince Turner to surrender his lifestyle and the income that accompanied it. After backing out he fretted about breaking the news to his mother and Geills – who then wanted him to run – and his sister Brenda. Now that it seemed Trudeau would be retiring again – presumably permanently – Turner, according to one friend, quietly prayed that the decision would vanish.

As Turner agonized, the Royal York group weighed the pros and cons. Turner started with political advantages other contenders could only dream about. He entered as the frontrunner, the heir apparent since 1968, and stood to benefit from the general feeling that John Turner's time had finally come. He had a beautiful wife and kids and a golden background. He had roots in Vancouver, Montreal, Ottawa, and Toronto. And he could rightly claim to be the last finance minister to bring down a surplus.

Two problems – aside from the danger of a backlash breaking out over his enmity towards Trudeau – bothered the Royal York committee. First, Turner refused to resign his corporate directorships. His boards included Canadian Pacific Ltd., Seagram Co. Ltd., Massey-Ferguson Ltd., Bechtel Canada Ltd., Sandoz (Canada) Ltd., Marathon Realty Ltd., Holt Renfrew & Co. Ltd., and MacMillan Bloedel Ltd. His advisers unanimously recommended that he get off all boards the minute he entered the race, but no amount of pleading, cajoling, or pressure could convince Turner to give them up when he didn't have to. He would sooner not run than resign his prized directorships. His stubbornness made him a sitting target for charges of conflict of interest and for snide comments about being the candidate from Canadian Pacific.

Something else threatened to embarrass Turner. Ticking away like a time bomb, ready to blow up his political prospects, was CFI Investments Ltd., a tax-shelter film company which had recently collapsed and was dragging its acrimonious way through court. CFI had flaunted Turner as chairman when selling shares to the public and now the whole enterprise had gone belly-up. Lee waited in dread for the day some hard-up widows would appear before television cameras with stories of how they had invested their savings because Mr. Turner had recommended it, and now they had lost everything. At the very best it would make Turner look like a bad businessman, and could easily depict him as a snake-oil salesman who had fleeced gullible investors, and besmirch his unstained image. All Turner could do was cross his fingers and hope for the best.

Turner and his Royal York advisers quickly agreed that he would not attack Trudeau publicly. Enough distance already separated the two antagonists; further sniping would damage Turner within the party. Many Liberals still regarded Trudeau as a great man and Turner needed their support, since he had to show that he could appeal to all wings of the party. When the Trudeau issue arose Turner would respond by calling him the most remarkable Canadian of his generation and leave it at that. The meetings also resolved to keep Turner above the fray by refusing to make deals with other politicians. Ministers and MPs who supported his candidacy would get no promise of reward. The "no deals" policy would leave him free to assemble the best talent for his cabinet.

The meetings continued through the fall of 1983 and into the winter of 1984, and Turner's enthusiasm picked up with each session. He complained less about surrendering a lucrative law practice and talked more about the political opportunity. The odds in favour of his running had grown to ninety per cent or better.

"All right," Turner said in early 1984, "if we're going to have a leadership campaign we've got to have a campaign manager – somebody who will run it."

"There's only one person in our group who has ever run a leadership campaign and that's Bill Lee," Foulkes responded.

"Hold it," Lee said. "Wait a minute."

Lee said the campaign needed somebody who was a woman, young, and bilingual and he flunked all three. Besides, he said, he had a business to run and had no desire to get so deeply involved in the political fray. Lee promised to suggest names, eventually proposing Heather Peterson, who worked in the Prime Minister's Office and was the wife of Jim Peterson, Turner's law partner. But everyone still awaited Turner's decision, which awaited Trudeau's.

"I don't think the son of a bitch is ever going to quit," Turner grumbled in early 1984, when Trudeau had nearly reached the end of his fourth year and continued to hang on. Turner and his advisers speculated about whether he was deliberately crowding their options or maybe worse; they took it for granted that Trudeau would not be going out of his way to do Turner any favours.

Turner left for Jamaica to holiday and ponder and, they hoped, make up his mind. The Royal York group met without him, and Swift announced that Turner had agreed, upon becoming prime minister, to appoint him principal secretary and Bob Foulkes – who was absent that day – his senior policy adviser for sums substantially above the public-service pay scale. In addition, Swift would be remunerated for a tax problem arising from his resignation from his law firm, and Foulkes would get compensation for a mortgage differential caused by the drop in the Calgary real-estate market. The salaries would put them well into the six-figure bracket and give them more than the prime minister. Swift wanted the group to understand that both he and Foulkes were earning good money in business and needed special arrangements to join Turner.

The room fell tensely silent. Finally Lee, the old Ottawa hand, objected that the planned salaries grossly exceeded what their predecessors made.

"Maybe so," Swift said, "but I don't give a damn. That's what we need to give up our positions in Vancouver and Calgary."

Swift and Lee sparred for a minute, glaring at each other, until Alway interjected: "I don't want to get into this thing. It's John Turner's decision. The main thing is we must never let this get out during the leadership campaign." A few amens were muttered, and the subject was dropped. The old John Turner, who was notorious for underpaying his staff and returning part of his office budget at the end of the year, never would have agreed to such a scheme.

Turner was gone about a week when, on February 29, Trudeau announced that he was retiring as prime minister and leader of the Liberal Party.

"Well," Turner replied when Payne phoned him in Jamaica, "I guess I've got to tell Geills."

Turner wanted more time to think about his decision. Payne issued an announcement saying Turner would not make a statement until March 16, believing that a public deadline would force Turner to stop dithering.

The dithering proved to be contagious. Geills Turner at first supported her husband's wish to run, and then changed her mind an hour later. After thinking it over, she didn't want to leave Toronto for the world of raw politics. Her change of heart seemed to kill the candidacy before it started. Turner's advisers couldn't believe it: who would be the next prime minister of Canada was being decided by where Geills Turner wanted to live. Then the Turner children rallied behind their father and persuaded their mother he should be allowed to run if that was what he wanted to do. After a lot of discussion, Turner was back in business.

Economic Development Minister Don Johnston was the first to jump into the race – only nine days after Trudeau's announcement – followed quickly by Justice Minister Mark MacGuigan. Before long Turner, Energy Minister Jean Chrétien, Indian Affairs Minister John Munro, and Employment Minister John Roberts joined the race. Even Agriculture Minister Eugene Whelan threw his hat into the ring.

On March 14, two days before the press conference, Lee handed Turner the statement that would officially tell the country he was running for the Liberal leadership and then told Turner he was off to Florida for some holidaying and a lot of spring-training baseball. Turner urged him – almost pleaded with him – to stay and see him through his declaration. Lee was surprised. Turner seemed awfully nervous for somebody who had first run for the job of prime minister at the age of 38. So he delayed his departure a couple of days, sending his wife to Florida alone and digging into his pocket to exchange his cheap air ticket for a regular one. Some people suspected that Lee was playing hard to get with all this Florida stuff and would eventually run the campaign, but he insisted that he was serious.

"Today I return to public life," Turner announced in the packed theatre in the National Press Building across the street from Parliament Hill. Reporters treated the announcement more as a coronation than as the launch of a contested campaign. The procession, however, was snarled by an ill-judged remark. While answering a question, Turner called bilingualism in Manitoba "a provincial initiative" which needed a provincial solution. His answer clashed in spirit with Liberal government policy, and the French-language press denounced him, as did Brian Mulroney and many others. Worse, Quebec MPs threatened to withdraw their support if he did not endorse Trudeau's policy of supporting the introduction of French-language services across the country. The following week – by this time Lee was in Florida, and out of the campaign – Turner issued a carefully crafted four-page clarification that found the right words to defuse the issue.

Chrétien said Turner had "fumbled the ball on the first play", and indeed he had. Furthermore, it soon became apparent that his fumble could not be dismissed as bad luck or a rare slip. Right from the start, Turner failed to articulate the leadership people expected of him. He nervously cleared his throat machine-gun style, wet his lips constantly, and generally seemed so awkward and uncomfortable that he became an irresistible target for parody. He stuck ploddingly to his pocket-sized cue cards and dared not speak without notes. While the other candidates circulated and chatted backstage before an all-candidates debate, Turner sat alone in a corner and read his cards, or just watched the others. Campaign watchers dubbed it "the rust factor".

Lee had expected some rustiness. Before Turner left for Jamaica to ponder his political future, Lee had dictated a synopsis of 74 issues a prime-ministerial candidate needed to know, and advised Turner to study them while on holiday. Each topic carried a brief historical background, the factors bearing upon it and a recommended policy position. Lee put the package inside a grey suede leather binder bearing the name William Davis in silver.

"Now if you leave it on the beach somewhere they'll blame it on Bill Davis," Lee chuckled. "They'll think he's trying to overthrow Mulroney."

"Holy Jesus," Turner replied, "Seventy-four issues. I've got to learn all these?"

Lee told him he needed to know more like 574, but 74 would do for a start. Turner flipped through the book and grumbled over the necessity for learning about Manitoba language rights. On the Manitoba language issue the book steered a careful course between the competing wishes of Quebec and Manitoba delegates and served up a politically safe answer. In the first hour of his candidacy Turner stumbled with an answer leaning in favour of Manitoba anglophones.

A month later in Montreal Turner gave the impression that he supported Quebec's Bill 101, the controversial language charter, which curtailed the use of English. Headlines declared Turner's support, throwing Quebec anglophones into a flap until Turner again backed off with a clarification. When Chrétien, as energy minister, was asked in the Commons about a Turner statement regarding offshore revenues for Newfoundland, he set the chamber roaring with laughter by saying: "Mr. Speaker, I will wait for the clarification."

For the first time it appeared that Turner could lose.

The rust had spread everywhere and perforated every part of his performance; eight years of neglect had taken its toll. Turner had once been a solid stump speaker, but now he appeared rough and disorganized on the podium. In contrast to Chrétien's rousing and inspiring speeches, he spoke in staccato bursts, pausing in mid-sentence as if gathering steam for another truncated outburst of words. The old Turner had handled questions from the audience adroitly, but now, as he groped for responses, it was clear that his old skill had abandoned him. He had fallen out of touch with politics and even with mainstream society. He raised Bobby Kennedy as a symbol, not realizing that the magic of the Kennedy name had long disappeared. Without the help of aides, briefings, and cabinet documents, John Turner was a shadow of the political figure he had once been. The man who as minister of justice had conceived the Victoria Formula had fallen so far out of touch that he had never read the new constitution. "It's so boring," he once admitted.

At least part of the reason Turner expressed himself so badly was that he had little to say. In the whole campaign, he produced not a single exciting idea or vision, and backed away from specifics whenever he could. His unfamiliarity with the latest issues earned him a reputation as a 1970s man running in the 1980s. The practice of corporate law had clearly narrowed his interests and cramped his perspective; while great leaders like Churchill and de Gaulle had used their periods of exile to ponder the use of power, Turner had chosen to live the good life, have a good time, and surround himself with sycophants. He brought no personal manifesto to the campaign other than a desire to chop the federal deficit and stimulate business growth. Audiences often dismissed him as indecisive without realizing that he fundamentally lacked an integrated philosophy, or the courage or ability to articulate it. His performance hit bottom in Richmond, B.C., where one delegate asked about the province's pulp and paper industry and Turner said he didn't know the answer. "Aren't you on the board of directors of MacMillan Bloedel?" the delegate asked. Yes, Turner replied, adding lamely that that didn't mean anything.

His shell-shocked staff watched him learn issues from week to week. They saw him mishandle questions and stumble from one mistake to another. Even Payne, the éminence grise who had known Turner as a young Montreal lawyer, had not realized how far he had slipped. Any other candidate would have been laughed out of the campaign, but two things saved Turner from the ignominious fate of an also-ran. First, he learned quickly, didn't often repeat mistakes, and improved as the campaign progressed. He was known as a "quick brief". Second, and more importantly, he was John Turner. The media clung to the notion of the exiled prince returning to claim his kingdom, and that alone made people take him seriously.

His campaign organization performed little better than the candidate. The sleek Turner machine, supposedly sitting in readiness for most of a decade, in reality ran more like an old jalopy with missing parts. It choked and stalled as quickly and as often as Turner did. He had surrounded himself with yesterday's political advisers, some of whom were as rusty as he was. Volunteers offering to work were turned away because nobody knew what to do with them; early delegate-selection meetings in Quebec produced disappointing results; the campaign had no buttons or posters. After three weeks the Turner team had failed to select something as simple as campaign colours.

From reading the Toronto *Star* and the *Globe and Mail* in sunny Florida every day, Lee could tell that things were going badly. Besides, people phoned him to moan about the latest foul-up, every night bringing in a new horror story and a plea to come back and clean up the mess. After a while Lee promised to come if Turner asked. Early in April, Turner called from Regina and told him the campaign was falling apart and needed him to pull it together. The old warhorse was back in harness.

Lee flew to Toronto and went directly to the Turner headquarters in College Park. "I want to start at eight o'clock tomorrow morning and I want to see everybody one on one," he told the assembled staff that evening. The next morning the root of the problem emerged: John Turner was both candidate and campaign manager. He ran the show from the campaign trail and made decisions on day-to-day matters over the telephone. That meant that each senior officer had a personal connection with Turner; at committee meetings they pushed their plans and fought for turf in Turner's name. Inevitably the meetings broke into petty feuds, with some staffers refusing to talk to each other, and Payne spending his evenings pacifying the various factions. Nothing happened because nobody agreed on anything.

The reason the campaign had no colours was that the colour committee had broken into two deadlocked factions. One bloc pushed for blue and the other for red. The committee finally succumbed to the lunacy of trying to resolve the impasse by commissioning a $12,000 survey into people's colour preference by the Winnipeg pollster Angus Reid. Meanwhile the campaign limped along with black and white. Lee disbanded the committee, cancelled the survey, and had a staffer line up the other candidates' colours alongside alternatives against the wall in his office. Lee pointed to red and yellow and proclaimed them the official colours, and instructed the staff to get the buttons, posters, and banners out.

Lee quickly convinced Turner that he had to stop intruding into the campaign and put everything into his hands, so that everything flowed through him. When asked for a campaign decision, he was to say "Check it with Lee." The only campaign player reporting independently to Turner was Payne, his political confidant and sounding board for more than twenty years.

With the three-month campaign not a month old, Lee discovered that two-thirds of the budget was either spent or committed, and that funds would run out before the halfway mark unless changes were made. While the Turner platform advocated development of Canadian technology, the campaign had ordered a $274,000 (in American funds) computer from New York. Customs duty alone amounted to $10,000. "We're going to be murdered in the press," Lee said. "And we can't afford it." He cancelled the order and for $24,000 bought, second-hand, the Canadian computer Brian Mulroney had used in his leadership victory the previous year. (As it turned out, the computer, intended for delegate tracking, went largely unused.)

Lee chose "Win With Turner" as the campaign slogan, calculating that it would appeal to delegates because above everything else the Liberal Party wanted to keep power. He added a schedule of policy pronouncements to give the campaign more substance, and began to control more closely what Turner said and when he said it. Although Lee personally shared Turner's right-wing philosophy, he moved him more to the centre and repeatedly told him to remember that two-thirds of the 3,400 delegates could fit into the NDP. Lee moved Turner to the left for the strictly pragmatic reason that the right wing already supported him. He urged him – not always successfully – to play down the deficit and other right-wing initiatives such as privatizing Crown corporations. Turner talked privately about eliminating universality for social programs, but Lee told him not to discuss it during a leadership campaign.

Lee next sought to scrape off some of the rust. He coached Turner on presentation and scheduled him to speak to more small groups, where he tended to relax. Since the polls showed that Turner's weakness among women stemmed from his macho demeanour and his apparent lack of sympathy for women's issues, Lee got him to curb his jock tendencies. Putting him in touch with the heads of influential women's groups, Lee told him to lay off his lusty language for the rest of the campaign. More than half the delegates were women, and he needed to improve his standing with them.

Finally, Lee sought to tame Turner's impulse for retaliation. Whenever opponents sniped at him, he instinctively wanted to lash back, especially when attacked over his refusal to resign his board memberships. "Be nice to them," Lee counselled. "They can't get you that way." Lee said he couldn't afford to be nasty to the other leadership candidates because he would need their delegates on later ballots. Every time he attacked an opponent he criticized the first choice of some of the delegates he would later be calling on. "Remember our credo," Lee told him before the policy debates. "They can say anything they want about you. But you don't say anything but positive things about them."

Above all else, Turner was not to criticize Trudeau, which was the policy set out right at the start in the Royal York meetings. Turner slipped once; in mid-May, when en route to a rally in Trenton, Ontario, he walked to the back of the campaign bus and chatted casually with a few newspaper reporters. Unfamiliar with the new rules in journalism, Turner thought he had engaged in some friendly off-the-record discussion until the front page of next day's *Globe and Mail* quoted him as saying that he had left the cabinet in 1975 because of Trudeau's failure to back his efforts to enlist labour support for voluntary wage and price controls. The story enraged Trudeau, who wanted to repudiate him in a news conference until aides calmed him down and arranged a telephone conversation between the prime minister and Turner, who apologized for the interpretation the press had put on his remarks. Still not satisfied, Trudeau issued a press release claiming that Turner's back-of-the-bus comments had misrepresented the facts.

As the convention approached Turner grew confident and started looking beyond the convention to plan the takeover of power. He had tapped John Swift to oversee the transition arrangements, but later also recruited the Ottawa duo Simon Reisman and Jim Grandy, his advisers on economic policy, to look after the same area. Turner had a habit of consulting widely and making everybody feel they had his exclusive ear – and hoping that they never bumped into each other. As a management style it was less than ideal, but handling people was not Turner's strength.

On a beautiful spring morning in the spacious back yard of his red-brick mansion in the exclusive Forest Hill district of Toronto, Turner, wearing Bermuda shorts, a golf shirt, and sandals and smoking a big cigar, presided over a meeting of Lee, Payne, Swift, Bill Macdonald, Reisman, and Grandy. They talked about what to do in power and how to cut down the size of government. Around noon Turner dismissed Macdonald, Reisman, and Grandy. Then, with Lee and Payne looking on, Turner turned to Swift and, with four-letter words flying, delivered an amazing tirade. Turner didn't like Swift's work on the transition arrangements and told him so, accusing him of botching the job and demanding to know what he was doing in the final weeks of the campaign. Five minutes passed, then ten, and Turner was still berating his former EA. The tongue-lashing probably lasted fifteen minutes or less, but seemed to take an hour.

Swift, a lawyer from Vancouver without a political background before becoming Turner's EA in 1973, was bright, and had administered Turner's ministerial office superbly, juggling eight in-baskets simultaneously. He always could be relied on to carry out Turner's instructions precisely, but lacked political feel and didn't stand up to him.

"You never say a bloody word at these meetings," thundered Turner. "This morning you didn't say one thing. You didn't contribute anything to the policy and where we are going to go with this government."

Swift said nothing. Payne stayed motionless, sitting in his usual Buddha-like posture, head thrown back and hands folded across his stomach. Lee sat frozen. The incident was revealing more about the character of Turner than the capabilities of Swift.

"I don't know what the hell you're doing and what you're up to," Turner persisted. "I don't even know if you want the job or not."

The job Turner referred to was as his principal secretary, the number two post in the Prime Minister's Office. Payne cut in and asked Swift if he wanted the job, and if he did to say so. Swift said yes – *and Turner told him it was his*.

Turner had just appointed as his principal secretary the person he had spent the previous fifteen minutes decrying as useless. If Turner became prime minister, Swift would assume the job Bill Neville had had with Joe Clark and that Jim Coutts had had with Pierre Trudeau. Nobody in the country would work more closely with the prime minister than he. Lee began to wonder if berating Swift and then hiring him as his top aide was typical of Turner.

By the time delegates gathered in the Ottawa Civic Centre in mid-June, the Liberal Party had done what Brian Mulroney feared most; astonishingly, it had caught and passed the Conservatives in the Gallup poll. Turner, meanwhile, had successfully shed much of the ungainliness that had dogged his early campaign, and he had finally started sounding like a politician instead of a lawyer. In the final ten days the Liberals sensed the inevitability of his victory, and people with no particular affinity for him climbed aboard the bandwagon. The strong-arm tactics in Quebec that had hurt Lee in 1968 now helped him because this time they favoured his candidate, and confounded Jean Chrétien's valiant attempt to come from behind. Lloyd Axworthy, though he had almost abandoned Turner in mid-campaign to run himself, figuratively beat western delegates into supporting him. Lee felt sorry for Chrétien because he had experienced life on the other side and knew how tough it was to fight the pillars of the party.

"Guess who called?" an excited Turner told Lee a few days before the convention. "Marc Lalonde. He's ready to declare if necessary."

"Jesus, John, we don't want Marc Lalonde," Lee replied. "We'll lose our western voters. I thought you hated the guy."

This sudden enthusiasm for Lalonde baffled Lee. Next to Trudeau, Turner loathed Lalonde more than anybody else in the party and for most of a decade had shamelessly disparaged him in private conversation. He told stories of how he used to win battles in cabinet committee only to have Lalonde visit 24 Sussex Drive in the evening and overturn him on the priorities and planning committee the following week. Turner never got invited to 24 Sussex and he resented Lalonde's access, and the use he made of it.

Lee considered Lalonde as toxic a political poison as Trudeau himself. Lalonde and Trudeau represented precisely the same political symbol the polls showed the public rejecting. It was no coincidence that Trudeau's retirement was coupled with one of the most dramatic turnarounds in the history of the Gallup poll. People wanted a fresh, new leader and no cabinet minister epitomized the Trudeau government more vividly than Marc Lalonde. The campaign had deliberately set out to separate Turner from Trudeau. Lalonde's offer only undermined this strategy, and had to be avoided at all costs. So when Lalonde told Lee he was ready to endorse Turner if the campaign needed it, Lee thanked him politely but didn't rush to take up his offer.

The day before the vote, Turner called Lee to report with delight that Allan MacEachen, the deputy prime minister, had decided to endorse him. MacEachen ranked just behind Lalonde as a token of the Trudeau government; if he had to support somebody, Lee would have preferred him to endorse the other side.

"John," Lee replied, "we've got nineteen ministers now. We have Monique Bégin, for crying out loud."

Lee couldn't understand Turner's new liking for the traditional power-brokers he had campaigned against. Nor could he understand why the Trudeauites themselves would do it; it made no philosophical sense for left-leaning ministers like Bégin and MacEachen to choose Turner. So Lee told Turner that MacEachen would do him more harm than good. Turner told him to call MacEachen and resolve the problem.

"Chrétien has been putting heavy pressure on me, but I've really decided that John's the one who can win for us," the wily MacEachen told Lee on the phone. "I think we can make up our differences in policy."

MacEachen wanted Lee to schedule a press conference at 10 the next morning to announce his decision, but Lee talked him into accepting a handshake with Turner when he took his seat in the convention hall and a place beside him (from which Lee planned to whisk him out of camera range within minutes). So many cabinet ministers and MPs now supported Turner that his campaign threatened to sink from the weight of the government he wanted to avoid.

Later that day, as delegates filed into the Civic Centre to hear the final speeches, Chrétien workers stood at the entrances and waved placards bearing the latest poll results, showing the Liberal Party under Chrétien beating the Tories 45 per cent to 43 and losing 42 to 45 under Turner. On the eve of the vote Chrétien was trying to undermine Turner's strongest suit, his "winnability". The figures disputed Turner's claim that only he could conquer Mulroney. The poll, commissioned by the developer Robert Campeau and conducted by Martin Goldfarb, the Liberal pollster, was distributed to all corners of the convention, and Lee was hastily called to put out the fire. The media wanted to know how Turner could claim to be the only winner in light of these results. "Just a second," Lee told reporters as he looked for Angus

Reid, Turner's official pollster. "Okay, gentlemen," Lee announced a few minutes later, "here's Mr. Angus Reid, the President of Reid and Associates." Reid read out the results of *his* poll, which showed the Liberals winning 45 to 43 under Turner and losing 35 to 52 under Chrétien. The battle of the polls was fought to a draw between the two frontrunners. The Reid results had defused the crisis.

The five second-tier candidates delivered their speeches first. Johnston, Roberts, MacGuigan, Munro, and Whelan hoped for a respectable showing on the first ballot. They were running for third place in hopes of becoming kingmakers and perhaps contenders. They pinned their ambitions on a sudden quirk of fate that might propel them to the forefront of the convention. Their dreams hinged on Chrétien's running a strong second and forcing subsequent ballots so that their momentum as compromise candidates had time to build.

Of the second-tier candidates Don Johnston, the Montreal tax lawyer turned politician, had the best chance of generating a groundswell, since he seemed to have taken over third place in the final weeks of the campaign. Some called Johnston the PAI candidate. PAI never made a corporate decision to support Johnston, but appearances strongly gave the impression that it had. MacNaughton came aboard first as campaign chairman, then Michael Robinson, then Rick Anderson, followed by Marjory Loveys and Joe Thornley. MacNaughton did the strategy and planning while Rick Anderson ran the campaign on a day-to-day basis. (PAI's Ava Wise worked for Turner and so did Torrance Wylie, who had recently left the company.) But Mike Robinson quickly dropped back because somebody had to run the company. Some felt PAI showed guts backing a candidate who wouldn't win. Others felt it raised Johnston up the flagpole so that he could flap in the wind for it, and boost its profile – and indulge its officers' passions to play in politics.

Before the race started, Johnston and MacNaughton had hardly known each other. On Rod Bryden's recommendation, Johnston dropped in on PAI's gala Christmas party in 1983 and asked MacNaughton straight out whether he would run his leadership campaign. MacNaughton took five or six weeks to examine his options and look at other candidates. During that time Wylie tried to recruit him into the Turner camp, but Mac-Naughton declined. Turner already had Lee, and MacNaughton had never bought the Turner legend. He remembered an old cartoon of Turner standing at a lectern about to make a speech with somebody sticking a cassette into his back, and thought that image pretty well summed up the man. He also believed that Turner's resignation in 1975 had inflated his reputation into something he couldn't sustain back in the real world of politics. Chrétien was out, too – he already had Eddie Goldenberg, his trusted EA, and John Rae, the Power Corporation executive. Lloyd Axworthy could not make up his mind, and Paul Martin Jr., the most promising outsider next to Turner, chose not to run. Johnston was thoughtful and open and had more to say than other contenders. At the end of January 1984 Mac-Naughton, no more immune to the political bug than Lee or Neville or Edmonds, said yes to Johnston.

As the "issues candidate", Johnston announced two new policies a week and often criticized existing government policy, yet managed to do so without overly irritating the Trudeau wing. PAI carefully positioned him as the reform candidate and kept him free of both the pro-Trudeau label of Chrétien and the anti-Trudeau stigma of Turner. Yet not a single cabinet minister or MP supported Johnston, and that glaring deficiency bedevilled his candidacy. MacNaughton spent hours coaxing Judy Erola, and sadly watched her declare for Turner even though she felt more comfortable philosophically with Johnston. She claimed she could exert more influence backing a winner.

Turner strode onto the rostrum to the theme music from *Chariots of Fire* accompanied by a parade of provincial flags and the obligatory loud demonstration from his cheering supporters. Lee's mind flashed back sixteen years, to when Paul Hellyer walked onto the same stage in the same building in search of the same job, and squandered everything with a rotten speech. He wouldn't let it happen again. Payne, a former journalist, had written the first draft; on the previous weekend Turner had polished it himself and then practised in his back yard with only some squirrels as his audience.

"It will not be easy for any of us to succeed Pierre Elliott Trudeau as leader of our party and prime minister of our country," Turner began. "No Canadian deserves more credit today than the prime minister in his search for peace. I have said on several occasions, but never face to face with him, that he has surely been the most remarkable Canadian of his generation." Trudeau, sitting directly in front of the stage, smiled shyly and nodded a salute.

Turner promised "no easy solutions, no quick fixes", but assured the audience that he believed in the "Liberal heritage" and would never "dismantle or tinker or destroy what we Liberals have built". Turner spoke confidently, gave an uplifting speech, and delivered it superbly, interrupted often by the roars of his supporters. He had started the campaign terribly but now he peaked perfectly, delivering the best speech of the campaign at the crucial moment. His early flubs no longer mattered. Timing is almost everything in politics and he could not have timed it better.

Jean Chrétien mounted the stage last, which seemed fitting, because delegates looked forward to his speech the most. His feisty campaign had made him the undisputed sentimental favourite. For nearly three months Chrétien had hung out his heart and had touched delegates across the country. The race had started as Turner versus The Pack, but the seventeen-year cabinet veteran who looked, in Dalton Camp's phrase, like the driver of the getaway car had turned it into a Turner versus Chrétien contest. He had generated momentum to the point where, given a few breaks and a Turner stumble or two, he might win it all.

Chrétien had campaigned more doggedly and more effectively than anybody else. He had outperformed Turner at the five regional all-candidates' meetings but could not destroy Turner's "crown prince" image. He loudly touted himself as the man from Main Street and never hesitated to mention that Turner came into the race from Bay Street. He fought Turner explicitly the way Turner fought Trudeau implicitly. When asked why he was running, Chrétien answered: "Because I know Turner." He emphasized that he was no quitter and had stuck it out in Ottawa while Turner ran off to Toronto and fattened his wallet. Chrétien, however, did not shy away from the Trudeau record, and that put him at a disadvantage; Turner had no record to defend. Two other things also hindered him. His timing was wrong – given the consistent alternation of Liberal leaders (Laurier, King, Saint-Laurent, Pearson, then Trudeau), many thought it was an anglophone's turn to lead the party this time around. Also, many delegates harboured doubts about his intellectual depth. Chrétien was a people person; as a cabinet minister he had never been renowned for his mastery of the details of his department's background papers.

That morning Chrétien had gotten the best reception of any candidate when he promised a special session of young Liberals that he would stay and fight whether he won or lost. In response to the same question, Turner had hedged. Before he gave his final speech, Chrétien's camp had analysed the numbers and come to realize one stark reality: while delegates loved the MP for Shawinigan they would vote for Turner. Chrétien's only hope lay in doing something so dramatic that it would sweep up uncommitted delegates and shake loose wavering supporters of other candidates. Chrétien could aim at Turner's solar plexus and deliver a zero-sum speech warning delegates that he could not in good conscience support the party's dangerous drift to the right. He would be playing high-stakes politics, undoubtedly alienating some delegates in the hope of winning others, but he was losing anyway, and losing by a little or a lot did not change the final outcome. Everyone in the audience knew that he had to deliver a classic speech.

"Of course you will vote with your hearts," Chrétien said. "If our forefathers had not listened to their hearts we would not have the great country we have today."

It soon became clear that Chrétien was playing it safe, trotting out his "Canada is number one" speech one more time. Delegates had heard it before, and while it was good, it fell short of greatness. Chrétien read from a text rather than telling it "straight from the heart" and failed to ignite the crowd the way he had during the campaign, in fact he fell somewhat short of Turner's performance. Some observers thought that Chrétien and Turner had fought to a draw on the podium. Whether he had fought to a draw or had lost didn't matter. He needed a knockout, and at best had scored a split decision.

The next day, while the convention awaited the results of the first ballot, President Ronald Reagan phoned to congratulate Turner in anticipation of his victory. But he could not get past the redoubtable Sandra Severn of ECL, who controlled Turner's convention logistics from a trailer on the Ottawa Rough Riders' football field. "Mr. Turner is waiting for first-ballot results, he can't talk to anybody," Severn told a Reagan aide and hung up. Two other calls came back from more senior aides until Severn finally told them to stop bothering her.

First-ballot results were announced in alphabetical order.

"Chrétien, 1,067," party president Iona Campagnolo announced amid cheers.

"We've won," Lee shouted, calculating that Chrétien needed 1,300 votes to challenge Turner seriously.

"What are you talking about?" Turner replied, stone-faced. "We haven't even heard our vote yet."

"Don't worry," Lee assured him. "He can't win. We've won."

The announcement continued: Johnston 278, MacGuigan 135, Munro 93, Roberts 185, Turner 1,593 and Whelan 84. Turner had fallen 125 votes short of a first-ballot triumph. The Turner troops erupted into wild cheering, and Turner broke into a broad smile. The other candidates huddled with their top advisers.

Some MacGuigan supporters had started streaming over into the Turner section and donning Turner regalia even before the results were announced. Lawrence Decore, the mayor of Edmonton and MacGuigan's key supporter, declared what everybody already knew, that he was joining the Turner camp. There was an argument in the MacGuigan box, and minutes later MacGuigan himself walked over to join Turner.

Lee picked up the phone and tried to call John Rae, Chrétien's campaign manager, but couldn't get through. He sent a runner with a message asking Rae to meet him outside the back of the building.

When they had both finished fighting their way through the crowds, Lee came straight to the point.

"John," he asked, "are we going to subject this crowd to an unnecessary ballot? You're not going to win."

"Chrétien wants to go," Rae replied.

"Okay. But it won't work. You know that."

Rae said nothing.

Sandra Severn's delegate-tracking operation in the trailer had forecast the first-ballot outcome within four votes. Turner now needed only a quarter of the delegates from the second-tier candidates to win a majority on the next ballot, and Severn's projections easily predicted that. She abandoned her trailer, walked into the convention and shook Turner's hand.

"Hello, Mr. Prime Minister," she said.

"Are you sure?" he asked.

"Yes, you're going to win."

"Really?"

"You've won," Severn assured him. "You can't lose. I promise you, you can't lose. You're it. You're prime minister of Canada."

Whelan, wearing his green stetson, waved at Turner as he walked past his box en route to Chrétien's spot at the other end of the arena. Throughout the campaign Whelan had hardly concealed his hostility to Turner. But a few days earlier Lee had quietly met Greg Ashley, Whelan's campaign manager, and been assured that at least half Whelan's delegates would swing behind Turner. The small Whelan bloc sat next to the Turner section and Turner delegates now swarmed into their space distributing Turner paraphernalia.

Munro, the most liberal candidate, went to Chrétien, too, but Isabel Finnerty, his aide, moved straight to Turner.

Roberts sat tight for the moment. He had never hinted what he would do in this situation, because he never expected to have to face it. He genuinely expected to pull off a "Joe Clark" 1976-style come-from-behind win, believing that the two leading candidates would stalemate each other and allow him to sneak through the middle. But that required a solid third-place performance. His fourth-place showing, nearly 100 votes behind Johnston, crushed those hopes. Now Chrétien phoned Roberts and pleaded for his support, and eventually Nick Taylor, the Alberta Liberal leader, ushered him to Chrétien's box. But Lee already had assurances from some of Roberts's top organizers that many of his delegates would come to Turner.

As for Johnston, he refused to budge and announced that he was hanging in for the second ballot. He liked neither Turner nor Chrétien as an option. Turner stressed "winnability", which

Johnston denied was the major criterion, while Chrétien promoted the tried and true, which Johnston had spent three months running against. Johnston's decision didn't surprise Lee because a week before the convention some of the PAI guys in the Johnston camp had informed the Turner camp it could not expect his support in later ballots.

"It's not Mission Impossible," Chrétien told reporters from his box. But it was. If Chrétien got every one of the 497 votes from the four withdrawn candidates – including MacGuigan, who now supported Turner – he would still trail Turner. But the cold arithmetic did not stop the Chrétien supporters from trying. The Chrétien section, including Chrétien himself, turned towards the Johnston section right beside them and shouted appeals for them and their leader to come over. Finally Chrétien pushed his way to Johnston's seat and implored his cabinet colleague to join him, or else everything was lost. The short-sleeved Johnston, perspiring in the muggy arena, smiled and patted Chrétien on the back and told him firmly that he was staying put. "Are you off your beam, Don?" Chrétien asked. As he shrugged his shoulders and walked back dejectedly to his box, Chrétien knew that Johnston had scuttled his only hope.

During the long wait for the second ballot Turner's moods switched back and forth. He brimmed with confidence one minute and fretted the next. Lee switched television channels briefly to the Saturday afternoon baseball game between the New York Yankees and the Baltimore Orioles. Finally Campagnolo read out the figures: Chrétien 1,368, Johnston 192, Turner 1,862. Turner jumped up, shook Lee's hand, and hugged his wife.

Plainclothes Mounties popped up from all directions to protect the prime minister designate and clear a path to the stage as the arena roared and leaped to its feet. Only Lee remained seated. He had tried to get up but his legs collapsed beneath him and caused him to fall back into his chair. The sixteen-hour days had exacted their toll on a man who had celebrated his sixtieth birthday two days earlier. So Lee sat hidden among the standing crowd and out of sight like a true backroom boy, while Turner hugged Chrétien on stage and exchanged a correct handshake and a smile with Trudeau.

Campagnolo introduced Chrétien as "the man who came in second – but first in our hearts". It was an amazing statement from the president as she prepared to introduce the party's new leader, but wholly true. The convention had to choose between sentiment and power and had chosen power. One television commentator said that the convention voted with its head rather than its heart. Had it not been for Turner's overwhelming support from the thousand or so unelected ex-officio delegates, Chrétien probably would have won. Ironically, the party establishment abandoned the candidate who defended the Trudeau legacy in favour of the one who sought to repudiate it.

As the audience cheered Turner, Trudeau stood sedately in the background, his hands lightly clasped in front of him, among the defeated candidates. The convention co-chairman, Rémi Bujold, invited him to the front to say a few words – and presumably to perform the ritual raising of the new leader's arm. Trudeau took one step forward, flashed his enigmatic smile, waved quickly and stepped back against the curtain to resume his quiet pose. That was it. Sixteen years earlier Lester Pearson had generously welcomed Trudeau on the same stage. A year earlier on the same spot, Joe Clark had bravely swallowed his disappointment at losing to Brian Mulroney and had magnanimously welcomed the man who had dumped him.

Trudeau's rebuff hardly worried Lee. Quite the opposite. Trudeau had emphasized the gulf that separated the two men, which would help Turner win the coming election. Reid's polling showed that 71 per cent of Canadians wanted the Liberal Party to change, and Allan Gregg's polling said much the same thing. Canadians had grown tired of the Trudeau government, the insider system, and the comfortable network of old boys. Having his arm raised by a smiling Trudeau would only lose votes.

In Lee's estimation, Turner was well positioned to take the election and run the country on his own mandate. The struggle to win the country promised to be tougher than Lee imagined; he would discover that putting Turner into the Prime Minister's Office was easier than keeping him there.

FIFTEEN

PRIME MINISTER TURNER

Until Prime Minister Pierre Trudeau formally resigned on June 30 1984, a full two weeks after the convention vote, John Turner worked out of the living room of Room 494 of the Château Laurier, sticking telephone messages into picture frames and clipping his daily schedule to a lampshade. The Monday morning after Turner's leadership victory, Jean Chrétien walked down the long corridor to see him in his $420-a-night VIP suite. It was vital for Turner to reach an accommodation with Chrétien. The convention had created bitterness and division within the party, which had to be resolved before the election. Chrétien's heart-winning campaign had made him a party treasure who could heal most of the rifts, attract popular support across the country, and ward off Brian Mulroney in Quebec. Turner needed Chrétien more than Chrétien needed him. Chrétien understood that reality and sought to parlay the bargaining advantage into every concession he could get.

Turner, unfortunately, started negotiations with his final offer – deputy prime minister and whatever cabinet portfolio he wanted – and that mistake weakened his bargaining position. Chrétien wanted assurances that the deputy prime ministership was not a figurehead post and sought guarantees for the seven ministers who supported him during the leadership race and the three candidates – John Roberts, John Munro, and Eugene Whelan – who joined him on the second ballot. But, most important, he wanted the powerful position of Quebec lieutenant which controlled millions of dollars in patronage spending. Nothing important happened in Quebec without the okay of the Quebec lieutenant, who approved every political payoff. The first demand gave Turner no difficulty, the second pushed him further than he wanted to go, and the third beset him with a horrendous problem. So Turner hedged.

They met again the following day, and to Turner's dismay Chrétien extended his demands. He now wanted the heads of André Ouellet, Marc Lalonde, Monique Bégin, and Serge Joyal, all of whom, he felt, betrayed him during the leadership campaign by supporting Turner. Chrétien remembered 1968 when Quebec MPs overwhelmingly endorsed Pierre Trudeau as their native son. This time they had split their support almost evenly between him and Turner, and that division at home cost him victory. But it was more than just the votes that rankled with Chrétien. Lalonde and his band dismissed him as an intellectual lightweight, frowned at him for laughing at himself and calling himself a pea-souper, and resented his popularity outside Quebec. Chrétien had felt every slight from his francophone colleagues and now he wanted revenge.

He had now seriously complicated the talks by demanding more than Turner could pay. Turner could not give away the post of Quebec lieutenant, because to do so meant abandoning André Ouellet, who had delivered the Quebec vote that undermined Chrétien. Ouellet had supported Turner loyally for years and was one of only three Liberal MPs with the courage to tell Trudeau to stay retired in 1979. Turner could not turn his back on an ally who had served him so well. One could argue that Ouellet was legitimately in line for the job even without his Turner credentials, since he had paid his dues as deputy Quebec lieutenant under Lalonde. But since Chrétien felt that as runner-up he had the most legitimate claim, negotiations reached an impasse. "Why doesn't he [Turner] step in and slug the son of a bitch," Marc Lalonde muttered as he waited his turn to see Turner.

Turner got a break from John Munro and Roméo LeBlanc, who announced they were leaving the cabinet and thus saved him the task of dropping them. Eugene Whelan tried to hang on but found himself dumped. According to his memoirs *The Man in the Green Stetson*, Turner said: "Big Gene, I gotta let you go. I got too many cabinet ministers and there's too many from Windsor and I have to let you go. I just can't keep you in the cabinet." Whelan lacked Chrétien's clout. Turner neither wanted him nor felt that he particularly needed him. Whelan begged, but couldn't change Turner's mind.

Turner and Chrétien met a few more times and on each occasion the encounter put Turner into such a foul temper that his aides could tell whenever he had been seeing Chrétien. The negotiations hovered only a notch short of open hostility. The Quebec minister not only negotiated hard but showed himself a bad loser, making no effort to be pleasant and showing no pretence of sympathy or loyalty, not even when talking to the press. Turner, who subscribed to the old-school rules of social etiquette, could not believe Chrétien's lack of grace.

In addition to his miseries with Chrétien, he faced difficult decisions over his cabinet. Twenty ministers, more than half the Trudeau cabinet, had supported his candidacy and now expected their old posts back – or better. Turner could not appoint them all and still show freshness; being newer than Mulroney meant freeing himself of Trudeau's baggage. He had promised nobody anything; the "no deals" policy gave him a free hand to pick and choose. Yet Turner hated to sack ministers who had rallied behind him, and as he wrestled with the problem he vacillated.

For example, he called Mark MacGuigan the Tuesday after the convention, praised his performance as minister of justice, and solemnly assured him that he had a place in the cabinet. Six days later MacGuigan was out.

"Wait a minute," MacGuigan protested, "last Tuesday you and I had a conversation in which you said –"

"I hope you didn't stake your hopes on that," Turner replied.

Turner was firing the only leadership candidate who had supported him. While Whelan, John Munro, and John Roberts marched to Chrétien, MacGuigan alone came to Turner, saving him from the embarrassment of getting nobody. But that was history. Turner had since bent to the desires of Herb Gray, who wanted no other cabinet ministers from Windsor, and Lloyd Axworthy, who had clashed with MacGuigan in Trudeau's cabinet.

When MacGuigan and his campaign manager, Jim McDonald, threatened to call a press conference to expose the broken promise, Turner changed his mind again. MacGuigan, he said, could remain minister of justice if he wanted, but MacGuigan, appalled by the way Turner was performing, foresaw a short

Liberal spell in power and opted for an appointment to the Federal Court instead.

His cabinet-making took days of back-and-forth negotiations and damaged several friendships. What exacerbated matters was that the makeup of the cabinet changed daily and even hourly, depending on who pressured him last; people who saw Turner in the morning and left convinced that everything was set learned by noon that it was off. The Turner government was coming together in a most unpromising manner.

As for Chrétien, Turner needed twelve days to reach an accord with him. Finally, forty-eight hours before the swearing in, they came to an agreement. The controversial "Quebec lieutenant" would now become a committee of three, with both Chrétien and Ouellet as members. The solution patched up the problem, but showed that Turner could be pushed around.

Lee saw Turner only sporadically during the two-week transition as he tried to catch up with work at ECL. His partners, Steve Markey and Rick Bertrand, had been running the company while he and Sandra Severn worked on the leadership campaign. Now Lee was free to return to work, as he no longer had an official role with Turner. With Lee gone and Payne returned to Montreal, Turner started relying on advisers from his past, most of whom, like Turner himself, had been out of government for a decade.

While Turner built his cabinet, negotiated with Chrétien, and mapped out an election scenario, he grappled with the mechanics of government. The new structure of government amazed and even bewildered him. When he left Ottawa in 1975 the government did not run its finances through "spending envelopes", and central agencies had not wholly supplanted the authority of line departments. Dazed by the way things had changed since the good old days when cabinet ministers ran their departments and were left alone to do it, Turner struggled with briefings from the Privy Council Office. Gordon Osbaldeston, the nation's top civil servant, brought huge briefing books outlining the operations of government. Tom Axworthy handed over thick red binders detailing the workings of the prime minister's Office. Gerald Bouey, the governor of the Bank of Canada, visited his hotel suite and so did Mickey Cohen, the deputy minister of finance. The stream of official visitors never seemed to end. "I'm dealing with a massive structure here," Turner told reporters at the end of his first week as prime minister designate.

Aside from his gutsy plan to contest a seat in British Columbia, which had been settled early on at the Royal York meetings, Turner made one bold decision in the run up to power. He decided to disband outright Trudeau's top-heavy system of central agencies that controlled cabinet's social and economic spending "envelopes" and to return their powers to the individual departments. He decided to announce it fast and enact it summarily, and he showed decisiveness and strength in doing so. In other matters, he waffled. Turner had been training for the prime ministership for years. His mind had been set on attaining the job and now that he had got it he was unsure of what to do.

In contrast to the stormy relationship with Chrétien, Turner and Trudeau dealt with each other cordially, though formally. Victory had softened Turner's antipathy toward his old enemy; aides heard him denigrate Trudeau only once, and that concerned Trudeau's slowness to vacate the prime minister's two residences: 24 Sussex Drive and the country retreat at Harrington Lake. Apart from that, only one other factor threatened to complicate their relationship.

Lee happened to be talking to Turner about the composition of the cabinet when John Swift walked into the room with a list of Liberal MPs. Turner said they were last-minute patronage appointments Trudeau planned to make upon leaving office, which he had agreed to make on Trudeau's behalf. Why? Well, Turner explained, if Trudeau made the appointments the Liberal caucus would lose its parliamentary majority and might deny him the strength to form a government. So Trudeau was deferring the appointments in return for Turner's promise to make them after he dissolved Parliament for an election. And, oh yes, Trudeau wanted the agreement in writing.

Lee couldn't believe it. What Turner described might come up in a political-science classroom, but not in real political life. The Liberals held 139 seats and the combined opposition had 132 votes. It was true that after the appointments were made the opposition, in unison, could outvote the remaining Liberal MPs and the governor general would want to know which party commanded the confidence of the Commons. But the next biggest bloc belonged to the Conservatives who, with 100 seats, would still lag two dozen seats behind. No governor general would give the second-place party the chance to form a government.

Lee told Turner not to sign Trudeau's agreement. Turner said it was a legal matter. Lee said it was political and he didn't care what fifty lawyers said – the governor general would not refuse him the right to form a government. It was a matter of common sense. He couldn't understand why Turner was spending precious time worrying about something like this, especially when Parliament was not in session. But Turner was afraid that he would have to call a quick election if he lacked a majority, and he didn't want to be boxed in that way; to keep his election options open he felt that he would need a majority of MPs. So Turner signed the agreement and later told the Liberal caucus that seventeen MPs would receive appointments. Even Payne couldn't talk him out of it, although he tried.

Trudeau left office in one final orgy of patronage. On the evening of June 28, with one full day remaining in the life of his government, the Trudeau cabinet slipped through 56 appointments. Cabinet normally bestowed between 300 and 400 jobs a year but Trudeau in his final month quietly awarded 215 jobs and stuffed virtually every opening he could find.

Trudeau arrived at Government House early on Saturday morning, June 30, in his official armour-plated black limousine and tendered his resignation. He promptly returned across the street to 24 Sussex Drive, which he would occupy for a few more days, and jumped into his Mercedes sports car and disappeared. He had been gone exactly ten minutes when the Turner family arrived with a crowd of aides and plainclothes Mounties. Shortly after 9 a.m. Turner took the oath of office and became the seventeenth prime minister of Canada. "I felt both humble and proud at the same time," he told reporters.

Turner clung to his corporate directorships until the last minute – and even beyond. He allowed himself to be re-elected to the board of Canadian Pacific Ltd. during the actual campaign, and hung onto all his boards even after winning the party leadership. Finally, he resigned his directorships en masse, effective the end of the month, which coincided with the end of the second quarter – about 15 hours after his swearing in. Directors' fees are paid quarterly, so for fifteen hours Turner ran the country while sitting on the boards of directors of nine companies. He knew all the time he was walking an ethical tightrope. During the two-week transition he told officials not to brief him on government business involving his companies until his director's terms had expired.

Despite his talk about newness that day at Rideau Hall, Turner unveiled a cabinet that bore an uncanny resemblance to Trudeau's old cabinet. It contained no outsiders and only five new ministers, and none of those five made it onto the cabinet's powerful priorities and planning committee, effectively the inner cabinet. Twenty-three of his twenty-nine ministers had been Trudeau ministers and no fewer than fourteen of these kept their old portfolios, including the key ministers: Finance Minister Marc Lalonde, Transport Minister Lloyd Axworthy, and Health and Welfare Minister Monique Bégin. Allan MacEachen stayed in the cabinet.

"I would need a larger mandate from the people of Canada to move farther than I have today," Turner explained somewhat defensively at the unveiling.

Brian Mulroney summed up the new government in one sentence: "What has happened is that the old bunch went out one door and came right back in the other."

The so-called new cabinet shocked Lee, especially the reappointment of Marc Lalonde as minister of finance, which meant that the most senior and most powerful post had gone to the biggest Trudeau symbol. He had urged Turner to break away from the Trudeau era by dumping ministers visibly identified with the former prime minister and by appointing to his cabinet four or five prominent non-parliamentarians. He proposed people like Iona Campagnolo from British Columbia, Bob Blair from Alberta, Roy Romanow or Doug Richardson from Saskatchewan, and Raymond Garneau from Quebec. Such dramatic appointments would bolster the party in the West and Quebec and would send a signal that the Liberals were starting with a clean slate.

Typically, Turner hesitated and wavered. Although such appointments were acceptable both politically and constitutionally, the plan bypassed Parliament and carried the potential for controversy. He first consulted Iona Campagnolo as party president and as a potential appointee, and that proved a mistake. Campagnolo savaged the plan. She said that someone who couldn't get elected to Parliament shouldn't sit in cabinet, and promptly repeated her views to the press. Turner dropped the idea as soon as Campagnolo's warning hit the newspapers. Lee pressed him to proceed anyway, arguing that every prime minister in modern history had appointed unelected ministers. "If she doesn't want to be a minister we'll put somebody else from British Columbia into the cabinet," Lee told him. But Turner believed in Parliament, and while he felt able to bypass the institution for a few weeks, he didn't feel comfortable carrying on with outsiders in the cabinet until fall. Turner wanted a fall election and didn't want to go to the polls early simply because he wanted to get some cabinet ministers into the Commons. He wanted to keep his election options open.

Having rejected non-parliamentarians, Turner, despite his leadership campaign promise of change, found that he had to build his cabinet from the available wood. Trudeau left behind mostly a pile of warped and sagging two-by-fours full of cracks and stains and dry rot. Throwing out the old was easy from the boardroom of McMillan Binch, but painful from the Langevin Block.

Real change required the sacking of Lalonde, MacEachen, and Axworthy just for starters. Although Turner loathed Lalonde he had always respected him. Lalonde had an impressive grasp of the finance portfolio, cabinet experience, and unquestioned control of Quebec. Turner liked the idea of having Lalonde work for him instead of against him; he could be just as formidable an ally now as he had been an enemy before. As for MacEachen, the veteran from Cape Breton did not want to stay in the cabinet, yet Turner persuaded him to come in as Senate leader. "We need the old hands who can deliver seats," Turner said. Axworthy had been his leadership campaign co-chairman and although he spent the first two months threatening to jump ship to run against him, he worked hard for Turner in the final month. The Liberal Party had only two MPs from the West, which meant that Turner couldn't drop him even if he wanted to do so.

Lalonde, MacEachen, and Axworthy were only the start. The list was long and the decisions became tougher the further down he went. More caucus members and more cabinet ministers had supported Turner than any other candidate. These people had invested their careers in Turner and delivered him the Prime Minister's Office and now he could not look them in the eye and wield the axe. Most of the people who supported him symbolized the past he had run to change, and that created anguished conflict between personal loyalty and political need. It was hard to be supported by the party establishment and act as the agent of change. The Liberal "establishment" had captured his campaign, and Turner could not muster the courage to clean the slate. The price for being an agent of change came too dear.

"It's just an interim cabinet," Turner assured Lee. "Don't worry. Watch me after I win the election."

Throughout the leadership campaign Turner had vowed to banish Senator Keith Davey. He mentioned Davey by all but name when he publicly promised to brook no rainmakers, and no junior G-men. Davey, on his part, who grew up with the gospel that elections were won from the left, found Turner's triumph as party leader alarming. Repeating that the Liberal Party would never go for a right-winger like Turner, that he came from Bay Street and had fallen out of touch, Davey supported no one during the leadership race. So when Turner won the leadership the question was not whether he would replace Davey as the party's election strategist, but with whom. Lee was the logical successor. Everybody assumed that Lee would run the coming election campaign despite his repeated denials. Some key people in the Turner camp felt that the old fox was engaging in manoeuvres to get the job on his own terms.

In an incident that would become significant some weeks later, a doctor who was an old friend of Lee's dropped into the ECL office and asked whether Lee would be running Turner's election campaign. When Lee assured him that he would not, the doctor replied that he was glad to hear it, and left without further explanation.

Lee officially told Turner exactly what he told the doctor, that he would not run the Liberal election campaign. He said he was wrong for the job, had long been too long out of touch with the party, and needed a rest after the the gruelling schedule of the leadership campaign. Lee then suggested a series of names: Jerry Grafstein, Royce Frith, Sandra Severn, Al Graham, Alf Apps, and even Keith Davey. "Christ, I can't do that," Turner replied indignantly at the mention of Davey, citing his promise to banish rainmakers. (Lee had raised the idea earlier with Davey, who dismissed it just as summarily with the quip that "the optics would be all wrong.") Finally Lee proposed John Rae, Chrétien's campaign manager, and twice talked to Rae, who initially declined but seemed to be coming around at the second meeting. When Turner dined privately with Lee the evening before the swearing in, he agreed to meet Rae over lunch and apparently accepted Lee's decision to bow out. "You know and I know I wouldn't be prime minister if it wasn't for you," Turner said.

The next morning Lee wrote Turner a farewell memo telling him it had been a pleasure to serve him, and inviting him to call should he need his advice. But the day after that, in his first full day as prime minister, Turner called Lee to his hotel suite in the Château Laurier and told him: "It's got to be you."

"I've decided I can't take Rae," Turner told him. "What if he threw the election?"

The statement dumbfounded Lee but Turner painted a gloomy scenario for his political future: he would lose the election, his leadership would fall under attack, and then Chrétien would be "waiting in the wings" to take his place.

"I know John Rae," Lee pleaded. "This man has as much integrity as anybody I've ever met in my political life. I can assure you that if he takes it on he will give it his best."

Lee failed to convince him about Rae, and Turner rejected every other name he suggested, saying he wanted him. Lee protested that he had to get back to his company, that his wife was soon undergoing serious surgery which weighed on his mind, and that the leadership campaign had exhausted him. Turner accepted none of his reasons.

"Everybody is agreed it's got to be you," Turner responded. "You did it last time. I don't want any last-minute rescue jobs."

"No, John," Lee said. "No."

Turner gripped Lee with his famous double armlock handshake and held him tight, like a wrestler going for the count, and stared piercingly into his face, eyeball to eyeball.

"You've got to go the next mile," Turner said. "You've got to go, and everybody thinks so."

Lee succumbed and said okay. Before he left the room he got

Turner to agree to an election team to oversee the campaign. It would have Doug Frith (Ontario) and Lise Saint-Martin-Tremblay (Quebec) as co-chairs, and a few days later Izzy Asper (the West) would join it.

Lee immediately recruited his colleague Sandra Severn as his executive director, and together they toured the Liberal Party office at 102 Bank Street. Lee walked upstairs and stepped into the premises for the first time since he had argued with Pierre Trudeau on the night of the 1972 election. The sight astounded him. Cramped and dingy, the office lay in shambles from the chaos of the leadership convention. But that didn't disturb him nearly so much as the fact that he could see no facilities – no "machine" – with which to fight an election.

"Where's the machine?" Lee asked.

"This is it," came the reply.

"C'mon," Lee said.

There were no computers, no electronic mail system – the party relied on the post office – and only an old-fashioned addressograph kept track of mailing lists. Lee saw a lot of scarred desks, chairs, and other routine office equipment, but nothing with which to contest an election.

"This is a God-damn disgrace," Severn blurted out.

The National Office had put all its energies into pulling together a leadership convention on fourteen weeks' notice, and during the scramble nobody had sat back to plan for an election. Gordon Ashworth and Tom McIllfaterick, the party officials conducting the tour, explained that they had been denied a budget to do anything more. Nobody mentioned the cleavage that had developed between party headquarters and the Prime Minister's Office. The division had grown and become hostile. About eight months earlier, when the party bought fifteen Hyperion computers for Ottawa to communicate with the provincial offices, each province received a unit and several were scattered around Ottawa; because of the inter-office rivalry, everybody got one – except, of all places, the National Office. Keith Davey had run his recent campaigns out of the Prime Minister's Office instead of party headquarters.

Turner assumed that a well-oiled Liberal machine awaited

his decision to call a national election. He believed, as Lee had believed until his horrifying visit to the Bank Street office, that the party stood poised to fight. In fact it lacked any weapons beyond some bows and arrows. A few blocks away Norm Atkins and the Tories waited with space-age machinery ready for the flip of a switch. The Tories had gone high-tech, while the plodding Liberals languished in the Stone Age. Lee, wondering what mess he had gotten into, left the Liberal office believing that Turner had to put off an election.

The next morning Lee phoned the party president, Iona Campagnolo.

"What gives?" he asked.

"Well, the PMO didn't want me to do any more than that," Campagnolo explained.

Campagnolo had cleared off old debts, but had not built up a campaign chest. The party's bank account hardly contained enough money to run the office.

Lee later had lunch at the Four Seasons with Tom Axworthy, who had been Trudeau's principal secretary in the PMO.

"Tom," Lee asked, "am I wrong? Is there no election readiness in the Liberal Party HQ?"

"No," Axworthy replied, "you're not wrong. There's nothing."

"But what the hell would you have done if Trudeau had decided not to retire and you had to fight an election this year or next?"

"Very simple," Axworthy answered. "We knew that 102 Bank Street was a wasteland, so we set up the whole machine in the PMO."

Axworthy bore more bad news: the election machine in the PMO no longer existed. In taking it over, Turner had dismantled the whole system.

"You've got nothing," he said. "Absolutely nothing."

Axworthy's answer so dumbfounded Lee that the propriety – or otherwise – of Trudeau's using public funds to establish an election machine in a government office did not occur to him.

Lee walked from the Four Seasons to the Langevin Block, where a cursory look inside the building confirmed Tom Axworthy's claims. The Prime Minister's Office felt more like a morgue than the humming nerve centre of Canadian politics it had been under Trudeau. Empty boxes littered the hallways. Doors were open and offices stood empty with closet doors ajar. More than half the staff had quit, and in Turner's zest to put a new face on government most of the rest were fired. Trudeau had not left Turner much to work with, and Turner had devastated most of what remained. Lee took the elevator and headed for one of the areas where voices were to be heard, to find John Swift sitting inside his office interviewing secretarial candidates. That illustrated Turner's predicament. The PMO now had to replace personnel from the ground up. The transition of power had cleaned out virtually everybody, and the election machine – such as it was – had disappeared in the cleanout. Lee would have to put together an election organization piece by piece and get it up and running. That required time. The Tories took more than a year to build their organization, and Lee had a few months at best. He would face disaster if Turner called a quick election, as some aides were advising him to do.

The next day, July 3, Lee wrote Turner a personal and confidential memo outlining three potential election windows. The memo was surprisingly dispassionate, given the fact that the Liberal Party cupboard was bare. Turner could squeeze the last drop of life out of Trudeau's old term and wait until early 1985. Lee dismissed the 1985 option as too risky; Turner would be riding Trudeau's mandate to the end of the fifth year, and Lee didn't think he could do that after what he had said about Trudeau. That left two alternatives: late summer or November. The choices narrowed down to going almost immediately or waiting for two months.

Aside from the Liberal Party's lack of readiness, two problems clouded the horizon for an early election. In eleven days the Queen was to arrive in Canada for a thirteen-day tour ending on July 27, and on September 9 the Pope would appear for an eleven-day tour. Not even Houdini could shoehorn a two-month election campaign between the two visits. The Queen, who had to be seen to remain above the world of politics, would not set foot on Canadian soil during an election campaign. An early election knocked off the Queen. Waiting for the Queen to leave ran Turner smack into the Pope's visit. Disrupting either visit carried political risk. The Queen and the Pope both had their fol-

lowings, and many communities across the country had enthusiastically made local plans for the trips. Forcing a postponement
of either tour for partisan electoral reasons would inevitably
alienate some voters. Election campaigns were supposed to win
votes, not lose them. Turner had little room to manoeuvre;
whether by accident or design, Trudeau had left him a lousy set
of choices.

If he moved quickly, Turner could call a summer election for
August 27 or September 4 and get it finished in time for the Pope,
which would disrupt only the Queen's visit. That was the early-
election option. Lee preferred the fall option. Turner could wait
for both the Queen and the Pope to clear the country and then
call an election for November 12 or 19. That way the election
writs would not be issued until late September, and would inter-
rupt and offend nobody.

Lee's memo listed the pros and cons of both options. An early
election had attractive features despite the conflict with the
Queen. It maintained the momentum built up from the leadership convention and harnessed the popular goodwill that inevitably accompanied a new leader. It also settled the issue quickly
and allowed Turner the freedom to restructure the economy. It
required no legislation and minimized his affiliation with the
Same Old Gang cabinet. Turner did not have to worry about
running in a by-election to get a seat in Parliament. Except for
the Queen, the early option was clean and simple.

But disadvantages outnumbered advantages. The memo mentioned: no election machine; difficulty getting new candidates;
exhaustion of the prime minister and key workers; unhealed
wounds from the convention, particularly with Chrétien; lack of
nominated candidates; no platform; uncertainty of polling data;
and political fallout from interfering with the Queen's visit. By
contrast, a fall election had nine advantages and only three disadvantages.

"You obviously want to go later," Turner said after reading the
memo.

"That's right," Lee replied. "You're not ready. I'm not ready.
The party is not ready. We don't have candidates nominated. You
can't go ahead and kill the Queen's visit."

Turner instinctively disliked the notion of a quick election.
He hated acting impulsively and he knew that he needed a rest.

Even casual observers could tell that the grind of a three-month leadership campaign had sapped his vitality and clouded his judgement. He needed time to recover. He had hardly settled into the Langevin Block and was still waiting to move into 24 Sussex Drive. He had been prime minister only four days and needed to consolidate his grip on the government machinery before plunging into another campaign. Payne also advised against an early election, telling him to take some time off to rest and think at the prime minister's country retreat at Harrington Lake. While Lee put an election organization into place he could collect his thoughts and make some policy announcements and put his stamp on government. All these factors made Turner inclined to wait, which was his decision that day. But hardly twenty-four hours had passed before he changed his mind and leaned toward an early election.

Three main factors had converted Turner from a dove to a hawk. First, the polls in the aftermath of the convention put him ahead of Mulroney. Gallup had him as high as 49 to 38. A 49 per cent share gave him not only victory but a sweeping majority. Trudeau received only 44 per cent in 1980 and in five elections never exceeded 46. The party had languished 22 points behind when Turner announced his candidacy in March and now it led by 11. The polls also showed Turner leading Mulroney personally two-to-one as the man Canadians judged best suited to lead the country and find jobs. He wanted to strike before public support cooled.

Turner's showing in the polls also impressed the Liberal caucus, which was the second factor in his conversion. Liberal MPs applauded the turnaround in public opinion just as enthusiastically as he did. Their electoral fates lived and died with the leader's popularity and now they urged him on to victory. They did not look forward to returning to their home ridings for the summer to hear complaints about the low dollar, high interest rates, and high unemployment when Turner could campaign to clean up the mess. The cabinet, with a few exceptions, most notably Chrétien, also pressed for an early election, advising him to jump before the convention's halo effect wore off. Calling an election immediately would send voters to the ballot box in two months, and the cabinet pros remembered that Brian Mulroney peaked in the polls two months after he won the Tory leadership the previous year. Lalonde particularly urged Turner to move fast; Trudeau did in 1968 and triumphed.

The third factor that significantly influenced Turner was a briefing from the Department of Finance that scared him silly. Marc Lalonde's Finance Department solemnly predicted that by autumn unemployment would jump to 15 per cent, interest rates and inflation would skyrocket, and the dollar would drop to 65 cents. The numbers frightened and even haunted Turner. If voting was delayed until fall, the economy would plummet exactly at the same time as Canadians headed for the polls.

"You want me to hold an election (in November)?" Turner asked Lee incredulously after reading the report. "We'll be creamed."

Bad economy or not, Lee told him he was further ahead waiting.

"The economy is a bag of shit," Turner retorted. For dramatic effect he cupped his hands and extended his arms as if holding the economy itself. "I've inherited a bag of shit."

Turner quoted his current lead in the polls, but that failed to impress Lee. One poll coming off a leadership convention was not much on which to pin a political fortune, especially after all the negative polls that preceded it. The polls showed extreme volatility and could easily swing the other way within two months. Gallup put Turner ahead by 11 points nationally, but other pollsters disputed that finding. Angus Reid gave him only a 7- or 8-point lead and stressed that it was soft. Reid said television coverage of the Liberal leadership race had skewed the results because during that period Mulroney had the profile of a ghost, and that would change in an election campaign. Martin Goldfarb put Turner ahead by only 4 points. In all polls the Liberal lead rested partly on the party's commanding edge in Quebec. The Liberals led only slightly in English Canada.

Worse, Lee argued that since the favourable Gallup poll was taken, Turner had done some things to dampen the public's enthusiasm and hurt his prospects. He had feuded with Chrétien in public and been pushed around. His patronage deal with Trudeau had leaked out and had rebounded adversely. Most of all, he had installed the Same Old Gang in the cabinet and was already seen by many to be picking up where Trudeau left off. The public started to wonder whether it had a Trudeau government led by John Turner. Lee felt that Turner could not call an election with such an image, and contended that he needed a few months to prove his freshness.

Lee also told him the country still did not see him as prime minister. For a brief second neither did Lee when he walked past a newspaper box and saw a headline "PM says ...' and immediately wondered what Trudeau was up to, before realizing the PM was not Trudeau but his boss Turner. After nearly sixteen years of Trudeau, the public needed time to absorb the new reality and get used to the words "Prime Minister Turner". A November election would allow Turner to be photographed with the Queen and the Pope, and give him an opportunity to visit Prime Minister Margaret Thatcher or President Reagan and bask in the glory of a world statesman. Lee argued that he needed to build up a record and show himself as prime minister before he could confidently ask for public support.

"You don't understand, Bill," responded Turner, still terrified by the gloomy economic projection, "if I go to the polls in November I probably won't get more than eighty seats."

Lee warned him that the party could not mount a campaign without an apparatus, but Turner countered that Lee had started from scratch during the leadership campaign and pulled it off, and could do it again. Lee explained that it had worked only because everybody else in the leadership race began from the same standing start, and that it would be different against the Tories in an election, that this time they were pitting themselves against a superbly organized adversary who was ready to roll at the drop of a writ. The Tories had already chosen 222 of their 282 candidates.

"We've got about 40 candidates," Lee protested. "We're going to have nominating fights."

"Well, you'll do it," Turner assured him. "You'll do it."

Turner believed that the Queen would never postpone the tour if he asked her not to. He knew her personally, had visited her in recent years, and kept her autographed picture in his den. He had once dated Princess Margaret. He was confident that his personal relationship would carry the day if he, John Turner, promised not to campaign while she toured the country. The

Queen would understand his predicament once he explained the plight of the Canadian economy.

"I think I can control that situation," he kept saying.

Lee's relationship with Turner had changed after he won the party leadership and had changed even more after he was sworn into office. Lee no longer dealt with the lawyer from McMillan Binch or the candidate for party leader but with the prime minister of Canada. Turner had started to chair cabinet committees and now relied on advice from the Privy Council Office, the Department of Finance, cabinet colleagues, and his own staff in the Prime Minister's Office. Lee had become less important to him.

On Friday July 6, without telling Lee, Turner boarded a government Challenger jet and departed for London to plead his case with the Queen. When Lee learned from an aide that he had left for the airport he instantly realized the consequences of the trip. It meant a summer election, because the moment Turner stepped aboard the airplane he surrendered his option for the fall. If the Queen said yes he had to carry through and call the election, because after putting her through the fuss he would look foolish to change his mind. If the Queen said no he still had to go ahead and call an election. The prime minister of Canada could not be perceived as taking orders from the Queen in England about when to call a Canadian election. Either way the country would be going to the polls sooner rather than later. The hasty trip to London, aboard a small plane so that no reporters could come along, made it a fait accompli.

Turner now faced a summer election after paying dearly to preserve the fall option. He had first submitted to Trudeau's patronage appointments partly because he mistakenly believed it necessary to maintain his government majority into the fall. Then, partly for the same purpose, he had ruled out non-parliamentarians in his cabinet and appointed the Same Old Gang. In order to buy a few months until fall he had swallowed his repugnance for the Trudeau government and abandoned the strategy set out in the Royal York meetings. Both actions had diminished his image as a fresh, new leader. Now, ten days after paying a hefty price to preserve the fall option, he impetuously discarded it for a quick election.

On July 8, Lee arrived in Turner's hotel suite at 6:30 p.m. to await his return from London. The flight was late and Lee waited for nearly an hour before Turner walked through the door. He had bags under his eyes and looked exhausted. Crossing the Atlantic twice in two days in a small plane had taken its toll.

"So she's coming?" Lee asked.

"No, she's postponing," Turner replied. "But it's just as good."

Lee shook his head but it was too late. Turner revealed to the other close advisers in the room that he would be announcing an election in the morning for September 4.

"Everybody with me?" Turner chirped as they all laid their hands on each other's like a boys' softball team at a big game. There were Turner, John Swift, Torrance Wylie, and André Ouellet.

"How about you?" Turner called over to Lee.

"Okay, John," Lee sighed, walking over to put his hand in, "you're the boss."

Turner proclaimed himself the CEO (chief executive officer), his three national co-chairs the board of directors, and Lee the COO (chief operating officer). At their eyeball-to-eyeball arm-locking session nine days earlier, Turner had accepted Lee's choices for the two national co-chairs: Doug Frith, the new minister of Indian affairs and northern development, for English Canada; and Lise Saint-Martin-Tremblay, a vice president of the Liberal Party, for Quebec. Turner said then that he had already promised Marc Lalonde the Quebec post, but quickly agreed to replace him with Saint-Martin-Tremblay.

Now, on the eve of the election announcement, Lee and André Ouellet accidentally discovered that they disagreed over who was the Quebec co-chair. Lee said it was Saint-Martin-Tremblay and Ouellet said it was Lalonde. As they turned toward Turner a look of horror crossed the prime minister's face. He shoved both hands into his jacket pockets, closed his eyes and winced. "Marc thinks he's Quebec," he murmured in a slow and barely audible voice. "I forgot to tell him [he's not]." In the meantime Saint-Martin-Tremblay had started organizing the Quebec campaign and had told friends she had the job, while Lalonde was also organizing and had held several meetings. For more than a week Quebec had two chief organizers preparing the campaign with neither knowing about the other. One of them had to be dropped, and the meeting debated who had to go. "You can't do this to the guy," Ouellet said about Lalonde. "It's his last fling in politics."

Turner decreed that Saint-Martin-Tremblay had to go and told Lee to inform her. That was bad enough. But dropping her created a new problem. With her gone, the national co-chair level had no woman. After more discussion it was agreed that Doug Frith would be dropped in Ontario and replaced with Judy Erola. Unable to find Frith that night, Lee intercepted him on his car telephone the next day as he was driving to the press conference to announce his appointment. On the eve of the election call, the Liberal Party had changed two out of three co-chairs, with only Izzy Asper, of Winnipeg, remaining in place. The Liberal election campaign was getting off to a shaky start.

When Turner announced the election the next day, July 9, he simultaneously unveiled the patronage appointments he had dreaded to make. He appeared apologetic and emphasized that with one exception the appointment of the seventeen Liberal MPs belonged to Pierre Trudeau. Two appointments stood out above the rest: Bryce Mackasey, who was named Ambassador to Portugal, and Eugene Whelan, who became Canada's representative to the Food and Agriculture Organization in Rome. Trudeau had previously appointed six Liberal MPs to various posts, which meant that altogether one-sixth of the Liberal caucus got pork-barrel payoffs. It made the Turner government look old and tired and little different from the one it had replaced.

"It's something out of an Edward G. Robinson movie," Mulroney scoffed. "You know, the boys cuttin' up the cash. There's not a Grit left in this town. They've all gone to Grit Heaven."

As if anticipating such a response, Turner implied that Trudeau had forced him into it, and he promised that from here on in things would change. Turner gamely tried to portray himself as the fresh wind that was blowing into town.

Mulroney countered with a statement claiming that Turner represented the ruling Liberal Party and only the Conservatives offered "true change, true attitudinal change, not cosmetic change". Ed Broadbent called Turner and Mulroney "Visa and MasterCard" and offered the NDP as the only vehicle of change. All three parties tried to position themselves as the real agents of change.

It was clear from the start that no substantive policy issues divided Mulroney and Turner. Both promised jobs, economic growth, more efficient government, and a reduced deficit. The battleground became Turner's image. Turner tried to show renewal and change, while Mulroney painted him as a blue-eyed Trudeau. The winner of the battle for the "freshest" image would win the election on September 4.

SIXTEEN

THE ELECTION OF '84

John Turner's decision to call a summer election baffled and delighted the Conservatives, who seemed to know more about the Liberal Party's lack of readiness than Turner did. They knew the Liberals were going into a national campaign from scratch, in violation of all the rules. The decision surprised nobody more than Brian Mulroney himself. "I kept saying he wouldn't go until fall," Mulroney said later. "He knew we were ready and he wasn't. I couldn't believe it when he made the announcement."

Nothing better illustrated the two parties' differing situations than the film footage on that evening's television news. One minute viewers saw people working quietly and purposefully in a glossy office at Conservative election headquarters, aided by a variety of sophisticated electronic devices. The next minute they saw an empty room at Liberal campaign headquarters at 130 Slater Street with workers installing telephones and people standing next to crates, watching movers carting in office equipment. The Tories' headquarters hummed while the Liberals' chugged and coughed.

Bill Lee scrambled to build an election machine. He had to get 242 candidates nominated, find campaign staffers in Ottawa and across the country, and put in place a communications system to connect up the provincial headquarters and the 282 ridings. The Liberals had no posters or brochures, and for the first three weeks relied on Turner's leftover placards from the leadership campaign. Turner had no speeches, and the party lacked a platform. Lloyd Axworthy headed up seven strike forces to rush out party policy. Turner promised to unveil the direction of his government as the campaign progressed, for the good reason that at first he had no policy to unveil.

As Liberal headquarters rushed to charter an airplane, produce an itinerary, book hotel rooms for Turner's entourage and the press, and do the hundred and one things needed to mount a national leader's tour, Turner stunned Lee and other campaign officials with a bizarre and totally unprecedented decision. Turner told his senior people that he would not tour during the month of July. He said he was too tired and needed to attend to government business in Ottawa.

"We have an election on," Lee protested. "You can't do that."

Turner said he needed to concentrate on cabinet matters and required a few long weekends of rest. Besides, he added, election campaigns were too long.

"This is madness," Lee exclaimed. "I'll give you long weekends, long rest periods, emergency cabinet meetings of some kind to get you back here. You can't just not campaign."

After the leadership battle Lee well understood Turner's fatigue. He had felt it himself. But an election campaign was absolutely the last time to rest. Having climbed into the ring, Turner now proposed to sit in the corner while his opponents won the early rounds by default. Lee took Turner aside and privately pleaded with him to change his crazy plan, but Turner would not yield. In his dismay, Lee remembered Pierre Trudeau being obstreperous and even bitchy in 1968, but he always showed up at the sound of the bell. Later Payne called to protest the silly decision, but Turner refused to listen even to his most faithful and trusted adviser.

Hours after calling the election on Monday, Turner boarded an Air Canada commercial flight and headed home to Toronto for rest and some seclusion. He told people not to expect him back before Thursday's cabinet meeting. That night television viewers saw Turner throwing steaks onto a barbecue in his back yard. Meanwhile Izzy Asper was flying to Toronto with a one-page statement he had written outlining a parliamentary screening process for patronage appointments. In Turner's house later that evening he implored him to release it, arguing that it represented his only hope of sidestepping the political backlash of the patronage appointments. Turner refused. Two weeks later Mulroney promised a nearly identical set of controls, which effectively gave him the high ground.

Dennis Baxter, Turner's press secretary, asked Lee how he should explain Turner's absence to the media. Lee, stuck without an answer, said he didn't know and needed time to think. The leader's tour focused the campaign not only for the leader but for all 282 candidates. Paid television commercials wouldn't kick in for another month; the leader's movements and speeches were supposed to prop up the national campaign in the early going when the public saw little else. With Turner resting, the Liberal campaign would run on empty for three weeks while Mulroney and Ed Broadbent barnstormed the country.

Turner returned to Ottawa days later and took an "unofficial" trip to Vancouver to pick a riding. His early bold decision to contest a seat in British Columbia had earned him broad respect. Now he frittered away much of the acclaim by dithering over which Vancouver riding to choose. He wavered between Vancouver Quadra and Capilano, and his hesitation added to his growing image as a weak and indecisive prime minister.

En route to Vancouver he stopped off in Edmonton to fulfil a leadership-campaign promise to inaugurate the Liberal Party's Western and Northern Council. In front of the audience, and a television camera, Turner gave Iona Campagnolo an amiable kiss and then a quick pat on her derrière. Campagnolo, much less amiably, slapped him back as the audience chuckled. "That's from woman-o to man-o," Campagnolo quipped, mocking Turner's self-description as a "mano a mano" (hand to hand) personality.

Bum-patting and Turner were hardly strangers. People had complained about it for years. John Turner slapped women's bottoms as Brian Mulroney made promises. He did it without thinking. It was a handshake for women. Lee got it stopped during the leadership campaign but, unknown to him, Turner started again after the convention. Sandra Severn dispatched a handwritten note in a double sealed envelope: "Bum-patting is not fun. It's not on, so stop it. Women don't appreciate it. Don't leer. Don't pat." Turner treated it as a joke. "I'm not leering," he grinned when he saw Severn.

On Sunday night Lee and other senior campaign officials waited at 24 Sussex Drive for Turner's return. When he arrived

Lee learned about the bum-patting exchange in Edmonton. A rumour floated around that CTV would air it that night. Turner and his entourage gathered anxiously around a television set for the CTV News, and everybody sighed with relief when nothing appeared. CTV had dismissed the exchange as an isolated event and decided not to use it.

"Look," Lee told Turner, "we've dodged that bullet. For God's sake, don't do it again."

The following week Turner slapped the bottom of Lise Saint-Martin-Tremblay at a press conference in Montreal, and that proved too much for CTV to suppress. It aired the Saint-Martin-Tremblay incident and pulled out the earlier encounter with Campagnolo in Edmonton. People across the country witnessed Turner's slap and Campagnolo's comeback again and again on newscasts that evening. It got more replays than the winning Grey Cup touchdown. Viewers watched it at regular speed and in slow motion. NBC's Today Show televised it across the United States. Mail poured in. Some women wrote to say they wished Turner would pat their bums, but most expressed outrage. Turner didn't understand what the fuss was about and remained unrepentant.

"I'm not apologizing for that," Turner told his handlers. "It is nothing more than the way I shake people's hands. I'm a tactile person."

Bum-patting dogged Turner for weeks. He shrugged off public criticism but radio and television reporters badgered him and soon had him dodging and weaving and sinking deeper into the mire. The incident gave the impression that Turner was out of step with modern society, and was incapable of admitting a fault.

Equally significantly, the whole incident demonstrated Bill Lee's lack of authority with Turner and his inability to bring him into line on a contentious issue. Turner no longer put himself in Lee's hands the way he had during the leadership campaign. He ignored his advice on the patronage list, on the date of the election, on when to tour, and now on the response to bum-patting. Turner kept saying he was the CEO who made the policy and Lee was the COO who carried it out. The "Check-it-with-Lee" days were over.

The day Turner called the election Mulroney challenged him to a face-to-face debate on television. The networks pursued the idea and so did Norm Atkins of the Conservatives and Gerry Caplan of the NDP. Turner, with Lee's support, stalled for time. He wanted to duck out entirely because he lacked command of the issues and spoke the worst French of the three leaders. Lee thought that, at best, Turner could manage a tie, and might well lose outright. With nothing to win and much to lose, a debate made no sense for Turner. Meanwhile Atkins and Caplan were dying to get their leaders into a studio with him. Atkins proposed a series of three debates – on foreign policy, social policy, and economic policy – which amounted to six debates when repeated in French. Atkins wanted them late in the campaign. For Lee, one debate was bad enough, three were out of the question. He couldn't prepare Turner for six sessions, and the thought of his screwing up late in the campaign worried him.

Lee countered with a proposal that he hoped would be rejected: one debate (two including English and French) early in the campaign – no more. It was a take-it-or-leave-it offer. If rejected, the whole thing was off. If accepted, he had a convenient cover for Turner's failure to tour, namely that he was busy preparing for the debate. So far Lee had fooled the press. The western trip to look for a riding was camouflaged as a campaign swing even though there was no chartered plane and Turner made almost no public appearances. The following week he surfaced in Toronto and Montreal. But Lee was running out of excuses for Turner's lack of travel, and the sleight-of-hand stuff couldn't last. So Lee insisted on staging the debate early if there was to be a debate at all.

The Tories and the NDP accepted Lee's proposal with surprising haste. So desperate were the Tories to get Turner on television with Mulroney they would clutch at anything. The media wondered why the candidates were debating so early when nobody had said anything yet. They also asked why Turner required a week to prepare when Mulroney and Broadbent needed only a couple of days.

Turner had once spoken good French but had let it slide, and now he needed to relearn much of the language. During the leadership campaign a private instructor had tutored him before each tour of Quebec and now, in preparation for the debate, she coached him daily. The French debate preceded the English one by a day. Lee, unilingual, watched the French debate on television. As far as he could see, Turner committed no gaffes, but he looked nervous and seemed often to be groping for the right word. His francophone advisers called it a draw. In fact he lost decisively. Both Mulroney and Broadbent outperformed him. He came across as a clumsy anglophone who could cope in French, whereas Mulroney spoke the language like the native Quebecker he was. Mulroney also demonstrated a superior grasp of Quebec issues. Polls later pinpointed the French debate as a turning point in Turner's fortunes in Quebec, and Allan Gregg's Decima Research called the impact "historically startling". Decima's tracking showed an unprecedented 12-point swing in Quebec overnight. But the reports sent back to Liberal headquarters in Ottawa claimed that Turner had held his own.

The next morning Turner sat at the head of the table in the prime minister's boardroom with Lee next to him. It was Turner's last English briefing and the advisers around the table debated the role he should play that evening as he confronted Mulroney in the all-important English debate. Should he be statesman or fighter? Aside from Turner and Lee, the group included John deB. Payne, John Swift, Torrance Wylie, Rick Alway, Izzy Asper, Jim Grandy, Simon Reisman, and Serge Joyal. Despite his promise of "no rainmakers" Turner had also invited Keith Davey, who had recently joined his lengthening list of informal advisers.

Turner wondered aloud whether it would be a good idea to attack Mulroney on patronage. He had grown irritated at defending his infamous appointments of the seventeen Liberal MPs, especially making Bryce Mackasey the Ambassador to Portugal. He had failed to shake off the controversy or pin the blame on Trudeau; now he looked for a way to turn the tables and flatten Mulroney with the issue. Eleven days earlier, Mulroney had committed his own faux pas on a campaign flight to Montreal. At the back of the plane Mulroney casually acknowledged to reporters that he had promised Tory patronage during his leadership campaign because "that's what they wanted to hear" and admitted that he was now taking a different tack and was lambasting Turner for doing the very thing he had once promised.

"There's no whore like an old whore," Mulroney said. "If I'd been in Bryce's position I'd have been in there with my nose in the public trough like the rest of them." Mulroney thought he was talking off the record, but reporter Neil MacDonald disagreed and embarrassed Mulroney by reporting his comments on the front page of the Ottawa *Citizen*. Mulroney had fumbled away the patronage issue but was smart enough to contain the damage several days later by apologizing for joking about it. Now Turner wanted to rub Mulroney's nose in those comments and get further milage out of his embarrassment.

Lee advised him to forget it because on patronage he had more to lose than to gain. The less said the better, he thought.

"Take the high road," he cautioned.

"Kick him in the nuts," Davey responded.

Lee said that Turner had won the leadership campaign by being a good guy and must remain a statesman.

"They want a tough guy," Davey argued. "Why don't we really put it to him? He said it, and he can apologize all he wants, but he said it."

Turner cut off the argument and left the issue hanging. He said he understood what both were saying and ended the briefing before noon. Lee told him to take the afternoon off, rest up, and not accept calls.

That evening, before Turner left for the studio, Lee slipped him a card with "dos" on one side and "don'ts" on the other. "Suggest you stick this card in your pocket and glance at it before you go into the studio," Lee wrote in an accompanying note.

DON'TS:
- Laugh (Joe Clark style)
- Place hands behind your hips
- Clear your throat after making a point
- Clench your jaw
- Squint your eyes when listening to a question
- Ever appear rattled

DOS:
- Keep calm, cool and relaxed
- Maintain a pleasant half-smile most of the time

– Use your terrific smile when appropriate (as often as possible)
– Look into your (red circle) camera lens during opening and closing statements
– Ignore cameras during debates

– Remember: *You* are the prime minister

Bruce Phillips raised the patronage question in the first portion of the debate while Mulroney and Broadbent shared the stage. Both leaders condemned the government over patronage and then the subject was over. Atkins, from his vantage point, quietly cursed Phillips for not waiting until Mulroney and Turner faced each other in the final segment. When Turner and Mulroney appeared together the debate had moved on to other issues.

Turner stood his ground and maintained a proper prime-ministerial stance. He said he represented change and freshness, and eluded real damage over bum-patting by stressing his record of commitment to women's issues. The debate seemed headed for a draw when, to Lee's horror, Turner turned toward Mulroney and suddenly lashed out at him over patronage, accusing him of saying one thing to his party and another to the country.

"He told his party last year that every available job would be made available to every living, breathing Conservative," Turner said.

"I beg your pardon, sir," Mulroney interjected.

"I would say, Mr. Mulroney," Turner retorted, "that on the basis of what you've talked about – getting your nose in the public trough – that you wouldn't offer Canadians any newness in the style of government. The style that you've been preaching to your own party reminds me of the old Union Nationale, it reminds me of patronage at its best. Frankly, on the basis of your performance, I can't see freshness coming out of your choice."

Mulroney could not believe his good fortune. According to L. Ian MacDonald, his biographer and later his aide, he told himself: "I just got lucky." Mustering every ounce of self-righteousness he had, he pounced.

"Mr. Turner," Mulroney responded, "the only person who has ever appointed around here, for the last twenty-odd years, has been your party and ninety-nine per cent of them have been Liberals. And you ought not to be proud of that. Nor should you repeat something that I think you know to be inaccurate. You know full well that that was a figure of speech that was used and I don't deny it. In fact I've gone so far – because I believe what you did is so bad I've gone so far, sir, as to apologize for even kidding about it. I've apologized to the Canadian people for kidding about it. The least you should do is apologize for having made these horrible appointments. I've had the decency, I think, to acknowledge that I was wrong in even kidding about it. I shouldn't have done that and I've said so. You, sir, at least owe the Canadian people a profound apology for doing it. The cost of that, $84.4-million, is enough to give – the cost of that to the ordinary Canadian taxpayer – we could pay every senior citizen in this country on the supplement an extra $70 at Christmas rather than pay for those Liberal appointments. And I say to you, sir, two things: (a) you should produce that letter, because you keep coming back to this situation. Please produce the secret letter you signed, that you undertook to make these appointments and (b) may I say respectfully that I think that if I felt I owed it to the Canadian people – and I did – an apology for bantering about the subject, you, sir, owe the Canadian people a deep apology for having indulged in that kind of practice with those kinds of appointments."

"I told you and told the Canadian people, Mr. Mulroney, that I had no option," Turner insisted, his voice raspy and defensive. Mulroney's counterattack had caught him off guard and had seized the initiative.

The moderator said: "Mr. Trueman, your next question, please." Mulroney ignored the moderator and continued to attack.

"You had an option, sir," Mulroney shot back, his voice rising and his pace quickening. He stabbed his finger and Turner seemed to reel back. "You could have said 'I'm not going to do it. This is wrong for Canada and I'm not going to ask Canadians to pay the price.' You had an option, sir, to say no and you chose to say yes to the old attitudes and the old stories of the Liberal party. That, sir, if I may say respectfully, that is not good enough for Canadians."

"I had no option," Turner sputtered. "I was able –"

Mulroney cut him off.

"That is an avowal of failure. That is a confession of non-leadership and this country needs leadership. You had an option, sir. You could have done better."

Turner, wilting under the barrage, remained silent.

"Mr. Turner, your response, please," the moderator announced in an official voice.

Here, Turner worsened matters by withdrawing into a defensive shell.

"I – I've just said, Mr. Moderator – taken the Canadian people through the circumstances. Mr. Trudeau had every right to make those appointments before he resigned. In order that he not do so, yes, I had to make a commitment to him, otherwise I was advised that, with serious consequences to the Canadian people, I could not have been granted the opportunity of forming a government."

Mulroney would relive the exchange over and over. "I hit him once," he later recounted, smacking his open hand with his fist. "I hit him again, pow" – Mulroney smacked his hand again – "he went down."

John Payne, watching from the booth, could not believe what had happened.

"Oh my God," Payne gasped, "Why? Why? Why did he do it?"

Lee, watching on television from his office, couldn't believe it either. The shaky man behind the podium bore no resemblance to the figure he had seen dominate corporate boardrooms. Turner liked to enter a boardroom late, timed for dramatic impact; he banged people on the shoulder and took charge; jaws hung open and everybody marvelled at the future prime minister of Canada. Now he *was* prime minister and, without cigar and four-letter words, he looked weak, nervous, and pathetic. He had been whipped in front of 7.5 million Canadians.

"Don't say a thing," Turner told Payne as he left the studio. "I did it on my own and I was stupid."

The next morning Turner called Lee into the Langevin Block. Turner was staring out the window with his back turned as Lee entered his office. When he slowly spun around he looked grey and awful.

"Bill, I let you down," he muttered.

"John, it's water over the dam," Lee replied. "I'll be candid with you, it wasn't a too thrilling performance. I think we lost the debate."

"I don't know why I did that," Turner said. "I don't know why. When I was up in the pre-box with Payne I kept hearing 'Lee says take the high road, Davey says kick him in the nuts.' 'Tough leader.' 'Statesman.' 'Tough leader.' 'Statesman.' Then I get down there and am waiting for this to happen and all of a sudden it goes by during Broadbent. I thought if I decided to kick him in the nuts, how am I going to get into it again? I kind of felt I was losing to Mulroney and I didn't know how to regain the advantage so I just decided to kick him in the nuts with what he said to reporters in the back of the plane."

The Big Mistake changed the campaign's very complexion. From then on everything shifted. Mulroney scoffed at Turner on the campaign stump. "I had no option," he mimicked, throwing up his hands in mock despair. "The devil made me do it." The audience roared. Meanwhile Turner was having to apologize for erroneously claiming that Manitoba was losing population, and also living down an accusation that Mulroney would fire six hundred thousand public servants, when the whole government didn't have that many employees. Angus Reid reported a "frightening reversal in our electoral chances".

Turner had started with an 11-point lead in the Gallup poll, but patronage and the Same Old Gang cabinet had helped put nearly four out of ten voters into the undecided box as Canadians re-assessed Turner. They harboured doubts about Mulroney, too, so they sat on the fence. The television debate confirmed their earlier worries about Turner enough for them to jump off the fence and into the Tory fold.

The first post-debate polls put Mulroney ahead as much as 45 to 36 across the country. The English debate became the axis on which Liberal and Conservative fortunes turned. It facilitated the swing but fundamentally did not cause it. The issue was patronage and the root cause was Turner's identification with Trudeau; voters in English Canada suspected that Turner had jumped into bed with Trudeau and was a weak prime minister to boot, and the English debate confirmed their suspicion.

As for Quebec, it abandoned Turner en masse. Liberals led 61 to 28 in Quebec before the debates and trailed 37 to 49 two weeks later. The French debate gave Mulroney legitimacy and actually caused Quebec to shift. It exposed Turner as an outsider and earned Mulroney his political credentials as a native son in a province where that counted.

The day after the debate Turner departed on a two-day shakedown swing through the Maritimes. The real tour finally kicked off in Vancouver the following Monday, July 30, and needed to go well if Turner hoped to turn things around. But Turner was complaining that Lee had jumped the gun on him by starting the tour two days before the end of July. Lee told him he had to get onto the campaign trail because they were getting murdered. Turner would fly to British Columbia (with a stop in The Pas, Manitoba) on Monday for three days, spend Thursday in Prince Albert, and arrive in Toronto that evening, and then visit Orillia on Friday before returning to Ottawa for the weekend.

Lee outlined the coming week's itinerary from a lawn chair in the back yard of 24 Sussex Drive on a beautiful sunny Sunday afternoon. Turner agreed to it. No problem. Then Lee raised the wearisome problem of finding a co-chair to join Barbara Sullivan for the plagued Ontario campaign. Turner had originally stipulated that one male and one female would head up each province and Lee had enlisted the Turner loyalist Norman McLeod, but a personality conflict made McLeod and Sullivan an unworkable pair. He then recruited Paul Klee until Klee's employer vetoed it, then abandoned the sexual balance and got Kathy Robinson, a lawyer, until a prolonged court case unexpectedly disqualified her. The campaign was one-third finished and the search was still continuing; the Ontario post seemed snakebitten.

Keith Davey's name popped up. Turner had to do something and Davey knew Ontario better than anyone. In many ways he was the natural choice. His concept of a national campaign was to concentrate on Ontario, let Marc Lalonde look after Quebec and Allan MacEachen the Maritimes, and forget the West. Ontario was what he did best and this post used precisely that strength. Turner liked the idea and promised to ask Davey personally. He realized that Davey's identification with Trudeau might create an image problem, but said he could handle it. Lee went along with the appointment, happy to see the Ontario problem resolved.

That night at about 11:30 Turner called Lee at home with the news that Davey had accepted. But, Turner added, he had given Davey the title national co-chairman.

"Wait a minute, John," Lee protested. "This will cause an awful lot of confusion. He's a very high-profile guy. You said no rainmakers."

A "national" title meant trouble, he warned. First, Davey carried a lot of baggage and such a title would cause the media to raise another Trudeau connection; the reinstatement of a symbol from the past like Davey was exactly what the campaign didn't need. Second, Lee said, the appointment would arouse morale problems within the party. It would raise the number of national co-chairs to four; the Atlantic provinces were already upset at having none, and now Ontario had two.

"It's just for the guy's ego," Turner replied. "There's no change in function – and I've already agreed."

Then Turner mentioned one other development: he had agreed to let Davey keep the chairmanship of Red Leaf Communications, the party's election advertising vehicle in English Canada. Turner's decision defied practice and upset Lee as much as the national title. Traditionally the person who ran the campaign presided over Red Leaf, as Davey himself acknowledged earlier when he offered to resign in favour of Lee. But at that point Lee had not taken over as national campaign director and didn't expect to, so he advised Davey to wait until Turner announced the successor. Now Davey had reversed himself and wanted to keep Red Leaf. That was alarming. Lee told Turner he needed the chairmanship of Red Leaf to keep it accountable.

"It's too late, I've agreed," Turner said. "Get together with Keith and work out the announcement."

"All right, okay," Lee moaned. "But I tell you, this will be misunderstood. It's going to hit the fan. People will say, 'Davey's back.'"

Lee thought then about resigning. He had considered it before, first when Turner slipped off to see the Queen without telling him, and again when he refused to campaign during July. A rift had developed between Lee's campaign office and the Prime Minister's Office which Turner did nothing to resolve. Increasingly Turner's aides in the Prime Minister's Office were making decisions affecting the campaign without consulting

Lee. But the return of the Rainmaker topped them all, because it was public and symbolic and undercut him in full view. First the Same Old Gang cabinet, then the patronage scam, the bum-patting blunder, and the TV debate fiasco; now Turner was restoring still another Trudeau symbol. Lee had lost control. He considered quitting but it was almost midnight and he was tired. Turner left for Vancouver first thing in the morning. There was no time.

The news that Davey was clinging to the chairmanship of Red Leaf disturbed Lee as much as his "national" appointment, because it killed any hope of bringing the agency to heel. Lee and Red Leaf were already engaged in what amounted to a battle for control of advertising policy. Red Leaf operated independently under Senator Jerry Grafstein, who disagreed with Lee on almost anything to do with politics. Lee wanted to incorporate Red Leaf into the overall campaign structure and tie advertising directly to the principal campaign, but Grafstein fought it. It was as if Lee commanded the army and Grafstein the air force, with the two bickering over which targets to attack. Lee knew that as Red Leaf's chairman Davey would support Grafstein, because he had given him his independence in the first place.

At the outset Lee, as national campaign director, had given Red Leaf two broad advertising guidelines: first, emphasize John Turner and not the Liberal Party; second, no black advertising – in other words no gutter tactics that maligned the opposition. Grafstein had a reputation for slinging mud and in 1980 had produced ads that ruthlessly disparaged Joe Clark. Lee told Grafstein to build up Turner rather than tear down Mulroney. He wanted ads featuring Turner addressing the issues of women, young people, natives, farmers, and fishermen.

The campaign had hardly started when Grafstein sent Lee an invoice for $2.8-million to cover Red Leaf's advertising program. The invoice represented 40 per cent of the entire campaign budget and contained no cost projections, budgets, or other details. Lee refused to pay until Red Leaf broke down the spending. Grafstein, complaining that Keith Davey never demanded such detail, had Red Leaf send him a rough explanation, but in a telecopier message on July 20 Lee rejected it as "totally unacceptable" and demanded answers to fifteen questions by 6 p.m. the next day.

Lee thought Grafstein was stonewalling and Grafstein thought Lee was poking his nose where it didn't belong. Red Leaf met the deadline with a twenty-four-page reply which Lee turned over for examination to André Masse, his Director of Communications. Masse could not account for $300,000, and wrote a searing memo charging Red Leaf with a series of deficiencies. The Masse memo urged Lee to appoint a special controller: "Surely the auditing process cannot be left in the hands of Red Leaf." Lee called in Murray Kierans, a Toronto lawyer and accountant with whom Lee had stayed during the early weeks of the leadership campaign. The showdown with Red Leaf had reached a climax the very day Turner informed him Davey would remain chairman of Red Leaf.

Earlier that day, at an executive-committee meeting, Grafstein held a preview screening of his ads and surprised and infuriated Lee by showing some black ads. Lee said he thought he had killed black ads and Grafstein replied he had made a few just in case. Lee said they violated Turner's instructions and advocated destroying them; not only were they black ads, they were bad black ads. Marc Lalonde and Judy Erola, two of the three co-chairs, rallied to Grafstein's defence and convinced the committee to keep the ads as insurance. Lee conceded defeat but vowed he would keep them off the air. Now, hours later, he had learned that Davey would preside over Red Leaf.

The media jumped on the Davey appointment with all the skepticism Lee had predicted, and maybe more. They demanded to know what it meant and why Turner had appointed Davey after promising "no rainmakers". Lee defended the appointment as common sense given Davey's wealth of experience, and urged reporters to take the news at face value. The media did not buy the "Ontario only" scenario.

When the news broke Turner happened to be standing in the pilot house of a ferry at Prince Rupert, B.C. Television crews and reporters stationed themselves on deck below and blocked his only exit as they waited for him to come down. Turner stayed up in the pilot house, steering the boat, while aides frantically tried to herd the crowd on to the waiting buses. The reporters stood their ground and grew loudly insistent: why did the prime minister who promised an open and accessible government refuse to discuss the most important appointment of his campaign? The standoff lasted fifteen minutes until Turner stopped hiding and descended to face the mob. Why did he do it? Because, Turner replied, he was using the best talent he could find. Is the Davey appointment a sign the campaign is faltering? No, the campaign is doing quite well. Turner added that Davey had been advising him for a number of weeks but that he himself controlled the content. After three questions Turner hastily deserted the scene.

"What the fuck have you done?" Turner screamed at Lee when he reached a telephone.

"John," Lee replied, "I did what you told me to do."

"Didn't you tell them it was Ontario?" Turner demanded.

Lee replied he hollered Ontario until he was blue in the face and nobody believed it.

That night a telephone call from Stephen LeDrew, the tour director, wakened Lee in the middle of the night.

"Guess what?" LeDrew said. "He ain't going to Orillia."

"That's ridiculous," Lee replied, sitting up in amazement.

Orillia represented a kingpin stop in Ontario. Candidates from about two dozen ridings were to assemble, people were being bussed in from all directions, and the party had taken out radio, television, and newspaper ads to promote the giant rally. Turner would leave Vancouver the next morning, stop in Prince Albert, and then fly to Toronto that night to unveil a government training program for youth unemployment. He was supposed to visit Orillia on Friday and return to Ottawa for Lloyd Axworthy's wedding that evening. LeDrew now revealed that Turner had decided to fly directly to Ottawa and bypass Orillia.

Lee waited until 7:30 a.m. Vancouver time before calling Turner: the PM said that Orillia was really unnecessary and could be picked up later. Lee asked why, and when he pressed the real reason emerged: the stop in Orillia left Geills Turner no time to get her hair done before Lloyd Axworthy's wedding. Lee could not believe what he had heard: the prime minister was cancelling the day's major campaign appearance so that his wife could get to a beauty salon. Lee resolved the problem by arranging a special plane to fly Geills Turner to Ottawa early while Turner campaigned alone in Orillia, but the incident resonated in his mind.

Later that day, as Turner flew to Toronto, Lee started drafting a long and unpleasant memo to Turner detailing why the campaign was floundering and how it could be turned around. Izzy Asper got hold of the first draft and toughened it with additional material.

Dated August 3 1984 and marked "STRICTLY PERSONAL AND CONFIDENTIAL, TO: PRIME MINISTER, FROM: BILL LEE", the final draft began: "With only your best interests in mind, I must place my views on this election campaign squarely before you." In numbered paragraphs, Lee noted that the Liberal Party had no election apparatus or plan in place when the election was called and that party headquarters was a disaster area. Starting from scratch, by working long hours, the campaign had built a working machine in remarkable time. The memo went to on say that the leader's tour stood out as the most serious area of concern, and advised Turner that he could not decide every aspect of the campaign.

"We whom you have assigned to manage your campaign must be given the authority to do just that," the memo said. "We are not asking for a blank cheque; you will be consulted on *major* matters. But, I am not being melodramatic when I say: If we continue to operate in this manner, you will become the Prime Minister with the shortest reign in Canada's history ..."

The memo added that there were several parallel campaigns running at cross purposes: the official campaign, the PMO, the airplane tour, and side campaigns such as Goldfarb versus Reid and Grafstein versus the world. Lee proposed "to lay down the law and require all factors and factions to blend into and be responsible to" his organization at 130 Slater Street.

"Your approval of this course of action is sought," the memo concluded. "The current situation is intolerable to me."

Lee took the five-page memo and the latest polling report from Angus Reid and stuffed them into a big envelope for delivery to 24 Sussex. His distrust of the Prime Minister's Office had grown to the point where he now sent correspondence directly to Turner's residence.

Turner performed well in Toronto on Thursday night and again in Orillia on Friday. But on Friday morning a story by Bob Hepburn in the Toronto *Star* reported bitter infighting among the Turner crew and blamed it on the fact that nobody seemed in charge aboard the plane. Ninety minutes after Turner's plane landed in Ottawa Lee convened the five tour handlers at Torrance Wylie's house in the West End of Ottawa. Lee said he wanted to know what was behind the report. Everybody remained silent. After some questioning the story unfolded, and so did the reason for their reluctance to talk. Lack of advance work had already beset the tour with gremlins. Now it appeared that Geills Turner had started countermanding orders and changing the itinerary along the way, throwing the tour off schedule. Nobody, not even John Turner, overruled her.

Lee decided to get her off the plane and wrote her a memo suggesting she start campaigning on her own. The memo said she was in demand as a speaker. Lee attached a list of places and assigned Diane Laham as her escort. Then he slipped the memo into the envelope containing his five-page ultimatum and the Reid poll results and sent the package off to 24 Sussex Drive. At the wedding that night Asper asked Turner if he had read Lee's memo.

"No," Turner replied, "it's on my desk at Sussex."

"Well, John," Asper said, "Bill's being polite. It's far worse than you imagine."

While the tour floundered over the details of getting Turner to the right place at the right time with a suitable speech, Mulroney's tour, backed by a healthy PC Canada Fund, unveiled the most sophisticated and effective national election campaign in Canadian history. The Tories had been polishing their campaign for more than a year, spending whatever it took to acquire the best technology and the talent to run it, and then having the time to fine-tune it. Each Tory candidate had a Texas Instruments computer to plug into a telephone for the latest policy line from headquarters or a copy of Mulroney's most recent speech. The Conservatives left nothing to chance. Mulroney's briefing book, sometimes thirty pages for a day, scripted every movement and covered every minute of the day. Mulroney received background notes on every official he met and a detailed analysis of local issues for each constituency. "We knew we were going to kill them once we got going," says one Tory.

Meanwhile, three weeks into the campaign, Lee had rounded up a few personal computers and installed an electronic mail system which constituted his centralized communications. He had no on-line communications with provincial headquarters, and the candidates needed no portable computers because the campaign still had no policy for them to check with. And if Liberal candidates didn't know what Turner was saying, neither did Lee, and even Turner himself was not always sure. Lee felt happy that he had finally gotten all the candidates nominated and no longer had to play referee over divisive nomination fights and to hear charges and countercharges of rigged voting.

The Liberals' makeshift election machine, thrown together in three weeks, sputtered and misfired a lot. Party workers out in the field had never experienced anything like it. Candidates wondered what Ottawa was doing and marvelled how a party with such a successful tradition could operate so ineffectively. Turner took the blame from the press, but Lee and his executive director, Sandra Severn, became the lightning rods for complaints from inside the party.

On Wednesday morning, August 1, the day after reporters confronted Turner on the Prince Rupert ferry, the cabinet met for its weekly meeting, with Herb Gray, the President of the Treasury Board, chairing in Turner's absence. The twelve ministers dispatched the affairs of state quickly and got down to the subject on everyone's mind: the disastrous campaign. They agreed that it was a mess and that the party had fallen behind and would lose on September 4 if something dramatic was not done soon. The discussion focused on problems and on errors and on what was needed to make things better. Everybody blamed Lee. Lalonde said Lee had bungled not only logistically but strategically. The ministers concluded that the campaign could be rescued only by firing Lee. Some argued that Lee had tilted the campaign too far right and cut off the party from its traditional small-l liberal roots, but most simply felt that the campaign was not functioning.

The worst time to fire a campaign director is in the middle of a campaign. Even the most hawkish ministers realized that it carried a huge risk of provoking a backlash that could divide the party and intensify the damage. Nor would it be easy to pull off. The only person who could fire Lee was the man who picked him in the first place, and he would not be eager to own up to a mistake, especially during an election campaign. Besides, Turner was semi-incommunicado and in the hands of the man they wanted to dump. The cabinet decided to consult John Payne, Turner's friend and closest adviser. They figured that if they could convince Payne they had a good shot at winning over Turner.

The cabinet met again at 5 p.m. with the same ministers except Gray, because somebody forgot to tell him the time. On this occasion the group gathered not in the cabinet room but in the prime minister's boardroom on the second floor of the Langevin Block. Payne, who had been briefed by Lalonde about the morning meeting, presided as chairman. Payne said he wanted to hear the complaints of each minister.

"We'll go around the table from my right," he said.

Unable to contain his eagerness, Gerald Regan jumped out of his chair and scurried to Payne's right. He kicked off the session by saying that the campaign had no strategy, the ridings were getting no help from Ottawa, and basic things like printed material were not arriving. Don Johnston, who arrived late, Charles Caccia, Bob Kaplan, Judy Erola, and Lalonde were the most vocal in their complaints, but the anti-Lee echoes resounded everywhere.

"We have a good mechanic," Lalonde said. "We need an architect. We can buy mechanics."

Payne listened for two hours. He was aware that there had been problems but had not blamed Lee. Instead he blamed Sandra Severn, Lee's executive director, whom he had unsuccessfully tried to keep out of the campaign. He had seen Lee operate during the leadership campaign and knew how effective he could be. Now he looked for a compromise such as bringing somebody in under or alongside Lee, with a lesser title, to share or take over the duties, but the ministers refused to entertain any accommodation. They wanted Lee out, and wanted it done that weekend, while Turner was in Ottawa. The ministers didn't just ask for Lee's dismissal, they demanded it. Furthermore, they said he should be fired and not allowed to resign. Some even mentioned that Turner's mettle for carrying it out was a test of his capacity as a leader, that firing Lee would show his leadership.

Payne concluded that since Lee had lost the confidence of the campaign committee he had therefore lost his usefulness. He hesitated to go any further without consulting Turner's immediate circle, and after the meeting he phoned Bill Macdonald at his cottage in Muskoka. He told Macdonald that Lee would be gone by Saturday if things didn't improve quickly. Macdonald abandoned his cottage and flew to Ottawa. The next day Payne sent Rick Alway to Toronto to meet the Turner flight from Prince Albert and to brief Mike Hunter, an old Turner aide aboard the campaign plane, about the latest poll results, but instructed him not to inform Turner about the Dump-Lee plot. He didn't want to distract Turner while he was campaigning. As a final step Payne invited Lalonde, Erola, and Herb Gray to meet in the Château Laurier Saturday morning. He also invited Jim Grandy, who agreed to come, and Simon Reisman, who was out of town.

On Saturday morning, the morning after Lloyd Axworthy's wedding, the Dump-Lee group assembled in Room 473 of the Château Laurier. Aside from Payne, there were Marc Lalonde, Judy Erola, Herb Gray, Rick Alway, Mike Hunter, Bill Macdonald, and Jim Grandy. They knew that John and Geills Turner would be breakfasting down the corridor in Room 495 with Senator Jerry Grafstein and his wife.

The Turners entered the lobby together at about 9:30 a.m., but Geills lost her temper on her way up and became separated from her husband. As Turner walked down the fourth-floor corridor alone, Mike Hunter intercepted him and said that a group of people had to see him on urgent campaign business. Turner promised to drop in after breakfast.

At around 11 Turner came to the door of Room 473. One look at the glum faces assembled there gave him a fair idea of what was on their minds. He had heard complaints from candidates in the field and he knew a storm was building; in fact, Lalonde had already written him a letter urging him to sack Lee. Turner had complaints of his own; in his opinion Lee had bungled the announcement of the Davey appointment, and he was still furious at him for releasing the news without warning. But Turner had miscalculated the depth and vigour of the anti-Lee feelings, and was amazed that events had progressed so far.

"We've got a real problem and you're going to have to act on it," Payne said as he and Alway outlined the problem.

"Is there another answer?" he asked.

"No," Payne replied.

Even the usually low-key Jim Grandy was vehement; if Grandy was vehement it had to be serious. The group relayed and endorsed the cabinet's contention that Lee should not escape with a resignation, that he should be fired and should be seen to be fired. Lalonde in particular argued that Turner had to show himself to be a strong leader; any face-saving formula to ease Lee out and spare his feelings made Turner look weak. Nobody spoke up in opposition.

"I want to do this alone with the guy," Turner said. "He's a good friend and I want to do it in a way that's as gentle as possible."

Turner could not bring himself to fire people. Aside from his painful cabinet-making experience six weeks earlier, Turner had fired only one person in his life – a secretary while he was minister of finance – and for that he had needed a year (and a lot of nagging) to screw up his resolve.

Before the hour ended Turner phoned Keith Davey, told him he was about to fire Lee, and asked him to take over. Much as he and Davey differed, Turner had nobody else with experience to turn to, which summarized the organizational depth of the Liberal Party. At the same time Mike Hunter called Lee at campaign headquarters and asked him to meet Turner at the prime minister's Harrington Lake residence at 3 o'clock. Lee, who now wanted to quit more than ever, understood the high-noon dimension to the meeting. He was waiting for Turner's response to the ultimatum he gave in his five-page memo.

Lee had an early afternoon glass of wine at the Four Seasons with Linda Diebel, a reporter with the Montreal *Gazette*, and left directly for Harrington Lake without giving Diebel a hint of the breaking crisis. Donald Wilson, his neighbour and 23-year-old errand boy in jeans, drove Lee in his Lincoln into the Gatineau Hills. A waiting Mountie unlocked the gate and in a separate vehicle escorted them down the mile-long driveway. Lee walked around to the back of the rambling white cottage and stepped onto the porch. It overlooked the lake, where he could see Geills, off in the distance, sunning herself on a rock below. Turner, wearing shorts, sandals, and sunglasses and, as usual, smoking a cigar, hurried out to meet him. He clapped Lee on the shoulder and forced a macho grin. Turner looked haggard and puffy. Lee had never seen him look so bad, not even during the worst stretches of the leadership campaign.

The two sat down alone on porch chairs and immediately got down to business. Lee asked if he had read his memo. Turner said he had and told him it was pretty rough.

"By the way," Turner added, flicking a finger toward Geills sunning herself on the lakeshore, "you didn't fool her one bit with that other memo you sent."

Lee said Geills had to get off the plane because her presence interfered with the tour and made everybody's job more difficult. Turner pretended not to understand what he was talking about.

"You know what is going on," Lee said. "Don't give me the 'you don't know' because you sit there and you don't do anything about it."

"It's a very difficult situation," Turner replied in a tone of resignation.

"I don't care," Lee barked. "I can't have it. I cannot have the prime minister's wife running the election tour."

Lee asked if he had read Reid's latest poll results. "Oh shit, it's inside," Turner replied as he jumped up to get it. He emerged a few seconds later with the Reid envelope and tore it open and studied the results. As he digested the numbers he grew increasingly distraught. While Lee and most other campaign workers had watched their standing skid from first to second, Turner was still labouring under the illusion that he was ahead. Only now did he realize for the first time that he had fallen behind Mulroney; what was worse, the figures showed the Conservatives nine points ahead and gaining. The results stunned Turner. In one month public opinion had shifted from majority Liberal to majority Conservative. Never in the history of Canadian politics had campaign polls swung so dramatically.

"I've screwed it up, I've screwed it up," Turner muttered as he scanned the summaries.

"Can we save it?" he asked Lee.

"In my opinion, only if we return to our leadership [campaign] system," Lee replied.

"You know you have enemies in cabinet," Turner said.

Lee said he knew about opposition from Lalonde, Judy Erola, Herb Gray, and Gerry Regan, but said that he also had supporters in the cabinet, the caucus, and the campaign structure. The conversation continued further before Turner finally told Lee that he could not accept his demands. Lee said that was okay and picked up the brown Reid envelope and scrawled his resignation on the back.

"In light of media reaction to Senator Keith Davey's appointment, I felt I had no alternative but to resign as National Campaign Director effectively immediately," the statement said. "My resignation was accepted and the Prime Minister and I left each other on the best of terms."

Two hastily penned sentences above his signature ended Lee's command of the campaign. Turner looked at the envelope and questioned the mention of Davey's name. Lee said it was the truth and would only lead to further questioning if omitted.

"Besides," Lee added, "I presume you're going to make him the National Campaign Director."

"Well," Turner admitted, "there is nobody else."

Barely twenty minutes had passed, but Lee had no reason to linger and stood up to leave. Turner put his arm around Lee and pulled him close to give him the famous blue-eyed stare.

"When we win the election you and Chatty will be our first dinner guests at Sussex Drive."

Lee remained silent and walked back toward his car. Tagging along, Turner said he didn't know what to do. Finally, as they rounded the corner of the house, with tears in his eyes, Turner said: "Bill, tell me honestly. Do you think I have sold out to the party establishment?"

"Yes, John," Lee replied, "I'm sorry, but I do."

Turner embraced Lee and clapped him on the back as he got into the car. Wilson, the driver, had picked up Lee from meetings with Turner often enough, and couldn't help noticing that this time Turner did not come around to his side of the car to shake his hand.

As Lee left, Turner called Payne at the Château Laurier and

announced that he had just completed the firing. Payne told Turner to go and have a whisky and then phoned Mike Hunter to relay the news and have him issue a press release.

Back at 130 Slater Street Lee handed the resignation envelope to his administrative assistant to type up, and then he personally released it to Canadian Press. After that he cleaned out his desk and left.

Several others quit along with him, including Sandra Severn, his executive director. Turner could not have designed a more dedicated worker than Severn. She idolized him. She had first glimpsed him at the 1968 leadership convention and immediately wondered what she was doing in the green dress of one of Robert Winters's girls. Later, as a Liberal Party employee during the Trudeau era, she raised people's eyebrows by somewhat imprudently hanging a picture of Turner in her office. She left that job in 1974 and took a pay cut to become a special assistant to Turner in Finance. She joined Lee at ECL in 1981 and was headed for a partnership when she took a leave to organize Turner's convention plans. She scheduled daily committee meetings at 7 a.m. and, when busy, at 6 a.m., and concocted possibly the most elaborate convention plan ever seen. That time her dedication paid off. She was out of the office when Lee returned from Harrington Lake but when she got back and heard the news she quit on the spot. She refused to work for Keith Davey and, with her knowledge of the Red Leaf shenanigans, she doubted that Davey would want her.

Over in John Swift's office in the PMO, a team of Turner aides debated the wording of the press release announcing Lee's firing. Mike Hunter eventually called in Payne to peruse the draft. At that moment Lee's "resignation" statement appeared on the Canadian Press newswire, which changed everything. Turner's "firing" was supposed to be announced before Lee could declare he had "resigned", but the group had been too slow drafting the announcement. Now Payne knew that cabinet ministers would be calling to demand why Lee had been let off with a resignation.

"This is going to be an issue," Payne told Turner over the phone. "Did you fire him?"

"Yes," Turner replied.

"Are you sure you fired him?" Payne pressed.

"Yes," Turner responded.

Payne asked yet again.

"I fired him, I fired him, I fired him," Turner declared.

With that assurance the group issued Turner's press release.

"I have decided that changes must be made in our national campaign," Turner's terse statement said. "I invited Bill Lee to meet with me at Harrington Lake this afternoon. As a result of that meeting, I have accepted his resignation as National Campaign Director. I have asked Senator Keith Davey to take charge of the campaign effective immediately."

The statement was not only tough and sly (since the word "fired" was never used) but callous, especially for someone who had worked hard and without pay. It showed no appreciation for past service and expressed no regret or good wishes for the future. The Turner forces hoped the incident would show decisive leadership and then drop off the front page and die, but Turner's "firing" declaration contradicted Lee's "resignation" claim and that inconsistency kept the story alive. The media wanted to know who was fibbing. Television crews patrolled Lee's house and the networks urged both Turner and Lee to come before the camera and explain their story. Turner, touring the Gaspé, heated up the story further the following Monday by saying straight out that he had requested Lee's resignation.

"I wanted to reorient the campaign so I asked Mr. Davey to replace Mr. Lee," Turner told reporters.

"Mr. Turner's statement is simply not true," Lee responded hours later. "This is not the John Turner that I know."

The dramatic events astounded the Tories more than anybody else. They couldn't believe that Turner, on his deathbed, would deliberately embarrass Lee and hasten his own demise by embracing the tired old Liberal formula of calling in the Rainmaker. They thought that such internal squabbling happened only to themselves. Norm Atkins, Lee's opposite number in the Mulroney camp, didn't understand what the Liberals were doing. He didn't think the fault was Lee's, and in any case believed that senior people should never be let go in the middle of a campaign no matter how serious the problem. Atkins phoned Lee and told him, one pro to another, that he was sorry to hear what had happened.

Instead of helping Turner, the change of campaign directors perpetuated the chaos and even aggravated it, which set back the campaign even further. Public support for Turner collapsed outright and Reid's polls showed him sinking faster than ever. For a while he dropped a point a day. The Davey appointment sent out exactly the wrong signals and reinforced people's growing disenchantment. Turner's callous statement about Lee exposed the campaign's internal disarray for all to see and cast doubt on his managerial competence, once his trump card over Mulroney. It also revealed a streak of coldheartedness and made him less likable. Voters wondered how Turner could run the country if he couldn't manage an election campaign. Whether Davey was more competent didn't matter; the public was comparing Turner's competence with Mulroney's and saw Turner always stumbling while Mulroney glided along. People started thinking of Turner as the summer prime minister.

Davey moved into the Prime Minister's Office as he had done during the Trudeau elections and directed the campaign mostly from there. But no Rainmaker could save the campaign at this point. A bagful of gimmicks couldn't transform Turner's discredited image in the space of a month. The Liberal leader came close to becoming an object of ridicule. People focused on his throat-clearing and staccato delivery instead of what he said, and reporters started looking for accidents. Davey persuaded Turner to apologize for bum-patting a month after the crime. He started de-emphasizing fiscal responsibility and the need to reduce the deficit. Instead Davey moved Turner to the left with an emphasis on traditional Liberal values, as if he was remoulding Turner into a blue-eyed Trudeau. He also dug out Grafstein's black ads and put them on the air.

"The high road was a no road," Davey told Roy MacGregor of the Toronto *Star*. "When he became a streetfighter, we got a campaign."

One of the black ads showed the northern Quebec town of Schefferville standing forlorn and ghost-like following the closing of the Iron Ore Company of Canada mine. An announcer's voice reminded viewers that Brian Mulroney, the company president, had closed the mine and killed the town. Viewers also saw an advertisement featuring a shopping cart full of boxes labelled promises and a man, presumably Mulroney, giving them away like candy. The Liberals had launched a desperate campaign, and the dirty tactics didn't work. By now Canadians had made up their minds and were cheering for Mulroney; the black ads gave them one more reason to question the character of John Turner.

On September 4 1984 Turner suffered the biggest election collapse in the history of the Liberal Party. The Tories took 49.9 per cent of the popular vote compared to 28.2 per cent for the Liberals and 18.7 for the NDP. The seat breakdown ran: Conservatives 211, Liberals 40, NDP 30, and one independent. Quebec seats swung from 74 to 1 for the Liberals to 58 to 17 for the Tories. Turner, who captured Vancouver Quadra by more than three thousand votes, showed dignity in losing. He conceded defeat graciously and spent the evening buoying the spirits of crushed Liberals.

Turner resigned as prime minister on September 17, eighty days after he was sworn in, thus escaping by eleven days Lee's warning that he might be prime minister for the shortest time in Canadian history. (In 1896 Sir Charles Tupper lasted only sixtynine days.) The leader Lee sold to Liberal delegates as a winner in June proved to be the party's biggest loser ever in September. Turner had run the most inept election campaign anybody could remember; the old adage "elections are lost, not won" might have been coined for his performance.

Lee made strategic errors. He gave people little reason to vote for Turner other than the negative one that he was different from Trudeau. He allowed control of the campaign to slip out of his hands and demanded it back only after it was too late. He let Turner, the self-proclaimed CEO, run the campaign knowing it was the road to ruin. Taking on Red Leaf Communications in confrontational style when he might have massaged it with tact and diplomacy was another mistake. And he employed two pollsters, Reid and Goldfarb, whose rivalry created tension and cost the campaign unnecessary expense. The Tories spent $2-million on polling and got $2-million worth; the Liberals spent $1.2-million and got $600,000 worth. While the Tories got a motion picture of public opinion, the Liberals had to settle for a series of snapshots with two prints per frame.

Knowing that Turner couldn't win it, Lee should have vetoed the television debate instead of using it to paper over Turner's July holiday. Despite Tory taunting, Keith Davey didn't allow

Trudeau into a TV studio with Joe Clark during the 1980 election, and rode to victory. At no time did Lee's failure to seize control hurt more than the briefings in preparation for the debate, where the sessions were large, unwieldy, and unfocused. Turner brought in old friends and Lee didn't stop it, until at one point seventeen people crowded into Turner's briefing room, with no single person coaching him step by step. Consequently Turner received conflicting advice on issues such as his patronage appointments. By contrast Mulroney sat down with four advisers who grilled him on issues and drilled his answers until they had straightened out every kink. As the man in charge, Lee had to accept responsibility for letting his candidate enter the studio unprepared.

But the absolutely critical mistakes belonged solely to Turner. Lee did not appoint the "same old gang" to the cabinet, nor submit to Trudeau's patronage, nor call an ill-advised election, nor pat bums, nor throw rocks at Mulroney from a glass house. Those were the decisions and actions that killed Turner, and the CEO executed those disasters on his own in defiance of Lee's advice. On the major decisions Lee proved to be correct. Turner never understood the underlying reason he inherited an 11-point lead in the Gallup poll, and because he never understood it, he promptly squandered it. Turner threw away his big advantages – newness and competence – in spite of Lee, not because of him. The fact that Turner had no plan allowed him to be buffeted by the latest air current, usually in the direction of short-term expediency. Turner, above all, was the one who charged into a campaign without policies, money, or a machine. Turner fell onto his own sword.

Or was he pushed? And was the sword planted in the path of his falling body?

It is hard to think how Pierre Trudeau could have made things more difficult for his successor. From the timing of the regal and papal visits to the handling of the patronage list, Trudeau's actions unquestionably hurt Turner, and that raised the question of why. Everybody knew Trudeau disliked Turner, but few attributed a conspiratorial motive to his actions. They believed that in his final year Trudeau did whatever he wanted to do and damn the consequences, that John Turner was a big boy who could look after himself, and that whatever happened after he left office was Turner's problem. Nobody laboured under the illusion that Trudeau had gone out of his way to do Turner any favours, but few believed that he had actively sought to harm his successor and fellow Liberal. Lee took a less charitable view. He came to believe that Trudeau had deliberately set out to destroy Turner; during the 1984 election campaign he came across some evidence that disturbed him.

On July 30, five days before Lee and Turner parted company, Lee's office at ECL received a phone call from Eric Boyd. An old Air Force friend of Lee's who later became a senior official at the Canadian Radio-Television and Telecommunications Commission, Boyd wanted to pass on an incredible story. An ECL staffer took notes and dashed off a memo, which was dispatched to Lee by runner. The memo, which referred to Turner by his initials JNT, said:

Eric Boyd called today. [July 30]

He says that according to a usually reliable source and confirmed indirectly by Marc Lalonde, the following took place: There were a number of meetings held at Trudeau's house in Montreal. Attending (at various times) were ... [At this point the memo mentions five names.]

Following these meetings Lalonde called JNT and said if Keith Davey didn't come back in, Quebec would ease off its support and assistance to him.

It appears that the assessment being made of these meetings is that JNT is to be set up so that he loses or has a minority which he subsequently loses. JNT would then be squeezed out. Then Lucie Pépin who by then would would have received needed profile would come in as the perfect candidate – francophone, woman. (I doubt Chrétien is aware of this part).

Lee put the memo aside. A lot of contentious reports crossed his desk in the course of a campaign.

The following day a long-time friend of Lee's, a distinguished Ottawa doctor,* phoned and said he had to see him immediately. Lee said he was busy and had no time, but the doctor insisted it was urgent and said that if Lee didn't come to him, he would go to his office on Slater Street.

---

*The doctor has discussed this matter with the author on the understanding that he would not be identified.

"I'll be there in ten minutes," the doctor announced.

It was the same doctor who five or six weeks earlier had stopped off at Lee's ECL office and sought assurance he would not run Turner's election campaign, and had then left satisfied when Lee told him he had no intention of doing anything of the sort. This time when the doctor arrived he closed the office door, and looked Lee straight in the eye.

"Bill, you are exhausted," he said. "You're going to resign from the campaign."

"I'm not exhausted," Lee protested. "I'm tired but I'm not exhausted. This is a crucial part of the campaign."

Then the doctor came to the point. He explained that he had reason to believe that Trudeau, Lalonde, Davey, and several others were plotting to bring down Turner. He said the plot started at meetings in 24 Sussex Drive soon after Turner announced his candidacy for the party leadership, and at that time was directed towards denying him the nomination. When that failed, the secret meetings shifted to Trudeau's new home in Montreal and now, in mid-campaign, were concentrated on bringing Turner down to "an ignominious defeat" in the election. The doctor refused to divulge where he had learned the information but revealed that he had got it first-hand.

"There is no question that this is fact," the doctor asserted. "No question. You are the one person standing between Turner and that ignominious defeat – and all of the other Turner loyalists. So they are out to get rid of you and separate Turner from his loyalists. That's why I want you out of this thing. I want you to resign immediately on grounds of exhaustion. Your loyalty and commitment are exactly what I would expect of you, but the matter is within their control."

Lee had known the doctor for years and trusted him implicitly. His story matched Boyd's account, but Lee was simply too busy to do anything about it. Turner was on the first week of his tour, and the controversy surrounding Keith Davey's appointment as national co-chairman had just broken. Everything was going badly and Lee had no time. He told the doctor he appreciated his concern but would not resign – at least until he had it out with Turner personally on the weekend.

Lee was out of the campaign by week's end. He then had time to visit his old friend Eric Boyd to inquire how he knew of the alleged meetings. Boyd said he had been told by Lucien Saint-

Amand* who worked for him at the CRTC. Saint-Amand grew up with Lalonde and knew him intimately; Boyd reported that when he learned about the plot from Lalonde, he was so shocked that, after wrestling with his conscience, he brought the story to Boyd because he knew of his friendship with Lee.

Lee returned to the doctor and showed him the memo. "It's the same story, but the basis of my belief is more substantial than Saint-Amand's," the doctor assured him. The doctor's response satisfied Lee that the story had substance; two unconnected channels had produced essentially the same story. It convinced him that there had been a plot to bring down Turner, a plot by Liberals to damage the Liberal campaign.

If Trudeau had plotted to bring down Turner, it explained a number of things. It explained why he clung to power until the eleventh hour and left no election machinery for Turner. It might explain why he in effect called Turner a liar during the leadership race, why he refused to embrace him on the convention podium, why he sandbagged him on the patronage appointments, why he hurried to fill hundreds of patronage posts in his final month, and why he boxed in Turner over the royal and papal visits.

If Lalonde was involved in the plot, it might explain his eagerness for an early election, his insistence on controlling the Quebec campaign but not running as a candidate, and his decision to freeze the Chrétien workers out of the Quebec campaign. Possibly it might even explain why Lalonde's finance department panicked Turner with the doomsday briefing on the economy that proved astoundingly false. Unemployment, according to the forecast, would jump to 15 per cent, interest rates and inflation would skyrocket, and the dollar would plummet to 65 cents. The economy did not plunge. It surged forward in central Canada and the Mulroney government claimed the credit. Interest rates and inflation dropped, and even unemployment eased off. The dollar held steady, and even advanced marginally.

As far as the economy was concerned, November would have been a good month for Turner to fight an election.

---

*Saint-Amand later said he might have to deny the story if it became public; however, a taped conversation, in which Saint-Amand confirms this account, is in the author's possession.

SEVENTEEN

MULRONEY IN POWER

But for the Turner campaign, Lee could have retired from business and politics unscathed by defeat. His brilliant career had never experienced failure. He had overwhelmed the Armed Forces, advanced Paul Hellyer, and wowed Pierre Trudeau. He had turned lobbying on its ear and amassed a personal fortune, and had just finished making a prime minister. In effect, he had hit home runs every time at bat. Now, after being called off the bench, he had struck out in the seventh game of the World Series with the nation watching. It didn't matter that he still had one of the best batting averages around, nor that he was struck out by spitballs; his team had crashed and that was what counted. After a career full of triumphs staged from the back room, he had stepped into the public arena and fallen flat on his face – and this one failure became his public identity.

Politics is a game of winners and losers, of ins and outs. The game is rough, unfair, and fickle, and the players take risks; you are a genius if you win and an incompetent if you lose. Lee had played in 1968 and won big, and had parlayed his political success into business success. By winning with Turner in 1984, he could have boosted ECL's sagging fortunes, reversing his company's slide by attracting new clients, and gaining ground on PAI. From late June to mid-July, when Turner looked like a winner, a few PAI staffers moaned that ECL had climbed back into the driver's seat, that Turner would win the election and clobber PAI. PAI was dead in the water trying to compete against Bill Lee, the king, operating out of the Prime Minister's Office. But Turner lost. That aggravated ECL's plight and brought on an immediate crisis.

Lee had been talking of personal retirement for years. Exhausted and demoralized by the experience with Turner, he now told his two younger partners, Steve Markey and Rick Bertrand, that he wanted to get out of the business no later than 1988, and sooner if possible. Markey and Bertrand realized that they confronted a dilemma for which neither had a resolution. If the company faced problems with Lee, it faced bigger ones without him. Bill Lee was the senior partner and the reason corporations paid big fees; without him ECL could foresee trouble in attracting clients. With him the company was waving a Liberal flag in a suddenly Tory town, which was the last thing the company needed. ECL had failed to cover its political bases and now faced the worst four months in its corporate history. But the problem went deeper than a simple lack of Tories in the firm. Lee had not established an independent corporate identity for ECL the way MacNaughton had with PAI. PAI brought people in and moved them around; MacNaughton could come and go and PAI stayed the same. By contrast, when people thought of ECL they still thought of Bill Lee. Neither Markey nor Bertrand had the profile with which to attract clients. The success or failure of ECL still hinged on Lee, and at the moment Lee's political currency had suffered devaluation.

Markey and Bertrand debated their options. Both understood that ECL would undergo change whatever happened. The new partner replacing Lee – the person to whom Lee sold his shares – would make or break the company. After thinking it over, Markey and Bertrand decided to pursue an accommodation with PAI, and asked Lee if they could negotiate the sale of his shares to PAI. Lee gave them his blessing, as long as the sale met his price.

ECL and PAI had talked merger four years earlier, but under very different circumstances. Then ECL sat on top of the market and it was the scrappy young upstart PAI that wanted to deal. The intervening four years had changed everything; the small company down the block had grown up, and now towered over its older neighbour. This time ECL made the approach. Markey told PAI's Mike Robinson that ECL's interest in merging had nothing to do with the election, but Robinson did not believe it. He knew that ECL was worried.

Agreement would not be easy because some formidable obstacles stood in the way. The two sides had different corporate cultures. PAI sought growth while ECL sought profit, and those conflicting objectives made for different evaluations. In ECL's view, PAI's bureaucracy constituted a drain on profit, whereas PAI saw it as essential to expansion. For its part PAI wondered exactly what it would get from ECL; with Lee retired, why should it pay big money for a company that was two partners and a client list? One side's assets were the other's liabilities. Each side had a different approach to servicing that it thought was superior, and a different management structure. Predictably, each side put a premium on the value of its own system.

A merger meant hammering out a common personnel structure, and that raised a separate set of problems relating to people's egos. The company could not have two chief executive officers. ECL would have to defer, and that would require Markey and Bertrand to sacrifice their existing authority in favour of PAI's structured hierarchy. Then there was the major problem of amalgamating client lists. Two sets of clients would inevitably produce overlaps and conflicts of interest that would have to be resolved. A merger would be uneconomic and pointless if too many clients had to be dropped; PAI would have little reason to buy ECL if it couldn't keep most of ECL's clients.

On the plus side was the fact that Markey and Robinson were old and dear friends. They did most of the negotiating and that made things easier. They agreed from the start to open their books and reveal their client lists. ECL hesitated momentarily about unveiling its deepest secrets to its chief competitor, but PAI promised not to touch their clients for at least a year. The show-and-tell session disclosed surprising results. Conflict of interest proved less irksome than either side expected; in fact, it proved to be hardly a problem. PAI could devour ECL's clientele virtually intact without any conflicts. The chief obstacle was overcome.

The show-and-tell unearthed one other surprise: ECL made more profit than PAI – not only a higher rate of profit but higher profit totals. The raw figures alone were a little misleading because as a matter of policy ECL partners drew modest salaries and big dividends, whereas all senior PAI management earned six-figure salaries; the different policies skewed profit figures in opposite directions and artificially widened the gap. Nevertheless, the results were amazing considering the relative sizes of the companies. PAI pulled in about $3-million in annual billings compared to about $1-million for ECL. But PAI carried such high overhead that ECL earned more net income at year-end. PAI's inferior profitability astounded Markey and Bertrand and made them think twice about the wisdom of a merger. They knew that PAI had deliberately forgone income but had not realized how much. ECL always paid big dividends and PAI never paid any. The two ECL partners could not see themselves trading their money-making shares for no-dividend stock. Their personal incomes would drop. They had other reservations too, regarding their role in the enlarged PAI. They could not bring themselves to surrender managerial authority and exchange a big chunk of ECL for a thin slice of PAI. Lee, who would be walking into retirement with a $300,000 windfall from the sale of his shares, supported the deal; but Markey and Bertrand mulled it over and pulled out. The deal was off; the companies would not merge. ECL would have to resolve its predicament some other way.

As ECL pulled out of these negotiations, Lee received a phone call from Pierre Fortier, a well-known Tory lawyer in Ottawa. Fortier had heard that ECL was overseeing the Canadian Association of Broadcasters' search for a new president to replace the retiring Ernie Steele and wanted to recommend a friend. Soon the telephone talk turned to other matters, since at that moment Fortier happened to be leaving the practice of law to set up a lobbying company with another well-known Tory, Paul Curley, who had been Mulroney's campaign secretary during the election. Lee saw instantly that a pair of plugged-in Tories like Curley and Fortier could work miracles for ECL. Curley was better known but either one would do, and both would be a coup, something PAI could not match. The prospect of getting two high-profile Tories into ECL in one sweep excited him. Lee wasted no time arranging a meeting for some merger talk.

The Markey-Bertrand team again represented ECL and met Fortier at the Four Seasons for an exploratory breakfast. Unlike the ECL-PAI match-up, this alliance held potential for a perfect fit: an established but troubled company with a good client base embracing two Tories new to the game but with the political connections and energy to turn it around. It should have worked. But the two sides started off on different planes and never found common ground; that doomed the talks. Markey and Bertrand were not prepared to let the newcomers in cheap – ECL made too much money for that – while Fortier didn't want to spend a lot of money buying into an existing operation, and felt he didn't have to. Curley and Fortier already had several clients and were confident that their Tory status would attract more and save the need for buying clients for a high capital start-up cost. The eggs had hardly arrived when both sides realized that an alliance was not on. They could enjoy breakfast, but ECL would have to find another solution.

Two days after he thumped John Turner, Brian Mulroney sent Bill Lee a handwritten letter saying that he and Mila wished him well and especially wished the best for his wife now that she was undergoing surgery. The note went on to say that politics was tough but that being in one party did not prevent him from having the highest regard for a person in another party. Lee appreciated Mulroney's compassionate gesture. Norm Atkins, Mulroney's campaign chairman, phoned a week later to report that he and some Mulroney advisers had just finished lunch with Mulroney and they had all received instructions to "let the word get out to all the cabinet ministers that as far as I'm concerned Bill Lee is persona grata." Lee asked Atkins to relay back his sincere thanks to Mulroney, and quickly followed it up with a note expressing his gratitude and wishing him well in office.

ECL could not have hoped for a more gracious response from Mulroney. But benevolence from the incoming prime minister did not solve the firm's problems. Mulroney's attitude, paradoxically, didn't matter nearly as much as what the corporate community thought his attitude was. Mulroney could write a thousand notes saying he held no grudges and it wouldn't matter unless he sent them to the companies that retained firms like ECL and paid their fees. The election débâcle caused ECL more problems with clients than with the Tory government.

In the world of corporate clients political connections are vastly overrated. By and large, propositions still get advanced on their merits, not on the basis of friendships with the prime minister. There was no reason why a Liberal who operated professionally could not work effectively with a Conservative government; in fact Lee enjoyed more goodwill from Mulroney than he had had from Trudeau in the last decade. Prime ministers change and so do the goals of government, but the system remains in place and continues to function more or less as always. As a Liberal Lee lost maybe half a step when dealing with Tory ministers' offices, but that hardly affected his ability to service clients. Only ten to fifteen per cent of ECL's dealings were at the ministerial level, and even there no minister would cut off ECL and risk bad press for using public office for partisan discrimination. Most of the contacts were with the bureaucracy, which hardly changed, and there, after sixteen years in the corridors of power, ECL could outmuscle recently arrived competitors who entered the market with political connections.

While Lee lacked access to Mulroney, he had maintained a string of friendships among prominent Tories like Finlay Mac-Donald and, more recently, Norm Atkins – who were close to Mulroney. Lee could claim long associations with Deputy Prime Minister Erik Nielsen, a fellow airman during the war, and Finance Minister Michael Wilson, who had sought his advice while in opposition. Some of his closest contacts over the years were Conservatives. Any long-standing Liberal operator with credibility had friends among Tories.

What Lee had lost was *the mythology of the political connection*. ECL encountered, not unfriendliness from Tories, but fear from clients. Corporations needed assurance that their Ottawa consultants were plugged into the senior decision-makers, and were afraid that a Grit firm would bring frowns to governing Tory faces. Lee and his colleagues faced a tall order convincing the marketplace that it could safely choose ECL over one of the new Tory firms.

The fact that corporations worried so much about political access said plenty about the state of business-government relations. For years ECL and PAI had preached the gospel of enlightenment, that effectiveness hinged on merit and presentation and not on connections, that a legitimate case backed by solid documentation would triumph over inside access. But the people behind the preaching were hotshots who ran leadership campaigns and worked in the PMO between times, which perhaps lessened the impact of the message on their corporate listeners. The corporate community may have believed the gospel when they first heard it, but now church was out, and it felt it had to cover its bets. Deep down, businessmen felt a little nudging and winking would help their case, and wanted guys with political pull on their side.

ECL would not collapse overnight. The system didn't punish losers so swiftly and brutally. Most old clients would show basic loyalty and would allow ECL to stumble once or twice; they had built up relationships and would stay, providing ECL serviced them well and didn't get into scrapes with the Mulroney government. New clients were another matter. The new-client market would evaporate almost instantly unless the company moved quickly. As clients dried up, ECL would wither and shrivel up before Mulroney finished his term.

ECL had survived the 1974 election when Bill Neville had left the firm to tilt at windmills and arouse the wrath of John Turner. It had also survived the 1979-80 Clark interregnum unscarred, for which it could partly thank the same Bill Neville, who was then in the Prime Minister's Office as Joe Clark's right-hand man, a circumstance that helped to preserve the mythology of the political connection. Clients wanting to leave ECL had nowhere to go in 1979, because at that time PAI had worse problems with its all-Liberal political cast. That was Clark's 1979. Mulroney's 1984 was dramatically different. Lee's decision to throw in his lot with John Turner had strengthened his Liberal ties and now new competitors with impeccable Conservative credentials had come out of the woodwork to prey on ECL's difficulty. ECL would not escape unscathed the way it had five years earlier under Clark.

In sixteen years ECL had made millions of dollars helping clients resolve crises with government, always counselling them to look forward, to anticipate events and prevent problems before they occurred. Now, ironically, it had failed to follow its own advice, and faced its own crisis with government. Since the Tories had spent most of the previous four years ahead in the polls, it didn't take a genius to predict that Mulroney would win. It made good business sense to prepare for a Conservative government whether the party led in the polls or not. PAI had spent four years carefully stocking its staff with Tories. ECL, busily preaching foresight to its clients, had gone on living without fire insurance knowing that sooner or later the Liberal government would burn down.

ECL needed more than vision and foresight. More than anything, it needed the self-discipline to turn its back on today's big dollars in return for secure earnings tomorrow. The firm had not been able to make that sacrifice; the partners each took out more than $150,000 a year and didn't want to tamper with a winning formula. Now ECL badly needed radical surgery. With Lee leaving, the firm would be down to two partners, neither of whom had senior government experience. How much confidence would clients have in two people who had never been in government? Lee's replacement would have to be good.

Lee first tried to recruit the former Clark minister Bill Jarvis, but he didn't want the work pace. ECL decided that if it couldn't purchase an entrée to the Mulroney government it could buy into the business community; it turned next to Sam Hughes, the president of the Canadian Chamber of Commerce. Hughes had conservative views but carried no political label. What he lacked in partisan identity he made up for in corporate status, since he brought with him national stature as one of the top business spokesmen in Canada. Whenever the government introduced a new budget, Sam Hughes popped up on the television networks to voice the business reaction almost the minute the minister of finance finished his speech. If the *Financial Post* needed business comment, it quoted Hughes. He was the voice of business and always spoke well and looked good on panels. He also happened to be looking for a change of career. His job at the Chamber required him to travel week after week meeting local business groups across the country, and the pace had worn him down. So when Lee offered to bring him into ECL as president he accepted.

Lee sold his shares to the company and signed a contract making him chairman. He would retire slowly, and each year would spend progressively more time in Florida until he was phased out entirely on July 1, 1988. Hughes was given an option to buy Lee's old shares from the company after fourteen months. ECL could have acquired a Tory, but settled on a businessman who didn't satisfy the mythology of the political connection. The company had decided to project a neutral look and put its recovery on a non-political footing. Hughes arrived in 1985 as the latest year-end figures showed ECL's profits down for the first time in history.

With his eye fixed firmly on becoming prime minister, Brian Mulroney started his bureaucratic takeover of power long before the voters of Canada awarded him the job. When he became Conservative leader in June 1983, without waiting to consolidate his grip on the party, he set up an elaborate series of committees to clear his administrative path to office. With that background Mulroney should have been ready to run the country the minute he slid behind his desk in the Langevin Block. But he was far from ready. Mulroney had overplanned the transition and was suffering some of the same glitches that befell John Turner's ill-fated transition to power. Finlay MacDonald, the man Mulroney first appointed to oversee the project, fell victim to internal Tory squabbling and was replaced by Erik Nielsen, the deputy Conservative leader. He saw politics as war and he turned the undertaking into a military operation. Nielsen, who later earned the title "Velcro Lips", buried the planning in so much secrecy that nobody – not even some of the participants – could figure out what was happening. By August 1984, when even the man in the moon foresaw the impending Mulroney sweep, Nielsen's operation had disintegrated into a shambles. Mulroney knew that a bad transition could devastate him as it had done Turner, bringing him to office looking weak and incompetent. Only once since 1957 had a new Conservative government been installed in power, and that occurred in 1979 when Joe Clark became prime minister. The man who handled that transition was Bill Neville. So early in August 1984, in the middle of the election campaign, Mulroney called Neville and asked if he would take over the mess and prepare him for office.

Mulroney believed that he had finally picked the right man. He had gotten to know him after his 1976 leadership loss when Neville first started working for Clark. Mulroney quickly sized him up as a talent and put him onto his well-used telephone network of friends and advisers. Mulroney always understood that Neville's loyalty lay first with Clark. Never hiding the fact that he was a Clark man, Neville became one of the rare Clark loyalists accepted into the Mulroney clan. Once a year or so Neville and Mulroney went fishing together at the Iron Ore Company camp in Labrador. Neville and his wife Marilyn found the Mulroneys a charming couple, and frequently flew down to Montreal for dinner and a hockey game. The Neville-Mulroney friendship survived even the Dump-Clark period, when they supported opposite sides. When Neville left Clark in 1981 Mulroney opened the door that led to his senior job as vice president at the Canadian Imperial Bank of Commerce, and as the assistant to the chairman on public affairs and strategic planning.

At the Commerce in Toronto, Neville worked on one of the most exclusive and prestigious office floors in all Canada. For most of his time only three Commerce officers occupied the august fifty-fourth floor – the chairman, the corporate secretary, and Neville. A butler in red jacket and white gloves padded along the hushed corridors to serve Neville coffee on a silver tray. The glassed-in executive dining room at the top of the silver tower took in as much of Lake Ontario as the eye could see and served some of the city's finest cuisine to its select clientele.

During the 1984 election Neville forsook his princely surroundings at King and Bay Streets each Monday morning and flew to Ottawa. There he sat on an élite strategy committee of top Tories that assembled once a week to advise Mulroney on campaign issues. Norman Atkins chaired the group, and its members included Senator Lowell Murray, Allan Gregg, Finlay MacDonald, Mulroney's aides Charles MacMillan and Jon Johnson, and a few others. The committee checked Mulroney's campaign itinerary, assessed the policy and speeches for the coming week, and recommended issues and themes. It also got involved during times of crisis, such as when Mulroney made his ill-advised patronage statement on the back of the plane. On top of this Mulroney sometimes phoned Neville personally, as he did in early August to ask him to patch up the transition arrangements for his imminent arrival in office.

The bank was eager to maintain its non-partisan profile and Neville didn't think it would free him to undertake this highly political job. But Mulroney had been a member of its board of directors, had used his influence on Neville's behalf before, and now did so again. The bank approved Neville's leave of absence but instructed him to avoid publicity. So Neville started his new duties in Ottawa without announcement and quietly spent August and the first half of September preparing the government apparatus for Mulroney.

When Mulroney returned to Ottawa after his big victory a crowd of television crews staked out Stornoway, waiting for news footage of important officials arriving to brief the prime minister elect. They didn't bother to turn on their portable floodlights or roll their cameras as Bill Neville quietly walked up the laneway. He carried a briefcase containing Mulroney's agenda for the next six weeks, but nobody stirred as he walked past. The man the press mistook for a Mountie or a chef was Mulroney's de facto chief of staff, and was the most important official he would see that morning.

Once inside, Neville stayed through lunch, outlining how Mulroney should proceed, what needed to be done immediately, and what could wait. He described the choices before him and advised him how to meet with Turner. From his experience with Clark, he was able to brief Mulroney on the requirements of the Prime Minister's Office, how it related to the rest of government, and how it might be structured. Finally, he unfurled what amounted to a thirty-day program for getting the government on its feet, starting with an agenda for the first cabinet meeting. Over the next few days he delivered a set of briefing books describing the mechanics of organizing a cabinet system. Neville warned Mulroney not to tamper with the cabinet's structure until he had some cabinet experience. He suggested forming the cabinet by settling on the key portfolios and assigning them to the ablest MPs, and then using the remaining slots for regional and political balance. Finally, he urged Mulroney to resist caucus pressure for a purge of the public service. The hawks in caucus, who saw the bureaucrats as unrepentant Liberals, were Mulroney's own supporters, but Neville, backed by others, persuaded Mulroney to work with the bureaucracy and not against it.

The transition went smoothly and set Mulroney into office on a solid footing. The unveiling of his cabinet would later draw wide praise from the media and the party. Mulroney, impressed, asked Neville to stay on, but Neville declined so quickly that Mulroney never got to finish his offer; consequently, Neville never learned exactly what he had in mind. He had been in the Prime Minister's Office before and had no interest in returning to government. The bank had made him a senior vice president a few months earlier, and he told Mulroney he planned to stay there. As his last act, the day before Mulroney was sworn in, he spent three hours briefing Bernard Roy about the ins and outs of being principal secretary to the prime minister of Canada and then flew home to Toronto, missing the swearing-in ceremony and the gala celebration he had helped to organize.

The new Mulroney government was hungry for ministerial aides and helped satisfy its appetite by snapping up a couple of PAI staffers. This was a switch; usually PAI took ministerial aides away from government. It had honed the practice into an art form, and now suddenly it came out on the losing side. The energy specialist, Harry Near, joined Energy Minister Pat Carney, and Elizabeth Roscoe went to work for Barbara McDougall, the minister of state for finance. Murray Coolican, PAI's Atlantic manager, took a leave of absence to help Indian and Northern Affairs Minister David Crombie organize his office. PAI nearly lost Michael Coates, its transportation specialist, but Coates, after thinking it over, turned down an offer of a $70,000 chief-of-staff job to stay with PAI for less money. PAI couldn't complain about being raided, since the government had only recovered two of the many people PAI had snatched away from it first. In fact, PAI quietly approved of such movement and benefited from it. Former employees acted as goodwill ambassadors and opened new contacts. They would probably return, with more experience and knowledge. And PAI didn't take long to reverse the flow by taking directly from Mulroney's staff. Mike Robinson asked around who would be the best Tory on Parliament Hill to bring into PAI, and the answer that came back most often was Jon Johnson.

Son of a medical doctor who spent twelve years as a Tory cabinet minister in Manitoba, Johnson was the youngest EA in the short-lived Clark government (who also happened to be working for the youngest minister, Perrin Beatty). He lost his bid for a federal seat in the 1980 election that followed, and returned to the London School of Economics to finish the Ph.D. that the Clark government had interrupted. He had already worked on Mulroney's leadership campaigns in 1976 and 1983 and, after the 1983 victory made Mulroney leader of the opposition, he joined his staff, acquiring such responsibility that he oversaw Mulroney's speeches during the 1984 election and wrote his briefing book for the television debate with Turner. Now he became PAI's consultant on financial services, and rose to vice president within a year.

Unlike ECL, PAI had actively prepared for a Tory government. David MacNaughton had been caught flat-footed by Joe Clark's victory in 1979 and had vowed never again to let that happen. Since March 1980 he had methodically stocked PAI's ranks with Conservatives and by 1983 reached approximate parity between Liberals and Tories. Aside from making the firm bi-partisan, MacNaughton had also set out to make PAI's appeal corporate rather than personal. Now PAI could look around at its competitors and see itself as better positioned than anybody else. It had no problems compared to ECL; MacNaughton was a Liberal but had not burned himself personally the way Lee had. So PAI should have been in good shape with Mulroney's victory.

But questions lingered. MacNaughton had indeed broadened the working ranks to include Tories, but the senior management stayed prominently Liberal. MacNaughton remained the chairman, Michael Robinson the president, and Torrance Wylie the recently retired founder, and all were partisan Liberals. The marketplace saw them, rather than the bevy of Tories who worked anonymously in the background. MacNaughton and Robinson never hesitated to tell anyone who would listen about their stable of Tories, but PAI didn't have a Tory look. The outside world still viewed it as mostly Grit. The firm had to do something. The Tory hirings had not created a mythology of Tory connections. PAI required a high-profile Tory at the top of the firm, someone seen as opening a pipeline into the Prime Minister's Office; someone whose mere presence would dispel the rumours.

Once MacNaughton concluded that PAI needed a prominent Tory he went straight after the one he wanted. Bill Neville. MacNaughton could think of nobody who would satisfy the need better than Neville, or as easily turn the political mythology in PAI's favour overnight. Neville not only knew the Prime Minister's Office, he had designed it. He knew who the wheels were and how they turned. Mulroney relied on Neville for advice and liked to have him on hand to give him an outside 'read' on major decisions. Neville still talked regularly to his old boss, Joe Clark, now the minister of external affairs, and a string of other ministers. When it came to government sources he had more pipelines than an oil company. Few people in government or out knew the key players better or could discover what they were thinking as well as Neville could.

Not only was he the ultimate insider, he also happened to be one of the foremost authorities on government relations. Saying that Neville knew about public-affairs consulting was like saying that Thomas Edison was familiar with the light bulb. Neville and Lee had invented the practice in 1968. He was a first-rate analyst and prodigious worker who was informed, hard-nosed, and able to write. He kept a good sense of proportion and didn't bend to the crisis of the moment. Nobody could match his list of credits. He would bring in new clients and command higher fees from existing clients. His mere presence at PAI would dispel the gossip and kill the rumours.

MacNaughton set out to get Neville whatever it took. He had first tried to hire him as he left Clark's office in 1981, but his non-competition agreement with ECL had not quite run out, and at that stage PAI could not compete with the Commerce. But Neville respected MacNaughton for trying, because in the spring of 1981, with Clark on the wane, Neville was less than hot property. The two had kept in touch during the intervening years and Neville had arranged for the Commerce to become the banker for PARG (the Public Affairs Resources Group), the holding company that owned PAI and Decima Research, its shares held by Allan Gregg (who ran Decima), Mike Robinson (who now ran PAI), and MacNaughton, who was increasingly consumed by PARG, which he had moved to Toronto, with the thought of eventually moving there himself.

In September, about ten days after Neville arrived back from his transition job in Ottawa, MacNaughton invited him for a drink. They met at the Wellington House next to Neville's Commerce Court office tower, MacNaughton showing up with his partner Allan Gregg, Neville's old colleague in the Conservative Party. MacNaughton quickly got to the point by offering Neville his job as chairman of PAI. Having made PAI the number one firm in town, MacNaughton had turned his attention outward and started to build up PARG, which he saw as the vehicle of the future. The coming of the Mulroney government had convinced him it was desirable for a prominent Liberal like himself to fade out of the daily Ottawa scene sooner rather than later, and leave the chairmanship of PAI in the hands of someone like Neville.

Executives didn't usually build up multi-million-dollar corporations and offer to vacate their posts at 35 in favour of someone else, so the offer surprised Neville. It also intrigued and interested him. If Neville was perfect for PAI, then the chairmanship of PAI was cut out for Neville. Despite his success at the bank, he wanted to return to Ottawa and be near the government. He was also looking for more income and now, three and a half years after MacNaughton's first approach, PAI could afford to outbid the Commerce. The bank couldn't pay performance bonuses; PAI could. Neville had no interest in buying into the company, so MacNaughton offered salary incentives based on revenue generation in the first year and on company profit the following years. If Neville triggered new growth his income would top a quarter of a million dollars.

Neville mulled over his options. He could stay at the bank, which he enjoyed. He was aware that he also headed the list for the presidency of the Canadian Association of Broadcasters. The CAB had made him a tempting offer, which was ironic because exactly ten years earlier it had turned its back on him after John Turner blackballed him in the aftermath of the 1974 election. In those days Neville was treated as a leper while Turner reigned as the almighty minister of finance. Now Neville entertained competing offers while Turner licked his wounds in humiliation and pondered his future.

The broadcasters wanted Neville as much as MacNaughton did, and kept offering more salary and adding perks. The CAB competed as hard as it could, but it was tough for an association not geared to profit to match a private company in offering bonuses. The CAB virtually pleaded with him and even enlisted friends to persuade him. He was sorely tempted. Broadcasting had always fascinated him; this was the only trade-association job in the country that attracted him. But while he liked the job and the people, heading an association would restrict his political freedom, and he wanted to keep active in politics, especially now that the Conservatives held power. He was too enthralled by the Tory back rooms to stay out of them and he couldn't be chief lobbyist for the broadcasting industry and serve its interests faithfully if he was simultaneously keeping the unquestioned trust of Brian Mulroney. The CAB wanted him to be a neutral friend of the prime minister – which was impossible, since Mulroney had no neutral friends.

Neville decided to accept MacNaughton's offer, and become the chairman of PAI. His announcement astounded the lobbying community. The reactions ranged from bursts of amazement, through spurts of cynicism to expressions of admiration, each with a measure of justification. The appointment worked as effectively as MacNaughton had hoped. Neville's hiring killed the gossip about PAI's future and put the firm back onto the offensive. PAI no longer needed to reassure clients. It no longer needed to defend itself. It no longer needed to explain. It no longer needed to say anything about its political status. It had regained the mythology. MacNaughton had pulled off the coup of the year. PAI returned to its familiar task of chasing new clients and pursuing growth, and Neville set about proving himself worth every penny of his salary.

EIGHTEEN

THE BLACKLISTING

One consultant with no worries about the coming of the Mulroney government was Duncan Edmonds. He had already established his Tory credentials and had paid dearly for doing so, having taken up political arms on behalf of Joe Clark in 1977 when the Conservatives still laboured in opposition. He had sold his profitable fifty-per-cent stake in PAI and turned his back on the ruling Liberals when there was nothing in it for him. His sojourn with Clark had not been a success, but nobody could deny or belittle the price he had paid to help the Conservatives. On the morning after Mulroney's victory he was in good standing with the new ruling order.

After leaving Clark in 1978, Edmonds had suffered through some ups and downs during the ensuing six years. As a first move he reactivated JDE Consulting from his pre-PAI days and set out to reclaim Canada Safeway as a client. PAI still had Canada Safeway, and a good sportsman didn't sell a firm like PAI for cash and then try to steal the clientele back from the new owner. But to Edmonds Canada Safeway was different. It was a special client, one that he had originally recruited into PAI and had always serviced more as a personal client than as a corporate one. He had sat on its board of directors; it seemed natural for the two to be reunited now that Edmonds was back in business. It surprised nobody that Canada Safeway switched to JDE Consulting and restored Edmonds to its board of directors. He had defied etiquette, but everybody pretended that it had never happened.

It didn't take Edmonds long to get back on his feet and substantially improve the $40,000 income he had earned under Clark. But it was not the same as before. Having lost all his blue-chip clients except Canada Safeway, he had to start over again in 1978, and he found it tougher the second time around. Edmonds picked up Coca Cola, a major coup, in 1979 when the Clark government banned the exploding 1.5-litre soft-drink bottle, and eventually he accumulated several clients. But it dawned on him that consulting was no longer his chief love, and was not really what he wanted to do.

On a visit to South Korea he had become intrigued and captivated by its economic vitality, entrepeneurial spirit, and general bustle. He was so impressed that he started a company called Canada-Korea Ventures Ltd. to concentrate on international business opportunities. Canada-Korea Ventures was a trading company that introduced Canadian businessmen to projects and joint ventures in Korea and financed its operations through fees from its clients, and possibly a slice of the take. Edmonds did enough consulting to keep him in touch with Ottawa and to finance his Korean dealings.

In June 1980 Edmonds travelled to China with the former Defence Minister Jim Richardson, who was a guest of the Chinese. When Edmonds checked out business opportunities in China he discovered that Canadians were mostly out of the picture while U.S. multinationals were busily establishing themselves. The most active American individual was Cyrus Eaton Jr., of Cleveland, son of the famous industrialist. Edmonds met Eaton and after several meetings moved to Cleveland to become president of the Cyrus Eaton group of companies. He was on the point of rolling up JDE Consulting in Ottawa when he discovered that Eaton was effectively broke; Cyrus Sr. had used up most of his money and left little for his son. So Edmonds moved back to Ottawa, mothballing the Chinese idea, but still excited by the prospects of Korea.

Later he met Peter Pocklington at a businessmen's dinner in Toronto and the two hit it off immediately. Within a month Edmonds started to act as a consultant for Gainers, Pocklington's meat-packing company. The two of them flew around in a corporate jet playing backgammon and exploring different ventures for Gainers, such as establishing a joint-venture meat-packing plant in Cuba with the Castro government. Cuba showed keen interest but ex-President Gerald Ford, recruited by Pocklington as a board member of his ill-fated Fidelity Trust, opposed the deal, solemnly advising Pocklington that the United States disapproved of business deals with Castro. The Pocklington-Edmonds relationship withered in 1983 when Pocklington ran for the leadership of the Conservative Party while Edmonds, unimpressed by his grasp of the issues, supported John Crosbie.

Edmonds got involved in other diversions but devoted most of his energy to Korea. South Korea was the kind of country where everybody was working on a deal, and as a regular visitor Edmonds became swamped with projects. In fact it overextended him and drained his energy. Each trip swallowed two weeks of precious time and the 21-hour return flight landed him back in Ottawa exhausted and backlogged. He found himself waking up in the middle of the night for a week afterwards, until after a dozen trips he realized there was only so much one could do. Canada-Korea Ventures financed a dozen trips to Korea at $10,000 to $15,000 per trip and recouped expenses through fees, but did little more than recover costs. The company generated lots of activity but had no big successes.

In 1979, South Korean Ambassador Hahn Byung Kie, son-in-law of President Park and a golfing partner of Edmonds, asked him for help in starting a Canada-Korea parliamentary group among Canadian MPs. Evidently the ambassador was trying to counteract Korea's growing reputation for civil-rights violations. Edmonds put Hahn in touch with Bob Coates, a long-time Tory backbencher from Nova Scotia and diehard Diefenbaker loyalist who happened to be president of the Conservative party. Coates gladly flew to Korea on an expense-paid trip, accompanied by his trusted aide and confidant, Rick Logan, and by Edmonds, who paid his own fare. South Korea treated Coates like royalty. Motorcycle outriders and wailing sirens accompanied his limousine and the government honoured him with a state dinner. The fanfare embarrassed the Department of External Affairs, but Coates enjoyed a grand week and basked in esteem he didn't get in Ottawa. He happened to be the president of Canada's ruling party, but in reality he wallowed in Joe Clark's doghouse, stuck in the back benches of parliament. The Koreans gave honour to titles, and either did not understand or deliberately chose to ignore Coates's real status.

The trip captivated Coates and kindled a love affair with Korea. He started to promote it unabashedly and returned many times. Later that year he founded the Canada-Korea Parliamentary Friendship Society, which eventually attracted as members more than a quarter of the MPs.

En route to Seoul, while sitting in the first-class cabin from New York, Edmonds, Coates, and Logan met the chairman of the Korean multinational Daewoo, one of the largest shipbuilders in the world. As the flight dragged on, Coates and Logan developed a good relationship with the Daewoo chairman and sought to parlay the connection into a business deal; Logan eventually proposed to help sell Daewoo ships in return for a fat commission. Both Coates and Logan had private companies and tried to swing deals much as Edmonds did with Canada-Korea Ventures, and they often relied on Edmonds's office and telex machine to help them. But unlike Edmonds, Coates and Logan earned no ongoing fees from Korea, and banked everything on the big payday that never came. At one point Edmonds bought shares in Logan's company for $2,500 as a means of lending the perpetually broke Logan some money. Later he had to write off the investment. He saw little of Coates and Logan through most of 1983 and 1984. While he got involved in the John Crosbie leadership campaign, Coates was busy campaigning for Brian Mulroney. With Clark gone and Mulroney in power, Coates suddenly became a man to watch.

As president of the party, Coates had stumped the country from 1977 to 1979 working for Joe Clark, and he never forgave Clark for excluding him from his cabinet. After Clark and Neville fumbled away power Coates joined the Dump-Clark movement and aligned himself with Mulroney. He firmly believed that the Conservative party needed a winner and gave his support to Mulroney as loyally as he had to Diefenbaker. In 1979 Coates, as president of the party, and Mulroney, as president of the Iron Ore Company of Canada, travelled to Romania together and returned as firm allies.

After the 1984 election Mulroney owed Coates something. Still, many people were startled when Mulroney appointed him minister of national defence and put him onto the priorities and planning committee, the de facto inner cabinet. Coates knew little about defence, and Elmer MacKay, who temporarily gave up his seat for Mulroney in 1983, seemed a more logical political minister for Nova Scotia. After sitting in parliament for twenty-seven years, Coates had reached the cabinet at last.

On September 18 1984, the day after he was sworn in, Coates invited Edmonds to the Four Seasons for lunch. Before they met, Edmonds quickly drafted a short memo outlining his views on a review of defence policy and gave it to Coates in the restaurant. Coates studied it briefly, and without saying more invited Edmonds to join his staff. "I need you to come and be the senior policy adviser and do this defence policy for me," Coates said.

Edmonds mulled the offer over at home that evening. His income would drop to $65,000, but that was the least of his concerns. Canada-Korea Ventures had failed to take off, while JDE Consulting had started to bore him. Defence policy had always interested him, and it tied in with his experience in external affairs. He still yearned for government involvement and wanted a successful stint after his failure with Clark. And he had retained some of his idealism and still believed in duty to country. The next morning he called Coates and said he would be happy and honoured to join his staff. After signing a one-year contract, he resigned his corporate directorships and put JDE Consulting into a blind trust under a defeated Liberal MP, Louis Desmarais, who would handle the clients and run the business. In less than two weeks Edmonds had rolled up his business affairs and was ready to help Coates conduct a much-needed review of Canada's defence policy.

Hundreds of political aides signed on with the Mulroney government in the first few months, and only a handful of them attracted press mention. But three days before Edmonds was to show up for his first day at work the *Globe and Mail* reported that the "man who once advocated integrating the Canadian Forces with those of the United States as part of a continental common-market system has been appointed senior policy adviser to the Minister of Defence." The newspaper reminded its readers of Edmonds's role in championing the Treaty of North America under Clark seven years earlier. Coates liked the Treaty of North America and had once even advocated it in the Commons, but now he smelled political trouble. The night before Edmonds was to show up for work, he called him at home and told him to stay away from the office for now. This behaviour annoyed Edmonds, but he couldn't quit after having just finished rearranging his business affairs, so he obligingly stayed home the next couple of days. The story died quickly, and Coates called Edmonds a few days later to give him the okay to start work.

That initial incident worried Edmonds. His doubts about his boss grew within the first few weeks. When he accompanied Coates and Logan, now the chief of staff, aboard a military plane for a NATO nuclear-planning meeting in Italy, he sat in the front section with Coates, Logan, and General Thériault, the chief of the defence staff, and his wife. In Edmonds's opinion, Coates drank too much and behaved boorishly. He also thought Coates and Logan were making a habit of throwing their weight around and bullying the top brass in the department and the military.

Once the NATO business was finished, Edmonds went with Coates to London instead of hopping straight back to Ottawa aboard the service flight. He took the long route back so that he would have time to brief Coates privately about the contentious issue of military uniforms. Coates could not wait to replace the military's single green uniform with different outfits for the army, navy, and air force, and in his first meeting with his officials he had ordered a report on the issue. General Thériault returned a sophisticated memo resisting new uniforms and warning of the implications, but Coates didn't read it. A new generation of soldiers had entered the military since Paul Hellyer imposed unification two decades earlier, and the new generation had grown up in green uniforms and become accustomed to them. New uniforms would cost about $50-million and not bolster the military's capability one bit. Coates ignored the arguments, and grew antagonistic to anybody who took issue with him. He said Mulroney had made an election promise. Edmonds hoped to have a quiet in-depth discussion with him during the long flight from London to Ottawa; but when the time came Coates gave his senior policy adviser the same curt backhanded response he gave everybody else.

Coates planned to unveil the new uniform policy officially to the military commands in December, and in his haste he jumped before receiving full approval from cabinet. Mulroney learned of it and at the eleventh hour cancelled the notice, much to the horror of Logan, who collapsed and was taken to hospital with a (wrongly) suspected heart attack. There was some speculation that Coates was falling out of favour with the prime minister, because around the same time he had to apologize to Mulroney for embarrassing the government with some derisive comments about the peace movement. Mulroney's veto gummed up the process for a month. Edmonds ultimately helped Coates implement the measure on the grounds that the government had the right to change the uniforms even if the plan was dumb.

While Edmonds disapproved of what Coates was doing, Coates harboured similar feelings about Edmonds. He did not like Edmonds's tendency to side with the bureaucracy, and particularly resented his interference over a patronage contract for engineering on the northern warning system. Coates had given the contract without tender to the Montreal firm of Ray Doucet, brother of Fred Doucet, one of Mulroney's closest friends and his senior policy adviser in the Prime Minister's Office. The bureaucracy felt Doucet's firm lacked the capacity for such a large project, but Coates awarded it anyway, and became furious when Edmonds backed the civil service in opposing it. Eventually Doucet's company received a smaller contract as a compromise, but tension was building between Edmonds on one side and Coates and Logan on the other; they saw Edmonds as part of the bureaucracy they so disdained, and felt that he was frustrating the political process.

Edmonds again supported the bureaucracy when Coates planned to travel to Turkey on a sales trip. The Department of External Affairs questioned the need for such a trip and warned that it would cause problems with Turkey's arch-rival Greece, and Edmonds agreed. By late November relations had so deteriorated that Coates and Logan made it clear that they didn't want Edmonds with them on their upcoming NATO trip. So while Coates, Logan, and Jeff Matthews, the press aide, flew off to the Canadian Forces Base in Lahr, West Germany, for the start of a four-country trip, Edmonds went to Florida and played golf near his condominium in Boca Raton.

A few weeks later General Thériault dropped into Edmonds's office at about 6 p.m. and informed him that Coates had left the base one evening for a visit to a nearby strip club. Thériault said he tried to warn Coates of the dangers, especially the security dangers, of this kind of behaviour but got nowhere. He hoped Edmonds would try. By this time Edmonds had heard of an expensive trip to New York and knew that Coates and Logan were planning to spend part of their Christmas break in Hawaii at government expense on the pretext of making a speech. So Thériault's news about Lahr didn't surprise him; he had already concluded that Coates and Logan, whose staggering expenses soon excited comment in the press, were not averse to having a good time at public expense. He knew he would have no more luck than Thériault, especially since Logan as chief of staff had cut off his access to Coates; several weeks had passed since his last private meeting. So Edmonds did nothing about Thériault's information except file it away in his mind.

Edmonds returned from his Christmas holiday in Florida determined to patch relations and open a channel with Coates. He needed to see Coates to get his advice for the green paper he was to write on defence policy. Edmonds met Logan for a long lunch at Nate's Delicatessen on Rideau Street. If the setting lacked elegance, so did the conversation.

"You know," Edmonds said, "we've got some problems."

"Duncan," Logan replied, "the only problem is you. The prime minister thinks Coates is doing a wonderful job. He's the best performer in the cabinet, the PM thinks, and you are a problem for us."

Edmonds raised the Lahr incident, but Logan brushed it off. He later agreed to arrange a dinner with Coates to get relations back on track, but Coates kept cancelling the appointments. It seemed extraordinary that the senior policy adviser couldn't get to see his own minister. Then Bev Dewar, the deputy minister, came into his office complaining of Coates's poor management of his time, and Edmonds learned that Coates couldn't cope with his schedule and was cancelling other meetings as well. Coates was one of the longest-serving members of parliament but was new to government, and knew little about how it operated. Suddenly he found himself overloaded and seemingly unable to keep a schedule as he shuffled from one cabinet-committee meeting to another.

On January 17 1985 Logan sent Edmonds a surprise memo stripping him of his assistant. The memo came without consultation or warning and amounted to an insulting vote of non-confidence. It left him little alternative but to quit. Edmonds dashed off a two-paragraph letter announcing his resignation and submitted it an hour later, naively believing that Coates would now try to work things out. The next morning the administrative secretary handed him a slip terminating his contract with one month's salary. Edmonds had lasted less than four months and was gone before he fully realized what had happened.

Over the weekend Edmonds wrote himself an eight-page memo setting down his complaints. At 9 a.m. the following Tuesday, January 22, he visited the Langevin Block and told his old friend Gordon Osbaldeston, the clerk of the privy council, that he had resigned. "Gordon, I don't know if you want to know the whole unhappy story," he began. "It's a mess as far as I'm concerned." He said that he was leaving for Florida with his wife Nancy the next morning but would put himself in Osbaldeston's hands if he or the prime minister wanted the reasons. Edmonds left the office scarcely ten minutes after his arrival.

Edmonds went home and read the *Globe and Mail*, wondering whether Osbaldeston would call. He read the paper a second time, then started smoking his pipe, and at around 11 a.m. the phone rang. It was Osbaldeston's secretary. She invited him back to the office immediately and told him that they would provide lunch, because it might take a few hours. When Edmonds showed up half an hour later Osbaldeston closed the door. He explained that he had briefed the prime minister, who was disturbed and told him to prepare a complete report by the end of the day. Osbaldeston took out a stenographer's notebook and assured him that Mulroney wanted to know everything: "Both the prime minister and I would be very grateful if you could give me a full briefing on the reasons for your resignation and your general views and observations on the whole situation in the Department of Defence."

Edmonds gave Osbaldeston his eight-page memo and spent the next two hours substantiating the allegations and spelling out his concerns one by one. He cited sloppy use of the signature machine and Coates's failure to read files, listen to briefings, or understand the complexity of issues such as Star Wars or the nuclear arrangements between Canada and the United States. He recalled that Coates had informed the U.S. Defence Secretary, Caspar Weinberger, of a Canadian decision regarding NATO commitments in Europe without telling his own department. The bureaucracy eventually learned about his decision through

External Affairs, which heard it directly from the Americans, via the embassy in Washington. Edmonds went on and on.

After about half an hour Edmonds mentioned Coates's nightclub visit in Lahr as evidence of injudicious behaviour. Osbaldeston blew up like a Roman candle. "This constitutes a potential security risk," he fumed. "This means that Coates has left himself open to blackmail in the future. This is a really serious matter." The furious reaction surprised Edmonds because he had casually assumed that Osbaldeston knew all about Lahr, since the top ranks of the defence staff knew about it and Osbaldeston sat as chairman of the committee on security and intelligence. Until now Osbaldeston had taken the view that Coates as the duly installed minister had the right to behave stupidly. Lahr was different. Osbaldeston now changed the tone of his questioning and expanded the nature of his inquiry.

Edmonds left shortly after 2 p.m. and Osbaldeston spent the rest of the afternoon interviewing General Thériault and Bev Dewar. He phoned Edmonds at home early that evening to thank him for his co-operation and to advise him that Thériault and Dewar had confirmed his story. He told him that he had submitted a report to the prime minister and the matter now rested with him. The next morning, January 23, Edmonds and his wife started driving for Florida before the outside world knew he had quit. The story would blow up soon and he felt it best not to be around when it did.

To his surprise Edmonds found nothing changed when he arrived back in Ottawa on February 4. Coates was still minister of national defence and Logan his chief of staff. Strong rumours, however, had started to spread, and late the next day a reporter from the Ottawa *Citizen* woke him at about 11 p.m. to inquire whether he had resigned after being pulled out of a brothel in Brussels with NATO documents in his possession. Edmonds declared that the story was nonsense, that he was not even on that trip, and then slammed down the phone. Word had filtered through the Press Club and around Ottawa about a big event in Brussels, and rumours sprouted everywhere.

On February 12 1985 the *Citizen* carried a front-page story that in the early morning hours of November 29 Coates, Logan, and Jeff Matthews had spent about two hours in a questionable nightclub outside Lahr called the Tiffany. That afternoon

Coates, dressed in a dapper blue suit with pocket puff, stood up in the House of Commons. Choking with emotion and staring down at his text, except for occasional sideways glances at Mulroney, he read a ninety-second statement announcing that he had resigned as minister of national defence and was initiating a libel action against the *Citizen*. After Coates had finished, Mulroney graciously ushered him out of the chamber and through a throng of reporters without comment.

Mulroney thought that Coates had been indiscreet but defended him by saying that everybody had human failings, and denying that Coates had ever breached security. Mulroney pinned much of the blame on Logan. Like almost everybody else, he believed that the gregarious and boastful Logan had brought Coates to the Tiffany in the first place and later, in front of others on the plane, had imprudently embellished the event. Chiefs of staff, Mulroney said, were supposed to keep their ministers out of trouble, not get them into it.

But Mulroney directed most of his wrath not at Coates, not at Logan, but at Edmonds, whom he fingered as the whistleblower and the real cause of the fuss. The affair would never have exploded had Edmonds not quit and tattled. Mulroney felt that he should have kept his gripes within the political arena, instead of running to a public servant like Osbaldeston. He accused him of disloyalty and maliciousness, and branded him an enemy of the government.

Mulroney phoned Secretary of State Walter McLean and ordered him to keep clear of Edmonds at all times. This was a great deal to ask. Although unconnected with the events, McLean happened to be one of Edmonds's closest friends, and had named one of his sons Duncan, but Mulroney didn't care about that. It was scorched-earth time. Mulroney then went before the national caucus and declared Edmonds persona non grata in front of all Tory MPs, calling him a disgruntled ex-Grit who had maligned an innocent man and embarrassed the government. A few choice words from the prime minister could inflate or destroy the prospects of almost any consultant. Mulroney had just put the power of his office behind the command to ostracize Edmonds. He had been blacklisted by the most powerful figure in the country.

Word quickly drifted out to the rest of the political world

that Edmonds had been blackballed from on high. A public-affairs consultant could not function after the head of the government declared him an enemy of his administration. Edmonds hired a lawyer and contemplated legal options; he even considered releasing the eight-page memo he had showed Osbaldeston, but decided against it. He gave one interview to *Maclean's* about the reasons for his resignation and decided to carry on with JDE Consulting. Although he had not lost his ideals and still believed in good government, he had lost his appetite for consulting, and spent most of his time pondering his future.

The resignation of Robert Coates proved to be the first in a series of scandals that rocked the Mulroney government, raising questions about its ethics. Mulroney's reprisal against Edmonds revealed a deep character flaw. As this trait gradually seeped into the open, it corroded his image and his credibility. Before long it undermined his standing with the public, until his government eventually plummeted in the polls. The blacklisting of Duncan Edmonds was an early symptom of that decline.

NINETEEN

THE NEW LOBBYISTS

In the spring of 1984, while the Tories waited for the coming election, John Laschinger unexpectedly resigned from the Conservative campaign team to take a position as president of an insurance company. Laschinger, a veteran of many campaigns, had been the director of national operations, and his unexpected departure opened a crucial hole near the top of the organizational chart that the party had to fill. Paul Curley, the campaign secretary, asked David MacNaughton whether PAI would lend them Harry Near for the job. MacNaughton, then quarterbacking Don Johnston's campaign for Liberal leader, paused briefly. He was not concerned about contributing a weapon of war to the other side, but he was concerned about losing Near at PAI where, as vice president, he managed the company's energy clientele, the most lucrative portfolio of all. The Tories would keep Near at least four months – longer if the incoming Liberal leader put off an election – and MacNaughton wondered how it would affect PAI. But he wavered for only a few seconds before saying yes, for above all MacNaughton supported the political system. He gave Near a paid leave of absence to join the Tory campaign. "Well," Curley replied, "I owe you one."

The day after Mulroney captured his 211 seats Curley invited MacNaughton for a drink at the Four Seasons and told him that he was establishing a public-affairs office in Ottawa. He already had Imperial Oil as a client. "I told you I owed you one and I owe you one," Curley said. "I won't take any business from you." If MacNaughton would reveal his energy-client list, Curley promised that he wouldn't touch them. Sitting on top of the heap with more energy clients than anyone else in town, Mac-

Naughton accepted the offer. He liked the gesture and thought Curley had played fairly.

Paul R. Curley & Associates moved into the same building as PAI and occupied a small space six floors below. Nobody who knew Curley's record doubted his ability to get results. An Ottawa native, he joined Imperial Oil in 1967 as a fresh commerce graduate from the University of Ottawa, and over the years quit three times to work on Conservative campaigns. He rose to become the party's national director under Joe Clark, and played senior roles in the 1980 election campaign under Clark and the 1984 campaign under Brian Mulroney. Curley was a detail man, somebody with savvy and good people sense who hustled his way through life and got things done. He made friends with everyone, whether they were up or down. For example, one of the lonely francophone Tories he befriended during the Conservatives' long stretch in the Quebec wilderness was Marcel Masse. When Masse became minister of communications in Mulroney's cabinet, Curley acted as an informal adviser and had more clout with Masse than some of his aides. When an RCMP investigation into Masse's campaign spending forced him to resign briefly in the fall of 1985, Curley was around to take him to dinner and cheer him up. He held a big party in honour of John Fraser after the tuna scandal forced his resignation as fisheries minister. He operated that way. Rod McQueen wrote in *Toronto Life* that "Curley holds more IOUs than a finance company."

Curley's company had started in Toronto in 1982 on the strength of his connections with the seemingly invincible Tory government in Ontario. When Mulroney won he added Pierre Fortier as a partner (later changing the firm's name to Curley, Fortier & Associates) and expanded to Ottawa. Fortier had practised law in Ottawa for fifteen years with such civic success that he was the president of the Rotary Club, sat on the boards of two hospitals, and was a director of the exclusive Rideau Club. Fortier knew Ottawa. The move to Ottawa saved Curley's company, because the following spring the Tories unexpectedly fell from power in Ontario, and Curley lost most of his business. But Ottawa worked out well, and more than made up for his setback at Queen's Park. Curley was flying higher than ever.

Curley headed the Conservative Party as national director

from 1979 to 1981, and Fortier, his new partner, held the post
from 1981 to 1983. Between them they knew every Tory of consequence in the country, and enjoyed close relationships with
the government in Ottawa; several Mulroney cabinet ministers
asked Curley and Fortier to find them political aides. They were
so close, in fact, that some critics didn't expect Curley to stay in
business once the Liberals returned to office. Like all public-
affairs consultants, Curley monitored government and gave
advice, but he also acted as a lobbyist. Some people called him a
door-opener, but he vehemently denied it.

Curley stayed in Toronto while Fortier operated out of
Ottawa and together they clicked like Lee and Neville in ECL's
grand old days. Curley, the friendly glad-hander, got the clients
and Fortier serviced them. Curley showed only cursory interest
in policy, but concentrated on communications (the Marcel
Masse connection) and energy (the Imperial Oil background),
while Fortier did most of the rest. When Masse moved from
Communications to Energy Curley became the most plugged-in
energy lobbyist in the country. The client list soon reached
about twenty and revenue topped $1-million. Besides Imperial
Oil (who hired Curley without informing Bob Landry, its vice-
presidential staff lobbyist in Ottawa), the clients included the
Government of British Columbia, Thorne Riddell, Crownx, Air
Canada, McLeod Young Weir, and Cantel. In no time the company caught up to ECL in billings and surpassed it in profits.
Curley kept overhead even lower than the tightfisted ECL. With
two partners and only a few employees, the firm didn't have to
worry that expenses would eat up its revenue.

One of Curley's underlings back in his Imperial Oil days happened to be Harry Near. Curley spotted him as a rising talent in
junior management and hand-picked him as a volunteer advance
man for the Ontario Premier, Bill Davis. Near seemed a good
choice. He was easy-going and affable and could fit in anywhere,
yet also had an analytical mind and superb organizational ability. Near proved himself and his star quickly took off, just as
Curley had predicted. A few years later he was running Joe
Clark's Ontario tour in the 1979 election victory. At the time
Near had never met Ray Hnatyshyn, and probably could not

even spell his name, but Hnatyshyn seemed to know about Near. Shocked at being named Clark's energy minister in 1979, he needed an aide who was Tory and knew the difference between oil and gas. Near fitted the bill perfectly, and over a three-hour moose-meat dinner Hnatyshyn hired him as his executive assistant. That one act proved to be the smartest thing Hnatyshyn did as energy minister. Near emerged as one of the premier EAs in the short-lived Clark government, and insiders credited him with whatever energy successes Hnatyshyn had. After the Clark government crashed, Near led a wave of Tories over to join PAI.

With the leave of absence that Curley had arranged, and MacNaughton had granted, Near joined the Mulroney campaign in May 1984. As expected, he stayed with the campaign through the election. But he never returned to PAI; instead he joined Energy Minister Pat Carney as chief of staff. The switch surprised some but not others. From the fall of 1983 to April 1984 Near had spent his spare time briefing Carney on energy issues to give substance to her role as energy critic for the opposition. During those months he promised to join Carney if she became minister of energy after the next election, with one caveat: he would not stay long. He would set up her office, help negotiate a new energy accord with the provinces, and then quit. He planned to return to private consulting and make some money.

In the meantime he did what he could about money. Treasury Board guidelines forbade ministers to pay their chiefs of staff more than $80,750 a year, but Carney asked for and received special permission to waive the limit for Near. She gave him a $50,000 contract lasting four and a half months – nearly double the top Treasury Board rate. Carney renewed the contract three times for one-to-two-month periods at roughly similar rates until Near left at the end of May 1985. He got out a few months before new conflict-of-interest guidelines imposed a cooling-off period that would have restricted his return to private practice.

At this point PAI hoped to get Near back, but he wanted double his old salary and told PAI he was examining his options. PAI did not subject its employees to non-competition clauses or cooling-off periods, which left him free to make the deal he wanted. The intervening period with Carney had enhanced his value as a marketable commodity and he wanted to test the market for his worth, since he believed he could better himself on his own, even if he had to compete head-to-head with PAI. MacNaughton found Near's salary demands excessive and felt that he showed little loyalty and even less gratitude for the fact that PAI had carried him on salary while he worked on the Tory campaign. He thought Near's experience at PAI had helped make him valuable to Carney in the first place; then, having enhanced his profile with Carney, he was auctioning off his services in search of the highest bidder. In the end Near decided to hang out his own shingle as a one-man firm. MacNaughton and Near had been close friends, even their families had been close, but this incident strained the bonds and cooled the friendship.

Near didn't wait long to launch a raid on PAI's energy clients. PAI had grown big and brassy enough not to fret about competition, but an attack from Near gave the company instant jitters. He was arguably the best energy consultant in town, possessing technical expertise, long political antennae, and, while Carney remained the minister, the best energy connections in town. More importantly, clients loved him and swore by him. If anybody could steal clients it was Near. There was no telling what damage he could do. PAI braced itself and waited for the storm. And nothing happened. Near approached the clients but landed no recruits. He struck out as clients one by one stuck with PAI. MacNaughton, Neville, and Mike Robinson could hardly contain their delight. If PAI could withstand a raid from Near, perhaps the ultimate test, it would prosper under the Mulroney government.

Near and Curley and the Tory lobbyists who set up shop following the Mulroney victory gave PAI and ECL a taste of competition they had never experienced before. But the Nears and Curleys paled in comparison to Frank Moores, another newcomer to Ottawa. Neville was close to Mulroney, but not as close as Moores. Few cronies were closer to Mulroney than Frank Moores.

Moores had lots of energy, street smarts, and a short attention span, along with a knack for wheeling and dealing. His father, Silas W. Moores, a well-to-do Newfoundland fish merchant who owned North Eastern Fish Industries Ltd., had higher professional aspirations for his oldest son and sent him to an exclusive school, St. Andrew's College in Aurora, Ontario; later he persuaded him to enrol at Boston University. The hyperactive Moores couldn't sit still for long and quit college after two months to work on a fish pier in Boston until his father relented and took him into the family business in Harbour Grace, Newfoundland. His father died a few years later and Moores took over the plant and parlayed it from a work force of fewer than 200 employees to more than 1,800, then in 1965 sold it for about $2-million to Birdseye, the frozen-food company owned by Unilever. He signed a ten-year contract to manage the plant, but hated working for others and left two years later when Birdseye installed quality controls and other institutional standards before he felt the plant could afford the overhead.

A person could do worse than retire as a millionaire at 34, but Moores loathed boredom, and the inactivity of retirement alternately drove him wild and depressed him. Moores needed adrenaline, and he went on drinking binges in Montreal and Toronto while looking for something that both challenged amd intrigued him. He started a little import-export business with Norway, but satisfying consumers in Toronto proved different from running a fish plant in Newfoundland, and it disintegrated into total disaster. Roy McMurtry, a high-school friend who later became Ontario's attorney general and Canada's high commissioner in London, suggested he run for office. He had never considered politics – he lacked political conviction, for one thing – but a federal election was coming up and, at wits' end, he gave it a try. He joined the Tories simply because the Newfoundland Premier, Joey Smallwood, was a Liberal. People thought him mad to run as a federal Tory in Smallwood's Newfoundland, but Moores believed that Smallwood had run the province too long. The province had always voted solidly Liberal both federally and provincially and had completely shut out the Tories in the last two federal elections. Facing a dim political future, Moores pulled together an aggressive campaign team of underage volunteers and jumped into a riding that had voted straight Liberal since Confederation in 1949. In the 1968 election voters across the country swung to Trudeau – except Newfoundlanders, who defied the sweep and elected Tories in six out of seven seats, including Moores.

Having amassed nearly sixty per cent of the vote in Bona-vista-Trinity-Conception, Moores soon began wondering what kind of victory he had won. In Ottawa he didn't fit, or enjoy, the role of a backbencher; he wanted to lead instead of follow, and complained of having nothing to do. Answering correspondence and sitting in the Commons chamber bored him silly, and the prospect of toughing it out on a parliamentary committee horrified him. In short, Moores found life as an MP dreadful, much like his experience as a retiree. When Dalton Camp stepped down as president of the Conservative party in 1969, Moores declared his candidacy on the spur of the moment. Nobody knew the rookie MP. He had not put in long years of party service or paid the political dues the post usually required, but he ran anyway and stunned everybody by winning.

Moores didn't stay long in Ottawa, but returned to Newfoundland in 1970 as leader of the provincial Conservative Party in order to confront the legendary Joey Smallwood directly. The Tories at the time counted a paltry 6 members in the 42-seat Newfoundland House of Assembly, and nobody – not even Moores himself – gave them much chance of knocking off a Father of Confederation. Yet Moores and his close friend Bill Doody spent a year organizing and building the base of the provincial party, and the experience changed Moores's mind about his prospects. He discovered that Smallwood had no political organization. Smallwood was the Liberal machine, and Liberal candidates won by clinging to his coat-tails. Now, after twenty-two years, he had overstayed his welcome and was vulnerable. The 1971 provincial election finished in a dead heat between Smallwood and Moores. After some recounts, changes of allegiance, charges and countercharges of buy-offs, and outright political trickery, Moores got one more seat and on January 18 1972 was sworn in as Newfoundland's second premier. Six weeks later he called an election and, facing a different Liberal leader, and a divided opposition, won a landslide victory. Moores had bounced from political obscurity to premier of Newfoundland in less than three years. A few years earlier he had been drinking melancholically at the bar of the Ritz-Carlton Hotel in Montreal wondering what to do with himself. Now he had something to occupy his time.

As premier Moores flew mostly by the seat of his pants and remained affable, charming and well liked. He was an adroit negotiator who got along with everybody from the Liberals in Ottawa to the unions in his province. He could step in and resolve labour disputes. He handled his cabinet well. And he was an excellent organizer. But he was not a detail man and lost interest once a project got past the conceptual stage. Some colleagues privately complained that he was lazy. Above all else he was controversial. He was soon divorced from his wife of two decades and the mother of his seven children and he married Janis Johnson, a young and attractive Tory from outside the province. He became embroiled in one patronage controversy after another. Everything he touched seemed contentious. Every time he toured the province his cabinet colleagues shuddered and waited for word on how many hockey arenas and community centres he had promised spontaneously out of an empty budget. Moores couldn't say no. The opposition found him a great target, but even his opponents liked him, although they complained that he didn't know where to draw the line. Through it all Moores never understood why controversy followed him everywhere.

Moores had a knack for relating to people and was uncannily good at remembering everyone's name. He would step in front of an audience and take off his jacket, loosen his tie, and, with perspiration dripping from his forehead, sway his listeners. He would flash his pearly whites and flutter his baby blues and moisten every eye in the house, or set them roaring with laughter and slapping their thighs with delight. He had been born with a silver spoon in his mouth, yet identified instinctively with ordinary people; he could move from an outport kitchen to a union hall to a multinational boardroom in New York without missing a beat.

Moores vowed from the beginning not to stay in office more than two terms. He liked the greasepaint and floodlights of public office but tired of the daily administration. He wanted to return to private business and make money and live the carefree and independent life that politics precluded. But for a fellow like him, getting out proved to be almost as hard as getting in. His Liberal critics hurled new accusations at him almost every day and he was determined not to quit under a cloud. He wanted to leave office with head high and no suggestion that scandal had driven him out. He also wanted to prevent Brian Peckford, his minister of mines and energy, from succeeding him. At the end of 1978 Moores asked a trusted friend and long-time Tory for advice on how to leave with honour. The friend was the president of the Iron Ore Company of Canada, Brian Mulroney, who enlisted Dalton Camp's help. The two of them flew to Newfoundland aboard Iron Ore's corporate jet, huddled with Moores for four days, and scripted his departure. Mulroney later hosted a glittering retirement party in the Starboard Quarter on the St. John's harbour front. In accordance with the tradition for retired premiers, both Pierre Trudeau and Joe Clark offered him a seat in the Senate, but Moores turned it down. He could not suffer the thought of vegetating in the chamber of sober second thought.

Moores and Mulroney had known each other for some years. Moores had nominated Mulroney at the 1976 Conservative leadership convention, had delivered all but a few of the Newfoundland delegates, and had been Mulroney's most prominent supporter. But it was after the convention, when Mulroney became president of Iron Ore, that their friendship really flowered. Iron Ore had huge holdings in Labrador and was Newfoundland's biggest employer, and that brought Mulroney to Newfoundland regularly. While he was there he made a point of dropping in on Moores.

Nothing in the world enchanted Moores more than fly-fishing. He frequently said goodbye to the world, headed for Labrador, and disappeared up a river wishing he could stay forever. Critics accused him, with some justice, of running off to the remote regions when he should have been working in his office in St. John's. His bi-partisan fishing guests included the likes of John Turner, Don Jamieson, and Jean Chrétien, but Mulroney was one of his favourites. The two escaped for long fishing trips during which they shared repartee and drink and developed a deep-seated friendship, so that the normally carefree Moores was able to console Mulroney during the black drinking binges that followed his 1976 leadership loss. Their personalities and styles matched. Both liked to live well, and to commiserate, exult, and entertain. Both liked money and political power, but Mulroney preferred power, while Moores leaned towards money.

Moores held no ill will towards Joe Clark and readily acknowledged that he was a decent and well-meaning leader, but he believed that Clark was a political liability who couldn't win.

He concluded that there was no point in keeping a leader who could not get elected, and secretly set out to dump him. Much of the money to finance Clark's ouster flowed through Moores, who spent most of a year raising funds and galvanizing dissident groups against Clark. He chaired meetings of Dump-Clark MPs in Ottawa and organized rebel groups everywhere except Quebec. He co-ordinated an inner circle of eight or ten Dump-Clark members who fed into other circles of participants. The core group met in Ottawa, Montreal, and Toronto, and once in Calgary. It assembled such an elaborate, wide-ranging machine that Moores couldn't understand how the media had failed to notice the troop mobilization. He lifted the cover slightly a week after the convention in an interview with the Montreal *Gazette*'s Claude Arpin. "When I woke up in Winnipeg the morning after the vote I had a real downer," Moores said. "... You don't destroy a guy's political career lightly. But it had to be done for the country's sake."

The 1983 Conservative leadership contest taxed even Moores's considerable political and diplomatic skills when both Mulroney and John Crosbie entered the race. Moores supported Mulroney and wanted him to win, but when a Newfoundlander launches out for national office every local boy must lend a hand at the oars. Protocol – not to mention tradition – required Moores to back the native son. He had known Crosbie since boyhood, and had appointed him minister of finance in his first cabinet. Torn between loyalty to Mulroney and allegiance to Newfoundland, he had to steer a delicate course.

At the convention Moores sat with his fellow Newfoundlanders in the Crosbie delegation, and moved to the Mulroney section, with most of the Newfoundland delegates, only after Crosbie was eliminated on the third ballot. But he had been working for Mulroney long before Crosbie was bumped from the ballot. L. Ian MacDonald, Mulroney's biographer and later his aide, wrote that "Moores may have been something of a double agent" but he didn't consider himself a double-dealer. "I genuinely didn't want to do Crosbie any harm," MacDonald quoted Moores as saying. "And I genuinely wanted Brian to win it." Moores led a double life during those months. In public he supported Crosbie but did no campaigning. But once he stepped behind the scenes and out of the spotlight he joined the inner council of the Mulroney campaign brain trust and worked tirelessly for the Mulroney cause. He shouted "Crosbie, Crosbie" when sitting in his seat at the convention, but connected with the Mulroney troops to help shift bodies over to Mulroney the minute he stepped onto the convention floor.

After he retired as premier in March 1979, Moores joined with Bill Doody and a former MP, John Lundrigan, to start a consulting company in St. John's called Torngat Investments, to help clients cut through red tape. The venture made little economic sense and never did significant business. The amount of consulting available in Newfoundland couldn't support three senior partners, even when one of the partners was a former premier and one a former minister of finance. Moores sat around the office talking politics all day, and the partnership folded after Doody went to the Senate. In the meantime Moores saw a boom in offshore oil and gas developments and with others poured money into preparations for land and port developments. But the developments never happened, partly because Premier Brian Peckford, the man he had failed to keep out of the premier's office, squeezed so hard for concessions that the oil companies stayed away, and Moores's plans turned sour.

Mulroney and Camp had successfully cleared Moores's path out of politics but Moores really needed guidance about what to do after he got out. The transition to private life staggered him and transcended the worst moments of his 1967 retirement from the fish plant. His celebrated divorce had cost him much of his fortune, and failed business ventures ate up most of the rest. His second marriage fell apart. Everything crumbled. After seven years as premier he suddenly re-discovered the hard specifics of the real world, and sank into the longest and deepest slide of his life. He also started running short of money, which was a new experience for him. In despair he left Newfoundland and settled in Montreal while he sorted himself out.

As he continued to flounder, three prominent businessmen took him aside. They had noticed his plight and believed that a former premier deserved a break, so undertook to pay him a salary while he worked through his difficulty, retaining him as a consultant on condition he sit back and do nothing but think. Moores had lucked into some benefactors. Most retired politicians found themselves dropped as soon as they left office, but he had stumbled across a happy example of the opposite. The financial backstopping enabled him to stay on top of events and to mess around in politics. In fact, it was during this period that he worked to unseat Joe Clark.

Moores needed a couple of years to rise out of his personal abyss, but things slowly turned around and he emerged in 1984 knowing exactly what he wanted to do. He wanted to be a consultant and lobbyist. He discovered that he loved high-level consulting on the national stage, since it opened the door to big, fast fees while leaving him free to come and go. He could travel and meet CEOs across the country while touching base with his network of political friends. It suited his personality and allowed him to dabble and liaise as much as he wanted. He surfaced from his personal purgatory feeling that he had found his calling.

Moores stayed close to Mulroney throughout his problem period and visited Ottawa regularly after Mulroney became party leader. His Ottawa visits also strengthened relations with old friends like Don Mazankowski, with whom he had shared an apartment (along with the renegade Tory Jack Horner) when both were freshman MPs. He also linked up informally with a small PAI-type company in Ottawa called Alta Nova Associates and used its office as his local base.

Alta Nova was a curious creature. Four Tory aides started it out of the ashes of the Clark defeat in February 1980. Jamie Burns, Pat Walsh, and Peter Thomson had all worked for Transport Minister Don Mazankowski, while the fourth partner, Fred von Veh, a Toronto lawyer with Stikeman Elliott, frequently flew into town to advise Mazankowski. When the 1980 election defeat left Burns, Walsh, and Thomson suddenly unemployed they started publishing a monthly newsletter for the business community called *Capital Briefing*, which was intended to be a meal ticket that would keep them in town until the Tories returned to office. *Capital Briefing* sold for $65 a year and had no editorial pretensions. The owners sifted through a month's worth of government press releases and reduced them into bite-sized items strung together as "a digest of federal actions affecting business in Canada". They wrote and assembled the first issue on Thomson's dining-room table and dug into their pockets to print and mail six thousand free copies with a subscription card attached. A critical last-minute spelling error nearly derailed the first issue, which was saved by quick fixing with boxes of white snow paint. Then a postal strike nearly killed the distribution, but the fledgling publication survived its founding issue and picked up enough subscribers to support Walsh and Burns full time by the following winter. Thomson left town and dropped out, while von Veh mostly stayed clear of operations, leaving the newsletter's fate in the hands of Burns and Walsh in a dingy office in the National Press Building.

Burns and Walsh neatly positioned themselves to expand beyond a subscription service by selling copies of the original press release to subscribers wanting more detail about particular items. That led to other things, and before long Burns and Walsh were handling all types of information requests. In no time they were not only digging out information but running errands, arranging announcements, and setting up press conferences. They moved out of their Spartan office and started promoting themselves as consultants. The fact that they were Tories in a Liberal environment did not deter them or hinder their effectiveness. They understood how the system worked and knew where to look. Both had excellent contacts in the transport bureaucracy. Wary of their political label, they didn't try to lobby but stuck strictly to giving advice on what arguments to use and who to use them on. Their modest little newsletter had expanded the company into a mini-PAI.

Alta Nova built up a handful of retainer clients and hired some office staff, but essentially remained a two-man operation. The company earned modest profits, which supported Burns and Walsh, but it never entered the arena with PAI or ECL. To do so required capital, and Burns sought to avoid long-term debt. He still wanted to return to government after the next election and planned to leave Alta Nova the minute Mazankowski returned to the cabinet. The Mulroney government swept to power on September 4 and took office on September 17, 1984. On September 15 Burns, about to become Mazankowski's new chief of staff, sold Alta Nova to Frank Moores. Impatient as always, Moores could not wait to set up shop in Ottawa, and Alta Nova gave him an established vehicle and a flying start.

Moores took control of Alta Nova with none of the grand

visions of growth that had marked David MacNaughton's take-over of PAI five and a half years earlier. He merely hoped to settle down and establish himself as a consultant and do some wheeling and dealing. But he loved action and excitement, and that psychological imperative ultimately guided the development of his company and launched it onto an aggressive path. Moores might not have set out to assemble a sizable shop, but he quickly proceeded to do exactly that; soon he passed ECL and Paul Curley, and showed signs of challenging PAI off in the distance.

Shortly after Moores bought Alta Nova, another Mulroney friend arrived in town to set up a lobbying firm. Gerry Doucet, a former minister of education in Nova Scotia, didn't know Mulroney as well as Moores did, but his brother Fred knew him better than almost anyone, having soldiered with him through the political wars and operated as his chief of staff in opposition. Now he was Mulroney's senior policy adviser. Gerry Doucet could expect to do well as a one-man Ottawa lobbyist, but instead arranged to go into partnership with Moores, becoming a minority shareholder and a part-time consultant who commuted between Ottawa and his law practice in Halifax. Before long Moores took in a third partner, Gary Ouellet, a Quebec City lawyer and long-time Tory organizer – and another old Mulroney friend. Ouellet had campaigned for Mulroney in both leadership races and organized eastern Quebec for the 1984 election. He then became chief of staff to Benoît Bouchard, the minister of state for transport, and was returning to his law practice in March 1985 when Moores steered him into his firm and made him a shareholder. All three partners carried impeccable Mulroney credentials.

Moores soon moved Alta Nova out of its cramped office and settled into plush quarters around the corner. He started a new company called Government Consultants International, Inc. – GCI – and rolled Alta Nova into it. GCI was a better name for an expanding company, although the name didn't matter much around Ottawa since people, surprised by the commotion he was causing in a community that usually operated subtly, simply called it Frank Moores's company.

Like Alta Nova, GCI monitored events, gathered intelligence, and gave advice, but GCI did something the old Alta Nova never did; like Paul Curley, Moores introduced "advocacy" as part of his package of services, and started to lobby. For an extra fee GCI would go directly to government, bang on doors, and plead a client's case. Clients could buy just monitoring and analysis. Or they could buy monitoring and analysis plus lobbying. Or they could forget the monitoring and analysis and buy only lobbying. A client with a specific objective could put down some money and put GCI to work. GCI would draft letters, write briefs, and argue the case face to face with the decision-makers in government.

By the summer of 1985 GCI had expanded to twenty clients, most of them foreign companies wanting to invest in Canada after the Conservatives' dismantling of the Foreign Intelligence Review Agency. Corporations chose GCI for several reasons. First, it lobbied, while its mainstream competition like PAI and ECL mostly didn't; the marketplace seemed to want advocacy and GCI offered it. Second, it pursued clients more aggressively than the established firms and tapped into hitherto overlooked markets, particularly in Quebec, Mulroney's home province. Quebec was PAI's Achilles heel, since it had no francophone officers, and its regional offices across Canada didn't include any in Quebec. Third, GCI engaged in some good old-fashioned price competition by charging lower fees. PAI never charged less than $3,000 a month, whereas GCI would take on clients for as low as $1,500 a month. But the biggest attraction by far was Frank Moores. Everybody knew that Mulroney and Moores were cronies who kept in touch, and that reality alone enhanced GCI's value in the marketplace.

Moores opened in Ottawa shortly before Neville came back to town as PAI's chairman. The two should have known each other well, considering the common links in their backgrounds. Both hung around the back rooms of the Conservative Party. Both kept close to Mulroney and were called for advice. Both loved to fish in remote areas around Labrador. They should have been buddies, but were not. They moved in different circles and seldom bumped into each other. Neville, since resettling in Ottawa, had moved into Rockcliffe Park while Moores, married for the third time, commuted from Montreal, arriving in Ottawa on Mondays and returning on Thursday night or Friday. The two had never fished together. Neither knew whom Mulroney called more often for advice; Moores could claim a closer friendship, but Neville, with his long Ottawa experience and analytical mind, gave more valuable counsel. Neville also kept his head down. Moores, by contrast, knew neither prudence nor caution and could be an unguided missile. Controversy had surrounded Moores all his life and in the summer of 1985 he started to run true to form in Ottawa, as the overblown Snarby incident demonstrated.

Ulf Snarby, a Nova Scotia fisherman and former sealing captain, invested his home and life savings into a down payment for a multi-million-dollar freezer trawler which he had bought solely for its fishing licence. He and his partner, Steiner Engeset, applied in October 1984 to transfer the vessel's licence to a bigger boat. The Department of Fisheries rejected the transfer at the end of December. The bureaucrats suspected that Snarby would return later for a bigger catch allowance to justify his bigger boat. Snarby tried to appeal directly to Fisheries Minister John Fraser, but the government bureaucracy claimed it couldn't book a meeting with Fraser until March, which was too late for Snarby. He needed approval by January 20 or he would forfeit his down payment. His MP was out of the country for three weeks, so Snarby looked for a lobbyist. A business friend gave him the names of five firms: three Liberal, one NDP, and one Tory, the Tory one being GCI. Snarby decided it would be foolish to go to a Tory minister with anything but a Tory outfit, so he flew to Ottawa, met Gerry Doucet and, briefly, Frank Moores, and signed a six-month retainer at $500 a month, the lowest fee GCI ever charged. PAI and ECL didn't touch such low fees, and normally neither did GCI.

GCI arranged a meeting in Fraser's office a few weeks later, and Snarby showed up with Gerry Doucet and the Nova Scotia minister of fisheries. "If you're willing to take a chance on this I'm certainly not going to stop it for you," Fraser told Snarby as he approved the application. Snarby didn't begrudge GCI the $3,000 in fees. GCI had spent a couple of weeks preparing the case for the Fraser meeting and had secured him a favourable result. The approval allowed Snarby and his partner to build up a work force of forty and to turn their operation into a business triumph. With partners, they later bought into a fish plant in Newfoundland which gave steady jobs to about 260 and occasional jobs to as many as 700.

The *Globe and Mail* broke the Snarby story in June 1985 and put Moores and GCI into the headlines. GCI had performed a routine, garden-variety lobbying service, of the kind that Ottawa sees in one department or other every day. But Fraser had overruled his bureaucrats and Frank Moores's firm had done the lobbying; those two factors, plus the publication of the fee, made it controversial. People assumed that Moores had used influence. MPs accused Mulroney of practising "government by cronyism", but Mulroney angrily brushed aside the accusations. "If the member keeps this up," Mulroney shouted across the House at Robert Kaplan, "you're going to give McCarthyism a bad name." Kaplan asked Justice Minister John Crosbie to check the Criminal Code of Canada for influence-peddling. The public saw Moores as the man who got a fishing licence for a few thousand dollars, and the image stuck. From then on his name could not appear in the newspapers without a background paragraph explaining he had opened John Fraser's door and secured a fishing licence for a fee.

Moores was still reeling from the Snarby affair when the Air Canada controversy levelled some serious charges at him. Linda Diebel started with a story in the Montreal *Gazette*, Michael Harris unearthed more in the *Globe and Mail*, and then Bob Fife of Canadian Press did some sleuthing. Each reporter focused on Moores's recent appointment to the Air Canada board of directors and how it might conflict with private clients' interests. Moores tried to ride it out, then made a concession by dropping Nordair and Wardair as clients. Instead of stopping, the press shifted its scrutiny to GCI's relationship with the German aircraft manufacturer Messerschmitt-Bolkow-Blohm.

Moores didn't know how to respond. To deny the allegations would keep the stories going, while saying nothing convicted him by his silence. For the first time people saw him chagrined, not because he thought he had done anything wrong, but because he had committed the political sin of embarrassing his friend the prime minister. Moores grew groggy from the battering and in September 1985 resigned from Air Canada. "There are occasions when a person cannot win the battle even when one is absolutely convinced of the rightness of his case," Moores said in his prepared statement. He said he hoped the media would now stop hounding him.

During the unravelling of the Air Canada story Diebel reported that Moores had picked up Bombardier of Montreal as a client while Don Mitchell, a well-known Liberal who had briefly been associated with Duncan Edmonds on some of his Korea ventures, had been dropped. A couple of days later Michael Harris reported in the *Globe and Mail* that Bombardier had dumped Mitchell in favour of Moores on the advice of the Prime Minister's Office. Bombardier denied the allegation, saying the Prime Minister's Office had nothing to do with the decision, but Mitchell claimed he had heard it straight from the Bombardier executive who fired him. Moores tried to lie low and avoid the press, but controversy followed him wherever he went. In under a year he had become the best-known – and the most notorious – lobbyist in town.

Now everybody watched to see how he would fare in the Gulf + Western case. In late 1984 Gulf + Western Industries of New York bought out the textbook publisher Prentice-Hall of Englewood Cliffs, New Jersey, for $934-million. The mammoth deal included Prentice-Hall of Canada, and that part of the transaction needed Canadian-government approval. By the time it reached cabinet almost a year later the government had adopted a nationalistic policy of fostering sensitive cultural industries such as publishing, and that policy ran counter to the Prentice-Hall purchase. Gulf + Western, the owner of Famous Players movie theatres and Paramount Productions, never had brimmed over with sensitivity to Canadian culture. Now it ran smack into Communications Minister Marcel Masse's bold new repatriation policy, which required foreign-owned buyers of Canadian publishers to transfer majority control to Canadians within two years. Gulf + Western refused to sell fifty-one per cent of its newly acquired Canadian subsidiary, and hired GCI to fight the policy.

Gulf + Western played rough, threatening to shut down the Canadian subsidiary if Canada didn't submit. Either Gulf + Western received approval or 230 jobs would be lost. Allan Gotlieb, Canada's ambassador to Washington, called it a scorched-earth policy. The Canadian government relented and gave Gulf + Western an exemption on the grounds that the takeover occurred before the government adopted its Canadianization policy. The government extracted no performance guarantees, although Gulf + Western reluctantly agreed to sell at least fifty-one per cent of Ginn and Company, a small textbook publisher which it had acquired as part of another purchase. Even that agreement came to nothing; the price Gulf + Western wanted for Ginn scared off Canadian buyers, so Ginn remained part of the U.S. conglomerate. The Gulf + Western case showed how aggressively GCI could pursue a client's case.

Even Gulf + Western's tactics didn't match those of the Pharmaceutical Manufacturers Association of Canada in its defence of the infamous multinational drug lobby. Compared to PMAC, Gulf + Western played strictly by Sunday School rules.

Canadian prescription drug prices were among the cheapest in the world after Parliament in 1969 amended Section 41-4 of the Patent Act to permit copycat generic drugs to be sold in return for a four-per-cent royalty to the patent-holders. This meant that consumers could buy the generic equivalent of Valium in Canada for less than one-tenth of the American price. PMAC, made up almost exclusively of large multinational drug companies based in the U.S. and Europe, accused the Canadian government of licensing legalized theft, and retaliated with one of the most odious lobby campaigns in the history of Canada. PMAC companies threatened to pull their plants out of Canada. They bullied cabinet ministers and public servants; they could be heard all the way down the hall, yelling in the office of Consumer and Corporate Affairs Minister Ron Basford. They spread scare stories about unsafe drugs killing thousands of Canadians, and managed to arouse a couple of provincial governments against Ottawa. They also bludgeoned the home-grown generic industry with expensive lawsuits. One multinational even started giving away Valium free in order to bankrupt a generic competitor. In short, with billions of dollars of profit at stake, PMAC pulled out all the stops to smash the hated amendment. The Trudeau government buckled under the pressure a few times and almost capitulated, but the provision remained.

The Mulroney government came to power promising stronger patent protection and supported the PMAC position, but once in office it hesitated over dismantling such a popular piece of legislation. The big Tory majority could push it through Parliament but Canadians would notice the impact at the drugstore counter, and would begin to protest. PMAC urged the government to make good on its promise but the government flinched at the prospect of defending such price increases. PMAC was well connected; President Reagan pressed the issue on its behalf at the Shamrock Summit in Quebec City in March 1985. The Mulroney government stalled while it looked for a compromise.

PMAC retained GCI to twist the Mulroney government's arm. Even without Moores's friendship with Mulroney nobody could rival GCI's connections on this issue. Gerry Doucet handled the PMAC file in GCI's office; his brother Fred handled the issue in the Prime Minister's Office. Gary Ouellet, the other partner, recruited Tory candidates in eastern Quebec for the 1984 election, and one of his committee members was Michel Côté, who had since become the minister of consumer and corporate affairs, and the man in charge of all changes in drug patents. If GCI couldn't help PMAC then nobody could.

The Canadian-owned generic companies fought back and resorted to political connections of their own. Ivan Fleischmann, a Liberal lobbyist and former executive assistant to John Roberts, had been representing them, but after the election the generic companies switched to E.F. (Skip) Willis, who had been Peter Pocklington's campaign manager in the 1983 Conservative leadership race. Willis operated out of Toronto and expanded to Ottawa following the Tory win, but he lacked real Mulroney connections and failed to attract clients. In the end he closed his Ottawa office. The fact that Willis couldn't get a toehold in Ottawa while GCI was expanding on all fronts seemed to symbolize the fates of their respective clients in the prescription-drug battle.

Côté tried to negotiate a truce. When that failed, he sided firmly with PMAC. In June 1986 he introduced legislation granting ten years of exclusive patent protection for new drugs, and tried to sneak the bill into the Commons a few hours before the summer recess. This clever ploy was intended to deny MPs any chance to debate the measure, or even to raise it in Question Period, until the fall, by which time other issues might have crowded it out of the news. But a last-minute delivery snag caused the bill to miss the deadline. When a similar bill was introduced in the fall, it was clear that GCI and PMAC had lobbied some more in the interval and had successfully managed to secure even more favourable terms. They had turned June's set-back into November's blessing. On May 6 1987 the Commons passed Bill C-22 and sent it to the Senate.

Whether the image was justified or not, Frank Moores symbolized the quick-fix school of lobbying. Nobody produced evidence of influence-peddling, but everybody suspected it. He made the government uncomfortable and enraged his competitors, who accused him of breaking the rules, and tarring their industry with a bad name. They said he catered to the worst instincts of business, and called him a menace to the system. Moores stoutly protested that he didn't sell influence, only knowledge, and never discussed GCI business with Mulroney. He didn't claim that he and Mulroney never talked politics; only a mute could sit down with Mulroney and not talk politics. Moores could proclaim his integrity all he wanted, but the majority of his competitors and the media refused to believe him.

His competitors boldly predicted that Moores would pick up the easy money, amass a small fortune, and quit to try his hand at something else. Moores would last only as long as his pals remained in office. A firm that acquired clients through political connections would lose them just as quickly. His rivals expected him to sell his client list and leave. But that didn't seem to be happening. Moores enjoyed his work and, rather than getting out, seemed to be digging himself further in. He also happened to be an effective practitioner. "He has a keen sense of what's going to wash and what's not going to wash," said one competitor who shared a client with him. "He has an analytical ability that is based on years of political experience, and also knowledge of individuals. And he has a quick grasp of issues. He's very, very good. Leave everything else aside, he's very good."

Moores was nothing if not canny. He realized that he had overbuilt his practice on political connections, and now had to sink roots into the bureaucracy and clean up his image in order to prosper in the long run. In setting out to acquire some respectability, he took a page out of David MacNaughton's book. In September 1985 he kicked himself upstairs to be chairman of GCI and elevated Gary Ouellet to vice chairman and chief executive officer. Ouellet ran the day-to-day affairs and tended the corporate machinery while Moores became chief marketer and super-consultant. Just as PAI had done five years earlier, GCI started to collect people of different political stripes. Moores hired two former Liberal MPs, Robert Gourd and Coline Campbell, in case the next election returned John Turner to the Langevin Block. Also in accordance with PAI practice, GCI started to hire staff who specialized in certain government sectors. Before long GCI had specialists in international finance, trade, procurement, communications, and transport. The managers at PAI wondered how Moores built an infrastructure so quickly. It belied the notion that GCI only opened doors. Within a year GCI had surpassed everybody in town except PAI, and had settled down as Ottawa's second-biggest firm.

Moores went a step further and did something PAI had not done. He appointed a high-profile board of directors. The board met a few times a year but was mainly a marketing device to pull in clients. Directors got ten per cent of the value of contracts they brought to GCI. The firm took out newspaper ads announcing the appointment to the board of Jean Marchand, an old Trudeau friend and former cabinet minister; Jack Armstrong, the former chairman of Imperial Oil; and George Hulme, a Calgary oilman. The Armstrong and Hulme appointments shrewdly helped consolidate GCI with the business community and made strategic sense, but the choice of Marchand left people blinking in amazement. What was Moores trying to do? Depoliticize himself? Marchand was one of the Three Wise Men – along with Pierre Trudeau and Gérard Pelletier – who trekked to Ottawa in 1965, but he had burned himself out the previous decade, being appointed to the Senate and later to the Canadian Transport Commission. As a former union leader he never had ties in the business world, and his Trudeau connection hardly secured GCI's future if John Turner were to become prime minister again. If Moores wanted a Liberal he could have done much better. For his part Marchand thought that he had really been recruited to give advice on how government worked, but, discovering the board existed to find clients, he quit after one meeting.

Moores astutely replaced Marchand with another former Trudeau minister, Francis Fox, who since his 1984 defeat was practising law in Montreal and keeping active in Liberal politics.

Moores later added Paul Robinson, the bombastic former U.S. ambassador to Canada, who outshone even Moores himself as a figure of controversy. Robinson made no pretence about his role; he said he was there to get GCI business in the light of the free-trade negotiations. Moores also appointed an unknown Boston insurance executive and entrepreneur named Robert Shea. This appointment mystified outside observers, until they learned that Shea, an American, had been at St. Francis Xavier University with Mulroney in 1955-56 and had remained a friend since. A document surfaced at the Sinclair Stevens conflict-of-interest hearings in which his name was recommended for patronage as "a friend of the prime minister".

Moores pulled off one other surprise that topped everything in terms of brazenness. After the 1985 Liberal victory in Quebec, he created a Quebec City subsidiary, Gestion Consultative Internationale – also GCI – and installed his Liberal allies Gourd as president and Fox as chairman. The Quebec City shuffle outdid anything Ottawa had seen.

In the world of consultants and lobbyists, it is a truism that corporate clients fear controversy almost as much as red ink. Clients would rather fail quietly than succeed noisily. For this reason critics believed that Moores had become too controversial for his clients' comfort, and would crash the minute he landed one more client into the news, as he had Wardair, Nordair, Bombardier, Gulf + Western, PMAC and Messerschmitt-Bolkow-Blohm. They could see clients deserting GCI and Moores fading off the scene; they waited for the collapse. Instead of collapsing, GCI picked up more clients than ever and added staff faster than anybody else in town. Business expanded each time the company hit the news. The controversy gave Moores free advertising and actually attracted clients, since every businessman seeking favours or influence called on GCI. Whenever people accused them of shoddy practices, GCI's officers said they refused more business than they accepted.

Moores's reputation did scare off some firms. A good many domestic corporations avoided GCI, and about fifty per cent of billings came from non-resident companies interested in investing in Canada. But some well-connected domestic firms put GCI on retainer to cover their bases; they wanted Moores – just in case. Even Nordair, which had been embroiled in controversy and dropped as a client during the Air Canada affair, returned to GCI. Airbus, the European aircraft-manufacturing consortium that Moores got into the news by representing one of its partners, later joined GCI as a client. Publicity didn't drive away as many firms as some had predicted.

Moores left his competitors dismayed, resentful, bewildered, and unsure about the meaning of his success. Whatever else GCI did, it managed to shake up the marketplace and introduce new competition. The genteel days when PAI and ECL carved up the market between them were over. Everybody now had to hustle harder because nobody knew what to expect next. Moores had joined the market in his own aggressive style and the old guard resented it.

Feeling the competition, PAI deliberated on how to meet the Moores challenge. PAI still had two to three times GCI's annual billings, sat alone in top spot, and, furthermore, continued to grow. But it had become number one by keeping ahead of the competition, and now GCI seemed to be the firm that was shaking things up. PAI briefly considered copying its high-profile board of directors, but dismissed it. It started toying with the notion of jumping into full-scale direct lobbying. It had already taken a half step into advocacy a few years earlier when it started advising clients on how to compete for major government contracts such as the Low Level Air Defence contract and the maintenance contract for the CF-18 fighter jet. In those instances it represented clients in front of bureaucrats and did engage in lobbying. But government contracts constituted only about twenty per cent of its business, and PAI treated them as a special case. It now started to think about going the whole way into lobbying, since the market seemed to want it. Moores had put the entire profession under scrutiny, and the bad publicity had rubbed off on PAI. If PAI was going to be hung for being a lobbyist, maybe it should start acting like one. But in the end it decided to keep the modus operandi that had made it number one.

One of the few Tories who didn't jump into the Ottawa market immediately after the Mulroney victory was Susan Murray, the young hotshot in Toronto who had helped rescue Massey-Ferguson a couple of years earlier. Murray also operated as an advocate, but the first thing she did when signing up new clients was to give them a copy of her firm's code of ethics, which made it clear that she didn't sell influence. She enjoyed impeccable Big Blue Machine connections, but when the Conservative government fell in Ontario in 1985 she built a relationship with the new Peterson government rather than chase after the market in Ottawa, and managed to expand her Queen's Park billings. Ironically, her Ottawa business grew even faster, and before long her office in Toronto did more volume out of Ottawa than from Queen's Park, until in the summer of 1986 she opened a staffed office in Ottawa. By this time her company had expanded to six consultants, which made her a force in the public-affairs industry.

The coming of the Conservative government and the rush of Tory lobbyists who followed Mulroney's footsteps to Ottawa changed the scene dramatically. It seemed that everybody who had ever voted Conservative had come to town and opened an office, including big Toronto and Montreal law firms who did more than practice law. Ottawa was swarming with lawyers, as most of the national firms had opened branch offices in the capital. Trade associations moved to Ottawa too, while those already in the capital beefed up their staffs. A lot was happening but nobody knew where it was going and when it would stop. Were the Mooreses, the Curleys, and the Nears riding a fad? Was Ottawa heading towards Washington's unabashed system of power lobbying? New players like Moores and Curley hailed the new style as a forward step in an unfolding evolution. Traditionalists like Lee and Neville saw it as a throwback to the bad old days of influence-peddling, the kind of practice that ECL in 1968 had tried to clean up. The change was manifested through Moores and Curley but sprang from more fundamental sources, such as the increasing intrusion of government into society, the demands of society for services, and the arrival of a new governing party in Ottawa. Without a hospitable environment the Mooreses and Curleys would not have succeeded. Nobody knew where things were leading.

TWENTY

THE COOPER
COMMITTEE

A small throng of lobbyists, reporters, and onlookers crowded into Room 307 of the West Block on April 24 1986 for the fifth public hearing of the Commons standing committee on elections, privileges, and procedure as it inquired into the need for a public registry of lobbyists. GCI was scheduled to appear that morning, and everybody was looking forward to seeing and hearing Frank Moores, the man who precipitated Prime Minister Mulroney's call for a lobbyists' registry in the first place. People called the registry the "Frank Moores bill". So it seemed fitting that the committee should have the chance to meet and quiz the man who started it all. But by the time Chairman Albert Cooper banged his gavel at 9:08 a.m., Moores had failed to show. Instead Gary Ouellet and Robert Gourd took the witness seats on behalf of GCI. The committee could not contain its curiosity, and halfway through the two-hour session a Liberal MP asked Ouellet where Frank Moores was. Ouellet replied dryly that as he was chief executive officer and ran the company on a day-to-day basis he thought it his position to appear.

Moores's absence failed to smooth GCI's reception, or to keep his profile low. John Rodriguez, the feisty New Democratic member for Nickel Belt, demanded to know who owned GCI, but Ouellet refused to answer, divulging only that it was a privately held company and that Frank Moores and Gerry Doucet were shareholders. "They are all secret," Rodriguez snorted. The session grew stormy as Rodriguez suggested that lobbyists such as Moores "are all a bunch of crooks" and several committee members challenged Gourd for wearing his MP's lapel pin when he was no longer an MP. Gourd, a former Quebec Liberal MP who fell in the Mulroney sweep, retorted that he wore his pin proudly but Rodriguez said it helped him as a lobbyist; that the committee was investigating whether lobbyists abused the system and Gourd's flaunting of his pin suggested that they did. It created a bad impression at the start.

Ouellet had tried to get the meeting off to a positive start with a reminder that the previous summer GCI had gone on record as supporting a registry. His formal brief proclaimed that GCI was the only company to endorse the principle, and he was right. The previous July, as he resigned from Air Canada's board of directors, Moores had suggested a registry. "A properly constituted regulatory framework in Canada for government relations people, or lobbyists, is an idea whose time has come, and is in the public interest," his statement said. But when the committee saw GCI's brief, it became evident that the firm supported the form of regulation but not the substance. GCI opposed the disclosure of anything more than the name and address of the lobbyist: no clients' names, no issues, and definitely no fees. "If a general provision requiring the disclosure of all clients and fees paid were required, there would be no open government relations business in Canada within a year," the brief claimed. "... No corporate client would tolerate the public disclosure of its corporate/consultant relationship, nor of the fees paid which, after all, is a private matter between the consultant, the client, and, eventually, Revenue Canada."

Several hearings later Sam Hughes led the ECL contingent before the committee and catalogued a series of objections to a registry. Nine days after that Bill Neville and David Mac-Naughton added their opposition on behalf of PAI. Susan Murray, of S.A. Murray Consulting, said that the amount of abuse did not merit government intervention, and proposed self-regulation under a board resembling the Better Business Bureau. The Cooper committee didn't have to beat the bushes for witnesses. Most of the consultant/lobbyist industry appeared to be only too willing to come forward and testify against a substantive registry. They complained that it represented a major intrusion and violated their promises to clients of confidentiality. They said that no law was any good if it was not workable, and a registry was totally unworkable, since the government would almost have to give out forms as businessmen got off the plane at the Ottawa airport. The plan would drive lobbying underground and make it more secret; only the honest lobbyists would register. They even questioned why Parliament was considering the issue. Many witnesses proclaimed to high heaven that they were not lobbyists and should not be lumped into a registry with the rest. Others said that if the registry included them it should also embrace lawyers, senators, unionists, social activists, and others who lobbied at one level or other. But almost all repeated the same thing: there was no problem, or, if a problem did exist – referring indirectly to Frank Moores – the solution was worse. The committee grew weary of hearing people say: "If it isn't broken, don't fix it."

Ouellet did have some easy moments during the otherwise tense session. Lorne McCuish, a Tory MP, disappeared for most of the hearing but not before tossing Ouellet a few marshmallow questions. McCuish, an insurance-claims manager from Prince George, B.C., flatly opposed a registry on principle. He didn't apologize for sitting on a committee mandated to produce a workable registry when he disagreed with its premise. He voiced his opposition at the first meeting by suggesting that a registry would only "make mankind more devious than he or she is now". Now he told Ouellet that no lobbyist should accept even a pro forma registry. "I do take strong, strong exception to a person's having to humiliate and humble himself by being put on a register – paying to suffer that humiliation – just so that he can talk to a Member of Parliament," McCuish complained.

"What you are saying is garbage," Rodriguez heckled from across the room.

It surprised no one that Rodriguez and McCuish clashed. They had collided before and would again, for Lorne McCuish and John Rodriguez disagreed on everything. Whenever McCuish looked up from his seat in the House of Commons and peered across to Rodriguez in the NDP benches he thought he was observing a raving socialist. When Rodriguez looked back he saw a rednecked, bigoted S.O.B. Rodriguez was a left-wing New Democrat and McCuish a right-wing Tory. The day McCuish and Rodriguez saw eye to eye on this issue would be the day Pierre Trudeau gave John Turner a friendly slap on the shoulder and told him to let bygones be bygones.

Rodriguez wanted a registry that captured every lobbyist,

every client, every issue, and every nickel and dime spent – with tough penalties for violations. It couldn't have too many bells and whistles for Rodriguez. He advocated registration so fervently that on December 5 1985 he introduced his own private member's bill in the House of Commons, Bill C-256, *An Act to Register Lobbyists*, which proposed covering every conceivable payment: money, loans, commissions, gifts, subscriptions, and even sexual favours. He formally proposed it to the committee two days earlier, and even appeared as a witness before his own committee. Rodriguez took the opportunity to thank Frank Moores for "letting the cat out of the bag" and provoking Mulroney into action. In that hearing it was Rodriguez who received the rough ride, specifically from McCuish, who accused him of conducting something of a vendetta against Moores.

Parliamentary committees usually act as lightning rods and then as rubber stamps. They absorb public hostility, and then approve government's bills with a minimum of tinkering. But sometimes, as with Mulroney on the registry issue, governments get cold feet, and before drafting a bill genuinely ask a committee for guidance about what it should say. In those exceptional cases, parliamentary committees can exert real influence, and MPs from all parties sincerely try to rise above their partisan differences to reach a unanimous conclusion. Unanimity becomes the overriding goal. In the world of politics nothing carries more authority and cuts through red tape faster than a report supported by all three parties.

The Cooper committee showed none of this non-partisan spirit, as its members bickered and postured and staked out ideological turf. Backing McCuish in outright opposition to a registry was Fred King, a fellow Tory who thought a registry would produce a bureaucratic nightmare and interfere with the right of business to operate freely. McCuish and King held that Canada was already overrun by government regulation and hated to add more, since both believed that the Criminal Code could handle unethical practices like bribery. King was more right-wing than McCuish and believed that Mulroney had climbed onto a left-wing limb with his crazy registry proposal.

On the other side, joining Rodriguez in favour of a tough registry, was Don Boudria, a member of the notorious rat pack, a group of four Liberal MPs who shrilly harassed the Mulroney government in its early years. Boudria insisted that a registry had to disclose everything, including fees, otherwise it would be useless. The five-man committee had only two non-Tories but Rodriguez and Boudria between them could overwhelm any committee.

Chairman Albert Cooper, the fifth member, stood out as the only voice of conciliation. Like his Tory colleagues he instinctively opposed a registry, but he kept an open mind and held his tongue. He could be a peacemaker if only the two sides would leave a little room for compromise, but as the hearings advanced it became clear that they couldn't shake off their ideological differences. Both factions left the committee room on some days muttering that there was no point in carrying on.

Besides the internal divisions, the committee faced the combined opposition of the lobbying profession. If anybody knew how to deep-six a registry it would be the lobbyists themselves. Furthermore, Mulroney, who had kicked off the debate with a ringing endorsement seven months earlier, when Frank Moores was making headlines, had lost his enthusiasm and was backing off. Mulroney had reason to stall. A registry would not revitalize the deteriorating image of his government or even cleanse the practice of lobbying. But he had made a pledge and couldn't retreat. Having rashly announced that he would confront lobbyists in the interests of openness and integrity, he had to carry through or be seen as surrendering to the forces he promised to curb. The very qualities that made a registry attractive in the first place made it hard to abandon. Because he couldn't afford to retreat, he stayed quiet and hoped that the committee would study the issue to death and then scuttle the whole thing, which now seemed an increasingly good bet.

As for the minister in charge of the issue, Consumer and Corporate Affairs Minister Michel Côté and his senior officials went along with the registry only because the prime minister had foisted it upon them. As the first witness, Côté kicked off the committee's hearings by advocating a minimal registry. "No more information than is absolutely necessary should be required," he said. "The system should not be so complicated that it discourages lobbying by anyone with modest means." He told the committee that he didn't favour the disclosure of fees, would settle for guidelines instead of legislation, and indeed would consider allowing the lobbyists to regulate themselves. Ultimately Côté would decide the matter, and his support looked dubious.

Few parliamentary initiatives could face the concerted opposition of the industry affected, the half-hearted support of the prime minister and the grudging endorsement of the sponsoring minister – not to mention ideological hostility from the parliamentary committee – and expect to survive. Everything pointed to a quiet death for the registry.

Worse was to follow when the veteran Tory MP Jim McGrath turned up as a witness. McGrath, who had recently finished a major study on parliamentary reform, had been an MP twenty-six of the last twenty-nine years, and enjoyed everybody's respect. Supporters of a registry expected McGrath's appearance to boost their sagging fortunes, because the previous June he had introduced private member's Bill C-248 advocating just such a registry, and proposing to punish violators with disqualifications and fines of up to $5,000 a month. Committee members expecting a rousing endorsement received a rude shock instead: McGrath came flat out and said he had changed his mind about a registry and no longer supported it. In fact he actively opposed it, even going so far as to to warn Côté against it. He said that the entire issue was complicated and tricky. From the witness chair he disowned his own bill, which still stood on the Commons schedule, and said he hoped it would never become law. He left committee members stupefied. He had staged one of the more notable conversions since Saul's journey to Damascus. If somebody with less moral clout had performed such a flip-flop people would have looked for the fix.

During his testimony McGrath advised committee members to travel to Washington to examine the American registry system for themselves. The committee planned to do exactly that. At an in-camera session a month earlier Cooper outlined a variety of travel plans, one of them a $100,000 world trip to Washington, Sacramento, Australia, the United Kingdom, and West Germany. Don Boudria leaked the $100,000 option to the press and scored some cheap political points by denouncing the cost as "obscene" without revealing that it was merely one of several alternatives. The public seized on the trip as a junket, and after a couple of weeks of hate mail and "sheer hell", the MPs chose to travel only to Washington and Sacramento, which, they claimed, they probably would have done anyway. The other MPs glared at Boudria, and even Rodriguez chastised him. The last thing the committee needed was more division and animosity.

The Washington hearing opened in the Canadian Embassy with two guests, Jim O'Hara, of the American League of Lobbyists, and John Zorach, of the Professional Lobbying Center. The committee had made a big catch in O'Hara, for eighteen years a Congressman and currently a partner in the well-connected Washington lobbying law firm Patton, Boggs and Blow. He had lobbied for General Motors on pollution, for Chrysler on loan guarantees, for California landowners on irrigation subsidies, for the Alaska lumber industry, the American Federation of Teachers, the boating industry, and the Business Round Table. The committee could hardly have done better than O'Hara.

Rodriguez knew that if anybody could convince free-enter-prisers like McCuish and King of the need for a registry it would be other free-enterprisers who had been even more successful at free enterprise. They would listen to O'Hara.

"If you were to give us advice," Rodriguez asked, "would you recommend that we establish a system of registering lobbyists?"

"Absolutely," O'Hara replied.

McCuish could hardly believe it. If his ears had not deceived him he had just heard the representative of the American League of Lobbyists advocate regulation.

"Are you sure?" McCuish inquired.

"Absolutely," O'Hara repeated without flinching.

"Well," Rodriguez continued, "your process here, your system, what would you recommend to improve it?"

"Make it tougher," O'Hara said. Zorach nodded approval. McCuish and King were stunned. As Boudria left the room that afternoon he turned to Rodriguez and said: "Gee, Johnny, some of these folks appear to be mellowing."

As the committee listened to more legislators and lobbyists it became obvious that O'Hara and Zorach were no eccentric gadflies. Just as virtually all the Canadian witnesses had opposed registration, virtually all the American witnesses supported it. In fact the Americans complained that their registry was weak and easily circumvented and needed fixing, urging the MPs to put teeth into their registry if they decided to have one. American lobbyists did not call themselves consultants or government-relations people the way the Canadians did; they proudly called themselves lobbyists. They advocated openness and disclosure and saw nothing intrusive or offensive about a registry. Unlike the Canadian practitioners, who seemed to lock their client lists in Chubb safes each night, the Americans paraded and even flaunted theirs, stopping just short of printing them on their business cards. The openness amazed the committee, and destroyed the Canadian claims that the system would fall apart if clients were identified.

The committee moved to Capitol Hill, visited the registry office, and met the clerk of the House of Representatives, who outlined the registry's scope. The Federal Regulation of Lobbying Act of 1946 required lobbyists to do merely two things: first, register themselves with the secretary of the Senate and the clerk of the House of Representatives, and, second, file quarterly financial reports on how much they spent influencing legislation. The act had no policing provision. The clerk and the secretary simply received the information. They lacked authority to investigate its veracity or even compel registration. Anybody could flout the act with impunity.

The committee learned that the Lobbying Act had more loopholes than a chain-link fence and that most lobbying in Washington escaped the system. For instance, the law covered only attempts at influencing Congress, and ignored lobbyists who concentrated on the White House or the bureaucracy, or even a congressman's aides. The financial-reporting requirements left all kinds of escapes; organizations and groups didn't have to declare their spending as long as their money was not raised specifically to persuade congressmen. Nor did they have to register if lobbying congressmen was not their "principal purpose", a clause that led many trade associations who regularly lobbied congressmen to refuse to register. The statute, as one critic put it, was "more loophole than law".

That evening McCuish turned on the television in his hotel room but didn't like the fare and went for a walk. He had strolled only half a block when a voice called out from behind: "Can I join you?" It was his old foe Rodriguez. Neither had eaten, so they stepped into an Italian sidewalk café and ordered ravioli. They shared the red house wine and talked and talked, and each discovered that a genuine person lived behind the ideological mask, as they joked and kibitzed about themselves and their families. That night Rodriguez and McCuish discovered that they liked each other. Later they walked to an ice cream parlour, ordered ice-cream cones, strolled to Capitol Hill, and got lost on the way back to the hotel. They hung around together for the rest of the trip. The man McCuish used to despise as a fire-breathing socialist became one of his truest friends in the Commons; a month later, when Rodriguez suffered a life-threatening heart attack, nobody in Parliament took it harder or fretted more about it than McCuish.

The evening in the Washington sidewalk café didn't change their political beliefs, but it opened up a line of communication and introduced a little give and take and a lot of respect at committee meetings. Rodriguez and McCuish no longer viewed each other with suspicion.

After witnessing the loose regulations of Washington, the committee travelled to Sacramento and got a look at possibly the strictest lobbying law in the world. California's Political Reform Act compelled lobbyists and employers to file certifications, registrations and reports with the secretary of state and to account for every expenditure over ten dollars. Business and labour originally led a massive lobby against the act but a statewide referendum gave it seventy-per-cent support. If Washington covered too little, California, perhaps, went to the other extreme. Every lunch and every meeting had to be reported, and even the Roman Catholic Archdiocese of Sacramento had to register. California demanded so much that some complained that the law was ineffective, that nobody bothered to look up the avalanche of details.

If lobbyists anywhere had cause to complain it was the highly regulated lobbyists of California, yet the committee discovered that none of them did, not even the wealthy firms with multi-million-dollar accounts. In fact they advocated tightening up the law further. A couple of lobbyists advocated the registry so aggressively that they turned the tables and started questioning the committee. They explained that the registry worked in their interest because it made them look professional and above board and prevented the suspicion that automatically accompanies secrecy. Sacramento surprised the committee as much as Washington had, not least when the members toured the office of the Fair Political Practices Commission and were amazed at how a small office handled thousands of files. Michael Salerno, a 1960s activist from Berkeley, enforced the act and impressed the committee with his missionary penchant for keeping everything squeaky clean. Salerno persuaded members that abuses would always occur and that lobbying needed monitoring.

Sacramento showed that lobbyists could live with a tough registry and even like it. This time it was Rodriguez and Boudria who searched their souls and started to mellow. They had arrived in California believing that one could develop a perfect registry that scrutinized everything, but Sacramento had taught them otherwise. They had been told how lobbyists circumvented the financial-disclosure requirements by offloading expenses to their clients, so that they had little to disclose. They came to accept that no system could be loophole-free, and gave up the idea that a registry should hold up every penny to public scrutiny. California proved that people could thwart even the most elaborate mechanism. They still supported financial disclosure, but Sacramento taught them to keep it simple and to concentrate on who was doing what and for whom.

The MPs, although split up, arrived back in Ottawa like a family turning into the driveway after a long journey. They had been through a lot together and were happy to be back home. A few days in the United States had changed everything, dramatically boosting the prospects for consensus. Both coasts of the United States – one with a weak system, the other with a stringent one – produced the same answer: a registration system was workable, and worked in everyone's interest. A philosophical gulf still divided the committee, but the gap had narrowed; the atmosphere was open and conciliatory and everyone realized that a little nudging and pushing might produce a consensus. Even Boudria, who had blown the whistle on the world trip, became a strong and loyal member.

Cooper had been making a shopping list of potential trade-offs. He now called the members together and started the negotiations. "Well," McCuish announced, "I am prepared to consider the premise of a registry in Canada and to work toward that." He said that registration was sure as hell necessary in the United

States but that nobody had shown him the need in Canada. But, he added, he was a firm believer in history and thought that Canada should get a registry now and see how it worked and review it in two years. Fred King still didn't like the idea but agreed to go along if everybody else wanted it. He could see the argument that Canadians had the right to know who was trying to influence the government, and on whose behalf.

Agreement in principle was one thing; fitting together the nuts and bolts proved another. The committee had to decide what to put into the registry and agree on who should be covered, whether to include unpaid as well as paid lobbyists, whether to include advisers like PAI and ECL, and a host of other questions. Did a lawyer who came to Ottawa once a month to represent a client have to register as a lobbyist? The registry had to cast a net that would catch lobbyists while letting through the general public; it shouldn't catch every businessman, union leader, farmer, and fisherman who occasionally came to Ottawa, and should never impede anybody's access to government. The Tories sought to minimize government spending and avoid a bureaucratic monster; Rodriguez and Boudria leaned towards giving the registry real teeth. Those two objects collided often enough to make everything difficult.

The MPs met in an off-hill committee room at 151 Sparks Street, and there the real horsetrading started. Rodriguez pushed for the names and addresses of both the lobbyists and the clients, the issue being lobbied, and the amount of the contract. He wanted financial disclosure backed up by receipts. McCuish balked at such sweeping disclosure and King supported him. McCuish, like GCI, wanted the name and address of the lobbyist and no more. He firmly opposed any financial disclosure, arguing that it would only cause lobbyists to undercut each other and lead to price cutting. King's commitment to the principle was still weak, and neither he nor McCuish wanted a nosy registry. The committee divided further on who should be classified as lobbyists. Rodriguez and Boudria wanted advisers like PAI and ECL included, while the Tories argued that they were not lobbyists, only experts. Rodriguez and Boudria maintained that they should be included because their advice influenced events. Such differences still blocked agreement.

Writing the report proved time-consuming and difficult.

Bruce Carson, the Library of Parliament research officer who attended all the sessions, drafted a skeleton report with alternatives, and the committee worked through it page by page, paragraph by paragraph, sentence by sentence, and even word by word, adding, dropping, and changing items. The Tories worried about leaving out essentials for fear of being laughed at, but dreaded even more putting in too much, especially since there would be no turning back once the report became public. Negotiations inched forward. The committee couldn't meet its deadline of June 30 1986 and asked Parliament for an extension that would allow it to resume its deliberations in the fall.

Parliament extended the committee's deadline and then played a dirty trick. The government, in an effort to start with a clean slate, prorogued Parliament. When the session ended so did the Cooper committee's mandate to report on registration. It could be resurrected only by unanimous consent at the new session. Cooper, Boudria, and Rodriguez had to lobby their respective House leaders to get their mandate back. Finally the committee resumed in November, nearly five months later – and members still faced the same disagreements that had immobilized them the previous June.

Shortly before Christmas 1986 the committee members resolved to set aside a full day for an ultimate all-or-nothing meeting. They holed themselves up in the West Block armed with a packed lunch, ignoring division bells. Starting at 9 a.m., they tackled the outstanding issues one by one. First they agreed to restrict the registry to paid lobbyists. That simplified matters and enabled them to dodge some serious philosophical questions. Then they whittled away at the pesky question of how much disclosure. McCuish still wanted the registry to reveal only the name and address of the lobbyist. He continued to oppose divulging the client, the issue, or the money involved.

"Well," Rodriguez asked, "then what would be the point of having a registry if that's all it's going to do? It doesn't create any transparency."

"All right," McCuish replied, "I'll go for the first three [lobbyist, client, and issue] but I'm not going for the contract sort of thing."

"You got it," Rodriguez answered.

Both McCuish and Rodriguez had made major concessions.

Rodriguez also backed down on including advisers like PAI and ECL, allowing the committee to word its report in a way that left them out as long as they didn't lobby directly. To overcome everyone's reservations, the committee recommended a review of the registry after two years. Everyone strove for a unanimous report; Rodriguez and Boudria realized that a minority report would do nothing to further their idea for a registry while the Tories knew that a minority report would undermine the credibility of their majority recommendation.

They emerged from the room around 5 p.m. worn out but elated. They went over to McCuish's office for a celebration and a Christmas drink. They felt proud that as an all-party committee they had tackled a tough issue and had overcome deep philosophical differences to find common ground. They all felt that they had made the parliamentary system work – all except one. Cooper was quietly seething. Nobody had seen the mild-mannered chairman angry before, and his fury over the committee's rejection of self-regulation surprised everyone. He had been such a conscientious mediator that he had forgotten to present his own views, which had been influenced by Susan Murray's presentation in favour of industry self-policing. Rodriguez had so adamantly refused to accept the idea that it had died. Later, Cooper sent Rodriguez a note saying that there would be no unanimous report without a recommendation for self-regulation. Rodriguez saw everything falling apart. He showed the note to Boudria, and together they decided to accommodate the chairman when the committee reconvened to approve the final draft.

The committee released its report on January 27 1987, and reporters immediately asked the members why they had not included PAI and ECL. "Isn't it strange that two of the biggest lobbying firms are not going to be captured by the legislation?" one reporter asked. The MPs replied that they were worried about casting too big a net. Reporters, who had earlier interpreted the committee's delay as evidence that it had succumbed to the lobbyists, now applauded it for producing a good report. The lobbying fraternity saw it differently.

The report did not add a single issue, or even nuance, to the substance of the registry debate. It didn't need to; the bureaucrats at Consumer and Corporate Affairs, who would ultimately write the bill, understood the various issues perfectly well. However, the report resolved the question of whether the government should proceed with a registry and, in general terms, gave guidance on what to cover. Mulroney's promised registry had been dying a slow death until the report breathed new life into it. The government couldn't ignore a unanimous all-party recommendation. The Toronto *Sun* columnist Claire Hoy and others had whacked Mulroney so badly with the "Lyin' Brian" image that he couldn't retreat now. By this time Harvie Andre had replaced Michel Côté as minister of consumer and corporate affairs. When the report formally reached the Commons two weeks later he promised to introduce legislation "in very short order". He said: "Unanimous reports are few and far between in this institution and when we get one we want to act on it. That is the intention of the government."

EPILOGUE

Five months after the committee released its report, Consumer and Corporate Affairs Minister Harvie Andre tabled Bill C-82, *The Lobbyists Registration Act*. The new bill proposed a two-tier registry. The first category of lobbyist – advocates who lobbied directly on behalf of a third party, appearing before ministers to plead a case directly – would have to list their clients and the issues being lobbied. Category Two lobbyists – staff people who lobbied for their employer as part of their jobs – would have to list only their names and companies or associations; in Andre's own words, they would have to provide "no more information than now appears on their business cards". The bill was very mild, milder even than the committee had recommended. The overwhelming majority of lobbyists would fall under the minimal requirements of category two – the bill did not outlaw contingency fees, or give the registry any investigative powers, or include the organizers of political mass mailings or advertising campaigns, despite what the committee had recommended.

"The basic goals of the committee are very much represented in this bill," Albert Cooper said loyally as he sat at Andre's side in the press theatre of the National Press Building. Sitting at the far end of the theatre, waiting impatiently for their turn, were John Rodriguez and Don Boudria, who took centre stage when Andre and Cooper left. Boudria called the bill "watered down" while Rodriguez complained about its "legalistic weasel words". Both noted that it contained no financial disclosures, while Rodriguez said he wanted to know "who was doing what to whom and for how much" and would try to amend the bill in committee.

The significance of their positions did not escape the notice of Canadian Press reporter Tim Naumetz who asked if the committee, of which they were members, had not unanimously backed away from fee disclosures. "That's correct," Rodriguez replied. "I wanted it and I fought for it in the committee. But I thought it was important to get a unanimous report so that we can get the legislation before Parliament, and so I compromised on that. But now that the bill is going to be before the committee, it's a whole new ballgame. And I think this is where I can resume the fight to have the 'for how much' included." Rodriguez and Boudria had shifted back into their adversarial roles against the Tory majority; politics always was a fickle profession.

The meekness of the bill greatly pleased most lobbyists. Firms like ECL and PAI had escaped the registry as long as they did not lobby. PAI would have to register only those clients it represented in an advocacy role, while it appeared that ECL would not have to register at all. Bill Neville and Frank Moores could live with the bill, but Bill Lee was taking no chances. He opposed the coming of a registry with the ideological passion of a militant businessman fighting government encroachment, and looked upon it as a personal affront to his integrity. Lee was 62, and abhorred the prospect of finishing his career lumped together with real lobbyists who button-holed officials and argued other people's cases. He maintained he would be perjuring himself by putting his name into a registry, because in nearly nineteen years he had never lobbied. He told Steve Markey and Rick Bertrand, ECL's remaining shareholders, that he would resign prior to his July 1 1988 retirement if the company listed itself in the registry.

The company Lee had built now faced a different future with Markey and Bertrand at the helm. ECL had scrambled to survive the 1984 débâcle and to hold its clients and, for the most part, had succeeded. Only American Express and Imperial Oil withdrew as clients, the latter blaming corporate cutbacks. The retainer-to-project revenue mix dropped from 80-20 to about 65-35 but, given the obstacles, ECL maintained revenue levels with remarkable success. Its 1984 billings of $1-million rose to about $1.2-million by the fiscal year ending June 30 1987. This didn't match the growth of the firms headed by Neville, Moores, Near, Murray, and Curley, but ECL had held on and marginally boosted revenues when everyone else had relegated it to the garbage heap. In November 1985, ECL held a glitzy party to celebrate its upscale move into elegant offices in Ottawa's latest glass tower, Heritage Place.

A good portion of the credit for ECL's survival belonged to Sam Hughes, the new president, whose arrival in 1985 helped start the revitalization. But if Hughes injected new life, he also introduced a problem ECL had never seriously experienced before, and at this juncture could ill afford. Hughes disagreed with Markey and Bertrand on fundamental business matters. Hughes was a natural leader with a strong personality who instinctively positioned himself as ECL's high-profile front man, whereas Markey and Bertrand sought to develop it into a partnership like a law firm where everybody contributed different skills and worked together. They believed that the débâcle of 1984 had proved the folly of embodying the firm in one individual. At ECL, senior officers worked jointly on clients' files, and the last thing the company needed was a breakdown in harmony between the two owners and the president – but such was the calamity that now befell ECL. By the summer of 1987, Hughes had left, to become chairman of Corporation House, and the Canadian director of Vickers Shipbuilding and Engineering Ltd., the giant British company that planned to bid on the estimated $10-billion contract for Canada's nuclear submarines.

After one more failed attempt to negotiate a deal with PAI, Markey and Bertrand launched ECL into an expansion that would have brought a smile to the lips of MacNaughton himself. Once resistant to innovation, ECL started adding new services and expanding on all fronts. First, it opened a Toronto office – staffed by a veteran Liberal, Norman MacLeod – to help clients deal with the new Liberal government in Ontario; then it bought a partnership in the Ottawa public-relations firm Waddell Solomon Associates as a means of selling communications strategies. Not content with that, ECL next purchased fifty per cent of COMPAS – Carleton Opinion, Marketing and Public Affairs Surveys, Inc. – a newly-founded polling company which used the facilities at the Carleton Survey Centre at Carleton University. COMPAS was starting from scratch, but ECL hoped to build up business through cross-selling, as PAI and Decima did. ECL also formed an alliance with Walter Gray, president of Henry &

Gray, Inc., and a low-profile Tory consultant who published several Ottawa newsletters and directories. Except for the Gray deal, all these acquisitions required capital, and Markey and Bertrand went out on a limb and signed large personal guarantees at the bank.

But ECL was not prepared to follow PAI's path on one crucial issue. Markey and Bertrand insisted on servicing clients from the executive level, which was the policy that had allowed PAI to outgrow it in the first place. Two partners could service only so many clients, and that restricted the company's expansion, whereas PAI could grow forever by hiring more consultants. In the good old days, ECL had never expanded beyond a small handful of partners because it had made so much money that the price of its shares scared off new partners. Fewer partners meant more profit for existing partners, which further drove up share prices, digging the company into a lucrative but ever-deepening rut. Now the market under the Mulroney government seemed to prefer big firms like PAI and GCI with lots of services, or, alternatively, small outfits like Curley-Fortier and Harry Near with hot connections. ECL fell into the no-man's-land in between, and had trouble competing at either end of the market.

After some soul-searching, Markey and Bertrand took a radical step and decided to convert ECL from a company with shareholders to a partnership like a law firm. That way ECL could continue to service its clients with partners and still add clients by merely bringing in more partners, the way lawyers and accountants do. This solved ECL's structural limitation on growth, but not without a stiff financial price to the two owners. Over the years Markey and Bertrand had each personally invested more than a quarter of a million dollars in acquiring their ECL stock, and now they were surrendering the equity value. Like lawyers leaving a law firm, they would have no shares to sell when they retired. New partners would join the firm rather than buy into it, and would share in the profits each year. The plan required Markey and Bertrand to make nearly a million-dollar sacrifice, but on reflection they decided that this was where the future lay. The Mulroney era had forced ECL to adapt, and after nearly two decades the firm had decided to adapt radically.

Duncan Edmonds also adapted to the new order of things. He faced greater difficulties than any ECL had in the wake of Bob Coates's downfall, when Mulroney's decision to ostracize Edmonds left him not only out of work but out of favour. He tried to salvage what he could out of the mess, by pulling JDE Consulting out of its blind trust and resuming his practice, but found the going tough. He still had Canada Safeway as a client, did some project work for Coca Cola, and regained the two directorships he had given up to work for Coates, but when it came to attracting new clients he encountered trouble. Not surprisingly, most potential clients stayed clear of him. They knew that he could still fall back on old connections in the public service and quietly call on friends, but they couldn't afford to take the chance of alienating Mulroney. Even a salesman like Edmonds could not overcome a blacklisting by the prime minister.

He agonized over his predicament. Still an idealist, he had trouble believing a government could behave so vindictively. He waited six months for Mulroney's anger to subside and then wrote him a four-page philosophical "Dear Brian" letter with a conciliatory recounting of events, and closed with a warm greeting. Mulroney didn't reply; he was not ready to forgive and forget. Edmonds's close friend Walter McLean, the secretary of state, who had been ordered by Mulroney to shun him, was later demoted to junior immigration minister, and eventually dumped altogether.

Edmonds had lost his enthusiasm for public-affairs consulting, and was looking to get out of Ottawa. He even tried to sell his company to ECL. So friends were not suprised when he leapt at an offer to be an unsalaried Visiting Associate of the Americas Society in New York City. The work took two days a week and kept him occupied when he was not in Ottawa servicing his few remaining clients. He sold his big house in Rockcliffe for a tidy $410,000 and moved into a nearby condominium, but spent increasing amounts of time at his condominium in Florida while he mulled over the prospects of relocating in the U.S. for good. Canada increasingly bored him; he read the *New York Times* and *Wall Street Journal* every day and found the news in the *Globe and Mail* tedious by comparison. In 1986 he moved to Yale University as Adjunct Associate Professor of political science and chairman of Canadian studies. He taught a graduate seminar on

Canada-U.S. relations while he serviced his Ottawa clients on the side. The appointment would last a couple of years or more and give him time to figure out his next move.

Frank Moores continued to keep in regular touch with his good friend Brian Mulroney. He also continued to thrive as chairman of GCI, but in a way that was uncharacteristic of him, namely by being uncontroversial. After spending much of 1985 in the headlines, he managed to lower his profile and fade into the background along with the rest of his industry. Some observers doubted whether he could maintain his new modest style but he seemed to be doing exactly that. At the same time he started hiring research staff and paying attention to the bureaucrats, the moves of a successful practitioner who was in it for the long term.

Allan Gregg faithfully abided by the terms of his pact with Brian Mulroney to hold his tongue until the end of the election campaign, keeping his side of the bargain perfectly, but not for a minute longer than he had to. Once Mulroney won his massive victory on September 4 1984 the covenant had expired and Gregg was free again to speak his mind. When he proceeded to do just that, his relations with Mulroney once again became strained and started to deteriorate. At one point there was talk within the anti-Gregg faction of the party of bringing back the American pollster Bob Teeter or importing the services of Richard Wirthlin.

Decima Research remained the party's pollster but Gregg's mercurial relationship with Mulroney hurt the company. Under Mulroney, Ottawa was looking to retain one company as the official government pollster which would conduct a monthly omnibus poll to handle the requirements of all departments. Everybody assumed that Decima Research would get the contract. The government requested proposals from the leading companies. Martin Goldfarb turned down an invitation to bid, claiming that the government wouldn't hire him anyway. Gregg, on the other hand, invested heavily in his presentation, at the expense of private-sector work, and won the competition on technical merit; but at that point Ottawa backed away from the whole concept, and awarded the contract to no one. As the Conservative Party's pollster, Decima would be a controversial choice, and the monthly omnibus poll was an easy target for journalists under the Access to Information Act. But many suspected the real reason was that Mulroney felt that Gregg was shooting off his mouth and getting out of line again.

David MacNaughton spent his time in Toronto running the Public Affairs Resources Group, the umbrella company that owned PAI and Decima Research, and operated them as divisions. Before moving to Toronto, he had bought a third subsidiary, a little company called McLean & Associates that packaged political commercials and communications strategies for Conservative politicians like Premier Bill Davis of Ontario, Premier Grant Devine of Saskatchewan, and Social Credit Premier Bill Bennett of British Columbia. Management deficiencies had pushed it to the edge of bankruptcy, and MacNaughton bought it from Nancy McLean and her partner as the bank was about to cut off its line of credit. While steering the company deeply into corporate work, he installed a new financial and administrative system and quickly transformed McLean & Associates from a problem into a moneymaker.

Meanwhile Mike Robinson quit as president of PAI and sold his shares to take a long sabbatical in France, leaving Gregg and MacNaughton as the two shareholders, with MacNaughton owning two-thirds and Gregg the rest. (If all PAI employees chose to convert their debentures into shares MacNaughton's holdings would decline to around 55 per cent and Gregg's to around 27 per cent.)

MacNaughton had big plans. He was determined to acquire more subsidiaries like McLean & Associates, and would seek to do it by leveraging PARG with debt. Beyond that he would move PARG onto the international stage and repeat abroad what PAI and Decima had done in Canada. He wanted to make PARG the largest public-affairs conglomerate in the world, starting in the United States, where he would first establish a base, and then expanding to Europe and later to Japan. MacNaughton had gambled before and planned to keep rolling the dice until PARG became big.

As his first foreign holding, MacNaughton bought Government Research Corporation, a money-losing firm in Washington that did much the same thing in the United States that PAI did in Canada. GRC, with a presence in Washington and an office in London, looked like the perfect launching pad for a worldwide takeoff. GRC's previous owner, Tony Stout, had had a disastrous fling with a futuristic worldwide intelligence-gathering scheme called IRIS – International Reporting Information Systems – which sought *Fortune* 500 clients and, working off a computer, presented itself as a kind of corporate equivalent of the CIA. The computer would hum and whirr and spit out up-to-date assessments about the prospects for rebellion in Tanzania, unemployment in Bolivia, or a change of interest rates in Japan. Unfortunately IRIS collapsed into bankruptcy before it got off the ground.

Despite the flop, MacNaughton liked the notion that underlay IRIS, and believed that an international network could succeed if it was refocused on more bottom-line issues, stripped of its gadgetry, and humanized. In his opinion it might have succeeded if it had offered face-to-face advice and strategy across a table, because corporate executives preferred picking the brains of an expert to reading a report out of a computer. Corporations wanted hard advice on things like when to get out of South Africa, and would also pay fees for the latest on an emerging tax bill in Washington or a defence procurement in West Germany or trade-policy changes in Japan. Strange as it seemed, the international consulting field remained in the same state of infancy that Ottawa had known domestically ten or fifteen years earlier. MacNaughton felt it could do nothing but grow.

But first he had to cure the ailing GRC. He believed he could remould it in the image of PAI and make it profitable by introducing PAI's management philosophy. He changed the structure of the client relationship and the content of the service, and instituted regular quarterly overview briefings for clients, like PAI's. GRC had little prominence in Washington, and since MacNaughton wanted to develop one, he urged the GRC staff, politically neutral to a person, to join the Democratic or the Republican party and become active in the political system. Now, he was confident that GRC would blossom into profitability the way PAI, Decima, and McLean & Associates had done before it.

But the recovery did not go as planned. GRC confronted Mac-Naughton with a bigger challenge than he had bargained for. He had underestimated the magnitude of its losses and the decay in the relationships with clients, now that Tony Stout's invitations to Scottish grouse moors were no longer forthcoming; GRC lost a quarter of its European clients within six months. Furthermore, its management personnel needed attention. It operated like a government bureaucracy and strove to compile quality research for its own sake rather than to turn a profit, or address the needs of individual clients. It had been losing a little money when he bought it; now it lost a lot.

As GRC kept bleeding red ink, MacNaughton began to worry, and the Washington staff became very familiar with his zero-base budgeting speech about making everything cost-recovera-ble. The GRC managers argued that Washington was more com-plicated than Ottawa, and worked differently. At the same time another of his recent acquisitions, Pension Finance Associates, which compiled data on the performances of about 450 major pension funds in Canada, continued to lose money. The com-pany had been heading for ruin when MacNaughton spotted it as a classic candidate for one of his patented turnarounds; but it too was failing to turn around and, together with GRC, was threatening the health of PARG itself. MacNaughton briefly doubted his magic, and began to wonder if he had made a big mistake with these latest takeovers. Maybe Washington was different, maybe his reach had finally exceeded his grasp. In two years GRC alone lost $700,000, which was more than the highly leveraged PARG could afford.

September 1986 proved to be a big month for averting further difficulty, for in that month MacNaughton bolstered PARG's financial position by unloading Pension Finance Associates for a capital gain. It was also the month that GRC began to turn the profit corner, and projected net income of $150,000 for 1986-87. MacNaughton concluded that Washington was bigger and more institutionalized than Ottawa but not fundamentally different, that public affairs in the two countries adhered to the same basic principles. After a few bumps and jolts, MacNaughton was back on course.

PARG reached $20-million in sales in 1987 and MacNaughton started the year by pressing the bank to drop half its security from the GRC loan in order to advance him another couple of million dollars. He wanted the money to buy a polling company in the United States so that GRC would have a polling sister, like PAI and Decima. After conducting a sophisticated canvass of available U.S. firms he set his sights on the *Cambridge Report*, an American equivalent of the *Decima Quarterly*. The *Cambridge Report* would give the *Decima Quarterly* a common data base with which to publish a North American *Quarterly*.

MacNaughton could borrow only so much money for PARG's continued expansion, however, so he decided to raise capital by selling shares to the public. But MacNaughton the businessman was still such a political animal that he could not sell the shares until after the next Ontario election. Since moving to Toronto he had become an informal adviser to the Ontario Liberal leader, David Peterson, who was now the premier. Peterson had tapped him, along with Penny Nash, to run his next election campaign, which could come at any time. So MacNaughton could not afford to lock himself into a schedule travelling to meet investment dealers. He had to keep his itinerary open, ready to drop everything and join forces with Martin Goldfarb, his biggest polling competitor, in fighting Allan Gregg across the election barricades. MacNaughton and Gregg were business partners, but during the Ontario election they would be political adversaries.

So the public issue of shares had to wait until MacNaughton completed his political commitments. Once he had bought a U.S. polling company, he would look next at London and Brussels and then at Tokyo, just as he had planned to do all along. He had missed a few steps but he was back on track, and it was a very fast track.

Bill Neville had reason to be satisfied at the beginning of 1987. The Mulroney era smiled warmly on PAI, more than on any other firm, even GCI. Two years of Tory rule had more than doubled its revenue. When Mulroney took office in September 1984, PAI billed just under $2-million. The figure jumped beyond $3-million after Mulroney's first year and topped $4-million after the second; PAI was now projecting $4.6-million for the fiscal year ending August 31 1987. Neville had joined PAI at a critical time and had ushered it through its most explosive growth ever. Lobbying always increases with a change of government, because political uncertainty causes businessmen to worry, which in turn motivates them to retain such firms as PAI. The company would have grown under Turner too, but it was hard to imagine that it could have done as well. The arrival of Mulroney in the Prime Minister's Office and Neville in their office had done wonders for PAI.

But the good fortune of PAI was running Neville off his feet. It had more than seventy clients, and each one wanted a piece of him, while the handful of clients paying $10,000 or more a month wanted big chunks of his time. As PAI's chief marketer, he also had to travel the country in search of new clients to meet the burgeoning payroll and to cover the fancy rent of the company's new office in the multi-cornered glitter of the Manulife Building, and to meet the ambitious revenue target imposed by PARG. Sean Moore had replaced Mike Robinson as president and spent little time with clients in order to concentrate on the internal management tasks which were needed now that PAI had grown into a fair-sized company. That left Neville doing all the senior counselling with clients, which even a workaholic like him found overwhelming.

To lighten his load, Neville compiled a list of senior civil servants in search of someone who could walk into corporate boardrooms to give overviews of government, and could talk authoritatively about the Mulroney government's impending tax reform and other issues. The bureaucrat near the top of his list was Mark Daniels, the deputy minister of consumer and corporate affairs, who had impressed Neville during the Clark government when, from the Privy Council Office, he helped extricate Clark from his Petro-Canada box. Daniels had since become assistant deputy minister of finance, then deputy minister of labour, was now deputy minister of consumer and corporate affairs, and was well-respected by his peers in the bureaucracy.

Daniels was lured away to PAI as vice-chairman in the spring of 1987. Conflict-of-interest rules prohibited him from giving advice on anything he had worked on in the previous twelve months, which meant that for a full year he would not be able to advise clients on the forthcoming lobby-registry bill, the patent-drug legislation, competition policy, or anything else in his department, because he had supervised them all.

At the same time as PAI hired Daniels, in another of Mac-Naughton's bold acquisitions, it bought Curley, Fortier & Associates. The takeover gave PAI sixteen more clients and $700,000 worth of new business, hoisting annual billings to a staggering $5.5-million. Only one client had to be dropped for conflict-of-interest reasons. In the bidding for the $350-million contract to build Terminal Three at the Lester B. Pearson International Airport near Toronto, PAI was working on behalf of Falconstar Corporation, while Curley, Fortier & Associates were acting for Huang and Danczkay Ltd., which now had to be given up as clients. (Huang and Danczkay, renowned for their controversial lobbying techniques on the Toronto civic scene, would not be left in the cold, however. In addition to Curley-Fortier, they had simultaneously retained three other firms with Tory connections: Frank Moores's GCI, John Lundrigan's St. John's company, and Biolink Management Consultants headed by Chester Burtt, a former aide to John Crosbie, who as Transport Minister was responsible for the final choice. On June 22 1987 Crosbie announced that Huang and Danczkay had won the contract.)

Fortier moved into PAI as counsel while Curley stayed in Toronto and became its second vice chairman. The personable Curley helped Neville with marketing and client relations while Daniels helped him with senior briefing. Some of Curley's clients, however, retained him for his lobbying skills and expected direct advocacy, so that the Curley acquisition moved PAI a little further into straight lobbying. PAI had once proudly claimed to do no direct lobbying, but had significantly backed off that declaration after the coming of the Mulroney government; by 1987 PAI acknowledged that fifteen per cent or more of its activity involved advocacy. It still maintained that strategic advice was by far its biggest service and represented the best choice for the majority of clients, but the company had trimmed its sails to accommodate the "Frank Moores shift" in the market winds.

Although Neville's salary had already vaulted him into Canada's income élite, in the spring of 1987 he was offered even more money to become the full-time lobbyist for the tobacco industry.

The offer from the Canadian Tobacco Manufacturers Council tempted him, and when it was sweetened so that he could establish his personal company – William Neville & Associates – and spend one-third of his time advising private clients, he couldn't resist, although it would not be a sinecure. His first challenge as tobacco's man in Ottawa would be to save the industry from the ravages of Bill C-51, the tough piece of legislation on Parliament's order paper that, once passed, would effectively ban all tobacco advertising in the country. Next, he would try to convince the government to stop using tobacco as a cash cow for its revenue needs, and to cease further tax increases. After that he would design a long-term strategy for the industry's future in the hostile environment of the 1980s and 1990s. The tobacco industry was under siege – from the public, from the government, and especially from Health Minister Jake Epp – and had come looking to Neville for rescue. With its problems, the tobacco industry needed a Bill Neville.

Neville left PAI at the end of August 1987, citing his health as the reason for his departure. Crohn's disease continued to plague him, and had recently put him into hospital for stomach surgery. He told friends that the switch was a matter of life and death, that if he didn't slow down and relax his lifestyle he couldn't expect to survive in the long run. The strain of heading a company with PAI's breadth of business was proving too much, and he was glad to hand over the reins to Mark Daniels.

Nobody questioned Neville's reasons, yet there was more to his departure – much more. He had already resigned from the board of directors of PARG over philosophical differences with MacNaughton. For some time he had been privately complaining that he was not enjoying public-affairs consulting any more. The corporate culture of PAI – and of the entire industry – had changed drastically from the time twenty years earlier when he and Bill Lee had controlled the market out of a hole in the wall on Slater Street. Now the cosiness with clients was gone. Like government, PAI had grown big and complex, and had spread itself across a variety of interests, becoming a machine that did volume business. Neville worried about MacNaughton expanding too much since the push to maintain growth, especially while keeping most of the ownership in the hands of two people, was causing serious personnel problems. In particular he disagreed with MacNaughton's decision to turn a personal-services corporation like PARG into a public company. Calculating profit margins and meeting corporate plans was not his idea of fun and fulfilment, so it was time for Neville to go. In fact Sean Moore, the new president, left a month before he did for some of the same reasons. PAI was suffering growing pains and had, perhaps, expanded too fast.

With the Trudeau government finally gone, some businessmen had hoped that a friendly administration would remove much of the need for consultants and lobbyists. But just the opposite proved to be true. Mulroney arrived in government with a forty-member cabinet which rarely met as a group, and contained junior and senior ministers with a variety of ambitions, capabilities, interests, and levels of influence. Business decided that it had to know who was up and who was down. The agenda of an officially friendly government could be just as challenging as that of an interventionist one, as industry's scramble for position over deregulation and for the rights to buy privatized Crown corporations soon showed. Furthermore, Mulroney continued to centralize power in the Prime Minister's Office, just as Trudeau had done after Pearson, who himself had done it after Diefenbaker. Clearly, politicians and the new generation of Tory backroom boys would be making the major decisions, not the bureaucrats. This centralization of power meant that Ottawa was increasingly following Washington towards the hired-gun approach to government relations.

Since Neville and Lee had started ECL in 1968, uncertain of the market for their services, the political and business culture of Canada had come to accept and legitimize such firms as PAI, ECL, and GCI. Over the intervening years, in fact, their services had become embedded in the cost of doing business, and had subtly altered the way Canadians were governed. Firms like PAI and ECL had provided a more sophisticated approach to dealing with government in Canada, and had benefited handsomely from doing so. The trend seemed to observers to be likely to continue, since it transcended the Mulroney government and went beyond

Canada. Significantly, the fastest-growing area of corporate development in the United States and elsewhere in the world was not economics, law, labour relations, production, or marketing – but public affairs. All the signs indicated that lobbying and public-affairs consulting would remain a growth industry, on into the future.

INDEX